Accusations from the West that China is tearing up the ⟨treaty⟩ over Hong Kong are serious calumnies. This book ⟨shows how⟩ opposed solutions were put together. The British war⟨ned they⟩ wanted a unilateral declaration of policy. The policy was enshrined in treaty form – in other words proving the maxim that a treaty between states is a disagreement put into writing. It is a riveting read, the work of a first class, razor-sharp mind, a distinguished academic as well as a prominent barrister.

– Anthony Carty, formerly Sir Y K Pao Chair of Public Law, University of Hong Kong, at present Chair of Public International Law, Beijing Institute of Technology School of Law, Beijing.

Treaty for a Lost City gives a timely, scholarly and thorough account of the constitutional history of Hong Kong from the time of the negotiations that led to the Joint Declaration of 1984 through to the present day with the enactment of the National Security Law of 2020. All this is seen through the prism of international law in general and the Joint Declaration in particular. Professor Lim guides the reader surefootedly through this thicket of law. Not every conclusion he reaches will be accepted but what he says is impossible to ignore.

– Christopher Forsyth was Sir David Williams Professor of Public Law in the University of Cambridge and is Honorary Professor of Law in the University of Stellenbosch

This is the best account of the Basic Law's relationship with the Joint Declaration, and the relationship between the Basic Law, international law and national law, dubbed 'the Holy Trinity'. It offers penetrating analyses of the constitutional controversies that have arisen. Based on archival work and an even-handed and fair reading of the relevant legal texts, this monograph offers a fresh perspective of Hong Kong's constitutional order. An elegant and compelling book.

– Hualing Fu, Dean, Faculty of Law, University of Hong Kong

This is an important book which vividly illuminates the bargaining process that shaped the Sino-British Joint Declaration. It gives full play to Chinese arguments about the Treaty and proposes an original counterpoint to the liberal argument about Hong Kong's constitutional identity. Treaty for a Lost City is an essential resource for people who wish to explore the debate about Hong Kong's constitutional treaty; or who wish to understand what Hong Kong has become.

– Ewan Smith, Christ Church, Oxford

TREATY FOR A LOST CITY

The Sino-British Joint Declaration was signed in 1984 and transferred control of Hong Kong to the People's Republic of China from 1 July 1997. This set the scene for the establishment of the Special Administrative Region (SAR) in Hong Kong, which has witnessed civil unrest in 2019–20, culminating in the National Security Law on 30 June 2020. In the twenty-fifth anniversary year of the handover of Hong Kong, C. L. Lim uses British archival sources to re-examine the Joint Declaration, the negotiations that led up to it and its resounding significance. Beginning with Margaret Thatcher's preparations for her Beijing trip, the book takes a chronological approach and offers a valuable, single-volume history of the Joint Declaration. In light of tumultuous current developments in Hong Kong, Lim provides a vital, clear explanation of the legal complexities that have underpinned the relationships between China, Hong Kong and Britain since 1979.

Chin Leng Lim is Choh-Ming Li Professor of Law at the Chinese University of Hong Kong, Visiting Professor at King's College London, Honorary Senior Fellow at the British Institute of International and Comparative Law, a member of the International and Comparative Law Quarterly editorial committee, and membre associé de l'Institut de Droit International.

Treaty for a Lost City

THE SINO-BRITISH JOINT DECLARATION

C. L. LIM

The Chinese University of Hong Kong

CAMBRIDGE
UNIVERSITY PRESS

University Printing House, Cambridge CB2 8BS, United Kingdom

One Liberty Plaza, 20th Floor, New York, NY 10006, USA

477 Williamstown Road, Port Melbourne, VIC 3207, Australia

314–321, 3rd Floor, Plot 3, Splendor Forum, Jasola District Centre, New Delhi – 110025, India

103 Penang Road, #05–06/07, Visioncrest Commercial, Singapore 238467

Cambridge University Press is part of the University of Cambridge.

It furthers the University's mission by disseminating knowledge in the pursuit of education, learning, and research at the highest international levels of excellence.

www.cambridge.org
Information on this title: www.cambridge.org/9781108838757
DOI: 10.1017/9781108976381

© C. L. Lim 2022

This publication is in copyright. Subject to statutory exception and to the provisions of relevant collective licensing agreements, no reproduction of any part may take place without the written permission of Cambridge University Press.

First published 2022

A catalogue record for this publication is available from the British Library.

ISBN 978-1-108-83875-7 Hardback
ISBN 978-1-108-97230-7 Paperback

Cambridge University Press has no responsibility for the persistence or accuracy of URLs for external or third-party internet websites referred to in this publication and does not guarantee that any content on such websites is, or will remain, accurate or appropriate.

To Lyn, once more

Contents

Preface	*page* xi
Acknowledgements	xiv
Table of Provisions in the Joint Declaration and the Basic Law of the Hong Kong S.A.R.	xvi

PART I   1982–1997

	Introduction to Part I	3
1	Negotiations Commence	5
2	The Joint Declaration	26
3	Twilight of Colonial Rule, Democratic Reform, the Basic Law and Bill of Rights: 1984–1997	56

PART II   1997–2014

	Introduction to Part II	79
4	The Court and the Canaries in a Storm	81
5	Foreign Treaty Relations	110
6	Acts of State, Foreign Affairs, Defence	129
7	Demos	147

PART III   2014–2021

	Introduction to Part III	175

8	Patriotism, Comprehensive Jurisdiction, Formal Allegiance: 2014–2017	177
9	Fundamental Rights and the 2019 Extradition Bill	200
10	The 2020 National Security Law	216
11	Aftermath	239
	Appendix - Text of the Sino-British Joint Declaration and Its Annexes, and the Sino-British Exchange of Memoranda of 19 December 1984	264
Index		288

Preface

It might once have been thought that a book on the Sino-British Joint Declaration would have been too exotic a legal-scholarly proposition. You could have said that in 2018. Yash Ghai's and Roda Mushkat's pioneering works at the University of Hong Kong were of great importance but these distinguished scholars who knew well their treaty law were most concerned with the Declaration's implications, more so than with the Declaration itself. It fell to non-legal writers to explain the Joint Declaration and there was, even when we read it today, Cottrell's impressive work, *The End of Hong Kong*. It was impressive because so much of what was said then was said most accurately and perceptively in advance of the thirty-year rule. However, the neglect by treaty scholars was as understandable as it was curious for a document whose treaty character, and thus its legal character, is a chief attribute. Still, the issue was unimportant. If the Declaration was significant in a practical sense it was so in another guise, in the form of the Basic Law of the Hong Kong Special Administrative Region (SAR). The courts hardly would have had occasion to speak of the treaty at all and so it lay there as just another piece of Hong Kong's history. Notwithstanding the UKFCO's six-monthly reports which by and large were viewed as a parliamentary ritual. Notwithstanding too some past allegations of treaty breach. The PRC had cited a breach before the handover in connection with the colonial government's eleventh-hour electoral reforms. Still, that storm passed just as Hong Kong's administration passed from Britain, and the British Empire receded. However, in 2014 there were some, though not the United Kingdom Government itself, who had started to speak of treaty rights and it piqued my interest (see 'Britain's "Treaty Rights" in Hong Kong' (2015) 131 *LQR* 348). In an emergency Commons debate on 2 December 2014 the Minister of State for Foreign and Commonwealth Affairs, Mr Swire, announced the UK Government's view that the UK had 'a legal interest and a moral obligation' in the Joint Declaration. The PRC rejected this view, of course, but what was notable was also a switch, even if still not enough to make a mountain, from 'a moral obligation and a legitimate interest', which was the precise phrase Mr Swire had used earlier in October in the Commons. Within a year things changed significantly. In the Six-Monthly Report on Hong Kong for July to December 2015, published in February the following year, Sir Phillip Hammond spoke of 'a serious breach' of the Joint Declaration. It was the first time the UK was to assert a treaty breach, at least publicly. Between 2020 and 2021, the UK formula had transformed into 'a clear and serious breach', something we have heard both Mr Johnson and Mr Raab say. The PRC denies all these assertions and claims, for only the second time to my knowledge, a breach by the UK in initiating and implementing a new policy for British Nationals (Overseas) passport holders.

Treaties often last longer than those who would remember them, then suddenly we are reminded that they do exist. I felt that it was time this treaty was explained but not as one might expect, clause by clause in a lawyerly way, although I would hope that my lawyerly ways have not escaped me entirely in writing a book that could, it is hoped, help to make sense of well-known and current events. Even so, it might be best to begin at the beginning, and there is no better place than Margaret Thatcher's notes on what she should wear on her 1982 trip to Beijing. The book takes a chronological approach and is broadly speaking divided into three periods – 1982–97, 1997–2014, 2014–21. In other words, from Thatcher's trip to meet Deng Xiaoping in 1982 to the 1997 handover, from the handover and resumption of Chinese sovereignty to the 2014 protests and from 2014 to the present day, thus encompassing the riots of 2019, which were unmistakably violent and uncharacteristic, the 2020 National Security Law for Hong Kong and finally its aftermath. The Joint Declaration in other words is sought to be explained here as a treaty document but against living events. No book on a subject as this will ever be adequate. I can only hope for the reader's forbearance for thinking that it would be worse not to have a book at all. While I have sought not to sway the reader's conclusions unduly, particularly on the law, at the same time I have not refrained from sometimes drawing my own and expressing them. Judges brook no interference. British judges owe their duty to the places abroad in which they serve and in this, they are admired. They should not be told whether they can or cannot perform their duties there, which involves telling them how to do their job. Lord Reed confirms that there has been no interference from the UK government in the face of doubt and criticism. Equally, members of the bar should not be told by members of the government whom they should or should not represent. No treaty disagreement can serve to justify that which in ordinary times would not need saying. I offer this defence of myself. Had this book been written for a different audience certain readers might have found its contents at times more to their taste, just as that other audience might find the present book more to theirs.

Although I completed the manuscript in July 2021, I have managed to include, while this book was in press, discussion of the resignations of Lord Reed and Lord Hodge on 30 March 2022 from Hong Kong's Court of Final Appeal.

The Roman numerals in Annex I of the Joint Declaration are referred to in this book as 'Article I', 'Article II' and so on, where they are also referred to commonly elsewhere as 'Section 1', 'Section 2'. I use 'China' and 'the PRC' interchangeably, and a final word is also in order on entirely Chinese names and Mandarin Chinese terms. I have placed surnames first, as is customary, as here in the Preface, in the main text and also in textual footnotes (e.g. 'Yao Guang, former Chinese ambassador to the French Republic'). However, for the sake of accurate citation, I have, when citing works by Chinese authors, placed surnames last in footnote citations – for example, for the late Professor Wang Tieya, 'Tieya Wang, "International Law in China: Historical and Contemporary Perspectives" (1991) 221 *Recueil des Cours* 195'. Throughout *pinyin* is used unless referring to Hong Kong figures, such as 'Sze-yuen Chung', or where a term is widely known under the Wade-Giles system it is also placed in brackets afterwards – for example 'Guomindang (Kuomintang) armies'.

All flaws, all errors, all of this book's shortcomings, all views are mine alone.

Acknowledgements

Although this is not a collection of past writings, it draws from my interest over the years in the subject of the Joint Declaration. I am grateful to two successive editors of the *Law Quarterly Review* and to Sweet & Maxwell for permission to reproduce the following short pieces which, although revised and amplified, remain substantially recognisable as they had first appeared – 'The Sino-British Treaty and the Hong Kong Booksellers Affair' (2016) 132 *LQR* 552–6; 'The Hong Kong Extradition Bill' (2020) 136 *LQR* 19–23; 'Hong Kong's New Law' (2021) 137 *LQR* 11–16. I would also like to acknowledge and thank Cambridge University Press for permission to reuse certain portions of a book chapter 'Judicial Rhetoric of a Liberal Polity' which appeared in advance in R. Abeyratne and I. Porat (eds.), *Towering Judges* (Cambridge: Cambridge University Press, 2021), chapter 6.

I have had the opportunity to review the files from the British National Archives on the negotiations from their inception until the period, in the following year, following signature of the Sino-British Joint Declaration. In the midst of a worldwide pandemic, when I should have been at Kew, providence intervened, or rather the Hong Kong Government, which had acquired the relevant archival records. For others who may wish to tread this same path, the records are TNA/PREM 19/1262–1267,1530 (Parts 1–18, Future of Hong Kong, New Territorial [*sic*.] Leases).

My debts do not end there and by now are many. Albert Chen and Michael Ng, former colleagues at The University of Hong Kong, eased my way into the declassified materials, while similarly Gary Cheung of the *South China Morning Post* kindly shared his own valuable archival investigations with me. I owe them, as I do Agnes Cheung at The Chinese University of Hong Kong's library and Sarah Monks and the staff at the Hong Kong Government Records Service, an enormous debt. I would also like to thank three anonymous reviewers at Cambridge University Press for their helpful and important suggestions, and also four of my distinguished peers who undertook to read the manuscript and offered not only valuable comments and needed encouragement but also generous advance reviews. They are, in alphabetical order, Anthony Carty, formerly of Hong Kong University and now the Beijing Institute of Technology; Christopher Forsyth, Robinson College, Cambridge, and honorary professor at Stellenbosch University; Fu Hualing, Dean at Hong Kong University; and last but not least Ewan Smith at Christ Church, Oxford, who offered not only extensive comments but saved me from error. At the Press, Finola O'Sullivan's phenomenal enthusiasm for the project and subsequently Marianne Nield's expert guidance made this book possible. My wife, Lyn, as always has been a source of strength.

Table of Provisions in the Joint Declaration and the Basic Law of the Hong Kong S.A.R.

SINO-BRITISH JOINT DECLARATION

Paragraph 1, 48–9, 264
Paragraph 2, 48–9, 264
Paragraph 3, 7, 145, 264–6, 208, 215, 221, 227, 230, 253, 258
    Paragraph 3(1), 49–50, 264
    Paragraph 3(2), 49–51, 129, 145, 230, 265
    Paragraph 3(3), 49, 51–2, 82, 145, 170, 226–7, 235, 265
    Paragraph 3(4), 49, 265
    Paragraph 3(5), 7, 49–50, 52, 145, 154, 170, 226–8, 235, 265
    Paragraph 3(6), 49–50, 265
    Paragraph 3(7), 49–51, 265
    Paragraph 3(8), 49, 265
    Paragraph 3(9), 49, 51, 116, 266
    Paragraph 3(10), 49, 51, 116–7, 266
    Paragraph 3(11), 49, 145, 170, 231, 266
    Paragraph 3(12), 6–7, 49, 79, 263, 266
Paragraph 4, 266
Paragraph 5, 266
Paragraph 6, 266
Paragraph 7, 50, 267
Paragraph 8, 53, 267
Annex I, 6–7, 9–10, 36–7, 39, 42–3, 50, 79, 92, 117–8, 157, 176, 227–8, 253, 266, 268–80
    Annex I, Article I, 14, 50–1, 65, 129, 155, 161, 167, 221, 231, 253, 258, 268–9
    Annex I, Article II, 51, 269
    Annex I, Article III, 51–2, 82, 270–1
    Annex I, Article IV, 271

Annex I, Article V, 50–1, 272
Annex I, Article VI, 272–3
Annex I, Article VII, 51, 273
Annex I, Article VIII, 51, 273–4
Annex I, Article IX, 274–5
Annex I, Article X, 51, 276
Annex I, Article XI, 51, 116–7, 129, 211, 231, 276–7
Annex I, Article XII, 52, 145, 231, 277–8
Annex I, Article XIII, 52, 88–9, 148, 154, 206, 208, 227–8, 278
Annex I, Article XIV, 51–2, 278–80
Annex II, 8, 36, 38, 42, 44, 52, 74–5, 281–2
Annex III, 42, 52, 92, 283–5

BASIC LAW OF THE HONG KONG S.A.R.

Article 1, 105
Article 2, 195, 214
Article 5, 8, 263
Article 11, 195, 214
Article 13, 87, 130, 215
   Article 13(1), 130, 137
   Article 13(2), 141
Article 14, 215
Article 17, 131–2, 146, 220–1
Article 18, 92, 144, 146, 195, 214, 220–1, 230–1, 236
   Article 18(2), 137, 144
Article 19, 86–7, 94, 130, 140–3, 211
   Article 19(3), 141
Article 22, 177–8
Article 23, 135, 230, 233–4
Article 39, 72–3, 90, 150, 152, 197, 202
Article 43, 70–1, 245
Article 45, 165–7, 179, 253
Article 48, 130
Article 52, 168–9
Article 62, 130
   Article 62(3), 130
Article 64, 169
Article 68, 253
Article 82, 82, 84
Article 85, 103–4

Article 95, 211
Article 104, 168, 245
Article 116, 118, 245
Article 133, 125–6
 Article 133(1), 125–6
Article 150, 118
Article 151, 118, 120, 125–6, 245, 251
Article 152, 118
Article 153, 118
Article 154, 191, 193
Article 157, 220–1, 223
Article 158, 9, 69–70, 79, 87, 91–2, 94–6, 131, 135, 140, 142, 163, 215, 220–1, 223, 234
Article 159, 9, 92
Annex II, 162–3
Annex III, 137, 144, 187, 196, 231

PART I
1982–1997

Introduction to Part I

This book begins with the origins and negotiation of the Sino-British Joint Declaration then turns to the immediate aftermath following its signature on 19 December 1984 and entry into force on 27 May 1985. That aftermath was a period during which the colonial administration pushed actively for democratic reform, following the conclusion of the Sino-British Joint Declaration but before Hong Kong was handed over on 1 July 1997. I have endeavoured to let recently declassified files speak for themselves. The result is not always as focused as one might like. There is a higgledy-piggledy quality which is common in any protracted treaty negotiation. Plans had to change, new makeshift plans enacted and adaptation became both frequent and necessary. In all this, China's negotiators might come across as certain and confident but this is only because, but for the occasional speaking role granted to them in the UK records, the files show little other than the silent, gleaming splendour of the national emblem above the Zhongnanhai's South Gate. In stark contrast, doubt and frailty, even occasional bigotry at the rag end of colonialism, are laid bare in the files from the National Archives. My only defence is that I have not set out to flatter my reader. Today, it is also widely assumed that the Joint Declaration ensures by treaty the protection of democratic and fundamental rights. The Joint Declaration did not grant democratic rights. These had been carved out on the UK side from the International Covenant on Civil and Political Rights during the period of colonial administration, and indeed even other fundamental rights the Joint Declaration spoke of in 1984 were but common law rights. The 1984 Joint Declaration contains instead a curious formulation which since has been repeated, in the Basic Law and most recently in the 2020 National Security Law. It states that 'the provisions' of that Covenant (and of the International Covenant on Economic, Social and Cultural Rights) 'as applied to Hong Kong shall remain in force'. It was only after the Joint Declaration had been concluded, and Hong Kong was lost, that the Covenant's rights were incorporated into domestic Hong Kong law.

Following events in China in 1989 this it was said was meant to assure the city's population. In short, there is almost as little on democracy as on genuine treaty rights, and when democracy did feature towards the end of the negotiations in the 1980s it soon was dropped, as always in favour of preserving British interests, the UK's relations with China and Hong Kong's stability, those being the prime considerations at the time. When it did re-emerge just before Hong Kong was handed over in 1997 the result was catastrophe.

1

Negotiations Commence

I SMOKY, FUCHSIA, GOLD BOWS, ENGLISH GARDEN, PLUM STARS[1]

The Island of Hong Kong, which is just a big rock with some land around it ... Then there are the leased territories including Kowloon which are part of the Mainland of China, from where Canton is only about 150 miles away. In Hong Kong a building boom started during the last 10 years because there was a serious shortage of space. As one of my friends explained to me, 'We are building on borrowed land, on borrowed time, with borrowed money.'[2]

Hong Kong, the last jewel of the British Empire, has been administered as a special administrative region of the People's Republic of China (PRC) since 1 July 1997. On 29 June 1997 the *Baltimore Sun*, a regional newspaper in Maryland, observed that young, well-dressed Chinese professionals dashed about chatting on cellular phones and luxury cars filled the streets while merchant ships traversed 'the roiling, turquoise waters of Victoria Harbor'. The *Baltimore Sun* asked how it would all work after the handover and what the Chinese government might do should Hong Kongers take to the streets to criticise its policies.[3] As it turned out nothing, protests were a regular feature of life in Hong Kong, until another twenty-three years had passed when events led – according to the Chinese authorities, they compelled – passage of the 2020 National Security Law for Hong Kong. The controversies surrounding

---

[1] Margaret Thatcher's dresses in her notes during preparations for her trip to Beijing in 1982; Thatcher MSS, Churchill Archive Centre: THCR 1/10/38 f68; also available publicly online, see 'Release of MT's Private Files for 1982 – China & Hong Kong', Thatcher Foundation, at: <www.margaretthatcher.org/archive/1982cac5> (last accessed 27 April 2021).
[2] Chef de Cabinet to three successive United Nations Secretaries-General. See C. V. Narasimhan, *The United Nations: An Inside View* (Delhi: UNITAR/Vikas, 1988), 131–2.
[3] Frank Langfitt, 'Hong Kong: Great Britain Returns the Last Jewel of Its Empire to China', *Baltimore Sun* (Maryland), 29 June 1997.

Hong Kong today, driven at times by statements from both Beijing and London, have been emotive.

An increasingly assertive British government claims that, at bottom, there lie treaty questions and that these include questions about the status and interpretation of the Sino-British Joint Declaration of 1984, a treaty in force since 27 May 1985. The government of China and the Hong Kong government decry what they consider a flagrant British intervention in China and in the Special Administrative Region. In substance, the Joint Declaration consists of a pair of declarations from both sides conjoined, and it was first presented formally to the UK side as such during the fourteenth round of negotiations between the two countries in the spring of 1984.[4] The first two paragraphs read as if they belonged to separate documents:

> 1. The Government of the People's Republic of China declares that to recover the Hong Kong area (including Hong Kong Island, Kowloon and the New Territories, hereinafter referred to as Hong Kong) is the common aspiration of the entire Chinese people, and that it has decided to resume the exercise of sovereignty over Hong Kong with effect from 1 July 1997.
>
> 2. The Government of the United Kingdom declares that it will restore Hong Kong to the People's Republic of China with effect from 1 July 1997.

The Joint Declaration, aptly termed, states in a further 'Chinese' part, in paragraph 3, that:

> The Government of the People's Republic of China declares that the basic policies of the People's Republic of China regarding Hong Kong are as follows ...
>
> ...
>
> (12) The above-stated basic policies of the People's Republic of China regarding Hong Kong and the elaboration of them in Annex I to this Joint Declaration will be stipulated, in a Basic Law of the Hong Kong Special Administrative Region of the People's Republic of China, by the National People's Congress of the People's Republic of China, and they will remain unchanged for 50 years.

The PRC appears to hold the Joint Declaration, which it does treat as a valid treaty, to have become fully executed, meaning that all its terms have been performed. Hong Kong has been handed over and much of the substance of the document is to be found in its first annex (Annex I) which is – and the PRC

---

[4] TNA/PREM 19/1265 (Pt. 14, Future of Hong Kong, New Territorial [sic.] Leases), 'The Sino-British Talks on the Future of Hong Kong after the Fourteenth Round', Hong Kong Department, 14 May 1984.

emphasises this aspect – entitled an 'Elaboration by the Government of the People's Republic of China of Its Basic Policies Regarding Hong Kong'. According to this view, we can stop reading anything too closely into the Joint Declaration after the second paragraph. The UK takes a different view, treating as substantive treaty commitments the PRC's (own) elaboration of Chinese policies in the third paragraph and in Annex I. The roots of this controversy run deep and have their origin in the treaty negotiations. This issue will also be discussed more closely later in this book, particularly where currently the UK has invoked paragraph 3 of the Joint Declaration following the passage of the 2020 National Security Law.[5] But it may be useful nonetheless to address one related point. The main text of the Joint Declaration also states a list of Chinese policies which will be preserved, and what occurs in Annex I is merely the elaboration of these. In which case the UK response would be, and has been, that (at the very least) the policies stated in the main part of the treaty, rather than in Annex I, are no mere 'elaborations' of Chinese policy, and that a state may commit not to change its policies as a matter of international law.

How then, it might be asked, can the PRC even suggest that all of the treaty's terms have been performed? For example, paragraph 3(5) of the main text of the Joint Declaration states that:

> The current social and economic systems in Hong Kong will remain unchanged, and so will the life-style. Rights and freedoms, including those of the person, of speech, of the press, of assembly, of association, of travel, of movement, of correspondence, of strike, of choice of occupation, of academic research and of religious belief will be ensured by law in the Hong Kong Special Administrative Region. Private property, ownership of enterprises, legitimate right of inheritance and foreign investment will be protected by law.

And where paragraph 3(12) in the main text then goes on to state, as I have just mentioned, that:

> The above-stated basic policies of the People's Republic of China regarding Hong Kong and the elaboration of them in Annex I to this Joint Declaration will be stipulated, in a Basic Law of the Hong Kong Special Administrative Region of the People's Republic of China, by the National People's Congress of the People's Republic of China, and they will remain unchanged for 50 years.

---

[5] See Chapters 9 and 10.

The Chinese view could be that (1) the PRC has indeed committed to preserving rights and freedoms and Hong Kong's way of life, and such, but (2) that by implementing the above 'basic policies' in the form of the passage of the Basic Law it has already performed its treaty obligation fully, noting as well that (3) the Basic Law itself, in article 5, states that '[t]he socialist system and law shall not be practised in the Hong Kong Special Administrative Region, and the previous capitalist system and way of life shall remain unchanged for 50 years'. Finally, (4) Annex II of the Joint Declaration concerns the Sino-British Joint Liaison Group, but that had ceased its operations by 2000.

Coming back to the negotiations in the early 1980s, the UK's approach was to squeeze as much detail as possible, in respect of a commitment in respect of Chinese policies after 1997, into a legally binding treaty. In a telegram reporting on the second day of the sixth round of negotiations on 15 November 1983, the British Ambassador in Beijing, Sir Percy Cradock, wrote:[6]

> I reiterated the three reasons I had offered yesterday as to why greater detail was vital ... and added a fourth reason: Yao[7] had argued that matters where further detail was required, such as the future court system and the independence of the judiciary from the executive, concerned only the actual implementation of basic policies. They were much more than this, and were, in fact, important points of principle.

Eight months later, on 31 July 1984, following the nineteenth round of negotiations held on 24 and 25 July, Sir Edward Youde was tasked to carry a letter from Margaret Thatcher to China's Prime Minister Zhao Ziyang. By then the UK was facing a breakdown in the talks over what was to become the Sino-British Joint Liaison Group after the handover. Youde reported to Hong Kong's Executive Council (ExCo) that:[8]

> The situation was developing by the hour and it was only on Monday evening that the documents were completed for the meeting with Deng. The results are recorded in the papers before you, as you will see from the text of the main agreement we achieved ... (c) A provision recording the (next word underlined) agreement of both sides that the Joint Declaration and its annexes will be put into effect. In other words legally binding. (d) A provision recording that the Joint Declaration and its annexes will be equally binding ... In

---

[6] TNA/PREM 19/1059 (Pt. 10 – Future of Hong Kong, New Territorial [sic.] Leases), Deskby FCO 1511OZ, FM Peking 151010Z Nov 83 to Immediate FCO, Telno. 1196 of 15 November 1983.
[7] Yao Guang, former Chinese ambassador to the French Republic.
[8] TNA/PREM 19/1266 (Pt. 15, Future of Hong Kong, New Territorial [sic.] Leases), Deskby 010730Z, FM Hong Kong 311900Z Jul 84 to Immediate FCO, Telno. 2182 of 31 July 1984.

return we had to drop the elaboration of the Chinese 12 points from the main agreement in exchange for agreement to bring the 12 points into line with the annexes. But this is offset by the provisions which I have just described which makes the annexes binding as the main agreement. We were able to accept the title of Joint Declaration once it was agreed that everything was binding. The whole is now a legally binding international agreement.

There was, in other words, an acute awareness on both sides during those negotiations of the Chinese view of the matter. Still, the question is not whether the annex is binding but what it means. These policies are despite the detailed nature of Annex I still to be implemented in the form of the Basic Law of the Hong Kong Special Administrative Region (Basic Law) which also contains a provision, article 158, granting the Standing Committee of the National People's Congress in Beijing the power to issue authoritative interpretations of the Basic Law.[9] Thus any intractable controversy, say over the meaning of 'defence' or 'foreign affairs' over which Hong Kong will not have autonomy, is likely in the ultimate analysis to be resolved by the Standing Committee of the National People's Congress (NPCSC). Furthermore, a British effort to have 'amendments' subjected to the scrutiny of an external body had to be dropped, as we shall see, during the course of the negotiations.[10] By the spring of 1984 a minute from Peter Ricketts[11] at the UK Foreign and Commonwealth Office (FCO) to John Coles[12] at Downing Street had stated that:[13]

> We should be able to preserve considerable negotiating flexibility because there are still elements which could be chopped, notably in paragraph 4 of the draft, describing the attributes of the Basic Law. Sir Geoffrey believes that we should keep open the option of discarding this section at the right moment in order to enable us to argue forcibly for the points which are of real concern to us.

The language of the British proposed text to the Chinese side reads 'Hong Kong (China) will enjoy autonomy within the People's Republic of China under the Basic Law which will be drawn up in accordance with the following provisions.'[14] That did not find its way into the final agreement.

---

[9] The amendment provision is article 159.
[10] TNA/PREM 19/1262 (Pt. 11), Minute from Howe to Thatcher, 'Hong Kong: Meeting of OD(K), 11 January 1984', PM/84/7, 2. Howe called the idea a 'non-starter'.
[11] Private Secretary to the Foreign Secretary, Geoffrey Howe, subsequently Chair of the Joint Intelligence Committee.
[12] Private Secretary to the Prime Minister, Margaret Thatcher, subsequently Permanent Under-Secretary of State for Foreign Affairs.
[13] TNA/PREM 19/1265 (Pt. 14, Future of Hong Kong, New Territorial [sic.] Leases), P. F. Ricketts to A. J., Coles, 'Hong Kong: Revised Draft Agreement', Secret, 1 May 1984.
[14] Ibid., enclosed British draft agreement.

Rather, what we have in Annex I of the Joint Declaration is the 'elaboration' of the basic policies of the government of the People's Republic of China that:

> The National People's Congress of the People's Republic of China shall enact and promulgate a Basic Law of the Hong Kong Special Administrative Region of the People's Republic of China (hereinafter referred to as the Basic Law) in accordance with the Constitution of the People's Republic of China, stipulating that after the establishment of the Hong Kong Special Administrative Region the socialist system and socialist policies shall not be practised in the Hong Kong Special Administrative Region and that Hong Kong's previous capitalist system and life-style shall remain unchanged for 50 years.

In short, at least from the PRC's perspective, it has done that which it said it would. The UK disagrees.

Following the defeat of the Guomindang (Kuomintang) armies and the establishment of the PRC in 1949, the new Government led by the Communist Party of China was faced with the problem of determining the extent of both its territories and treaty obligations. At the conclusion of the Sino-Japanese War (1894–5), the Treaty of Shimonoseki ceded Taiwan to Japan.[15] Hong Kong (including Kowloon and the New Territories) and Macau were under British and Portuguese rule, respectively. The Treaty of Nanjing had already ceded – or as the PRC would have it, purported to cede – Hong Kong Island to Britain in 1842 following the end of the First Opium War (1839–42).[16] Hong Kong had fallen to British occupation in the previous year. Subsequently, in 1860, the First Peking Convention ceded Kowloon to Britain following the Second Opium War.[17] The New Territories was thereafter leased

---

[15] Treaty of Shimonoseki, 17 April 1895, article 2(b): 'China cedes to Japan in perpetuity and full sovereignty the following territories, together with all fortifications, arsenals, and public property thereon: — ... The island of Formosa, together with all islands appertaining or belonging to the said island of Formosa.'

[16] Treaty between Great Britain and China, Nanking, 29 August 1842, reproduced in Yash Ghai, *Hong Kong's New Constitutional Order: The Resumption of Chinese Sovereignty*, 2nd ed. (Hong Kong: Hong Kong University Press, 1999), 501 (Appendix One), article 3 of which states: 'It being obviously necessary and desirable, that British Subjects should have some Port whereat they may careen and refit their Ships, when required, and keep Stores for that purpose, His Majesty the Emperor of China cedes to Her Majesty the Queen of Great Britain, etc., the Island of Hongkong, to be possessed in perpetuity by Her Britannic Majesty, Her Heirs and Successors, and to be governed by such Laws and Regulations as Her Majesty the Queen of Great Britain, etc., shall see fit to direct.' As for an English-language history of the First Opium War (and also of the second), see Julia Lovell, *The Opium War: Drugs, Dreams and the Making of China* (Basingstoke and Oxford: Picador, 2011).

[17] Convention of Friendship between Great Britain and China, 24 October 1860, reproduced in Ghai, *op. cit.*, at 505 (Appendix Two), article 6 of which reads: 'With a view to the maintenance of law and order in and about the harbour of Hong Kong, His Imperial Majesty the

to Britain for a period of ninety-nine years under the Second Peking Convention of 1898.[18] The Central People's Government, which had been established following the Chinese Civil War, reaffirmed the previous Chinese government's position; namely, that China renounces all 'unequal treaties' with the Western Powers. This view did not in fact apply to all treaty obligations, and to complicate matters further renunciation of specific treaties did not in the Chinese view necessitate any reassertion of immediate effective control over the corresponding territories. Rather, the Chinese legal view was that a sovereign may delegate under international law such control or authority to another for a limited period. Indeed, albeit a legal fiction, it can. A distinction was drawn between having sovereignty and exercising it.[19] Thus, China reserved the right to determine when and how it would resume the exercise of its domestic jurisdiction and control in due course. From this perspective, China never lost sovereignty over Hong Kong.[20] Various controversies today now implicate this Chinese legal

    Emperor of China agrees to cede to Her Majesty the Queen of Great Britain and Ireland ... to have and to hold as a dependency of Her Britannic Majesty's colony of Hong Kong, that portion of the township of Cowloon, in the province of Kwang-tung, of which a lease was granted in perpetuity to Harry Smith Parkes, ... on behalf of Her Britannic Majesty's Government'; Office of the Geographer, *International Boundary Study No. 13*, April 13 1962, *China-Hong Kong Boundary* (Washington, DC: US Department of State, 1962), 3.

[18] *Convention between Great Britain and China, Respecting an Extension of Hong Kong Territory*, 9 June 1898, *reproduced in* Ghai, *op. cit.*, 50, the relevant provision of which reads: 'the limits of British territory shall be enlarged under lease to the extent indicated generally on the annexed map. The exact boundaries shall be hereafter fixed when proper surveys have been made by officials appointed by the two Governments. The term of this lease shall be ninety-nine years.'

[19] See Tieya Wang, 'International Law in China: Historical and Contemporary Perspectives' (1991) 221 *Recueil des Cours* 195, 304 *et seq*. Not all scholars were agreed however on this point, which comes out clearly in the late Professor Wang's discussion. See, for example, Tieya Wang, 'A Criticism of Bourgeois International Law on the Question of State Territory', in Jerome Alan Cohen and Hungdah Chiu (eds.), *People's China and International Law: A Documentary Study*, Vol. 1 (Princeton: Princeton University Press, 1974), 322 at 333, for Wang saying that bourgeois international lawyers considered that 'sovereignty may be separated from jurisdiction' such that '[i]f a state lets another state exercise its territorial jurisdiction, the sovereignty of the [weaker] state is not violated', but that '[t]hese absurd theories try to conceal the imperialist criminal act of plundering territory with roundabout legal concepts, and they enable the territory of other countries to fall into the grasp of imperialist devils'. For a similar objection, see Tiqiang Chen, 'Book Review: Zhou Gengsheng's International Law (1981)', in Chinese Society of International Law (ed.), *Selected Articles from Chinese Yearbook of International Law* (Beijing: China Translation & Publishing Corporation, 1983), 240, 251. On legal fictions, see Jean Salmon, 'The Device of Fiction in Public International Law' (1974) 4 *Georgia Jo Int'l Comp L* 251. Tiqiang Chen was better known to English-speaking readers as T. C. Chen. Chen together with Wang and Li Haopei were the three key mid-to-late twentieth-century figures in the public international law field in the People's Republic.

[20] Deng to McLehose, speaking apparently from a loosely prepared statement, Suzhou Room, Great Hall of the People, 29 March 1979; Robert Cottrell, *The End of Hong Kong: The Secret Diplomacy of Imperial Retreat* (London: John Murray, 1993), 54; also Ghai, *op. cit.*, 47.

view. Thus, what is called the 1997 handover by the United Kingdom or the 'restoration' of Hong Kong, Beijing describes instead as Hong Kong's 'recovery' and the 'resumption' of Chinese sovereignty.[21] This eminently workable and constructive piece of treaty ambiguity was a part of the ingenuity of the Joint Declaration. As with many treaties disagreement had been reduced to writing.

The negotiations leading to the Joint Declaration began, in effect, in September of 1982. Signature and ratification took place finally on 19 December 1984 and 27 May 1985.[22] The pace of the negotiations was dictated by Deng Xiaoping who gave the UK two years to conclude the treaty negotiations. It should also be mentioned again in connection with this, recalling what had just been said earlier, that China maintained the position – the legal fiction, if you will – that the negotiations were not strictly speaking necessary. What was involved concerned only the manner – the modality, as Professor Yash Ghai calls it – of the handover. More importantly, the resumption of Chinese sovereignty was considered by Beijing to be essentially a Chinese internal affair. The UK, on the other hand, was concerned with the scope of the negotiations and, in fact, its expansion to include various matters.[23]

There was even the view, not proven entirely incorrect, that by the time the Chinese side realised the complexity of the undertaking, of managing an international financial centre, they would give up and come round to a quintessentially British view of how Hong Kong ought to be governed.[24] However, China refused to commence the negotiations without the UK conceding the issue of sovereignty first, whereas the UK initially was not prepared to discuss that issue until arrangements were first settled on terms which would be acceptable to the people of Hong Kong.[25] This led, during the Deng–Thatcher meeting of 1982, to Deng Xiaoping, China's paramount leader, issuing a directive that Margaret Thatcher should first be 'bombarded out of her obstinacy'.[26] Declassified materials show that the negotiations came near to collapse.[27]

---

[21] Compare Sino-British Joint Declaration, 19 December 1984, paras. 2 and 3(a).
[22] Ghai, *op. cit.*, 35.
[23] *Ibid.*, 44.
[24] For this approach see e.g. TNA/PREM 19/1057 (Pt. 8, Future of Hong Kong, New Territorial Leases), Folio 4A – 2 Notes for the File dated 5 September 1983, Note of a Meeting held at 1600 hours on Monday 5 September 1983 at No. 10 Downing Street ('Sir Percy Cradock said that the three rounds of talks held so far had gone much as had been expected. We had achieved part of our aim in that we had begun a process of educating the Chinese in the complexities of Hong Kong').
[25] Cottrell, *op. cit.*, 102–3.
[26] *Ibid.*, 88.
[27] Stephen Seawright, 'Hard-Fought Sino-British Negotiations over Hong Kong Revealed in Declassified Files', *S.C.M.P.* (Hong Kong), 18 August 2013.

Perhaps we now tend to forget it but the post-handover arrangements which today are portrayed in terms of the PRC's obligations to the UK were at bottom a Chinese idea. The notion of an autonomous Hong Kong with its way of life – including its own freedoms, its system of economic governance and the preservation of the common law – assured for a period of fifty years from 1997 was part of a Chinese blueprint for the recovery in due course of Taiwan. More than that, according to one contemporary view it reflected an approach stretching from the Qing Dynasty to the New China, following the establishment of the People's Republic, towards the administration of China's outer land and sea frontiers. These comprised the land frontier of Tibet and the sea frontiers of Hong Kong, Macao and Taiwan. Ultimately a system was required which granted local autonomy. Not least in light of Deng Xiaoping's belief that Western forces will never give up on the aim to subvert China, using Hong Kong as a base from which to do so.[28]

Mrs Thatcher was sceptical. She considered that the whole idea of having 'one country, two systems' would lead only to capital flight and the end of Hong Kong as a financial centre. On the UK side, there was the feeling that the Chinese were 'incorrigible', 'ineducable' and 'blinkered by dogma and national pride', and that continued British administration of the territory remained feasible.[29] It was only later that the view was to take hold that once the Chinese began to see the problems of Hong Kong's administration, once they were brought into the details, the Chinese would themselves come to see 'one country, two systems' from a British point of view, that (hopefully) Hong Kong's system of government and administration would remain 'unchanged' and that its legal system would remain 'basically unchanged'. In the main body of the treaty, paragraph 3 states that:

> The Government of the People's Republic of China declares that the basic policies of the People's Republic of China regarding Hong Kong are as follows:
>
> ...
>
> (3) The Hong Kong Special Administrative Region will be vested with executive, legislative and independent judicial power, including that of final adjudication. The laws currently in force in Hong Kong will remain basically unchanged.

---

[28] See further Shigong Jiang, *China's Hong Kong* (Singapore: Springer, 2017), 87–101.
[29] Cottrell, *op. cit.*, 88. At bottom was the issue of sovereignty (over Hong Kong and the Kowloon peninsula) which Thatcher would cede in exchange for continued British administration of the entire territory (i.e. including the New Territories, the lease for which would have lapsed). Percy Cradock who uttered these words was apparently the first to realise that the UK would not prevail.

In the all-important Annex I, we find the following 'elaboration' by the PRC Government of its basic policies in article I:

> ... after the establishment of the Hong Kong Special Administrative Region the socialist system and socialist policies shall not be practised in the Hong Kong Special Administrative Region and that Hong Kong's previous capitalist system and life-style shall remain unchanged for 50 years.

This treaty was eventually concluded, signed, ratified and registered with the United Nations.[30] Forgotten too was that Deng Xiaoping considered the whole idea to be an experiment, perhaps not unlike when it is said in the United States that there they too have only an 'experiment' at the end of the day. Until recently, no major differences had emerged, at least in public, about its operation and implementation. In 2015, a note in the *Law Quarterly Review* had discussed the question of any continuing British 'treaty rights'.[31] Since then a succession of events have shaped the terrain of legal issues which while Beijing considers to be entirely within its domestic sphere the UK contends are treaty issues which implicate the Joint Declaration. What these issues are will form the core of this book. Major differences now exist.

---

[30] U.N.T.S. vol. 1399, 1985, No. 1, 33. According to S. Y. Chung, who was then the Senior Member of Hong Kong's Executive Council, the Council had pushed for an assurance that the 'Joint Declaration' would be as good as a 'treaty'. He writes in his recent memoirs: 'Her Majesty's Government then brought in experts in diplomatic law who confirmed to us that the pact by the name of "Joint Declaration" was legitimate and equally binding.' However, '[t]o be double sure, the Executive Council suggested that the document be submitted to the United Nations for registration', Sze-yuen Chung, *Hong Kong's Journey to Reunification: Memoirs of Sze-yuen Chung* (Hong Kong: The Chinese University Press, 2021), 114. One need not go so far as to say that had the UK and China air-shipped a poodle and called it a treaty the UN Secretariat simply would have filed the dog away politely, or to suggest that registration lacks any legal significance. The Secretariat however does not confirm what it is you are supposed to have sent: 'Where an instrument is registered with the Secretariat, this does not imply a judgement by the Secretariat of the nature of the instrument, the status of a party, or any similar question. Thus, the Secretariat's acceptance for registration of an instrument does not confer on the instrument the status of a treaty or an international agreement if it does not already possess that status. Similarly, registration does not confer on a party to a treaty or international agreement a status that it would not otherwise have'; Treaty Handbook (United Nations Publication, Sales No. E.02.V2), 27. There is an obligation on the part of UN Members to register their treaties under article 102 of the UN Charter. Non-registration will prevent its invocation before any UN organ; article 102(2). Thus, the question should not be whether everyone thinks the instrument is a treaty, or indeed that someone might not. This in any case is not the issue with the Joint Declaration; its binding nature is not apparently in question.

[31] C. L. Lim, 'Britain's "Treaty Rights" in Hong Kong' (2015) 131 L.Q.R. 348. Cf. Ewan Smith, 'Constitutional Treaties in Hong Kong', 20 April 2017, available on SSRN.

II JOINT DECLARATION

One consequence of China's view that sovereignty over Hong Kong was never ceded to the UK is that there logically were no concessions which can be made in exchange for its recovery. There was nothing of real substance which the UK could give in exchange for any binding promise. The American China Law comparativist Jacques deLisle puts it elegantly – what was required was a 'special form' for the return of Hong Kong not a treaty transferring or ceding Hong Kong 'back to' China:

> The Chinese 'naturalist' claim here is two-fold: First, because there is, and can be, no *quo* of China's regaining its undisturbed and non-derogable sovereignty over Hong Kong, there is and can be no *quid* in the PRC's statements of its plans for Hong Kong. Second, the statements about how China will exercise sovereignty over Hong Kong cannot impose irrevocable restrictions (especially ones giving foreign powers enforcement rights) because that would be an attempt to 'carve up' sovereignty over Hong Kong, much as the nineteenth-century treaties had purported to do.[32]

Contemporary assertions of British treaty rights might tend to overlook this central complication. Be that all as it may, the evidence suggests that the PRC relented from adopting a hard-line position albeit only at the last minute on the question of 'unequal' treaties. Deng Xiaoping agreed in April 1984 that there would be a 'binding' document, if the sovereignty question was handled by way of the parties each stating their own individual position. There would be a common declaration only on points of agreement.[33] Hence a 'Joint Declaration'.

By December 1983, Sir Geoffrey Howe, whilst briefing cabinet colleagues, suggested that the negotiations should be based on the Chinese proposals.[34] Of course, that the UK and the PRC went on to negotiate strict treaty terms is an irrefutable fact. One question today as seen by the Department of Treaty Law and Affairs in the Chinese Foreign Ministry is, as I have mentioned, whether the treaty produced is now already fully executed.

In this, the legal architecture of the Joint Declaration as well as its legal nature have both become matters of contention. More to the point, the whole issue now complicates relations between London and Beijing. According to

---

[32] Jacques deLisle, 'Sovereignty Resumed: China's Conception of Law for Hong Kong, and Its Implications for the SAR and US-PRC Relations' (1998) *Harvard Asia Quarterly* 21, 22.

[33] Ghai, *op. cit.*, at 53; Cottrell, *op. cit.*, 149: 'while Deng agreed that the final document should be binding, rather than merely a statement of intent, he still favoured parallel declarations rather than a simple treaty'.

[34] Seawright, *op. cit.*

the usual understanding, or at least one which has for many years been expressed uncontradicted, the Joint Declaration is – by whatever name we call it – a treaty. A broad range of evidence has been cited for that proposition.[35] The recent rejection of its application to broader questions of what 'Western international lawyers' would call 'treaty succession'[36] will also need to be addressed.[37]

III THE NEW TERRITORIES LEASE

The story of the Joint Declaration begins in 1978,[38] even if Thatcher's visit to Beijing in September 1982 is usually taken as the start of negotiations, lasting until 1984. With the signing of the Joint Declaration in 1984 there was a period of thirteen years before Hong Kong's handover in 1997, before the commencement thereafter of the fifty-year period during which China undertook to preserve Hong Kong's capitalist way of life. Whether China's undertaking was not merely a unilateral declaration of policy or is the subject of binding treaty duties is a subject now of Sino-British controversy. As will be seen below in Section V, the issue was present from the beginning. The PRC's position was that, without an agreement with the UK, it would have declared the resumption of the exercise of Chinese sovereignty in or around 1984. Or that, at least, was what the PRC had informed the UK in 1982 about its intentions in 'one or two years' time'.

At the start of it, the progressive Labour Party-leaning Murray MacLehose[39] was Governor of Hong Kong. Preparations had just been made for his March 1979 visit to Beijing where it was hoped that he would meet personally with Deng who by December of 1978 had become China's paramount leader.

---

[35] See e.g. Roda Mushkat, *One Country, Two International Legal Personalities* (Hong Kong: Hong Kong University Press, 1997), 140 *et seq.*

[36] There being no 'succession' at all in the Chinese view.

[37] C. L. Lim, 'Fragrant Harbour and Oyster Mirror' (2015–16) *Yrbk Int'l Investment Law & Pol* 375.

[38] Cottrell, *op. cit.*, 35 *et seq*; Ezra Vogel, *Deng Xiaoping and the Transformation of China* (Cambridge, MA: Harvard University Press, 2011), 492–511; James T. H. Tang and Frank Ching, 'The Maclehose and Youde Years: Balancing the "Three-legged Stool" 1971–86', in Ming K. Chan and Frank D. Young (eds.), *Precarious Balance: Hong Kong between Britain and China, 1842–1992* (Armonk, NY: M.E. Sharpe, 1994), 149; James T.H. Tang and Frank Ching, 'Balancing the Beijing-London-Hong Kong "Three-Legged Stool", 1971–1986', in Ming K. Chan and Gerard Postiglione (eds.), *The Hong Kong Reader: Passage to Chinese Sovereignty* (London: Routledge, 2016), 41; Dick Wilson, *Hong Kong! Hong Kong!* (London: Unwin Hyman, 1990), 193–211.

[39] Who was at the same time against any move towards having a constitutional democracy, rather than a continuation of the colonial executive-led system.

III The New Territories Lease

Mao Zedong had died in 1976. What supplied the impetus to broaching the Hong Kong question was that the date loomed for the expiry of the UK's leasehold of the New Territories. The 1898 Convention Respecting an Extension of the Hong Kong Territory had envisaged, as previously mentioned, a lease of ninety-nine years until 1997. Its expiry was now less than twenty years away.

There were several suggestions about how China might be approached with the question. The more courageous, or preposterous, was the suggestion that a lease provided under a treaty whose existence and validity China rejected as being unjust could not after all contain any term for its expiration.[40] According to Professor Wesley-Smith,[41] the PRC would still be left to decide when it may wish to resume sovereignty but, assuming that it was in its own interest to delay, it would not have complained about continued British administration of the territory where the UK accepts, simultaneously, the Chinese claim that the nineteenth-century treaties were invalid and therefore the term governing the expiry of the leasehold was, likewise, invalid. What then would be the basis for continued British authority? The answer, according to this scenario which Wesley-Smith attributes to Anthony Dicks, would have been to invoke the Crown's prerogative to govern beyond the seas. That would have been the source of the authority to cede Hong Kong, while at the same time invoking the Foreign Jurisdiction Acts of 1890 and 1913 as authority for continued British administration. It comes down to the doctrine that if you are sitting on a rock and someone wants you off it, they will have to get you off. Perhaps it was not altogether preposterous when it is considered that certainly during the earlier stages of Sino-British negotiations Thatcher had held firm to the belief that absent actual British administration confidence in Hong Kong would simply evaporate.[42]

---

[40] Cottrell, *op. cit.*, 44; citing doubts in Peter Wesley-Smith, *Unequal Treaty, 1898–1997* (Oxford: Oxford University Press, 1980), 240. See further Anthony Dicks, 'Treaty, Grant, Usage or Sufferance? Some Legal Aspects of the Status of Hong Kong' (1983) 95 *China Quarterly* 427. Wesley-Smith remarked that Dicks' article was probably published too late to have had any impact on the course of the negotiations. All of this overlooks the fact that Britain had two years to conclude a deal or risk a unilateral statement of China's plans to recover Hong Kong; Cottrell, *op. cit.*, 89, observing that 'the British had not foreseen that the Chinese might choose to fix a deadline to negotiations'. By 15 August 1983, Hu Yaobang, the CCP General Secretary, informed a visiting Japanese delegation that '[w]e will recover Hong Kong on 1 July 1997' and that 'our attitude is one of respect for history'; quoted in *ibid.*, 114–55. Deng was to communicate the end date of 1997 to Edward Heath in September; *ibid.*, 117. Wesley-Smith had observed as well that it would have been an about face for the UK now to turn around and say that China was correct, that the nineteenth-century treaties were unequal and invalid.

[41] Peter Wesley-Smith, *Constitutional and Administrative Law in Hong Kong* (Hong Kong: Longman, 1994), 60–1.

[42] Quoted in Seawright, *op. cit.*

As it turned out the MacLehose visit was, in search of a lasting solution for the Hong Kong question, to raise the question of leases directly but not the New Territories lease itself. Rather, and this was a ploy, the question concerned the validity after 1997 of domestic leaseholds over land.[43] Albeit not lacking in subtlety, a child could see through it. As a matter which the Joint Declaration would eventually address, the spectre of Chinese immigration into Britain post-1997 had by then become an important factor.[44] It is noteworthy, also ironic, that almost twenty-five years after the handover, immigration into Britain is now presented as a British solution in the face of the PRC's objections.[45] Murray MacLehose's visit was intended merely as preparatory, paving the way for the Foreign Secretary, David Owen's own trip to Beijing. As it happened, it was Deng Xiaoping who initiated the discussion over Hong Kong's political future, emphasising China's sovereignty while recognising Hong Kong's special position and its treatment as a special region. Whereupon '[f]or a considerable length of time, Hong Kong may continue to practise its capitalist system while we practise our socialist system'.[46] Meanwhile in London the Government fell following the Conservative Party's victory over Labour in the UK elections of May 1979.

The notion of 'one country, two systems' was not designed with Hong Kong in mind but rather Taiwan, as a route to Chinese reunification, but with the apparent diminishing prospects for such reunification,[47] Chinese attention had shifted to Hong Kong instead. Settling Hong Kong's future arrangements presented the attractive prospect of a swift and easy victory. On this account, China's sights turned, starting at the beginning of 1982, to Hong Kong's political as well as its commercial future.[48]

By April of 1982, Deng Xiaoping had put his 'Nine Points' for Chinese reunification to Edward Heath, during the latter's visit to Beijing, as a possible solution for Hong Kong.[49] At the same time, that April, article 31 of the 1982 PRC Constitution had been circulated following approval by the NPC's Constitutional Revision Committee. It would authorise the CPG to establish special administrative regions. Geoffrey Howe who was himself to play a pivotal role in this entire affair describes the Deng-Heath

---

[43] Vogel, *Deng, op. cit.*, 491. So far as Chinese perceptions were concerned, whether Deng Xiaoping did see through it is questioned by Vogel, *ibid.*, 492; *cf.* however Cottrell, *op. cit.*, 55.
[44] Cottrell, *op. cit.*, 35–7.
[45] See Chapter 11 of this book.
[46] Quoted in Cottrell, *op. cit.*, 54.
[47] Vogel, *op. cit.*, 492 attributes this to the advent of the Reagan Administration.
[48] Cottrell, *op. cit.*, 66.
[49] See also David Akers-Jones, *Feeling the Stones* (Hong Kong: Hong Kong University Press, 2004), 110.

meeting in his memoirs: Deng's message to Ted Heath had been straightforward, if unwelcome. China, he said, intended to assert and safeguard her sovereignty over the whole of Hong Kong. All the unequal treaties would be abrogated. Britain, he implied, should withdraw completely. Special arrangements would be put in place to enable 'Hong Kong people' to maintain the prosperity of Hong Kong; its social and economic system will remain unchanged. Four words were enough to encapsulate Deng's insight: 'One country, two systems'. In this one phrase he set the scene for the next quarter of a century.[50]

However, any relinquishment of 'British sovereignty', which Beijing at least disputed on the ground of unlawful British treaties, would inevitably be a grave and complicated factor following the Falklands War in April to June of 1982. Sovereignty had loomed large in the public imagination in the UK, albeit not so large as in the British Prime Minister's mind, according to the fears of FCO officials.

Whatever the UK might have thought, there was no question of any form of continued British administration of Hong Kong so far as the Chinese side was concerned. Unnecessary legal ambiguity may have attended the PRC's position on unequal treaties, which is that while Chinese sovereignty remained uninterrupted its 'resumption' – I use only the word from the Joint Declaration – could be delayed until such moment when the time was ripe. Whether the date of expiry of the New Territories lease in 1997 would become that precise moment was unclear. At least in London where the evidence was that certain hopes were harboured still, or at least could not loudly be denied, for some form of continued British administration of Hong Kong after that date. The Chinese position had been put clearly in Ambassador Huang Hua's letter of March 1972, ten years before, to the United Nations' decolonisation committee:

> The questions of Hong Kong and Macau belong to the category of questions resulting from the series of unequal treaties which the imperialists imposed on China. Hong Kong and Macau are part of Chinese territory occupied by the British and Portuguese authorities. The settlement of the questions of Hong Kong and Macau is entirely within China's sovereign right and do not at all fall under the ordinary category of colonial territories. Consequently they should not be included in the list of colonial territories covered by the

---

[50] Geoffrey Howe, *Conflict of Loyalty* (London: Macmillan, 1994), 363.

declaration on the granting of independence to colonial countries and people. With regard to the questions of Hong Kong and Macau, the Chinese government has consistently held that they should be settled in an appropriate way when conditions are ripe.[51]

Despite criticism still heard today, removal of Hong Kong from the committee's list of colonial territories was at least in accordance with the salt-water theory of colonialism,[52] which defines it as 'white rule on alien peoples separated by a stretch of salt water from the imperial centre'.[53] Whatever else one might think, the idea that first mandates under the League of Nations Covenant then trusteeships under the United Nations Charter as some 'sacred trust of civilisation'[54] should authorise continued white administration is now discredited. The choice was between complete independence or autonomy, or absorption.[55] In any case, Thatcher, fresh from victory in the Falklands, now Prime Minister, took the position that in return for what she considered to be a 'transfer' of sovereignty – she calls it in her memoirs an 'exchange'[56] – the UK should secure a right to continue to administer Hong Kong. That view has been described amply elsewhere,[57] resting upon the rejection of any unequal treaties doctrine. In which case would it not be possible to retain Hong Kong Island and Kowloon while relinquishing the New Territories? The answer, as it turned out, was that it would have been impossible practically speaking.

IV FROM NINE TO TWELVE POINTS

Beginning sometime during or just after January of 1982, a working group of the PRC State Council's Hong Kong and Macao Office had been labouring on the original 'Nine Points' for Taiwan, eventually turning them into 'Twelve Points' for Hong Kong. This was the Sino-British Joint Declaration in its embryonic form. When Margaret Thatcher met Deng Xiaoping in September of 1982 the difference then came to this. For the UK, two valid treaties had ceded territory in perpetuity. In exchange for what the UK no

---

[51] Tang and Ching, *op. cit.*, 153; Zhenmin Wang, *Relationship between the Chinese Central Authorities and Regional Governments of Hong Kong and Macao: A Legal Perspective* (Berlin: Springer, 2019), 64; also Christine Loh, *Underground Front: The Chinese Communist Party in Hong Kong*, 2nd ed. (Hong Kong: Hong Kong University Press, 2018), 130
[52] See further, Chapter 7 of this book.
[53] Rupert Emerson, 'Colonialism' (1969) 3 *Jo Contemporary Hist* 3, 3.
[54] Emerson, *op. cit.*, 13
[55] Ali Mazrui, 'Consent, Colonialism and Sovereignty' (1963) 11 *Political Studies* 36, 36.
[56] Margaret Thatcher, *Downing Street Years* (London: Harper Collins, 1995), 259, 259–61.
[57] Cottrell, *op. cit.*, 70–1 especially.

doubt saw as a retrocession of these territories, which the PRC would deny, Britain wanted continued administration. The idea had its roots in the UKFCO prior to victory for the Conservatives at the recent elections. It appears to have been based in some part upon felt scepticism that China, fresh out of a Cultural Revolution, a period during which there was a hostility to cities and landlords, with a GDP per capita of USD 203.33, could in any case manage a modern financial centre like Hong Kong.[58] For the PRC there was never a valid cession of the territories of Hong Kong and Kowloon in the first place, but with the resumption of China's exercise of its sovereignty in 1997 it would, acting entirely on its own, maintain Hong Kong's prosperity afterwards.[59] This view was presented by Deng Xiaoping as early as the McLehose visit in 1979.[60] The key idea in the British Prime Minister's view however was, as she had said to the press during the main press conference during that visit, that 'we stick to our treaties'.[61] Yet the problem lay in China's view that they were unequal treaties which never were valid, whereas in the UK's view international law knows no unequal treaties doctrine.

More will be said of this point of treaty law, but by 2020, Mr Boris Johnson would come to adopt a similar approach to current events as Thatcher once did in the past. Ezra Vogel quotes Thatcher's BBC interview during her 1979 visit,[62] and Vogel goes on to describe the reaction of the 'China hands' so-called in the FCO:

> In a BBC interview before leaving China, she said, 'If one party to a treaty or a contract says, "I cannot agree to it, I am going to break it", you cannot really have a great deal of confidence that any new treaty they make will be honored.' China specialists in the British Foreign Office cringed when she repeated these comments at a press conference in Hong Kong, for they knew that these words would dampen the goodwill with China that they had been working to build.

Vogel's comment comes in fact from Cottrell's interview with a British official, who was reported to have said:

> '... stick to the facts, which are that the treaties are valid under international law, while the Chinese position, that they are invalid because unequal, is incorrect ... '
>
> But going on to talk about questions of trustworthiness was to add a gratuitous statement of opinion.

---

[58] Vogel, Deng, *op. cit.*, 491.
[59] Cottrell, *op. cit.*, 77–97.
[60] Vogel, *op. cit.*, 491.
[61] Cottrell, *op. cit.*, 90.
[62] Also by Cottrell, *op. cit.*, 93; see Vogel, *op. cit.*, 496.

The difference between the two situations then, in 1982, and now forty years later may be that the UK still feels that there is a disagreement to be thrashed out, while the PRC sees no basis at all for that supposition since Hong Kong is not any of the UK's concern. China at least has always been consistent in holding that firm view. If that is correct it is less in reality a question of the continued validity, which the PRC admits, and operation – which it denies – of the 1984 Sino-British Joint Declaration, rather than the fact that any Sino-British treaty differences today continue to be shaped by fundamental, unresolved issues given over by history.

Where the UK sees the contemporary international law on treaties as having rejected any unequal treaties doctrine international law in fact is rarely that simple. The PRC sees history rejecting the imposition of Western international law. Thus even if the whole issue is put, as it will be below in Section V, in modern terms of treaty interpretation that would only cloud the fact that history shapes legal arguments and not the other way round. We have seen this elsewhere, in the context of the South China Sea Arbitration, in relation to which the PRC has rejected the award outright, but while ancient mariners knew not to go where there be dragons, modern treaty law knows no such thing. Currently, we are faced with a treaty about unequal treaties which the UK, hewing closely to modern treaty law, claims has been broken.[63]

V IN ONE OR TWO YEARS' TIME

The Chinese position during Thatcher's visit was that, absent agreement, China would declare its position unilaterally and resume the exercise of sovereignty over Hong Kong. Margaret Thatcher referred to it thus, in recalling her meeting with Deng Xiaoping:[64]

> He reiterated that the Chinese were not prepared to discuss sovereignty. He said that the decision that Hong Kong will return to Chinese sovereignty need not be announced now, but that in one or two years' time the Chinese Government would formally announce their decision to recover it.

---

[63] Conceptually the issue is connected with what international lawyers once called the 'New States' problem, applying to the newly independent Asian and African States' supposed rejection of the European Law of Nations as a standard of civilisation. The PRC hewed close to this view. The articulation of that view is seen most profoundly in the late Tieya Wang, 'International Law in China: Historical and Contemporary Perspectives' (1990) 221 *Recueil des cours* 195, 333–44, on the Chinese view of a doctrine of unequal treaties.

[64] Thatcher, *op. cit.*, 261.

It was as China's Ambassador, Huang Hua, had also put it a decade prior to the decolonisation committee – the questions of Hong Kong and Macao are 'entirely within China's sovereign right' to decide. As reported in the British minutes, Zhao Ziyang during Thatcher's visit is supposed to have replied to the British Prime Minister's suggestion that continued British administration was essential: 'China would not allow others to administer Hong Kong on its behalf nor place Hong Kong under the trusteeship of others.'[65] This was again repeated in late 1983, that China would on its own accord unveil its plan by September 1984.[66] That feature made its way into the structure and content of the Joint Declaration where much that is substantive is to be found in paragraph 3 of the main body of the treaty and in Appendix I in which the PRC 'declares' and 'elaborates' upon its (own) 'policies' in Hong Kong. Much of the controversy today is therefore hardly new.

It had likewise been the case with the 1982 communique drafted for public consumption during Margaret Thatcher's visit to Beijing, in which the UK side sought constructive ambiguity as the path to continued negotiation. The Chinese side added a coda – according to Cottrell apparently without consultation of the British side – asserting China's sovereignty.[67] That acorn of fundamental disagreement had now become an oak tree.

That was to manifest itself initially between the second and third rounds of the formal talks, which had commenced by July 1983, ten months after Mrs Thatcher's visit. The Chinese side issued a detailed 'Twelve-point Plan' for Hong Kong, in effect pre-empting the negotiations. In September, Edward Heath visited Deng Xiaoping. It was to be Heath's sixth visit to China. Heath wrote in his memoirs:

> We started with a general discussion about the international situation, but then he turned to Hong Kong. I noticed that at this point his colleagues, far from relaxing against the backs of their chairs, immediately sat bolt upright and concentrated on listening to him. This gave me a cue that something significant was about to be propounded. 'I said that we had two years for this negotiation with the British', he began. 'A year has already passed and we have got nowhere at all. When you go home, go and tell Mrs Thatcher that there is only one more year left for us to settle these affairs. If she has not done so with me before another year is up, I shall settle it entirely on my own.'[68]

---

[65] UK's minutes of the meeting quoted in Seawright, *op. cit.*
[66] Vogel, *op. cit.*, 497.
[67] Cottrell, *op. cit.*, 89–90.
[68] Edward Heath, *The Course of My Life* (London: Hodder & Stoughton, 1998), 644.

In sum, the political future of Hong Kong had been sought to be presented in terms of the protection of domestic property rights, namely the security of land tenure. Underlying it was an unresolved difference on sovereignty, which in turn depended upon long rejection by China of nineteenth-century injustice. There is longevity to this aspect of the Chinese view of international law. China's reactions in recent times, not least in respect of the workings of the Hong Kong SAR, cannot be properly assessed otherwise. At bottom, there were the 'unjust treaties' which were the outcome of nineteenth-century British gunboat diplomacy. During the 1968–69 United Nations Conference on the Law of Treaties China sought to include an express term on the legal invalidity of unjust treaties but did not succeed. However, in its view the absence of such an express term does not preclude an unjust treaties doctrine in international law for in the end, certainly in the late Wang Tieya's view, perhaps the best known of the three prominent Chinese international lawyers of his time, it is implicit nonetheless[69] in the final product, the 1969 Vienna Convention on the Law of Treaties.[70] As for the UK, all three nineteenth-century treaties pertaining to Hong Kong, Kowloon and the New Territories lease were valid and needed to be addressed, two at least would require amendment, for in its view the UK would have to cede the respective territories of Hong Kong and Kowloon. For the PRC, however, Britain's recognition of Chinese sovereignty was a prerequisite to negotiations about the future arrangements for Hong Kong. Against this, the UKFCO and the British Prime Minister still held out hope for some form of continued British administration, which by itself need not exclude Chinese sovereignty.[71]

There was an altogether realistic prospect that China would, simply, have proclaimed its position unilaterally, although one might ask why the UK side should have accepted it as a genuine possibility rather than as a mere ruse. A question also lingers in some minds about whether any of this should matter now to the interpretation of the Joint Declaration. That is not to say that it should necessarily matter. Often a search for the background to the negotiations, the *travaux preparatoires*, yields only the same differences which had precipitated the treaty. In more formal terms, a treaty is to be interpreted by the ordinary meaning of its words, its text, unless that would be absurd in which case one cannot in good faith accept such absurdity, and in light of the object of the treaty as well as its purpose. Context is equally of importance by which

---

[69] Wang, *op. cit.*, 337.
[70] UN Doc. A/CONF. 39/27; Vienna Convention on the Law of Treaties, 23 May 1969, U.N.T.S., vol. 1155, 331.
[71] Cottrell, *op. cit.*, 98.

we mean that the context of a word or clause or article is to be found as a part of the document as a whole, the whole document including any annexures and appendices, and in light of any other agreement at the time of the treaty's conclusion.[72] A search for the negotiating background is, at least in principle, only triggered by ambiguity in the words not the fact that a treaty may have to be interpreted.[73]

As important as the 'internal' context of the treaty, meaning its whole structure and the words in it, and the 'external' context formed by any other agreement at the time of its conclusion, is sometimes any subsequent agreement modifying or clarifying its meaning, and also the parties' own subsequent conduct.[74] The subsequent two chapters turn to the 1984 Sino-British Joint Declaration thence to events in its aftermath up until the 1997 handover. The remainder of the book will discuss events following the handover, including various controversies, in the past twenty-five years. It will take us to the mid-point of the fifty years of autonomy which the Joint Declaration assures, and to contemporary Sino-British treaty disagreement and its possible legal ramifications.

---

[72] Vienna Convention on the Law of Treaties 1969, article 31.
[73] Vienna Convention on the Law of Treaties 1969, article 32. That is the principle, but in practice international lawyers turn routinely to the *travaux préparatoires*, the history of the negotiations. See e.g. Julian Davis Mortenson, 'The *Travaux* of *Travaux*: Is the Vienna Convention Hostile to Drafting History?' (2013) 107 A.J.I.L. 780.
[74] As with the *travaux*, resort to which is frowned upon only in principle, looking 'outside the treaty' is at times seen to be something of a poor person's guide to what the treaty means, see Georges Abi-Saab, writing on the approach of the WTO Appellate Body, 'The Appellate Body and Treaty Interpretation', in Malgosia Fitzmaurice, Olufemi Elias and Panos Merkouris (eds.), *Treaty Interpretation and the Vienna Convention on the Law of Treaties: Thirty Years On* (Leiden: Nijhoff, 2010), 99, 104–5. Professor Abi-Saab's suggestion of some hierarchy is contentious, however, amongst international lawyers.

2

The Joint Declaration

1 CHINA'S 'OWN POLICIES' TOWARDS HONG KONG

The negotiations following Margaret Thatcher's visit had commenced on 12 July in the former Austro-Hungarian Legation Building in Beijing. As we saw, Cradock may have taken the view that China's leaders were incorrigible, ineducable and blinkered by dogma and nationalistic pride, but to the Chinese side, Britain's negotiators demonstrated a 'colonialist and imperialist attitude', one which was 'outmoded, lacking in reality and would get nowhere'.[1] Midway through the formal negotiations in July and August of 1983, between the second round in late July and the third round in early August,[2] the Chinese delegation was to present publicly its position on the indivisibility of sovereignty and administration, that is, that there is no resumption of sovereignty over Hong Kong if Britain were to continue to administer it.[3] China also unveiled the twelve principles (or 'Twelve Point Plan') for Hong Kong.

Insofar as the Chinese position was concerned the formal talks were therefore only limited to discussion of Hong Kong's prosperity, both after Hong Kong's 'recovery' from Britain in 1997 as well as during a transition period prior to that date, that is, from 1984 to 1997. In any event, this too was to be a matter involving only China's own policies towards Hong Kong.[4] There would be no Chinese sovereignty without unfettered Chinese administration. That view has continued to be maintained consistently today in the face of fresh controversy between the UK and the PRC following passage of the new

---

[1] Stephen Seawright, 'Hard-fought Sino-British Negotiations over Hong Kong Revealed in Declassified Files', S.C.M.P. (Hong Kong), 18 August 2013.
[2] Robert Cottrell, *The End of Hong Kong: The Secret Diplomacy of Imperial Retreat* (London: John Murray, 1993), 98–118.
[3] Cottrell, *op. cit.*, 112–13, 119; also Dick Wilson, *Hong Kong! Hong Kong!* (London: Unwin Hyman, 1990), 210.
[4] Cottrell, *op. cit.*, at 115–16.

2020 National Security Law for Hong Kong. The PRC asserts that the law is entirely a sovereign, domestic matter and that UK has no right to interfere, that is, that Hong Kong is no longer administered by the UK. There is from the PRC's viewpoint as well no 'moral obligation' on the part of the UK in respect of Hong Kong. To the UK, however, there was an exchange in 1984; that Beijing will not intervene in Hong Kong affairs but for those concerning defence or foreign affairs, Hong Kong will elect its own Chief Executive and the socialist system will not be applied to Hong Kong.[5]

It is not to be supposed that all this can be analysed purely as a question of 'black-letter' international law. For example, by asking if indeed the UK retains certain treaty rights then can it be said that it is interfering in China's purely domestic, sovereign affairs at all?

There is much about the Sino-British negotiations during the 1980s which continues to inform us, not least about what words that are used today mean. Words such as 'responsibility', 'moral obligation', 'duty'.

II COLLAPSE OF THE BRITISH NEGOTIATING AND FALLBACK POSITIONS

Negotiations which had been adjourned following the third round in early August were not going well. The communiqué following that round had triggered a fall in the Hang Seng index.[6] Negotiations were to be recommenced in a fourth round in September 1983, amidst a harsh atmosphere in Hong Kong.[7] The UKFCO and the Executive Council (ExCo) in Hong Kong comprising the local 'unofficials' – officials who were appointed to advise and assist the Governor but did not hold any governmental office as such – were split on the question of continued British administration; the former having seemingly conceded the issue while the latter still clung to it with it seemed the British Prime Minister's support.[8] A review of the files in the National Archives will show that much effort was spent on bringing in and placating the unofficial members, led by S. Y. Chung in Hong Kong,[9] who were on the whole adamant that there should be continued British administration.[10] Earlier in February an alternative negotiating position had been dismissed

---

[5] Wilson, *op. cit.*, 210.
[6] Cottrell, *op. cit.*, 113.
[7] Ibid., 119.
[8] Ibid., 116–17.
[9] S. Y. Chung (1917–2018), of whom more will be said.
[10] TNA/PREM 19/1057 (Pt. 8, Future of Hong Kong, New Territorial [*sic.*] Leases).

as a 'sell out' by the Prime Minister who, according to the journalist Stephen Seawright's review of declassified files, had asked for a military assessment only to be told the obvious.[11] However, by September the Hong Kong dollar had lost a third of its value and the fourth round of talks was conducted, apart from its frigid atmosphere, in fraught economic circumstances.[12] The two sides had barely agreed on a fifth round of talks which were to be held in October.[13] At the British end, Chinese intransigence was viewed as a cause of the loss of confidence. The UK had already intervened in the currency markets but there were limits to what it could hope to achieve. What was needed, at least from the UK's viewpoint, was a show of confidence in Hong Kong's future by both the UK and the PRC. On 27 September, Geoffrey Howe met Wu Xueqian, the Chinese Foreign Minister, for an hour in what one telegram described as a 'lengthy rehearsal of respective positions':

> 4 ... but the obstacle was the question of sovereignty, the talks were stalemated because the British took the view that they could exchange sovereignty for administration, this was unacceptable. Sovereignty was not negotiable in any sense ... Deng[14] had told Mr. Heath[15] that his advice to the British Government was that China could not compromise on sovereignty, she would take back Hong Kong in 1997.
> ...
> 7. Invited by Wu to comment, Zhou Nan said that Britain had evaded the crucial question in the talks so far by insisting that while China could have nominal sovereignty, Britain should retain administrative control. This approach virtually closed the door to any discussion of practical arrangements to maintain Hong Kong's stability and prosperity after 1997. The Chinese side had been surprised and disappointed by the British position. If it changed, detailed discussions on all practical aspects of the issue could begin immediately. China could agree to a statement as we wished ... He added that the Chinese side had been particularly distressed by a recent statement by Sir P Cradock

---

[11] Seawright, *op. cit.*
[12] It was from these events that the Hong Kong dollar peg to the US dollar emerged; Cottrell, *op. cit.*, 123–7.
[13] TNA/PREM 19/1057 (Pt. 8), FCO Deskby 231030Z, Hong Kong Deskby 231030Z, Singapore Deskby 240110Z from Peking 230945Z Sep 83 to Immediate FCO, Telno. 933 of 23 September 1983 (Cradock); Deskby 250100Z FM FCO to Immediate Hong Kong (Howe).
[14] Deng Xiaoping.
[15] Who met with Deng Xiaoping earlier that month, 10 September 1983, to smooth the way forward. A record of the meeting appears in the National Archives files; TNA/PREM 19/1057 (Pt. 8), Deskby 101000Z from Peking 100915Z Sep 83 to Immediate FO, Telno. 879 of 10 September 1983.

II Collapse of the British Negotiating and Fallback Positions

that British administration was the only way for Hong Kong to remain stable and prosperous in the future.[16]

Another contemporary observer had put it this way – 'time was running out'.[17] Hope that Beijing would yield to the suggestion of continued British administration because of the Hong Kong dollar crisis, perhaps with a 'watered down' version of continued administration,[18] had been misplaced.[19] It might have seemed reasonable to suppose that Beijing would prefer a golden goose to a dead duck, but that supposition albeit in retrospect was misconceived. On 27 September, Sir Edward Youde, Governor of Hong Kong, had despatched a telegram:

> I am afraid we do not see any other means available at the present time to get over the message. The Chinese recognise that there is a crisis but believe we are trying to use it in order to bring pressure on them and are determined not to give way. They have also made plain their readiness if need be to accept considerable economic damage ... The only way to get their co-operation ... is to make a bow in the direction of the premise (see Para 7 of Peking Telco 937).[20]

The next round of talks in October 1983 were now clearly at risk. It may be useful to observe in passing that a similar notion that Hong Kong's economic worth to China could present itself as hostage was to re-emerge in some minds in post-handover Hong Kong in 2014 and again in 2019, and elements of 1983 were to be rehearsed, but that is to rush the story.[21] In late 1983, Britain, soon to realise the danger of this initial assumption, was compelled ultimately to cede

---

[16] TNA/PREM 19/1057 (Pt. 8), Deskby Hong Kong 280100Z, FM UKMIS New York 27222Z Sep 83 to Immediate Hong Kong, Telno. 006 of 27 September 1993, Info Immediate FCO, Peking, Washington (For Coles in PM's Party), paras. 4 and 7.

[17] David Akers-Jones, *Feeling the Stones* (Hong Kong: Hong Kong University Press, 2004), 145.

[18] These originally were 'Option A' and 'Option B', but were to evolve. See TNA/PREM 19/1057 (Pt. 8), Deskby 10100Z, FM FCO 091445Z Sept 83 to Immediate Hong Kong, Telno. 880 of 9 September 1983, para. 10 (Howe); TNA/PREM 19/1057 (Pt. 8), 'The Future of Hong Kong, Talks with the Chinese, A Reappraisal One Year On', Secret, FCO, August 1983.

[19] British fears about the seriousness of the crisis were genuine, see e.g. TNA/PREM 19/1057 (Pt. 8), Letter from J. O. Kerr to Andrew Turnbull, 30 September 1983 ('Charles Goodhart from the Bank ... will therefore fly to Hong Kong over the weekend'). At the same time there appeared to have been a British belief that the Chinese side was not taking the matter 'genuinely and seriously'; TNA/PREM 19/1057 (Pt. 8), Telegram from Private Secretary to the P.M. to Governor, undated in file (circa 29–30 September 1983).

[20] TNA/PREM 19/1057 (Pt. 8), Deskby 271200Z Ottawa, FM Hong Kong 271020Z Sep 83 to Immediate Ottawa, Telno. 12 of 27 September and to Immediate FCO, Washington (For Private Secretary to Chancellor of Exchequer), UKMIS New York (For Private Secretary) and Peking, para. 4.

[21] Chapters 7, 9 and 10 of this book.

on the issue of continued British administration, having effectively relinquished in March its earlier position on sovereignty. Thus, between March 1983 and September 1983, the assertion of UK sovereignty under two treaties and the UK's fallback position – continued British administration after 1997 – had both essentially collapsed.[22] Albeit 'conditionally' the UK now was ready to explore other options with China in the coming fifth round of negotiations in October. Geoffrey Howe wrote in his memoirs:[23]

> [T]he British side (including Hong Kong) was torn between two views. From Hong Kong most of the unofficials [unofficial or non-governmental members of the Executive Council], led by Sir S. Y. Chung ... and supported by Sir Philip Haddon-Cave (by now Chief Secretary), took the view that the Chinese were bluffing and should be pressed to accept our case [continued British administration of some sort, after 1997], even at the risk of breakdown. They were supported, cautiously, by Governor Teddy Youde. On the other side were ranged the London China hands led by Percy Cradock. Richard Luce and I shared their view that the Chinese were not bluffing, and that confrontation would lead only to disaster for Hong Kong.

24 September 1983 was to become a critical turning point. To Sir Percy Cradock in Beijing a (further) fallback plan was now required which would have to involve discussing 'the Chinese plan positively' however or 'the breakdown will occur during that round'.[24] There previously had been three options – Option A, continued British administration; Option B, accepting the Chinese plan; Option C, accepting the Chinese plan but to explore 'what flexibility there might be in the Chinese concept of administration, and what guarantees in the form of continued British links the Chinese would be prepared to build into their plan'.[25] Cradock's

[22] TNA/PREM 19/1057 (Pt. 8), Deskby 291200Z, FM FCO 291130Z Sep 83 to Immediate Washington and to Immediate UKMIS New York (Personal for Private Secretary), Info Immediate Peking (Personal for Chargé), Telno. 1614 of 29 September 1983 ('The Chinese are adamant that both sovereignty and administration will be recovered in 1997 and have characterised our insistence on British administration as an insuperable obstacle to progress. They have hinted strongly that they will break off the talks if there is no change in the British position ... In light of what the Chinese have said the following grave risks must be taken into account ... That the Chinese will be ready if necessary to sacrifice the economic benefits they obtain from Hong Kong in order to achieve their political objectives. It would be dangerously wrong to assume that they would back down in a confrontation once they saw the damage being done to the Hong Kog economy'). See also Cottrell's earlier treatment, op. cit., 129–30.
[23] Geoffrey Howe, Conflict of Loyalty (London: Macmillan, 1994), 367.
[24] TNA/PREM 19/1057 (Pt. 8), Deskby FCO 240800Z, Deskby H.K. 240730Z from Peking 240600Z to Immediate FCO, Telno. 937 of 24 September 1983, para. 7.
[25] TNA/PREM 19/1057 (Pt. 8), Deskby 291200Z, FM FCO 291130Z Sep 83 to Immediate Washington and to Immediate UKMIS New York (Personal for Private Secretary), Info Immediate Peking (Personal for Chargé), Telno. 1614 of 29 September 1983, para. 6.

II Collapse of the British Negotiating and Fallback Positions

view was that breakdown was not inevitable and that the UK should explore the last Option C – that is to say, PRC sovereignty, no British administration but to seek to preserve 'British links'.[26] Cradock added: 'I realise that this is a serious step, and that ExCo [the local Executive Council in Hong Kong] will find it difficult to contemplate. The Governor will, no doubt, give his views on how they should be consulted.' While it might be thought that such a step should be considered only after the breakdown of talks, it would in Cradock's view create an unacceptable risk (Cradock described it as 'extremely dangerous') since the UK would have then nowhere to fall back upon, a retreat would have to be conducted in public view and further havoc would be wrought upon the Hong Kong economy.[27] Cradock had also sent an earlier telegram on the same day reporting that during dinner on the previous evening with 'an unusually voluble delegation' comprising Yao Guang,[28] Ke Zaishuo[29] and Lu Ping[30], he had been assured 'that everything else was negotiable if the principle that sovereignty and administration should pass to China were accepted' barring however a Governor appointed by the UK which Lu Ping and the other Chinese officials made plain would be 'out of the question'.[31] So far as the point on continued British administration was concerned Yao Guang had put it even more strongly to Cradock the day before that, on 22 September 1983: 'Yao said that our insistence on administration amounted to out and out insistence on colonial rule. He referred to the Opium War and accused us of trying to replace the old unequal treaties with a new one, and adopting an imperialist attitude. We must be day-dreaming.'[32] A telegram by Howe on 24 September reads:

> It is our belief, and we are confident, the belief of the majority of people of Hong Kong that the best way to ensure the continued prosperity and stability

---

[26] In a way, 'Option C' was an inversion of a watered down version of Option A. Rather than to have British administration with 'Chinese flexibilities' one would have Chinese administration with 'British links'.

[27] TNA/PREM 19/1057 (Pt. 8), Deskby FCO 240800Z, Deskby H.K. 240730Z from Peking 240600Z to Immediate FCO, Telno. 937 of 24 September 1983, paras. 8–10.

[28] Vice-Foreign Minister, leader of the Chinese negotiating team until January 1984 and previously China's ambassador to France. His replacement subsequently was Zhou Nan, then Assistant Foreign Minister, raising at the time at least the question of a downgrading of diplomatic representation at the talks in early 1984. The question was swiftly dispelled by Yao Guang over dinner with Anthony Galsworthy.

[29] Later to head the Chinese delegation to the Sino-British Joint Liaison Group established under Annex 2 of the Joint Declaration.

[30] Head of the PRC delegation.

[31] TNA/PREM 19/1057 (Pt. 8), Deskby FCO 240800Z, Deskby H.K. 240600Z from Peking 240530Z Sep 83 to Immediate FCO, Telno. 935 of 24 September 1983, para. 4.

[32] TNA/PREM 19/1057 (Pt. 8), Deskby 221400Z from Peking 221100Z Sep 83 to Immediate FCO, Telno. 927 of 22 September 1983, para. 3.

of Hong Kong is to avoid disturbing the complex arrangements which now provide the framework of Hong Kong's success ... we believe that the talks should focus particularly on how future arrangements can guarantee the continuation of Hong Kong's free economy and way of life, and thus sustain the confidence which is absolutely essential to Hong Kong's success.[33]

Cradock's view was clear; the UK could not pursue options B and C in tandem. If under Option B it was to be Chinese administration in the future, the UK would want to propose changes to the current colonial system, but under Option C – continued British administration – the UK would be seeking to preserve those colonial elements.[34] The declassified files show however that insofar as the UK was concerned, acting on the advice of the local ExCo members in Hong Kong, Option B (allowing the possibility of Chinese administration after 1997) was to have been no more than a tactic to draw the Chinese negotiators in, while at the same time pursuing Option C, that is, continued British administration after 1997. In other words conceding on sovereignty only conditionally was a fig leaf, but an apparent concession concerning continued British administration was instead only a negotiating ploy.[35] Any risk of the PRC declaring that the UK had in fact conceded the issue of continued British Administration could and would have to be denied vigorously in public, and Ministers in London had agreed to all this.[36] Yet ploy had turned to reality and for Cradock the premise now lay in the preservation of the colony's existing features after the handover.

The fifth round of talks took place from 19 to 20 October but the UK's position was to be further diminished. British archival records show consternation over the PRC's suspicions that the UK still harboured hopes of continued British administration. In conversation with Gaston Thorn, the

---

[33] TNA/PREM 19/1057 (Pt. 8), FM FCO 231315Z Sep 83 to Immediate Hong Kong, Telno. 961 of 24 September 1983, Info Immediate Peking, paras. 4–5.

[34] TNA/PREM 19/1057 (Pt. 8), Deskby FCO 240800Z, Deskby H.K. 240730Z from Peking 240600Z to Immediate FCO, Telno. 937 of 24 September 1983, para. 6.

[35] The files show that the phraseology and precise articulation of the ruse had preoccupied Margaret Thatcher. A telegram from the Private Secretary to the PM to Geoffrey Howe's Private Secretary reads: 'We should avoid giving any impression that Britain has shifted its position ... the Prime Minister considers that rather than "maintaining our position in principle" we should "firmly maintain our position". She has counted that it must be clear that our own views on British Administration have not changed'; TNA/PREM 19/1057 (Pt. 8), FM The Hague 200840Z Sep 83 to Immediate FCO, Telno. 262 of 20 September 1983.

[36] TNA/PREM 19/1057 (Pt. 8), Deskby 210100Z FM FCO 201910Z Sep 83 to Immediate Hong Kong, Telno. 937 of 20 September 1983 (Howe); TNA/PREM 19/1057 (Pt. 8), Deskby 210100Z FM FCO 201910Z Sep 83 to Immediate Peking, Telno. 618 of 20 September 1983 (Howe); TNA/PREM 19/1057 (Pt. 8), Deskby 191400Z FM FCO 191318Z to Immediate The Hague, Telno. 112 of 19 September 1983 (Howe).

II Collapse of the British Negotiating and Fallback Positions

President of the European Commission, Deng Xiaoping had referred to the UK harbouring such hopes still of what he described as 'co-administration' and 'administration of the territory in disguise', and Thorn in turn had briefed European Community ambassadors.[37] Cradock wanted a statement on the record that the UK had relinquished the idea of any kind of continued British administration while Teddy Youde considered it unwise for the UK to be rushed into this by the PRC side.[38]

In any event, Cradock reporting on the second day of the sixth round of negotiations, stated that while the UK wanted to get into the minutiae of autonomy, the PRC refused to get into these treacherous details and was immoveable on first addressing the broad question of sovereignty and the non-negotiability of any continued British administration,[39] or more euphemistically any 'links of British authority'. During that sixth round which took place from 14 to 15 November a clear assurance was by then at least in the view of Britain's ambassador to Beijing clearly required, in order to allay Chinese fears, that there in fact would be 'no links of authority' from the UK's viewpoint, no links that is of any residual British authority assuming the satisfactory conclusion of talks on Hong Kong's handover. The Chinese side were especially perturbed by a radio phone-in interview which the Prime Minister had given, which would only deepen their suspicions notwithstanding any prior assurance by Cradock of Britain harbouring hopes for some form of continued British role.[40] Immediately after the sixth round, which he

---

[37] Future of Hong Kong, New Territorial [sic.] Leases), P. F. Ricketts to A. J. Coles, 10 November 1983.

[38] See e.g. TNA/PREM 19/1059 (Pt. 10), Deskby 111630Z FM FCO to Immediate Athens, undated (Howe). Interestingly, in this telegram Howe observes that Cradock's suggestion that the question of the Governorship of Hong Kong should be tackled early on 'will need very careful consideration'. Youde himself had something to say about the ultimate credibility of Cradock's suggestion at home in the UK, see Deskby FCO 110900Z, Deskby Athens 110700Z from Hong Kong 110440Z Nov 83 to Immediate FCO, Telno. 1707 of 11 November 1983. Cradock, in a telegram the previous day, wrote that the divergence in viewpoint had to be 'clarified if we are not to become completely stuck' since Youde's suggestion to hold firm will 'generate such suspicion and resentment on the Chinese side that we would have done better never to embark on it'. Cradock wanted the removal of 'any links of authority', rather than 'other links which are negotiable', in order to then pave the way for a discussion of 'the constitutional and administrative arrangements'. He added: 'All I am proposing is that we should tell the Chinese this now instead of waiting for it to emerge when we present a paper on this subject'; TNA/PREM 19/1059 (Pt. 10), Deskby 1010002 from Peking 100855Z Nov 83 to Immediate FCO, Telno. 1176 of 10 November 1983.

[39] TNA/PREM 19/1059 (Pt. 10), Deskby FCO 151130Z FM Peking 151010Z Nov 83 to Immediate FCO, Telno. 1196 of 15 November 1983.

[40] See also Cottrell, *op. cit.*, 131–2 whose work which was based on interviews does not appear to have had direct access to the currently declassified files-, and is all the more remarkable for it.

considered had gone very badly notwithstanding the fact the UK had kept the PRC in the talks, Cradock proposed the following formula which, while adhering to the Prime Minister's parameters, he would be willing to convey to the PRC side:

> The Chinese side have repeatedly asked us to define more clearly what we mean by the expression 'a substantial British role' which was used by the British Prime Minister in her message of 14 October. I wish to make it clear on instructions that the British side understands that the Chinese plan is based upon the premise that both sovereignty and the right of administration over the whole of Hong Kong should revert to China after 1997. For this reason the British side does not intend, in the course of the discussion proposed in the Prime Minister's message. To make any proposal on links between Britain and Hong Kong which conflicts with the premise that both sovereignty and the right of administration over the whole of Hong Kong should revert to China in 1997. In particular the British side does not intend to propose any link of accountability or authority between the Government of the Hong Kong SAR after 1997 and the British Government at any level. The British side would also be working on the assumption that any British subjects who continued to serve in Hong Kong as Government officials would be in the employment of the Government of the SAR and would owe their loyalties to that Government. They would not be appointed by the British Government, nor would they be responsible to London.[41]

The question of the abandonment of any 'British links of authority' is a critical point not least in light of contemporary assertions, assertions at the time of this book, of Britain's 'responsibility' towards Hong Kong and explains the strenuous PRC reaction. But all this is, again, to rush matters. Naturally such British assurances during the fifth and sixth rounds of negotiation in October and November remained 'conditional' but that is to state only the obvious since nothing is done until everything is done in any treaty negotiation, and as Cottrell calls it a 'fig leaf'.[42] The stage was set, the treaty would be for a lost city, and soon there was to be another radical development following these concessions by Britain's negotiators.

For the UK, all of these developments would now at least pave the way for detailed discussions on the post-handover arrangements for Hong Kong where previously the negotiations had been sterile and desultory. Indeed the seventh round held on the 7 and 8 December 1983 was by all accounts more positive: 'I

---

[41] TNA/PREM 19/1059 (Pt. 10), From Peking 170900Z Nov 83 to Immediate FCO, Telno. 1206 of 17 November 1983.
[42] Ibid., 134.

spoke first. I repeated for the record the formula I had delivered on instructions to Yao Guang on 28 November.'[43] Cradock was then to comment in a further telegram:

> This was perhaps the most positive session so far ... It would seem that the formula presented to the Chinese side on 28 November, taken together with the Prime Minister' message of 14 October and subsequent explanations of it, have finally brought the Chinese to the point where they are ready to discuss practical matters.[44]

British Cabinet Office minutes noted that:

> The Foreign and Commonwealth Secretary said that, although the seventh round ... had been conducted in an improved atmosphere, it was necessary to recognise the weakness of the United Kingdom's negotiating position. It was now clear that the Chinese Government were not prepared to accept what had been the original British objective of a continuing British presence in Hong Kong after the expiry of the lease of the New Territories in 1997. Nor would they accept any link of authority. The aim must now be to negotiate on the basis of the Chinese proposals in order to make them more acceptable and workable, even if at the end of the process the proposals might well not be such as the Government could positively commend to Parliament or to the people of Hong Kong.[45]

Insofar as Britain's negotiators were concerned, the talks should at least result in detailed treaty provisions. Alas it was, again, not how Beijing's negotiators saw it. The deadline set by Deng Xiaoping for a settlement by September 1984 now loomed. The Chinese side proposed that because of the need for a swift outcome the treaty should take the form rather of a joint set of declarations by the PRC and the UK. According to this proposal, the PRC will state its own policies in respect of the arrangements for post-handover Hong Kong. It all came as a surprise to the UK negotiators,[46] who had wanted instead to explain

---

[43] TNA/PREM 19/1059 (Pt. 10), Deskby FCO 071130Z FM Peking 070955Z Dec 83 to Immediate FCO, Telno. 1309 of 7 December 1983 (Cradock). The reader should be cautioned that this author has not had actual sight of a copy of the 'Cradock formula' as is here reported to have been presented to the PRC side.

[44] TNA/PREM 19/1059 (Pt. 10), Deskby FCO 071200Z FM Peking 071000Z Dec 83 to Immediate FCO, Telno. 1310 of 7 December 1983.

[45] TNA/PREM 19/1059 (Pt. 10), Secret: Most Confidential Record to OD(K) (83) 3rd Meeting Minutes, Tuesday 13 December 1983, Cabinet Office.

[46] As S. Y. Chung put it: 'Both Britain and the Hong Kong Executive Council initially and all along had thought of labelling the accord the terminology of "Sino-British Agreement".' Sze-yuen Chung, *Hong Kong's Journey to Reunification: Memoirs of Sze-yuen Chung* (Hong Kong: The Chinese University Press, 2021), 113.

the minutiae of colonial administration as part of a wider process of, first, securing China's agreement on the elements which ought to be preserved following the handover of Hong Kong. One could add that that was what 'conditionality' was after all about but it is unsurprising, albeit once again in hindsight, that China's negotiators were about to strip away all pretence. All of this was to emerge fully by January 1984 during the eighth round. Moreover, the Chinese side now sought to have the talks concluded by July.[47] More serious, from the UK's viewpoint, was the proposal of a Sino-British Commission, what ultimately became the Sino-British Joint Liaison Group, which would operate with some considerable powers during the period between 1984 and the actual handover in 1997. This was to become Britain's last bargaining chip as the negotiations drew to a close, to be traded for a more detailed Annex (Annex I) on China's policies towards Hong Kong after the handover, and which itself became the subject of Annex II of the Sino-British Joint Declaration.

The Joint Declaration's present structure, its very architecture, reflects these turns of events during the eighth round of talks. The main text consists only of three pages. Much of the substantive detail is contained in Annex I, consisting of some twelve pages but entitled an 'Elaboration by the Government of the People's Republic of China of Its Basic Policies Regarding Hong Kong'. An elaboration, that is, of its unilateral policies as the PRC would go on to emphasise when controversy was to emerge publicly in 2014.[48]

London was only too aware of this aspect of the Joint Declaration, almost from the beginning of substantive talks. From the UK's viewpoint, the issue was as if a continuous thread running through much of the negotiations. Sir Geoffrey Howe had briefed the Prime Minister in a minute dated 23 December 1983, attaching a policy review paper on the future of Hong Kong which reads:

> They [the Chinese side] will try to whittle away any agreement down to an acknowledgment of their sovereignty on our part, an undertaking on theirs to look after our "interests" and a joint undertaking to cooperate in a smooth transition. But we must make it clear that any agreed arrangement should include assurances of Hong Kong's effective autonomy and Chinese non-interference for 50 years after 1997. One way of doing this would be . . . a joint declaration referring to a more detailed statement, possibly a unilateral

---

[47] Howe, *Conflict of Loyalty, op. cit.*, 134, 140–3.
[48] See C. L. Lim, 'Britain's Treaty Rights in Hong Kong' (2015) 131 *L.Q.R.* 348. Subsequently the UK would claim a treaty breach publicly for the first time regarding a different matter; see C. L. Lim, 'The Sino-British Treaty and the Hong Kong Booksellers Affair' (2016) 132 *L.Q.R.* 552 and Chapter 8 of this book.

II Collapse of the British Negotiating and Fallback Positions

Chinese one, as its Annex which would describe the essential continuity of systems, freedoms and laws etc in some detail.[49]

'Possibly' a 'unilateral Chinese statement'. That formulation reappeared unchanged in early January 1984, in a further minute to the Prime Minister from Howe during preparations for the eighth round held on 25 and 26 January.[50] The UK, or at least Howe, had concluded in addition that the PRC could not be pinned down in the eventual drafting of Hong Kong's Basic Law, which would implement any eventual Joint Declaration, on subjecting future amendments to that law to the judgment of an international commission.[51] The serious consequence then would be this: UK acceptance that detailed commitments by the PRC might be unilateral, and that furthermore it would be for China to implement the treaty in more detailed terms in which it saw fit. By December, referring to this aspect, Geoffrey Howe was to inform the House of Commons two weeks before the signature of the Joint Declaration:

> It is of course the Chinese who must undertake the drafting of the Basic Law. But the Joint Declaration states that the basic policies for Hong Kong set out in the Joint Declaration itself, and elaborated in Annex I, will be stipulated in the Basic Law. The agreement thus provides clear guidelines for the drafting of the Law.[52]

'Clear guidelines', that was as much as could have been achieved. Finally, there was the question of Parliament's approval which, together with China's preference for a smooth transition, were the UK's only forms of leverage. Howe thought Parliament would not need to pass legislation on a transfer of sovereignty concerning what merely would be a Chinese unilateral declaration, 'unlike a formal agreement', although it would still need to approve and ratify the whole package, for which see below Section V.[53] However, insofar as the PRC negotiators would 'whittle away' the UK claim to sovereignty, promising

---

[49] TNA/PREM 19/1059 (Pt. 10), Future of Hong Kong: Policy Review', attachment to Minute from Howe to Thatcher, 'Future of Hong Kong', 23 December 1983, PM/83/102, para. 17.
[50] TNA/PREM 19/1262 (Pt. 11), 'Future of Hong Kong: Policy Review' (revised), attachment to Minute from Howe to Thatcher, 'Hong Kong: Meeting of OD(K), 11 January 1984', PM/84/7, para. 17.
[51] *Ibid.*, Howe-Thatcher Minute, 2.
[52] TNA/PREM 19/1530 (Pt. 18, Future of Hong Kong, New Territorial [*sic.*] Leases), 'Speech by the Rt. Hon. Sir Geoffey Howe, QC, MP to the House of Commons on 5 December: Hong Kong Agreement', 10.
[53] TNA/PREM 19/1262 (Pt. 11), 'Future of Hong Kong: Policy Review' (revised), attachment to Minute from Howe to Thatcher, 'Hong Kong: Meeting of OD(K), 11 January 1984', PM/84/7, attachment, para. 17.

in return to 'look after our "interests"', Howe advised that the UK should insist on Hong Kong's autonomy.[54]

At the most fundamental level, China's position had been consistent; that the negotiations should not extend into matters concerning the detailed policies that would apply to Hong Kong after the handover. For otherwise, from the PRC viewpoint, China would be negotiating the precise and detailed terms of a transfer from Britain which would be anathema to it. Rather, in the Chinese view, China would resume sovereignty and declare on its own terms its own policies towards Hong Kong. From a practical perspective, any dispute about the meaning and content of these policies in the future would be a matter entirely for China itself, as would questions about the Basic Law. Up until the final phase of the negotiations, on 5 July 1984, Len Appleyard at the FCO wrote to Charles Powell at Downing Street enclosing a strategy paper in which the 'Chinese position' was described as follows:

> On the agreement they take the line that the main document should not show their plans for arrangements after 1997 have emerged from negotiation between the Chinese and British Governments and that detail should be covered only in the annex. They say that the agreement and annex would be equally 'binding' but they do not explain how this would be made clear in a legal sense. Thus they are likely to continue to question paragraph 6 of our revised main agreement, which would provide such a binding provision. Nor do they state how much detail would be included in the annex. Their flexibility on this has yet to be fully tested.[55]

In the end the issue was to be resolved, traded would be a better word, for Chinese demands on the details, including the operative dates and location, of the Sino-British Joint Liaison Group which was to be provided for under Annex II to the Declaration. The key sticking point had been the PRC's demand for the Group to meet in Hong Kong against UK fears that it would have undermined the UK's authority in the period leading up to the handover – the fear of a 'creeping condominium' in international law terms with more than one power at once having dominium. In the end the Group was to meet alternately in London, Hong Kong and Beijing[56] albeit with its principal base in Hong Kong and operate from 1985 to 2000. In exchange the UK

---

[54] Ibid.
[55] TNA/PREM 19/1266, (Pt. 16 – 'Future of Hong Kong New Territorial [sic.] Leases'), L. V. Appleyard to C.D. Powell, Secret, 5 July 1984, enclosing 'Future of Hong Kong: Strategic Discussion Paper – July 1984, Chinese Position in the Negotiations', Hong Kong Department, July 1984, para. 2.
[56] Meeting at least once in each of the three locations in each year.

II Collapse of the British Negotiating and Fallback Positions

managed to secure greater detail than it otherwise might in Annex I. In a minute from Percy Cradock to Margaret Thatcher dated 3 August 1984, Cradock wrote, supplementing Geoffrey Howe's report to Thatcher on the state of the talks:[57]

> First, there was no question that for the Chinese this was a make or break occasion. Zhou Nan made this very plain to me at lunch on the first day when he outlined the Chinese offer: if we left Peking without settling the issue of the Joint Liaison Group, Chinese offers of concessions would be withdrawn and the talks as a whole would fail ... the question had therefore to be settled on the spot ... We went to the brink and even slightly beyond it. Once we had your telegram, the bargaining on the date of location of the Joint Group in Hong Kong was carried on ... During the two days in Peking when we indicate that we were interested in the Chinese offer but the precise date of the Joint Group location in Hong Kong was still being debated we enjoyed maximum leverage and were able to exploit it. In that time we pinned the Chinese down on issues which we had expected to take weeks, ie making the agreement legally binding, undertaking that its provisions and those of the Annexes would be in the Basic Law, calling the Annexes rather than exchanges of notes, and removing offensive Chinese language on sovereignty. The use of the word 'agree' governing all the provisions was particularly critical.[58]

This is not to say that the usual rules of treaty law and interpretation and the law on unilateral declarations will not of themselves apply in respect of the legal status of Annex I and its construction. On the other side was sovereignty and the traditional viewpoint of developing nations that international law itself is a contrivance of continuing colonial interests. These were two moving parts of an unstable machine in 1984, involving the negotiation of a treaty text and at a more fundamental, secondary level contestation over the principles and history of international law. To the PRC any commitment to principles concerning Hong Kong's governance can only be a unilateral Chinese statement of policy, or risk dividing sovereignty, that very thing which to Chinese eyes was indivisible. For the UK, not only must Annex I be binding, all would depend upon the level of detail that it would condescend to. It was patently

---

[57] TNA/PREM 19/1267 (Pt. 17, Future of Hong Kong, New Territorial [sic.] Leases), Cradock to Thatcher, 'Hong Kong', Secret, 3 August 1984, paras. 2–4.

[58] It is unclear how far the use of the word 'agree' went in the end when compared to the excitement evident in Youde's message. The final text of the Joint Declaration reads 'to this end, they have, after talks between the delegations of the two Governments, agreed to declare as follows ... 1. The Government of the People's Republic of China declares ... 2. The Government of the United Kingdom declares that ... '. In other words, they 'agreed' to declare separately their positions.

obvious however, even then, that room for doubt on interpretation and detail would tend to favour China's own view of Chinese policies after 1997.

III A LONG, BINDING TREATY

The ninth, tenth and elevenths rounds of negotiation then saw a divide over questions of form begin to play out fully, not least in British insistence that the treaty should contain sufficient detail rather than a preface attached merely to a Chinese twelve point plan. This then was to set the stage for Geoffrey Howe's visit to Beijing. He was to press the Chinese side for a binding treaty rather than a set of entirely separate declarations by the UK and China stating only their own respective understanding. The UK also wanted a detailed document rather than one which only contained broad statements of principle. It became a question about whether the agreement would be 'short' or 'long'[59] and also whether the treaty would be initialled by September of 1984 when Deng's two-year period was up.[60] The timetable was clearly foremost on Geoffrey Howe's mind. For the UK's part, the Ponsonby rule would require a treaty which requires ratification to be laid before Parliament itself and for important treaties to be subject to debate. It derives its name from the British Under-Secretary for State Arthur Ponsonby who had stated to the House in 1924:

> It is the intention of His Majesty's Government to lay on the table of both Houses of Parliament every treaty, when signed, for a period of 21 days, after which the treaty will be ratified ... In the case of important treaties, the Government will, of course, take an opportunity of submitting them to the House for discussion within this period. But, as the Government cannot take upon itself to decide what may be considered important or unimportant, if there is a formal demand for discussion forwarded through the usual channels from the Opposition or any other party, time will be found for the discussion of the treaty in question.[61]

As Howe recalled it:

> Peking on the afternoon of Sunday, 15 April 1984 looked very different from the city that Elspeth and I had last seen ... Our talks with Foreign Minister Wu Xueqian ... started the following morning and lasted all day ... My meeting with Deng – my first – was certain, I knew, to be more testing than

---

[59] Cottrell, *op. cit.*, 134.
[60] Howe, *Conflict of Loyalty*, *op. cit.*, 148.
[61] Hansard, 1 April 1924, col. 1999. See further, Ewan Smith, Eirik Bjorge and Arabella Lang, 'Treaties, Parliament and the Constitution' [2020] *Pub. L.* 508.

this ... I had secured provisional Chinese acceptance – by Wu or Ji or Zhao – of our timetable, which would enable Parliament to debate and approve (but not amend) a draft agreement before it was signed; our insistence that both drafts would remain upon the table, with many of the vital points of substance already in place; our demand that in the final document the details shall be set out in annexes that were to have the same force as the main Agreement ... We were still seriously at odds, however, about the dreaded Joint Commission[62] ... The real business began when I explained to Deng what had been agreed about the timetable. He readily agreed that the British Parliament should have time to consider the matter ... The real points that I needed to raise were few and your allotted two hours had to be filled somehow ... In due time I brought him back to our Agreement, and particularly to the need for detail in our final text. After some resistance, I was able to persuade him to endorse the formula that had been agreed by Zhao.[63]

As Cottrell, in the most comprehensive published work on the negotiations thus far, explains it: 'On some important points, however, the meeting was inconclusive: while Deng agreed that the final document should be binding, rather than merely a statement of intent, he still favoured parallel declarations rather than a simple treaty.'[64]

'Parallel' was to be distinguished subsequently from 'joint'. Still, by this stage, with the UK having conceded on sovereignty and the question of continued British Administration having already been put aside – albeit conditionally,[65] at least from the UK's viewpoint – the questions about the ultimate form in which a Sino-British agreement might take were by now fairly settled. Rather than a preface attached to China's twelve points or mere separate declarations by the UK and China, it was to be at least as perceived by the UK a binding treaty containing the twelve points, in one composite document albeit that the detail will be fleshed out in annexes which nonetheless would form a part of the whole. In a now declassified telegram to the FCO following Howe's visit, Sir Richard Evans wrote:

Both sides reviewed the understanding reached during your visit. Agreement on the timetable was confirmed ... Zhou [Zhou Nan] noted that the legal advisers of the two sides had held an informal exchange of views on the form of the agreement. It should not be difficult to solve this question. You had

---

[62] What became the Sino-British Joint Liaison Group after the Joint Declaration was concluded.
[63] Howe, *Conflict of Loyalty, op. cit.*, 369–72.
[64] Cottrell, *op. cit.*, 149.
[65] Such an expression of continued intellectual reservations could have provided only modest cover.

stressed that there should be adequate detail in the agreement. Deng had point [*sic.*] out that it should contain only matters of principle, which should not be dealt with in detail. Excessive detail would easily lead to mistakes and would be impractical. The idea that the agreement itself should cover only matters of principle while the annexes, in an exchange of notes, could deal with relevant matters in more specific terms, might be desirable. He recalled that Zhao Ziyang had also said that some agreed matters of principle could be included in the annexes as a component part of the Joint Declaration, with which they would be equally valid and binding ... Zhao Ziyang and others had pointed out that Chinese policies in Hong Kong after 1997 were an internal matter. There could be no impression created that the policies were subject to another country's approval and there could be no interference in the SAR's high degree of autonomy after 1997.[66]

In the end, there were three pages in the main body of the text, reflecting China's Twelve Point Plan, Annex I containing a more detailed elaboration of China's basic policies towards Hong Kong after 1997 as the UK had wanted, a further Annex (Annex II) on the Sino-British Joint Liaison Group which jointly would plan and discuss the transitional arrangements until the handover in 1997 still some thirteen years in the future, and Annex III on land leases. This last was an issue which had provided Murray McLehose's original pretext for bringing up the Hong Kong issue. There was finally, as had also been mentioned, an Exchange of Memoranda on British Nationals Overseas status for those born before the handover date, which today has become a source of considerable controversy between the UK and China with the UK's decision to admit BN(O) passport holders for resettlement in the UK.[67]

The questions about validity and form have themselves also become the subject of renewed controversy at the present time, starting from about 2016. From the Chinese viewpoint once sovereignty had been conceded,

---

[66] TNA/PREM 19/1264, (Pt. 13 – 'Future of Hong Kong New Territorial [*sic.*] Leases'), Deskby 271100Z FCO and Tokyo from Peking 270950Z Apr 84 to Immediate FCO, Telno. 810 of 27 April 1984.

[67] In his interview with the Times of London, on 19 July 2020, Liu Xiaoming, the Chinese Ambassador to the Court of St James stated, that: 'the UK goes back on its commitment. When we reached agreement with the UK, we have a separate document and the UK committed that they would not give right of abode to BNO holders. But now they have completely changed their position. So on the one hand, they criticize China for violating China's commitment – and it's a false accusation against China. We told them we are still committed to "One Country, Two Systems". "One Country, Two Systems" is our policy that has been incorporated into the national Constitution and the Basic Law of Hong Kong. It has nothing to do with the Sino-British Joint Declaration. On BNO, there is a very clear-cut commitment from the UK. We exchanged an MOU. But now they want to walk away from their commitment. So there are two elements here.' See further, Chapter 11 of this book.

Hong Kong's governance would become a matter internal to China, many of the detailed guarantees are contained in Annex I but those are, for the PRC, elaborations by China of its own basic policies towards Hong Kong. After all, that is what 'sovereignty', as the Chinese side saw it, in fact means. On the UK side however, all the parts constitute a whole,[68] this is – it is said – supported by treaty law and the rules of treaty interpretation, and the Sino-British Joint Declaration is a treaty which is as valid today as it was on the day of Hong Kong's handover. Furthermore, as had emerged as early as during the eighth round of talks earlier in January, the UK while conceding Chinese sovereignty would not have to further concede that it had never acquired sovereignty and that the nineteenth century treaties with China were unequal and therefore invalid.[69]

Coming back, however, to Howe's visit to Beijing in April 1984, it now remained for him to convey the news publicly that there would not be any continued British administration of Hong Kong, and thence to return to London to inform Parliament. There were two more months of negotiations before July with the aim of settling the terms of the Sino-British Commission proposed by China as a part of the eventual treaty itself.[70] Amidst these there was also concern about the ways by which there could be assurances that the terms would be complied with subsequently.

IV TO BE CONSULTED OR TOLD?

The account given thus far may be thought to be incomplete in one glaring aspect – what of Hong Kong and views from Hong Kong? That was an entirely British concern in these bipartite negotiations, a concern which from all accounts elicited only great suspicion on the Chinese side. Recall too that the world had in effect agreed to the removal of Hong Kong from the list of territories overseen by the United Nations' decolonisation committee.[71] That was done at China's initiative. In an important sense Hong Kong was unlike other new and newly decolonised nations of Asia and Africa which had emerged from their existing colonial administrative boundaries to become

---

[68] There is also Cradock's account in which he describes the UK's expectation that Annex I will have been fleshed out in detail by the Chinese side, but that in fact it ere as if the British had expected a roomful of Chinese treasure only to find the room empty, and that it was for the UK side to flesh out in detail the contents of that Annex; see Percy Cradock, *Experiences of China* (London: John Murray, 1994), 208.
[69] Cottrell, *op. cit.*, 142.
[70] Howe, *Conflict of Loyalty, op. cit.*, 375.
[71] See Chapter 1 of this book.

transformed into sovereign, new independent nations. The Opium War had been fought with an existing sovereign country, China. The post-war solution or remedy was to be its recovery. But for certain events that possibly could have happened much earlier, following the conclusion of the Second World War, had the American President Franklin Delano Roosevelt been alive to see it through.[72]

Still, every effort had to be, or had to be shown to have been, made not only to accommodate but to satisfy Hong Kong's wishes. The UK, as will be recalled, had conceded on continued British administration assuming that Hong Kong will be satisfied with the outcome. The records show a great amount of attention being focussed particular in the period from December 1983 to January 1984 on bringing the 'unofficial members' of ExCo in Hong Kong on board. Put differently, the onus fell upon Britain to make any eventual deal acceptable. Formally however while Hong Kong's native unofficial members were ultimately given access to information about Sino-British negotiations, they were expressly forbidden from taking soundings and were also required to maintain strict confidentiality.[73] Hong Kong could not in fact, despite whatever pretence or British conditionalities, be consulted rather than to be told simply about the negotiations and their outcome, and it fell to Geoffrey Howe to tell Hong Kong that there will be no continued British administration.

It was in those circumstances that there came a suggestion from certain quarters in Hong Kong, suggestions which were conveyed to London, in respect of the Sino-British Commission/Joint Liaison Group that would operate up until the date of the handover. It was during this phase that Howe had also been involved in drafting the terms for what was to become the Sino-British Joint Liaison Group, more or less as it now appears in Annex II of the Joint Declaration.[74] It was put to Howe that there ought to be a mirror image of such an entity operating until the handover, that there would be the continuation of such a mechanism even after the handover, thereby securing continued British surveillance after 1997. Clearly as far as the PRC was concerned, just as sovereignty was indivisible from continued British administration, continued British surveillance would be an unwarranted intrusion into China's internal sovereign affairs. The PRC also considers today that what was substituted for the mirror-image idea, the UK Foreign Secretary's current six-monthly reports to Parliament on Hong Kong, to be just such an

---

[72] Roosevelt would, it appears, have returned Hong Kong after the Second World War had Winston Churchill not held firm.
[73] Cottrell, *op. cit.*, 193–5.
[74] Howe, *Conflict of Loyalty, op. cit.*, 375.

interference. A contemporary example of the PRC's position is the Chinese Ambassador to the UK's statement, in 2020, that:

> The UK side knows well that Hong Kong is no longer under its colonial rule, and that Hong Kong has returned to China and is now part of China. The UK has no sovereignty, jurisdiction or right of 'supervision' over Hong Kong after the handover. However, the UK Government keeps making irresponsible remarks on Hong Kong affairs through its so-called 'Six-monthly report on Hong Kong'.[75]

Let us come back however to Geoffrey Howe. His trip triggered a move within Hong Kong for wider consultation. The cat was out of the bag and threatened to make a nuisance. A delegation from Hong Kong had made its way to London in January with a list of inconvenient questions. These included how acceptability to Hong Kong will be measured, the status of British Dependent Territories Citizenship in the future,[76] the ways to ensure the PRC's future compliance with treaty terms, and also a call for greater assurances that implementing legislation (the eventual Basic Law of the Hong Kong SAR which entered into force upon the handover) would in fact conform to the treaty. That delegation was rebuffed on both sides of the House of Commons, and for good measure it was also denounced by the National People's Congress in Beijing. As Cottrell again, who describes these events, put it memorably: 'They were, they discovered, colliding with a new geometry of power created by the approaching Sino-British agreement – a geometry which moved them from the centre to the margins.'[77]

S. Y. Chung, then the Senior Member of the Executive Council, recalling all this in his memoirs wrote that the delegation to London had six concerns, two questions and four requests. The four requests were, that:

The Agreement should:

(1) Contain full details of the administrative, legal, social and economic systems applicable after 1997;
(2) Provide adequate and workable assurances that the Agreement will be honoured;
(3) State that the Basic Law will incorporate the provisions of the Agreement;
(4) Guarantee the right of the British nationals.[78]

---

[75] Online press conference, 9 July 2020, transcript available on the embassy's website at www.chinese-embassy.org.uk/eng/dshdjjh/t1796269.htm (last accessed on 21 July 2020).
[76] The question of nationality had been raised by Howe in Beijing in April 1984, and entered into the discussions during the thirteenth round of negotiations; see e.g. TNA/PREM 19/1266, (Pt. 16), Geoffrey Howe to Margaret Thatcher, 'Future of Hong Kong: Nationality', PM/84/122, Secret, 13 July 1984.
[77] Cottrell, *op. cit.*, 153.
[78] Chung, *op. cit.*, 83–4.

Howe for his part described the Hong Kong delegation's London visit in the following way:

> This time they came armed with a manifesto, raising quite specific and legitimate points ... They may have felt dismayed by their welcome, if only because no parliamentary voice was raised in criticism of my approach. I was indeed commended by Denis Healey for the official Opposition. But no less than twenty-two back-bench speakers took part in a debate that lasted until midnight, all of them urging me to intensify my efforts on behalf of Hong Kong.[79]

In political terms at least Howe's mission had been a complete and utter success.

But just as the negotiations moved into their final phase, and which were now led by David Wilson, a further Hong Kong delegation this time to Beijing rather than London, and which predictably ended badly, now required Geoffrey Howe himself to undertake a further trip there himself. The unofficial members in Hong Kong and Edward Youde as Governor had all argued against the trip for fear that the UK had by then already conceded too much. In terms of tactics, the Governor favoured instead leaving all the outstanding issues to the very end in a final grand bargaining session.[80] Percy Cradock was again on Howe's side.

Howe's trip had been arranged for the end of July, 27–31 July 1984,[81] the target now being September 1984 for the conclusion of the deal. The fifteenth and sixteenth rounds of negotiation in late May and mid-June had dwelt still on the question of inserting detail into the agreement, while aside from the question of a Sino-British Commission/Joint Liaison Group operating in the transition before the handover 1997, there now lurked since Howe's earlier visit the question of stationing a People's Liberation Army (PLA) garrison in Hong Kong.[82] In London the firm position was that Hong Kong's views will not be ascertained by any kind of referendum, which clearly China was strongly against, and there would also be no prospect of Hong Kong amending

---

[79] Howe, *Conflict of Loyalty, op. cit.*, 374.
[80] TNA/PREM 19/1266, (Pt. 16), L. V. Appleyard to C. D. Powell, Secret, 5 July 1984, enclosing 'Future of Hong Kong: Strategic Discussion Paper – July 1984, Chinese Position in the Negotiations', Hong Kong Department, July 1984, para. 17.
[81] TNA/PREM 19/1266, (Pt. 16), Richard Evans to Richard Luce, 'Joint Group: Secretary of State's Visit', Secret, From Peking 130255Z July 1984 to Flash Hong Kong, Telno. 140 90F, 13 July 1984.
[82] Intense deliberations on the UK side on these two points are reflected in TNA/PREM 19/1265 (Pt. 14, Future of Hong Kong, New Territorial [sic.] Leases), covering the fourteenth to the sixteenth rounds of negotiations from May to June 1984.

the deal reached between Beijing and London.[83] The difficulty with the idea of a Sino-British Commission was that China would wield power over Hong Kong even before the handover, and thus the UK proposed that such an entity should only have a 'liaison' function. In Beijing, Zhou Nan on the Chinese side made a key concession in the interest of concluding the talks by September. There had been a darkened atmosphere leading up to that point, only two weeks earlier Evans in Beijing was to report in a telegram to Geoffrey Howe:

> Zhou Nan took me aside at the French ambassador's national day party on 14 July, we had a conversation of about 20 minutes, out of earshot of anyone else ... Zhou Nan said that he wanted to underline what was said to me at the dinner two days before about the danger of confrontation. Given the present mood of his leaders, he foresaw confrontation if you were to urge on them the acceptance of our proposals about a Joing [sic.] Liaison Group. Confrontation could lead to deadlock (semi-colon) deadlock to breakdown (semi-coln) [sic.] and breakdown to a very unpleasant situation.[84]

In the end, the Sino-British Commission originally proposed by the PRC would be renamed the 'Sino-British Joint Liaison Group', a liaison function had come to replace the risk of Chinese oversight in the period leading up to the handover and in a nod to the mirror-image idea the Group would operate after the handover until 2000.[85] This end date will in time reflect China's views about the practical importance of the Joint Declaration, after which insofar as the PRC is concerned the Sino-British Joint Declaration would have fulfilled its practical function. It is not the UK's view.

V THE ELEGANT SOLUTION

To be sure, Howe's visit, albeit successful, was not the end of it. There were further rounds subsequently. On 8 September Howe wrote to Evans in Peking: 'I have been following very closely the progress of the negotiations ... since my visit to Peking in July. Much was achieved during that visit ... The same spirit has enabled further progress', however 'I should like to tell you frankly that I have become increasingly concerned about difficulties which have arisen on three of the subjects left outstanding after my visit, namely nationality,

---

[83] Cottrell, *op. cit.*, 154–9.
[84] TNA/PREM 19/1266, (Pt. 16), 'Future of Hong Kong: Your Visit', Deskby 161000Z from Peking 160935Z July 1984 to Immediate FCO, Telno. 1439, 16 July 1984.
[85] Cottrell, *op. cit.*, 160–1.

constitutional arrangements and ratification.'[86] But by 17 September 1984 Evans could report that the final negotiated text was ready for the lawyers to pore over: 'agreement was reached at delegation level on the text of the Joint Declaration and all its annexes ... will not be subject to further examination by experts at a meeting this afternoon to ensure consistency of language, etc. Agreement on the exchange of memoranda on nationality will be confirmed this evening.'[87]

A considerable amount was owed however to Geoffrey Howe and Zhou Nan who worked together that summer on the text, on 30 July 1984. The formulation adopted eventually was that while the PRC declared its decision to 'resume the exercise of sovereignty over Hong Kong' (paragraph 1), the UK would declare simultaneously that it would 'restore' Hong Kong to China (paragraph 2). This 'joint declaration', appearing in the initial two paragraphs of the text, sidestepped the issue of the legality of British colonial administration, any question of a retrocession of territory and allowed each to maintain their own views regarding the validity of an unequal treaties doctrine. It was an elegant solution. The UK's position on this point had been outlined in a secret minute dated 2 May 1984 from Sir David Goodall[88] to the Prime Minister:

> The revised draft circulated with Mr. Rickett's letter of 1 May has been designed to retain the essentials of the British negotiating position, with ... the important provision that the agreement as a whole and its annexes should be binding. In order to make the draft more acceptable to the Chinese, however, some of their language has been adopted, as has the technique of parallel declarations with a joint provision that the future of Hong Kong must be settled in accordance with the declaration and annexes. The Chinese 'twelve point plan' is included, but this has been amended to remove reference to the 'unequal treaties'. A disclaimer would explicitly dissociate the British Government from the Chinese view of the status of Hong Kong.[89]

---

[86] TNA/PREM 19/1267 (Pt. 17), Deskby 080930Z BOTH, FM FCO 080901Z September 1984 to Immediate Peking, Telno. 1131 of 8 September 1984 (Howe). Howe had briefed Mrs Thatcher on the three issues two days earlier, see TNA/PREM 19/1267 (Pt. 17), Howe to Thatcher, PM/84/144, 6 September 1984, the same day the second day of the twenty-second round of negotiations had remained bogged down with the ratification issue, TNA/PREM 19/1267 (Pt. 17), 'Future of Hong Kong: Round 22: Second Day: Ratification', Deskby 061200Z FCO from Peking 061039Z September 1984 to Immediate FCO, Telno. 2133 of 6 September 1984.
[87] TNA/PREM 19/1267 (Pt. 17), Deskby 170730Z BOTH from Peking 170529Z September 1984 to Immediate FCO, Telno. 2457 of 17 September 1984 (Evans).
[88] FCO Deputy Under-Secretary.
[89] TNA/PREM 19/1265 (Pt. 14), 'OD(K): Strategy in Negotiation', Secret, B.06733, A. D. S. Goodall to Prime Minister, c. Sir Robert Armstrong, 2 May 1984.

Ricketts' revised draft of 1 May differed markedly from what now is the simple British declaration in paragraph 2 that it will 'restore Hong Kong to the People's Republic of China with effect from 1 July 1997'. The Ricketts draft reads:

> The United Kingdom declare that on 1 July 1997 and without prejudice to the position of either government before that date with regard to the status of Hong Kong, they will restore this Hong Kong area (including Hong Kong Island, Kowloon and the New Territories) to the People's Republic of China. Accordingly the United Kingdom Government declare that they will continue to administer Hong Kong until 30 June 1997 and will, with effect from 1 July 1997, terminate all powers of administration, which they exercise with respect to Hong Kong.[90]

At the same time the PRC's declaration that it will 'resume the exercise of sovereignty over Hong Kong' appears now in paragraph 1 preceding the UK declaration in what now is paragraph 2.

What had begun as a great stumbling block at the beginning, concerning a fundamental incommensurability between a Western conception of and a quintessentially anti-colonial perspective on international law, as well as a subsequent controversy over the ultimate nature and form of a Sino-British deal – specifically, as to whether it should consist of parallel declarations only or a singular treaty text – were all overcome.

Following on from paragraphs 1 and 2 as just described, in paragraph 3(1) to (12), exactly twelve Chinese points were 'declared' by the PRC. However, these do not correspond precisely to the original twelve points which had been made public on 29 July 1983 between the second and third rounds of the Sino-British negotiations.[91] Importantly, we do not as yet have an entirely complete picture of each step in the transformation of the twelve points although we know that Wilson and his counterpart Ke had worked on the drafts leading to the final product before they reached Howe and Zhou. Sub-paragraph 1 of paragraph 3 – paragraph 3(1) – in the Joint Declaration instead states the establishment of the Hong Kong Special Administrative Region by the People's Republic of China. It is in the all-important paragraph 3(2) however that we find the words 'The Hong Kong Special Administrative Region will enjoy a high degree of

---

[90] TNA/PREM 19/1265 (Pt. 14), 'Hong Kong: Revised Draft Agreement', Secret, P. F. Ricketts to A. J. Coles, 1 May 1984.

[91] For which, see *ibid.*, 112. For a further, authoritative, rendition of the twelve points, see also The Practice of the 'One Country, Two Systems' Policy in the Hong Kong Special Administrative Region, Information Office of the State Council, 10 June 2014 ('2014 State Council White Paper') http://english.www.gov.cn/archive/white_paper/2014/08/23/content_281474982986578.htm (last accessed 7 April 2021).

autonomy, except in foreign and defence affairs which are the responsibilities of the Central People's Government.'

The main body of the Joint Declaration consists of eight paragraphs in all, followed by three annexes and alongside these the exchange of memoranda already mentioned. The remainder of the Joint Declaration may usefully be introduced to the reader, even if a little loosely, through the framework provided originally by the Chinese twelve points. They lie at the core and also inform the framework as well as what ultimately, when fully fleshed out, became much of the substance of the Joint Declaration.

Turning to the first point in China's original 'Twelve Point Plan', that concerns the maintenance of Hong Kong's capitalist system. Recall that the Chinese position is that sovereignty had always stayed with China and that Sino-British discussions should therefore focus only on maintaining Hong Kong's future stability and prosperity. This point now appears in paragraph 3(5) of the main body of the Joint Declaration and is elaborated upon further in article I of Annex I which itself contains, as was previously also mentioned, China's elaboration of its policies towards Hong Kong. At this juncture a word of caution may be necessary. While Annex I contains China's own policies, stated unilaterally, the annex is nonetheless an essential part of the treaty.[92] Thus it may be suggested – and it appears to be the UK's position – that read as a whole, together with all annexes, the Joint Declaration is a collection of reciprocal rights and duties, carefully balanced. In any event, paragraph 7 of the Joint Declaration states that 'The Government of the United Kingdom and the Government of the People's Republic of China agree to implement the preceding declaration and the Annexes to this Joint Declaration.' It is not necessarily the PRC's position, and this goes back to its negotiating position that a pair of separate declarations should suffice. In the end there was a composite document. However, the composite document itself contains separate declarations, albeit contained in that one, single document. It has been said, for example, that whatever we make of the point about reciprocal rights and duties in the main body, clearly Annex I is precisely what is described in the title, no more than the PRC's 'elaboration' of its policies towards the Hong Kong SAR. We will have to return to this issue later, for now it is best just to flag it and to, first, have a firm overview of the entire treaty.

The second point in the 'Twelve Points' was that Hong Kong is to remain a free port and financial centre. That now appears in paragraphs 1, 3(6) and (7) in the main body, and in Annex I's articles V (Hong Kong shall deal on its own

---

[92] For which the reader might also wish to turn to for its full text in the Appendix at the end of this book.

in financial matters) and VI (capitalist economic and trade centre). Under the Joint Declaration, Hong Kong shall in addition also preserve its own previous system of shipping management and regulation (Annex I, article 8).

The third point was that Hong Kong will retain a freely convertible currency, now appearing in the main body in paragraph 3(7) ('The Hong Kong dollar will continue to circulate and remain freely convertible'), and in Annex I, article VII.

The fourth and fifth points were, respectively, that Hong Kong will not be run by Beijing's emissaries but will have a mayor elected by local inhabitants who must however be a 'patriot'. Especially following a 2021 decision to reform Hong Kong's electoral arrangements, to ensure that 'patriots will govern Hong Kong', that word has since garnered considerable attention in the UK.[93] Paragraph 3(2) of the main body of the Joint Declaration states that the Hong Kong SAR 'will be directly under the authority of the Central People's Government', while paragraph 3(3) states that the Hong Kong SAR 'will be vested with executive, legislative and independent judicial power' and that the 'law currently in force in Hong Kong will remain basically unchanged'. These are elaborated upon further in Annex I, in articles I, II and III.

Likewise, the original sixth point that Hong Kong will manage its own affairs except in defence and foreign affairs is stipulated now in paragraph 3(2) and in Annex I, article I of the Joint Declaration.

Hong Kong, under point seven, will however have a wide freedom to conduct external economic and cultural relations and the point is now found in paragraph 3(9) and (10), and in Annex I, in articles X and XI.

Point eight of the twelve points then permits Hong Kong after the handover to issue its own travel documents and this now is reflected in paragraph 3(10), and Annex I, article XIV.

The ninth point, the substance of which has since also become prominent in light of events in 2020, relates to the preservation of Hong Kong's common-law based legal system so long, however, that it does not come into conflict with China's sovereignty. Hong Kong will also have its own final appellate court. It is useful to bear in mind that transformation from the twelve points into treaty form entails that the construction of an international treaty is subject to legal interpretative rules such as those described earlier. In

---

[93] US sanctions have followed in its wake while in the UK the Foreign Secretary has characterized it as a treaty breach. See Chapter 11 of this book. In the UK, an episode of BBC's 'Hardtalk' aired on 23 March 2021 was devoted principally to this issue, in an interview with Hong Kong legislator and member of the Executive Council, and erstwhile Secretary for Security, Regina Ip.

particular the words of the treaty are to be given great, if not the greatest, importance. Point nine now appears in the Joint Declaration in paragraph 3(3), and in Annex I, article III.

Point ten had been that Hong Kong will be responsible for public order in the territory, and that such order is to be maintained by the police. That appears now in Annex I, article XII. More specifically, military forces stationed in Hong Kong shall not intrude into that sphere of domestic administration of law and order. This too has now become a point of contention following the passage of the 2020 National Security Law.[94]

Point eleven was that all political activities will be allowed, including that of the Taiwanese Nationalists, with the exception of sabotage. It does not appear in express terms on the face of the Joint Declaration but it is perhaps fair to assume that it is subsumed under the protection of civil and political rights in paragraph 3(5), and in Annex I, article 13.

The final and twelfth point was that Hong Kong shall conduct its own 'social reforms'. There is no express language on this matter in the Joint Declaration although it can be discerned at the broadest level from the assurance of Hong Kong's autonomy after the handover.

Beyond the translation of the original twelve points, the UK will administer Hong Kong until the 1997 handover date (paragraph 4), as previously mentioned provision is made for a Sino-British Joint Liaison Group (paragraph 5) which in addition is the subject of its own annex, Annex II, while Annex III deals with the original issue of land leases. Thus, the Joint Declaration handed Hong Kong over, guarantees Hong Kong's autonomy and serves as a bill of rights as well as an economic charter while the continuing role of the common law assured therein serves both of these latter aims. A final issue of substance which has since 2020 given rise to grave disagreement between the parties is the right of abode for all those born in Hong Kong or who have resided for seven years in Hong Kong within a stipulated period. This is found in Annex I, article XIV. It is, importantly, the subject of the Sino-British Exchange of Memoranda. According to the Chinese memorandum, the PRC recognises British Nationals Overseas (BNO) passports only as travel documents, rather than conferring British nationality upon the holder. Thus considered as PRC nationals Beijing did not then have to absorb three million foreign nationals overnight. In any event, Britain did not intend to grant a right for the vast majority of the population to reside in the UK. Absent this compromise, Chinese Hong Kongers would in effect have become stateless.

---

[94] Discussed further in Chapter 10 of this book.

V The Elegant Solution

The Joint Declaration was signed on 19 December 1984 by Margaret Thatcher as Prime Minister and China's Premier Zhao Ziyang, stipulating in paragraph 8 that it would be subject to ratification and that it will enter into force upon an exchange of instruments of ratification which shall take place in Beijing before 30 June 1985.

What can be said about the negotiations? Javier Perez de Cueller, the then Secretary-General of the United Nations called it 'one of the most outstanding examples of effective quiet diplomacy in contemporary international relations'.[95] There is however more than just the impression of the UK retreating quickly into a series of makeshift fallback positions as the talks went on, making only the most of what little leverage it possessed before managing to achieve what might have seemed impossible. A long, binding treaty. Rather than the initial options, for continued British administration and so on, being seen as deliberate moves from the outset which were meant only to distract the Chinese side. This is not to say that Britain's negotiators and the Prime Minister were without guile. The files show clearly that such a suggestion if made would be untrue. Others will always wonder why continued British rule, or at least British administration, was not preserved and ask if indeed the UK's position was so weak, and China's position so strong, as the UK's negotiators thought. They might ask if the two-year deadline and ultimatum which Deng Xiaoping had laid down at the beginning was no more than an empty ruse. After all, the Argentines had been humbled only recently. That we can only view things through the British archives and in so doing we see the frailty of the UK's position, that constant gnawing sense of doubt, while China's negotiators appear firm and confident is perhaps only because we do not know the doubts that the Chinese negotiators too might have had. How could those who were only earlier in that century considered widely to be but semi-civilised, which even the most distinguished works on international law attested to as legal doctrine,[96] and with one of the lowest GDP per capita

---

[95] TNA/PREM 19/1530 (Pt. 18), 'Conservative Research Department Brief: Hong Kong', prepared for the Debate in the House of Commons on Wednesday, 5 December 1984 (Ref: FA (84) 6), 1.

[96] By the nineteenth century, the European world (joined by the United States) viewed the non-European world in two principal ways, broadly speaking; as on the one hand consisting of established States like China, Japan or Siam in the Far East, for example, and tribal communities on the other. The former were treated as semi-civilised as they possessed a recognisable form of government, while the latter were considered uncivilised or barbarous. In respect of the former, the system of international interaction that was devised was a 'capitulary' system so-called whose name derived probably from the numbered *capitula* or chapters, as the late Italian jurist Cassese once explained, of treaties which typically included

figures on earth, have matched Britain? It should be remembered that China in the early 1980s is not what it is now.

As for why the UK negotiated at all the reason was, as has been mentioned, the fact that the New Territories lease would soon expire. Sir Geoffrey Howe, speaking in the Commons on 5 December 1984, explained to members of the House that:

> This 1898 lease covers 92% of the land territory of Hong Kong as it is now. And it expires, of course, on 30 June 1997. On that date, the New Territories will revert to China. The ceded territories, the other 8%, have – over the past eighty-seven years – become completely integrated with the leased territories. On their own, they would not be viable.[97]

On 27 May 1985 instruments of ratification were duly exchanged. This was only the beginning. Without pre-empting our next chapter a single line from one of Percy Cradock's books, which otherwise contains almost nothing on Hong Kong, leaps out:

> The result was a treaty ensuring the colony the most complete protection possible in the real world for at least fifty years after the hand-over. It was generally acknowledged that no better solution could have been achieved. Unfortunately, in this instance the effects were partially undone by a later change of policy under John Major, which his predecessor, reverting to her instinctive approach to the Hong Kong issue, too readily endorsed.[98]

The UKFCO's China hands had prevailed for the moment, with considerable help from Geoffrey Howe, but in the period from 1984 to 1997 things would

---

provisions preserving the European way of life, European commercial privileges and European jurisdiction and laws. All this within the territories of these established but semi-civilised entities. Barbarous communities in contrast were simply ripe for conquest. In a sense, the Joint Declaration owes something to the past in aiming to preserve the way of life, trade, and separate jurisdiction and laws existing under colonial rule. See further, Antonio Cassese, *International Law in a Divided World* (Oxford: Clarendon, 1986), 38 *et seq*. Within the capitulary system the non-European entity was 'sovereign enough' to enter into a treaty albeit still not as an equal; Robert Stern, 'Rethinking the History and Theory of Jus Publicum Universal: The Formation of China as a "Semi-civilized" Legal Subject' (2017) 12 *Frontiers of History in China* 181. More can be said, but this book is not the occasion for it.

97 TNA/PREM 19/1530 (Pt. 18), 'Speech by the Rt. Hon. Sir Geoffey Howe, QC, MP to the House of Commons on 5 December: Hong Kong Agreement', 3. Internal discussions on the possibility of separating the New Territories from the rest of the colony appears to have commenced in the immediate aftermath of the post-war period, as early as 1946, see Peter Wesley-Smith, *Unequal Treaty, 1898–1997*, 2nd ed. (Oxford: OUP, 1998), 239 *et seq*.

98 Percy Cradock, *In Pursuit of British Interests* (London: John Murray, 1997), 294–5.

soon come undone as the PRC and the UK descended into fundamental disagreement over the transitional arrangements. This was to coincide with the arrival of Hong Kong's last Governor, dubbed 'a serpent', 'whore of the East', 'tango dancer', 'a sinner who will be condemned for a thousand generations'.

3

Twilight of Colonial Rule, Democratic Reform, the Basic Law and Bill of Rights: 1984–1997

I DISLOYAL, DANGEROUS

Had Franklin Roosevelt lived after the Second World War, or if Churchill had not, China might have recovered Hong Kong earlier. Such determinations belong to the professional historian and fall outside the province of an international lawyer's account of events, yet there was also something far more significant to present-day events occurring just after the Second World War – what was called the Young Plan which could have introduced democratic governance as early as the post-war period but which was shelved by the colonial administration in 1952. There it could have stayed but in the twilight of British colonial rule – between the 1985 ratification of the Joint Declaration and Hong Kong's actual handover date in 1997 – steps towards democratising Hong Kong's legislature were taken suddenly.[1] Again it must be left to historians to decide how much of that accounts now for events since 2014, in which year there was a mass protest calling for a fully elected Chief Executive, being the successor to the colonial Governor. And accounting also for events in 2019 which have led to the UK's latest invocations of the Joint Declaration following Beijing's intervention with a national security law.

Cottrell cites the former Director of Home Affairs in Hong Kong, John Walden: 'Throughout the 30 years that I was an official myself, from 1951 to 1981, "democracy" was a dirty word ... In all those years, civil servants who favoured democratic reform (there were a few, usually from former British

---

[1] Although there had been reforms in 1982 introducing elections at the district council level previously, under Murray MacLehose. Apart from that, colonial Hong Kong's was a system of 'government by discussion', what Ambrose King formerly Vice-Chancellor of the Chinese University of Hong Kong described as 'synarchy', using J. K. Fairbanks' term for it; a consensual system of government which involved government co-optation of the Chinese elite; see Ambrose King, 'Administrative Absorption of Politics in Hong Kong: Emphasis on the Grass-Roots Level', in Ming Sing (ed.), *Hong Kong Government and Politics* (Hong Kong: OUP, 2003), 69, 72–73.

colonies in Africa) were regarded as disloyal or even dangerous.'[2] To introduce direct elections now to the Hong Kong legislature – there was no talk of electing a local successor to the post of colonial Governor, although more of this later – would, could only, have been viewed with grave suspicion. Yet this was the turn of events referred to by Cradock at the end of our previous chapter. Lord Patten puts it differently in his memoirs:

> In 1984 Britain had promised to implement the Joint Declaration by putting in hand the democratic development of the colony ... By 1987 the issue had boiled down to this: should directly elected seats be introduced in the 1988 elections or should direct elections be delayed until 1991? China's position was clear: there should be no direct elections until China had laid down the nature and pace of Hong Kong's democratic development in its Basic Law, which was to be adopted in 1990 ... What is impossible to defend is so-called realpolitik ... What anyway of realpolitik? Were 'practical politics' served by postponing the elections and allowing China to get its own way? ... it would surely have been better to allow the elections to go ahead in 1988, putting pressure on China.[3]

Was it however simply about what China would have wanted? There is a redacted file where the name is deleted and closed under the Freedom of Information Act's exemption. It concerns a statement delivered to Margaret Thatcher during the London visit of the unofficial members of colonial Hong Kong's Executive Council and Legislative Council (UMELCO) on 5 December 1984. There is little doubt that it was delivered by the late Sir S. Y. Chung:

> We must now look beyond the Agreement. The major task for the British Government and the people of Hong Kong is to move to a representative form of government ... We, the Members of UMELCO, support this move, but I hope you will agree with us, Prime Minister, that we must not move at a pace and effect such radical changes that would jeopardize the very reason of Hong Kong's existence, that is to say, our social stability and our economic prosperity. To do this would be to put at risk the overriding aim of the Joint Declaration ... If Hong Kong embarks on policies which put at risk our prosperity and stability, there would no longer be any justification for China to give Hong Kong this special status. So, whilst we must clearly move towards representative form of

---

[2] Robert Cottrell, *The End of Hong Kong: The Secret Diplomacy of Imperial Retreat* (London: John Murray, 1993), 178–9; quoting John Walden, *Excellency, Your Gap Is Growing* (Hong Kong: All Noble, 1987), 74.
[3] Chris Patten, East and West (London; MacMillan, 1998), 35–7.

government [sic.], we must do this cautiously, gradually, step-by-step, and reviewing progress at every stage.[4]

However, with Lord Patten installed subsequently as Governor and as 1997 drew ever closer, Britain suddenly was in haste and it would leave in place a population or a segment of the population that would go on to risk every possibility in the future of a direct collision with the Central People's Government in Beijing. Recall that a compromise had been achieved at the eleventh hour to replace Deng Xiaoping's proposal for a Sino-British Commission with a mere Sino-British Joint Liaison Group. China's role was to be limited to participation in a mere liaison entity for the duration of the period preceding the handover.

II 'THE UNITED NATIONS HAS NO RIGHT'

Clearly the PRC would be – and was – against any significant moves by the UK in the meantime. Unlike the usual colonial template for the emergence of independent entities, whereby self-government was introduced on the way to formal independence, Hong Kong was no Malaya or Nigeria. By the terms of the Declaration itself, even from the UK's perspective, what was involved was the 'restoration' to China of Hong Kong, which now was to be accompanied by nothing far short of a calculated provocation. The Joint Declaration had not provided, or promised, democratic reform. It was to be promised subsequently in China's Basic Law for post-handover Hong Kong. Equally the Joint Declaration did not prevent explicitly the UK from commencing democratic reforms once Hong Kong was lost to it. That was the door wherein Britain went.

Employing a British colonial 'template' would have suggested to the PRC a position contrary to its 'recovery' of Hong Kong, as well as being contrary to the removal of Hong Kong in 1972 from the United Nations decolonisation committee's list of non-self-governing territories. The full name of that body is the UN Special Committee on Decolonisation, and it usually is referred to as the 'Committee of Twenty-Four' or the 'C-24'. The Committee had been established following a watershed UN General Assembly resolution, resolution 1514, which called for the immediate grant of independence to colonial

---

[4] TNA/PREM 19/1530 (Pt. 18, Future of Hong Kong, New Territorial [sic.] Leases), 'Statement by ... [redacted] ... during the Meeting with the Prime Minister – 5.12.84', name deleted and closed under FOI exemption, signed Wayland, 3 July 2014, closed under the Freedom of Information Act 2000. The next file contains a press statement concerning UMELCO's call on the Prime Minister, 5 December 1984, whose delegation was led by the late S. Y. Chung.

countries and peoples. The UN Charter itself which came into being after the Second World War contained a 'Declaration on Non-Self-Governing Territories' which had imposed, in its famous article 73(e) in Chapter XI, a reporting obligation to the UN on the development of such territories under the control of what essentially were colonial, principally European, States.[5] Article 73 of the UN Charter imposed an obligation to promote the interests of these inhabitants as a 'sacred trust', and to a lesser extent their self-government. It was from this quaint conception of some part of humanity holding another part on trust[6] which grew into what was perhaps the most famous UN General Assembly resolution of the twentieth century, resolution 1514. That document was nothing short of an expression of African and Asiatic impatience, a demand for 'immediate' and 'unconditional' independence for colonial peoples and it was hailed as a Magna Carta for coloured people the world over.

As has been mentioned, the idea of a 'colonial people' was defined at the time by separation by a stretch of seawater from their colonial masters. Did Hong Kong's Chinese inhabitants have such a master? Clearly, there being vast oceans between Hong Kong on the Pearl River Delta and the UK more than 8,000 miles away. This was no doubt accepted from the British viewpoint. It was after the passage of resolution 1514 that the General Assembly, increasingly filled by newly decolonised, newly independent Asiatic and African nations, established the C-24 as a surveillance body by way of yet another resolution in 1962. At this juncture one might ask whether resolution 1514 should therefore not apply to Hong Kong, that is, for the immediate grant of independence. It cannot have been thought or suggested seriously however

---

[5] Unlike the pre-war situation under the League of Nations Covenant, the UN Charter now also provided for Trust Territories in succession to the previous concept of Mandated Territories which had applied to pre-World War I Ottoman and German possessions. But these in fact, as was the case with the League Mandates System, comprised a list of the possessions of the defeated powers in war. See James Crawford, *The Creation of States in International Law*, 2nd ed. (Oxford: OUP, 2006), 564–601.

[6] 'Non-self-governing territories' in Chapter XI of the UN Charter should be distinguished from 'trust territories' under Chapter XII. There is no reference in the case of the former to article 1 of the Charter, and that provision's reference to the principle of self-determination of peoples. It is therefore said that the obligations of the colonial administering authority are less burdensome, being obligated to develop only self-government rather than to foster independence. The freely expressed wishes of the population need not be respected but need only be taken into account. This no doubt served the UK's purposes well. See Bruno Simma *et al* (eds.), *The Charter of the United Nations: A Commentary*, vol. II, 3rd ed. (Oxford: OUP, 2012), Ch. XI, art. 73. In any case, as has already been mentioned, Hong Kong was subsequently removed even from this list of the non-self-governing. Any suggestion today that anyone's freely expressed wishes ought to be respected, let alone in respect of anything resembling independence, would be peculiar both legally and historically. Under the 2020 National Security Law, it is also unlawful. See Chapter 10 and Chapter 11 for the international controversy in its aftermath.

that this was, in any way, the UK's view. It may have been the view of some new nations that all – A-L-L – peoples of non-self-governing territories should be entitled to immediate and unconditional self-determination. As a rallying cry it was that neat and simple. The reality however was that the UN Charter itself is more vague and practice that grew from it was more nuanced. A related resolution, resolution 1541 (rather than 1514), had gone on to distinguish between self-determination through independence or through absorption on the basis of equality, as an equal people, into another existing State. This later resolution, 1541, was concerned with the obligation on the part of Member States to transmit information to the UN in respect of those non-self-governing territories under their administration.

In 1972 following the PRC's substitution for the Nationalists in the UN, Huang Hua who was then the PRC Foreign Minister first intervened within the C-24. The record there shows that at its 873rd meeting on 6 June 1972 the Committee had considered the recommendation of its Working Group relating to Huang Hua's letter to the Chairman of the C-24. The Working Group had reported that 'the Working Group after an exchange of views' had agreed to recommend to the C-24 that:

> The Special Committee should recommend to the General Assembly that Hong Kong and Macau and dependencies be excluded from the list of Territories to which the Declaration is applicable ... The Special Committee should defer consideration of these questions pending a decision by the General Assembly ... The Special Committee should instruct the Secretariat to defer the preparation of any working papers relating to these questions.[7]

The C-24 records go on to state also that at that meeting 'following statements by the representatives of Venezuela, Fiji, Sweden, Mali and Afghanistan, and the Union of Soviet Socialist Republics ... the Special Committee adopted without objections the above-mentioned recommendations ... it being understood that the reservations expressed by members would be reflected in the record of the meeting',[8] and that:[9]

> Accordingly, the Special Committee recommends to the General Assembly that Hong Kong and Macau and dependencies be excluded from the list of Territories to which the Declaration is applicable.

---

[7] Report of the Special Committee on the Situation with Regard to the Implementation of the Declaration on the Granting of Independence to Colonial Countries and Peoples, Vol. 1, U.N. G.A.O.R., 27th Sess., Supp. 23, UN Doc. A/87/23/Rev.1, para. 71.
[8] Ibid., para. 72.
[9] Ibid., para. 73.

Huang Hua then was able to raise the issue of Hong Kong at the General Assembly and succeeded, formally by a vote of ninety-nine for, five against and twenty-three members abstaining, with five non-voting, to have Hong Kong removed from the purview of the C-24.[10] Thus Hong Kong shall henceforth be treated as falling outside the list of such territories which otherwise would have been poised for decolonisation in the view of the numerous Asian and African representatives who would treat resolution 1514 as expressive of international law. It is easy to be incredulous and to ask how Hong Kong could even be said not to be a 'non-self-governing' territory or 'colony'. The simple answer is that this is a misconception; as a matter of law it was no longer to be placed in the category of territories poised for independence. Hong Kong was no 'trust territory'. There was no inconsistency in this. Pomerance, perhaps the greatest authority on the subject, writes:

> While 'self-determination and independence' is indeed the most usual formula, 'self-determination' sometimes does appear alone ... Where in this gradation a particular territory will land has much to do with the identity of the claimant to territorial integrity, and the assessment of the situation which will result from effectuating its claim – continued 'colonialism' or effective 'decolonization'.
>
> If independence may be disallowed in the face of a valid 'non-colonial' claim, it may also be rejected if the context in which it is granted or assumed is deemed 'colonial' or 'racist', as in the case of the Transkei, Rhodesia, or South West Africa (Namibia). These rejections are premised not so much on the invalidity of the methods as on the unacceptability of the results obtained.[11]

Thus:

> It is in this context that protests sometimes raised in the United Nations to the classification of avowedly 'colonial' areas as 'non-self-governing territories' are to be understood. The objections of China regarding Hong Kong and Macao ... were designed to abort any future claims by the inhabitants of those territories either to separate 'selfhood', or alternatively, to the exercise of the more usual rather than the 'classic alternative' form of self-determination.[12]

As Pomerance also puts it, the right to self-determination is negated in these instances insofar as United Nations General Assembly practice is concerned.[13]

---

[10] U.N.G.A. res. 2908 (XXVII), 2 November 1972. Vote recorded based on UN Doc. A/PV.2078.
[11] Michla Pomerance, *Self-Determination in Law and Practice* (The Hague: Nijhoff, 1982), 27.
[12] Ibid.
[13] Ibid., at 26.

Huang Hua put it thus in 1972 in a letter to the UN's C-24 in 1972:

> In connexion with the questions of Hong Kong and Macau, I have the honour to state the following:
> As is known to all, the questions of Hong Kong and Macau belong to the category of questions resulting from the series of unequal treaties left over by history, treaties which the imperialists imposed on China. Hong Kong and Macau are part of Chinese territory occupied by the British and Portuguese authorities. The settlement of the questions of Hong Kong and Macau is entirely within China's sovereign right and does not at all fall under the ordinary category of 'Colonial Territories'. Consequently, they should not be included in the list of Colonial Territories covered by the Declaration on the Granting of Independence to Colonial Countries and Peoples. With regard to the questions of Hong Kong and Macau, the Chinese Government has consistently held that they should be settled in an appropriate way when conditions are ripe. The United Nations has no right to discuss these questions. For the above reasons, the Chinese delegation is opposed to including Hong Kong and Macau in the list of Colonial Territories covered by the Declaration and requests that the erroneous wording that Hong Kong and Macau fall under the category of so-called 'Colonial Territories' be immediately removed from the documents of the Special Committee and all other United Nations documents.

That formulation, that the matter will be addressed when 'conditions are ripe', is consistent with the position previously discussed of successive Chinese governments, not just of the PRC, which is that the nineteenth-century treaties were unequal and they were invalid. Most importantly, removal from the C-24 list also removes the 'Hong Kong question' from British purview at least in the PRC's view. In a telegram eleven years later, Sir Phillip Haddon-Cave, then Chief Secretary of Hong Kong, quoted Sir Ian Sinclair[14] that Britain had never accepted 'and never would accept, that continuance of colonial status contravenes any existing or emerging norm of *jus cogens*' which under the Vienna Convention on the Law of Treaties the Chinese side had concluded makes Britain's claim to Hong Kong unlawful.[15]

In any event, in the early 1970s the C-24 duly reported all of this to the UN General Assembly which, while approving the committee's report on its work in 1972 in UN General Assembly resolution 2908 at its twenty-eighth session the following year, approved the PRC's view. The voting record shows a clear split between the developing, Eastern European and Latin American nations

---

[14] Legal Adviser to the Foreign and Commonwealth Office, 1976 to 1984.
[15] TNA/PREM 19/1057 (Pt. 8, Future of Hong Kong, New Territorial Leases), FM Hong Kong 210940Z Sep 83 to Immediate Peking, Telno. 539 of 21 September 1983.

on the one hand, and on the other hand the European and Western nations which either abstained or – as with the United States and United Kingdom – voted against. Whatever else may be inferred the Asian and African countries which had pushed for immediate colonial independence worldwide voted, overwhelmingly, for resolution 2908. Any suggestion that 2908 was just a routine resolution, or that it was voted upon absent-mindedly or was not properly scrutinised, is unsupported by the clear and concentrated differences in the voting record. The UK had lost the vote.

The matter was debated subsequently by Parliament in London.[16] Evan Luard, the Parliamentary Undersecretary of State in the FCO, read out to members Huang Hua's letter to the C-24. He explained that the UK, following resolution 2908, had now ceased to transmit information as previously had been required of it under article 73e. The die was cast; it is not – as it sometimes is said inaccurately – that Hong Kong was 'no longer a colony'. Rather here was confirmation that it was not and, it is fair to say, never was intended that Hong Kong would satisfy the international rules on achieving self-determination in any manner or form other than through its absorption into China. Haddon-Cave, in the 1983 telegram mentioned, reported Sinclair's view that at best such a rule would only have begun to form after the 1928 Kellogg-Briand Pact and that article 52 of the Vienna Convention on the Law of Treaties ('Coercion of a State by the Threat or Use of Force') was, first, in stating that 'a treaty is void if it is procured by the threat or use of force' restricted to the rule against the use of force in the 1945 United Nations Charter; and second, that colonialism after 1945 does not violate a peremptory norm of international law (a *jus cogens* rule).[17] Geoffrey Howe,[18] a former Middle Temple barrister, quoted Sinclair in a separate telegram stating that in the UK's view (at least) there was no such peremptory norm against colonialism:

> The General Assembly's decision in 1972 that Hong Kong be removed from the list of non-self-governing territories that article 73(e) applies did not alter the legal status of Hong Kong. The fact remains that it is a territory for whose administration the UK has responsibility and to allege otherwise is not in accordance with reality ... In any event a peremptory norm of international law can exist only when it is 'accepted and recognised by the international community as a whole as a norm from which no derogation is permitted'.

---

[16] HC Deb 14 December 1976 vol. 922 cc686-8W.
[17] TNA/PREM 19/1057 (Pt. 8, Future of Hong Kong, New Territorial Leases), FM Hong Kong 210940Z Sep 83 to Immediate Peking, Telno. 539 of 21 September 1983.
[18] Then Secretary of State for Foreign and Commonwealth Affairs

(Article 53) The alleged rule against colonialism is clearly not so accepted and recognised ... There is no rule of international law which would prevent two States from agreeing that territory under the sovereignty of one should be administered by the other ... Examples of some precedents were sent under cover of Davies' letter of 4th July to Clift, copied to Peking.[19]

It should be recalled that this was written during a critical turning point in the negotiations as the UK's primary position, that it should retain sovereignty, as well as its fallback position, that it should in any case continue to administer Hong Kong after 1997, had all but collapsed. Sinclair's opinion that continued colonialism does not violate a peremptory norm of general international law would only become increasingly isolated globally, and it is not a view which has improved since. The notion that the UK administered Hong Kong under an 'agreement' with the PRC also downplayed the PRC's view that rather than being by right the UK did so only by an act of grace. All of this, as we have seen, would come to a head in September 1983 when the PRC made plain that it would declare unilaterally its intention to resume sovereignty over Hong Kong by 1984 with or without British agreement. As far as concordance with reality was concerned, it was Sinclair's legal view which soon would be put to the test before the month was out.[20] Britain would have to leave with grace or without.

One official view taken in declassified files that it was not until September 1983 that China would articulate its legal position publicly is also open to some doubt.[21] The latter's view of unequal treaties was well known and public and had been for years. If by this was meant the view that China had not stated its legal position specifically on Hong Kong before that date that too cannot be entirely accurate, as Huang Hua's letter to the United Nations' C-24 eleven years before shows.

III HISTORY'S HAND IS SELDOM ABSENT

So far as the UN Charter is concerned, article 73 imposes obligations of trust upon a (usually self-declared) administering authority to see to the well-being and development of the territory and its people, while article 74 which is sometimes treated as if it were an afterthought requires the administering authority to attend as well to the development of the territory's self-

---

[19] TNA/PREM 19/1057 (Pt. 8), Deskby 220100Z, FM FCO 211715Z Sep 83 to Immediate Peking, Telno. 628 of 21 September 1983.
[20] See the earlier discussion of the collapse of the UK's negotiating position in the previous chapter of this book.
[21] TNA/PREM 19/1057 (Pt. 8), Deskby 201300Z, From Peking 2011457 Sep 83 to Immediate FCO, Telno. 913 of 20 September 1983.

government. As has been mentioned article 74 was subsequently given expression instead by the General Assembly's resolutions, including resolutions 1514, 1541 and 2908 which all have already been mentioned. Thus, the position as of 1973 was that neither provision, neither article 73 nor 74, could now be read other than in light of the eventual return of Hong Kong. In short, that this was not the UK's negotiating position until after the Thatcher-Deng meeting in 1982 sat ill with the 'new international law' as transformed by resolution 1514.[22]

History's hand is seldom absent. Controversy today between the UK and China may be said to stem from the echoes of the United Nations decolonisation period still, in that China's complaint today is that the UK continues to behave, albeit in an unwarranted fashion, as if it still held a sacred trust over Hong Kong, and that the UK has discovered somewhat belatedly a zest for Hong Kong's democratic development and reforms. This is perhaps not entirely an inaccurate view of the UK's approach towards the content and meaning of the Joint Declaration. For the UK it seems the whole cornucopia, the torrent, of United Nations General Assembly resolutions and other relevant United Nations laws,[23] vague as they are, have simply become bilateralised, or 'contractualised' to use that term very loosely, into the form of a binding treaty between China and the UK. This imported into the treaty all the tensions and ambiguities of international law. For the concept of a sacred trust the contemporary term which Britain might prefer is 'moral obligation' and 'self-government' has become 'democracy', whereas for China Hong Kong has achieved self-determination and its people are now on equal terms with other Chinese as a part of China, even on more than equal terms. As the German hermeneutician Hans Georg Gadamer might once have put it, each approaches the text with vastly different horizons and experiences.[24] The UK's argument hinges ultimately on the following language in Annex 1, Article I of the Joint Declaration: The legislature of the Hong Kong Special Administrative Region shall be constituted by elections.

---

[22] Pomerance quotes Emerson's 'New Higher Law of Anticolonialism' in describing the view of the large numbers of African and Asian States, see Pomerance, *op. cit.*, 13, and ch. 1 generally.

[23] I call it United Nations 'law' in the sense used by Dame Rosalyn Higgins, namely that United Nations practices shape the law more widely. See Rosalyn Higgins, *The Development of International Law Through the Political Organs of the United Nations* (London, New York and Toronto: OUP, 1963).

[24] Hans Georg Gadamer, *Truth and Method*, 2nd rev. ed. of 1989, Joel Weinsheimer and Donald G. Marshall transl. (London: Continuum, 2004).

IV AN ENORMOUS BLOW TO RELATIONS

By the time Chris Patten succeeded David Wilson as Governor in what were controversial circumstances, democracy was gaining ground globally. In advocating democratic reforms, Patten stopped short of introducing any sort of Westminster system by way of introducing an elected cabinet. There was not to be as once described so pithily by Walter Bagehot a 'committee of the legislature' forming the government:

> The efficient secret of the English Constitution may be described as the close union, the nearly complete fusion, of the executive and legislative powers. No doubt by the traditional theory, as it exists in all the books, the goodness of our constitution consists in the entire separation of the legislative and executive authorities, but in truth its merit consists in their singular approximation. The connecting link is *the cabinet*. By that new word we mean a committee of the legislative body selected to be the executive body.[25]

As we will see further below in Section V (footnote 40 specifically), even one of the most eminent Chinese scholars on the subject concedes that there might have been some basis in the Joint Declaration for saying that the PRC had agreed to the accountability of the executive branch in post-handover Hong Kong to the legislature. Ultimately, however, and as a matter of the final position adopted in the Basic Law, colonial Hong Kong was to remain 'executive-led'. In this its cabinet is appointed rather than elected. An elected cabinet would have meant a change to Hong Kong's executive-led system which, as Patten subsequently sought to explain in his recollections of that period, the PRC would have objected to. Perhaps it was not irrelevant that British colonial reforms themselves had already resulted in a divide between a now partially elected and increasingly vocal colonial legislature on the one hand, and an appointed Executive Committee on the other chaired by Patten as Governor.[26]

As it turned out, Beijing had far more to object to. There had already been consultations on democratic reform even before the Joint Declaration was signed,[27] but holding direct legislative elections as a practical matter first arose – from a British point of view at least – as one of timing. Should it occur in 1988 or await passage in 1990 of the Joint Declaration's implementing

---

[25] Walter Bagehot, *The English Constitution* (New York: Dolphin, 1867), 62.
[26] Patten, *East and West, op. cit.*, 56.
[27] See further, Ming K. Chan, 'Democracy Derailed, Realpolitik in the Making of the Basic Law, 1985–90', in Ming K. Chan and David J. Clark, *The Hong Kong Basic Law* (Hong Kong: Hong Kong University, 1991), 3, 9 *et seq*.

legislation by the PRC; namely, the Hong Kong Basic Law? This after all was to be a mini-constitution for Hong Kong.[28] Assuming the introduction of legislative elections for the first time had gone ahead in 1988, just four years after the Joint Declaration was concluded, three years after its ratification, it would have risked divergence with China's Basic Law for Hong Kong. Even if Patten's recollection that the Chinese had alleged a violation of the 'spirit' of the Joint Declaration was clarified subsequently by the Chinese side, which denied making that claim.[29] The decision taken ultimately was that elections of nearly a third of the Hong Kong legislature would take place instead only afterwards, in 1991. The Basic Law itself which was passed without any, at least formal, British participation, went on to make promises of democratic reform of its own.

Second there was the possibility that such reforms were they unacceptable to China would not last beyond the 1997 handover. China and the UK would have seen the wisdom of Oliver Wendell Holmes' famous insight, that time has upset many fighting faiths.

This issue was however to erupt in respect of the elections four years later, in 1995, a mere two years before the actual handover date. The whole matter having come to a head with Patten's reforms resulted in China setting up its own 'Provisional Legislative Council' which would and did immediately assume its place as the Hong Kong SAR's first legislature, the Legislative Council or 'LegCo', come midnight on 1 July 1997. The original idea had been however that the same legislature would occupy the period both before and after 1 July. That idea had now failed. The 'through-train' so-called had been wrecked.

Third, and for the sake of completeness, it should be added that the UK's plan that a deputy to Patten, a 'Deputy Governor' as it were, would simply assume the position of the Hong Kong SAR's first post-1997 'Chief Executive' (as that position is termed under the Basic Law) came also to naught.

Thus, the fraught but successful negotiations to resolve the question of how the interim period between the 1984 Joint Declaration and the 1997 handover should be managed ended, ultimately, in an enormous blow to the handover arrangements and did not help Sino-British relations.[30]

---

[28] See further, J. M. M. Chan and C. L. Lim (eds.), *Law of the Hong Kong Constitution*, 2nd. ed. (Hong Kong: Sweet & Maxwell, 2015).
[29] Patten, *op. cit.*, 68–9; *cf.* Chan, *op. cit.*, 12 citing Li Hou's press statement.
[30] One could say none of it mattered ultimately; that China still sought and obtained WTO membership in 2001, internal reform of the socialist system continued, and that the point of contention passed eventually. Hong Kong itself evolved to be not dissimilar in 1998 to the way it was in 1997.

This was not to be the last time even if it would take another quarter of a century, in 2020, for a similar occurrence in the relations between the two countries, again over the question of Hong Kong. Some twenty-three years after Hong Kong's handover to China, and the resumption of Chinese sovereignty. In 2020 the British Prime Minister, Mr Johnson, proclaimed to Parliament in response to a new National Security Law for Hong Kong, itself the culmination of a long sequence of events between 2014 and 2020,[31] that China had breached the Joint Declaration 'and the Basic Law'. It would be as if Beijing had pronounced a breach of the law in England, but if this is unfair it is at least apparent what Mr Johnson's statement meant, which was that if the Basic Law were but the implementation of the Joint Declaration then saying there is a breach of the latter would entail a breach also of the former. That would be to interpret Johnson's statement, and in any case the one need not follow from the other. If, as Beijing says today, the Joint Declaration has been executed fully as a treaty, then the Basic Law is China's affair entirely. Here lies a further significant point of contemporary, indeed current, legal disagreement between the two sides.[32]

How were the interim arrangements wrecked? To an extent elements of today's contemporary controversies, as the next section will explain, lie in events in 1988–89 which occurred during the drafting of the Basic Law for Hong Kong which would implement the Joint Declaration.

V AND THEN THERE WERE RIGHTS

Both the question of democratic reform and the drafting, passage and application of the Basic Law are matters which go directly towards the preservation of Hong Kong's post-handover autonomy. Put simply, Hong Kong people will govern themselves and this Chinese law for Hong Kong will guarantee Hong Kong's autonomy. This brings us to the Basic Law for post-handover Hong Kong, and also a sudden Bill of Rights which the British colonial authorities sought not only to enact but also – in an act which could easily have been perceived as sheer vanity – to entrench after the 1997 handover.

First, to the Basic Law. In terms of the process beginning in 1985 and leading finally to its enactment by the National People's Congress in 1990, a Basic Law Drafting Committee (BLDC) with 36 members from the PRC and 23 from colonial Hong Kong was charged with the drafting of the law, while for

---

[31] See Chapters 7 to 10 of this book.
[32] See further, Chapters 9 and 10.

outreach there was the larger and more broadly representative 180-member Basic Law Consultative Committee (BLCC).[33]

However, the reform issue promised to put the process of drafting the Basic Law for Hong Kong in a contentious light even without the UK's formal participation. This was only to be expected, for the Basic Law is PRC Law and therefore a piece of Chinese legislation. The UK as a party to the Joint Declaration would have to communicate any views it may have had as a non-participant through diplomatic means only.[34] At the heart of the drafting of this law was the issue of democratic reform itself, then subsequently that cataclysmic event, the Tiananmen Square or 'June 4th' incident in 1989, was to occur towards the final drafting stages.[35] These were the principal forces which shaped what in essence became the legal document that would translate the Joint Declaration into assurances under both PRC law and Hong Kong law, thereby involving a delicate juxtaposition of Chinese socialist legality and the Anglo-Hong Kong Common Law. Nowhere was this more so than in what became article 158 of the Basic Law:

> The power of interpretation of this Law shall be vested in the Standing Committee of the National People's Congress.
>
> The Standing Committee of the National People's Congress shall authorize the courts of the Hong Kong Special Administrative Region to interpret on their own, in adjudicating cases, the provisions of this Law which are within the limits of the autonomy of the Region.
>
> The courts of the Hong Kong Special Administrative Region may also interpret other provisions of this Law in adjudicating cases. However, if the courts of the Region, in adjudicating cases, need to interpret the provisions of this Law concerning affairs which are the responsibility of the Central People's Government, or concerning the relationship between the Central Authorities and the Region, and if such interpretation will affect the judgments on the cases, the courts of the Region shall, before making their final judgments which are not appealable, seek an interpretation of the relevant provisions from the Standing Committee of the National People's Congress through the Court of Final Appeal of the Region. When the Standing Committee makes an interpretation of the provisions concerned, the courts of the Region, in applying those provisions, shall follow the interpretation of the Standing Committee. However, judgments previously rendered shall not be affected.

---

[33] Chan, *op. cit.*, 7.
[34] *Ibid.*, 22.
[35] *Ibid.*, 9–20.

> The Standing Committee of the National People's Congress shall consult its Committee for the Basic Law of the Hong Kong Special Administrative Region before giving an interpretation of this Law.

Under article 158, the power of interpretation of the Basic Law itself does not lie with the courts because of their inherent jurisdiction as common lawyers might view it. Rather that power is vested elsewhere, in the Standing Committee of the National People's Congress (the NPCSC). However such power is delegated to the Hong Kong courts but there are limits to that delegated authority. Certain matters are excluded from the jurisdictional authority of the Hong Kong courts, where these fall instead within the responsibilities of the Central People's Government or concern the relationship between the Mainland's Central Authorities and Hong King as a Special Administrative Region. Who is to decide where a matter falls? That is a question dealt with in the next chapter. It goes not only to the preservation of the common law, but also the role of Hong Kong's common law judges and courts.

As a whole the Basic Law comprising nine chapters and three annexures contained as one might expect much of what had been discussed previously about the substance of the Joint Declaration.[36] After all, the Basic Law is intended to implement the Joint Declaration. Insofar as the lingering question of democratic reform was concerned, however, it threatened to cause a rupture in the Sino-British relationship. There had, first, emerged the proposal, following the release of a first consultation draft of the Basic Law in April 1988, containing what was dubbed the 'mainstream model'.[37] This would have a decision by the people of Hong Kong on having direct elections for the entire legislature and the post of Chief Executive delayed until 2011. It proved to be controversial and a number of other proposals were to emerge.

The second draft of the Basic Law, released in February 1989 during the second and final round of the drafting process, also caused controversy. The Joint Declaration had, reminiscent of Bagehot's unity of the legislature and the executive, referred to the accountability of the Chief Executive to the legislature. However the second draft was to refer to the Chief Executive's accountability to Beijing. That is its final form today. The Basic Law, in article 43, states:

> The Chief Executive of the Hong Kong Special Administrative Region shall be the head of the Hong Kong Special Administrative Region and shall

---

[36] See Chan and Lim, *op. cit.*, generally.
[37] Chan, *op. cit.*, 13.

V And Then There Were Rights

represent the Region. The Chief Executive of the Hong Kong Special Administrative Region shall be accountable to the Central People's Government and the Hong Kong Special Administrative Region in accordance with the provisions of this Law.

That second clause speaks of accountability to Beijing and to the Hong Kong Special Administrative Region. It was to remain unchanged beginning with what was article 43 of the first and second drafts.[38] One might imagine the Chief Executive as some sort of an emissary to Beijing and vice versa, but that would be an unsustainable legal interpretation. As a matter of PRC law, under the 1982 PRC Constitution: 'The State Council of the People's Republic of China, namely, the Central People's Government, is the executive organ of the highest state organ of power; it is the highest state administrative organ.'[39] An emissary would be a different creature, representing one sovereign power before another. In the case of Hong Kong, China is sovereign and the Central People's Government is the highest organ of state administration, whereas Hong Kong is but a mere special administrative region.

Disagreement between the UK and the PRC was to lie elsewhere. An eminent Chinese scholar has sought to explain that the accountability of the Chief Executive to the legislature had been written into the Joint Declaration where the Chinese side had failed to note its full significance, in terms of the idea of a cabinet government and cabinet accountability. They then sought to clarify the situation, indeed to rectify it depending upon one's viewpoint, when the Basic Law was drafted. Insofar as the drafting process was concerned, as has been mentioned, this was an entirely sovereign affair. That said, two of three international lawyers whose opinions were sought before the House of Commons' Foreign Affairs Committee, as to whether Patten's proposals conformed to the Joint Declaration, took the view that there was a 'link' between the Joint Declaration and the Basic Law.[40]

---

[38] Ibid., 21, that draft provision is reproduced at 73 of Chan and Clark, Hong Kong Basic Law, op. cit., 73.

[39] Art. 85.

[40] Interestingly one of the experts, Dr Peter Slinn, took the view that the PRC is hardly likely to implement any further suggestions regarding the constitution of the legislature. See the Minutes of Evidence, 3 November 1993, Foreign Affairs Committee, House of Commons, Sess. 1992–93, HC 842-ii, 1992/93 in *Relations between the United Kingdom and China in the Period Up to and Beyond 1997: First Report, Great Britain, Parliament, House of Commons, Foreign Affairs Committee*, vol. II (London: HMSO, 1994), 48, 49. Although that point was made in respect of the likelihood of any further obligation being accepted by China concerning democratic reforms arising from the Hurd-Qian letters, as a practical matter one would tend to think that it was an equally valid point in respect of the likelihood of the Basic Law establishing a Westminster-style form of cabinet government which is accountable to the

Be that so, there then occurred the June 4th incident in 1989 which tilted the balance decisively in favour of democratic opinion, just when the drafting of the Basic Law had entered into its final phase. Until then the UK's position had been that Hong Kong's inhabitants should have full confidence in the Joint Declaration. Following the June 4th incident so sanguine a view could no longer be maintained.[41] By the autumn two of the BLDC members had resigned.[42] That instrument which was to be a confidence building measure now risked becoming a principal source instead of insecurity.

There arose at least from the British viewpoint some further need to assure Hong Kong's inhabitants. The UK's answer was to push on with democratisation which ended with the derailment of the 'through train';[43] a limited number of passports granting full right of abode in the United Kingdom; and finally a Bill of Rights. In April 1990, the Basic Law was enacted by the PRC. In the same week, the colonial Government in Hong Kong published the proposed Bill of Rights.

VI A BILL WITHOUT VOTING RIGHTS

The idea behind the Bill of Rights Ordinance was to incorporate into Hong Kong law the international law on the protection of civil and political rights. The Bill of Rights reproduces, substantially, the rights contained in the International Covenant on Civil and Political Rights, excluding article 1 on the right to self-determination, and replete with such British reservations as would exclude immigration matters and, ironically, the provisions on the right to vote and to political participation. It was to be a Bill without voting rights.

Yet how would that sit with the Basic Law enacted by the PRC? Chapter III of the Basic Law now contained its own assurances of the protection of rights and article 39 of which states, that:

> The provisions of the International Covenant on Civil and Political Rights, the International Covenant on Economic, Social and Cultural Rights, and

---

legislature, rather than (as ultimately it was decided) an executive-led system akin to the preceding colonial system. Professor Shigong Jiang discusses the debate within the BLDC, apparently sparked by the phrase 'the executive authorities ... shall be accountable to the legislature' in the Joint Declaration. However, we are only told that in the end the executive-led system was adopted in the Basic Law, it appears as a compromise solution based upon the pre-handover position; Shigong Jiang, *China's Hong Kong* (Singapore: Springer, 2017), 143–4.

[41] Chan, *op. cit.*, 17–20.
[42] *Ibid.*, 23–4.
[43] The idea that the same pre-handover (partially elected) legislature would stay on as the post-1997 legislature was dead.

international labour conventions as applied to Hong Kong shall remain in force and shall be implemented through the laws of the Hong Kong Special Administrative Region.

The rights and freedoms enjoyed by Hong Kong residents shall not be restricted unless as prescribed by law. Such restrictions shall not contravene the provisions of the preceding paragraph of this Article.

According to China, the UK had sought to entrench the ICCPR's provisions and in doing so had created the risk of conflict with the Basic Law. This view was prompted by amendments made to the Hong Kong Letters Patent which, together with the Royal Instructions, had served as Hong Kong's colonial constitution. However, there was no question of the entrenchment of the rights contained in the Bill of Rights Ordinance (HKBORO) beyond 1997, rather than a need to ensure that the Ordinance would not be amended or superseded by subsequent colonial legislation.

Having said that the HKBORO does have a 'parasitic' effect. Article 39 of the Basic Law speaks of the provisions of the ICCPR as they applied to pre-handover Hong Kong being maintained after the 1997 handover. It is the HKBORO which states the application of those provisions before 1997.[44] Curiously perhaps the HKBORO has not been repealed after the 1997 handover and indeed it has been cited and relied upon by the courts, together with the fundamental rights contained in Chapter III of the Basic Law, ever since.

Insofar as the issue of democratic reform was concerned, a Sino-British understanding was reached through an exchange of letters at the height of controversy over the final phase of the drafting of the Basic Law. The letters were exchanged between Douglas Hurd and Qian Qichen in January and February of 1990 ('the Hurd-Qian letters') which then paved the way for the formula eventually adopted for the subsequent 1991 legislative elections to have eighteen (being 30 per cent of) legislators directly elected, which will move up to twenty legislators (33.3 per cent) in the 1995 elections, just in time for the 1997 handover. Patten however, without unsettling these actual numbers, sought amongst other things to lower the voting age from twenty-one to eighteen, and to enfranchise working voters in respect of the legislature's functional constituency seats. These were based upon not individual but corporate voting. The Patten proposal would also have such individual voters potentially being able to 'vote twice' both as individuals and through corporate voting.[45] As a contemporaneous House of Commons briefing paper put it:

---

[44] Chan and Lim, *op. cit.*, 569–71.
[45] John Fowler, *The Final Years of British Hong Kong* (Hong Kong: Macmillan, 1998), 109 *et seq.* See further, Chan and Lim, *op. cit.*, 33 *et seq.*

At the most general level, China is concerned that the UK has breached bilateral agreements and seeks to extend its influence over Hong Kong beyond 1997. Sir Percy Cradock summed up this position in his evidence to the Foreign Affairs Committee. 'The Chinese', he said, 'fear democracy. They are deeply afraid of it because they see it as a virus which will spread into their own territory ... They certainly fear it in Hong Kong because they see it as an attempt by the British to go back on the provisions of the Joint Declaration and make Hong Kong more independent than we had signed up to at that time' (p122).

The claim that the UK is in breach of the Joint Declaration has been made throughout the dispute which began in October 1992. It was denied by Foreign Office and independent lawyers in evidence to the Foreign Affairs Committee (HC 842-ii 1992/93) and, naturally, has been consistently denied by HMG and Mr. Patten. The current argument seems to be that the provision in Annex II to the Joint Declaration has been breached that in the second half of the transitional period there 'will be need for closer cooperation, which will therefore be intensified during that period'. However, Annex II relates to the Joint Liaison Group, a specific organ of the relationship, rather than to the relationship as a whole. The question as to which party has failed to cooperate is also, of course, a central point of dispute.[46]

The three independent British legal experts who gave evidence on the legality of Patten's plan under the Joint Declaration – the late Peter Duffy, Perry Keller and Peter Slinn – took the view that since the Joint Declaration imposed an obligation to have an elected legislature, there would be a corresponding obligation on the part of the UK to move in that direction as it were.[47] They went on to conclude that Patten's proposal to enlarge the franchise was thereby lawful. However, Dr Slinn pointed out the Chinese understanding of functional constituencies as a British invention to create corporate voting.[48] Viewed in that regard, the UK was shifting the goalposts.

The ensuing 'derailment of the through-train' which resulted from Sino-British acrimony meant that the legislature which was formed through the

---

[46] Paul Bowers, *Hong Kong and Democracy*, Research Paper 94/44, 10 March 1994, House of Commons Library, 13–14.

[47] This would conform to the principle of good faith under international law, the idea being that nothing ought to be done which would be inconsistent with the obligation undertaken. Still, it might be asked whether that principle could be cast as a positive duty on the part of the UK to promote democratic reform rather than a duty not to hinder (in other words, a 'negative' duty regarding) such reform in the post-handover period.

[48] HC 842-ii 1992/93, 52.

VI A Bill without Voting Rights

1995 election, colonial Hong Kong's second and last legislative elections, ceased to exist at midnight on 1 July 1997. Lord Patten has since stated that he was not at the time of his proposal made aware of the Hurd-Qian letters as he had not been briefed, adding however that he did not take 'too tragic a view of this'. In any event, he did not consider it anything other than a strict adherence to the figures agreed upon in the letters.[49] The PRC for its part established a Preparatory Committee and in December 1996 appointed a Provisional Legislative Council in preparation for the post-handover legislature drawing thirty-three of its sixty members from the existing pre-handover legislature. Patten's legislative reforms were abolished following the handover.[50]

In accordance with Annex II of the Basic Law, there were twenty directly elected members in the 1998 elections, rising to twenty-four in the 2001 elections and thirty (i.e. 50 per cent) in the 2004 elections. In 2008 there were thirty again, and in 2012 and 2016 thirty-five Legislative Council members were directly elected out of what now following a 2010 constitutional amendment is a seventy-member legislature.[51] At the end of July 2020, the Hong Kong SAR's Chief Executive invoked emergency powers to postpone elections to the legislature by a year.

Discussion of the difficulties over electoral reform, not least in electing the Chief Executive through universal suffrage, will resume in Chapter 7.[52] The HKBORO has remained substantially unaltered since the 1997 handover and, as has been mentioned, it is routinely cited and relied upon by the courts together with the fundamental rights contained in Chapter III of the Basic Law, and it is to Hong Kong's post-handover record of securing civil and political rights which we now turn in the next chapter. The singular contribution of the judicial protection of rights is summed up by the Cantonese aphorism appearing at the end of Cottrell's End of Hong Kong, published in 1993:[53]

> Those with cash
> Can always dash;
> And for the poor,
> the Basic Law.

---

[49] Patten, *op. cit.*, 66.
[50] See further Chan and Lim, *op. cit.*, 35 *et seq.*
[51] Chan and Lim, *op. cit.*, 1017.
[52] See Chapter 7 of this book.
[53] Cottrell, *op. cit.*, 188.

We might add 'the Bill of Rights'. In any event, many were to return subsequently. The question of confidence was not to emerge again until 2020. As for Lord Patten, the epithets quoted in his lively account – 'a serpent', 'whore of the East', 'tango dancer', 'a sinner who will be condemned for a thousand generations' – were selective, and his list was incomprehensive.[54]

---

[54] See Fowler, *op. cit.*, 131 – 'robber', 'thief' and 'a guilty man' should not go unmentioned.

PART II

1997–2014

Introduction to Part II

Part II begins with the UK's failure to secure a role for the Hong Kong judiciary in relation to the 1984 Joint Declaration. Part I had discussed the idea during the negotiations of subjecting amendments to the Basic Law to the judgment of an 'international commission', where Geoffrey Howe had considered it to be a non-starter. Instead, there was an attempt to have the Basic Law's terms dictated in detail by the terms of the Joint Declaration resulting in a short statement of China's 'basic policies' in paragraph 3 in the main body of the Joint Declaration, a more detailed 'elaboration' of these in Annex I and a clause in paragraph 3 (paragraph 3(12)) stating that both these basic policies and their elaboration will 'be stipulated' in 'a Basic Law' and will remain unchanged for fifty years. The declassified records show that following the release of the second draft of what was to become the Basic Law, in February 1989, the UK had proposed to the PRC through diplomatic channels (since it had no role in the drafting of the Basic Law) that a new article should be inserted to 'make the Joint Declaration a reference point for interpreting, and for limiting amendments to the Basic Law'. That proposal failed. There is often a thin line between interpretation and amendment but the UK's overall intent was clear, as much as it would be unacceptable to China. Put bluntly, it was to tie China's hands again by another treaty. In the end the Basic Law was to provide in article 158 that despite the Hong Kong SAR courts having the final power of 'adjudication' the ultimate authority to interpret the Basic Law would rest not with the courts themselves but with the Standing Committee of the National People's Congress. Still, a practice was instituted under which British and other common law judges would sit on Hong Kong's highest court as non-permanent justices. By 2020 however there were calls in the UK for the removal of these British judges. In the interest of maintaining the flow of the discussion the issue is included in this Part although it lies, strictly, in the period covered in the next Part of the book. It was to culminate in the resignations of Lord Reed and Lord Hodge at the end of March 2022, when this book was already in press. Quite aside from the role of the judges, from the outset foreign affairs and defence had been carved out of Hong Kong's sphere of autonomy altogether. A closely related concept is the notion of an act of State which it is not entirely clear is to be understood in the common law sense. Finally, there is the question of democratic reform. One complicated by the fact that it involves China's relations with the great majority of almost invariably Western democracies. In short, this part discusses what often are the most controversial issues – judicial authority, autonomy and democratic reform, more precisely their outer limits – paving the way for the discussion of contemporary events in Part III.

4

The Court and the Canaries in a Storm

I A NEW COURT

The Joint Declaration may have been concluded in 1984 but it was not until 1991 that agreement, or at least a first agreement, was reached between China and the UK on the composition of an altogether new entity, the Court of Final Appeal or 'CFA' for post-handover Hong Kong. It was to replace appeals to the Judicial Committee of the Privy Council from colonial Hong Kong. In that respect the new Hong Kong Special Administrative Region will begin where other former British colonies had evolved; the eventual abolition of appeals to the Privy Council when sufficient confidence in the local judiciary had been, or was felt to have been, achieved, or perhaps when national honour in some former colonies had demanded it. Barbados and Guyana have now joined Canada, New Zealand, Malaysia and Singapore, effectively Australia,[1] and also India, Pakistan and Sri Lanka just to name a few prominent examples of jurisdictions which have abolished appeals to the Judicial Committee.[2]

In Hong Kong's case this would place the CFA in the unenviable position of having to secure the confidence of other nations, foreign commercial interests and the people of Hong Kong themselves. The twelve points and their final incarnation, the Joint Declaration, provided only terse guidance. The original ninth point – which since has become prominent in light of events surrounding the new National Security Law in 2020[3] – is related to the preservation of

---

[1] For a contemporary survey focusing on developments in the Anglophone Caribbean Community, see e.g. Michael Anthony Lilla, 'Promoting the Caribbean Court of Justice as the Final Court of Appeal for States of the Caribbean Community', Institute for Court Management Court Executive Development Program 2007–2008 Phase III Project, May 2008, 25–6.
[2] For Hong Kong's record of appeals, see Oliver Jones, 'A Worthy Predecessor? The Privy Council on Appeal from Hong Kong, 1853 to 1997', in Simon N. M. Young and Yash Ghai (eds.), *Hong Kong's Court of Final Appeal* (Cambridge: Cambridge University Press, 2013), 94.
[3] Chapter 10 of this book.

Hong Kong's common-law based legal system so long, however, that it does not come into conflict with Chinese sovereignty, and states that Hong Kong will have its own final appellate court. The ninth point appears now in the Joint Declaration in paragraph 3(3), and in Annex I, Section III. The Joint Declaration states in part in paragraph 3(3) that:

> The Hong Kong Special Administrative Region will be vested with executive, legislative and independent judicial power, including that of final adjudication.

The corresponding elaboration of that clause in Annex I[4] refers to a:

> court of final appeal in the Hong Kong Special Administrative Region, which may as required invite judges from other common law jurisdictions to sit on the court of final appeal.

The idea of foreign judges sitting alongside local judges is credited to colonial Hong Kong's last Chief Justice, and the first Chinese person to hold that position, Sir Ti-liang Yang (T. L. Yang) who drew from the example of Brunei.[5] Perhaps that idea can also be understood differently and in light of the tradition of colonial 'mixed courts' in the Middle East and in the Far East.[6] In any event, the central notion was that such a substitute for the Privy Council should engender the same degree of confidence and therefore drawing from the same judges as those who would have sat on the Privy Council would have had a natural attraction. Unlike the mixed courts of old, there would be no hybrid laws but a continuation, indeed the very preservation, of the common law.

As for the Basic Law, it states in article 82 that:

> The power of final adjudication of the Hong Kong Special Administrative Region shall be vested in the Court of Final Appeal of the Region, which may as required invite judges from other common law jurisdictions to sit on the Court of Final Appeal.

The fierce debate over the number of foreign judges has been discussed elsewhere.[7] In essence an initial agreement in 1991 between the UK and

---

[4] Article III, fourth paragraph.
[5] Simon N. M. Young, Antonio da Roza and Yash Ghai, 'Genesis of Hong Kong's Court of Final Appeal', in Young and Ghai, *op. cit.*, 121, 124. There is, today, the Sir T. L. Yang Society at The Chinese University of Hong Kong.
[6] These included such nineteenth-century mixed courts as those of Cairo, Mansoura and Alexandria. See Mark S. W. Hoyle, 'The Mixed Courts of Egypt: An Anniversary Assessment' (1985) 1 *Arab Law Quarterly* 60.
[7] See Jonathan Dimbleby, *The Last Governor* (London: Little, Brown, 1997), ch. 15.

China following the conclusion of the Joint Declaration had been that there would be the Chief Justice, three local judges and one judge chosen from a list of Hong Kong and foreign common law judges. This was seen to have put a cap on the number of foreign judges where no such limitation appears either in the Joint Declaration or the Basic Law.[8] In the Legislative Council that agreement was rejected by thirty-eight to two votes. A second agreement in the Joint Liaison Group had originated in the Preliminary Working Committee of the Preparatory Committee for the Hong Kong SAR, a Beijing constituted body resulting directly from controversy over Patten's democratic reforms. The National People's Congress decided in conjunction with the Basic Law's passage in 1990 that there would be constituted a Preparatory Committee. Chaired by Qian Qichen, the PWC comprised fifty-seven members, thirty of whom were from Hong Kong. An eight-point plan which the PWC devised formed the basis of the Joint Liaison Group's agreement (at the diplomatic level) which in turn became the revised draft of the Court of Final Appeal Ordinance. According to this revised formula, there would be permanent judges so-called as before, and thirty non-permanent overseas judges or more. The judges would sit according to the formula devised in the first agreement; namely the four permanent judges, including the Chief Justice, together with one non-permanent judge.[9]

II JUDICIAL REVIEW, POWER OF FINAL ADJUDICATION AND ACTS OF STATE

Lying at the heart of the controversy over the judges to be appointed to the Court of Final Appeal was the fact that the initial 1991 agreement between the British and Chinese sides had been done in secret. The broader context was that on the Chinese side there was a three-prong proposal to (1) deny the courts the power to declare laws unconstitutional, (2) reserve the power to overturn the Court from Beijing and (3) exclude 'acts of State' from the purview of the Hong Kong courts.[10] Thus, an agreement to limit the number of foreign judges fell along these lines. This further Sino-British agreement to restrict the authority of the courts is what makes the contemporary suggestion, in the UK, that British judges should be prevented from serving on Hong Kong's CFA ironic.

---

[8] Young, da Roza and Ghai, *op. cit.*, 126.
[9] *Ibid.*, 125–38.
[10] Dimbleby, *op. cit.*, 275–6.

It is a stark reminder of the 1991 agreement. Ostensibly[11] that suggestion is justified by the recent passage, in 2020, of a National Security Law for Hong Kong. Recall that while the Joint Declaration requires the CFA to be established, article 82 of the Basic Law states that: 'The power of final adjudication of the Hong Kong Special Administrative Region shall be vested in the Court of Final Appeal of the Region, which may as required invite judges from other common law jurisdictions to sit on the Court of Final Appeal.' If this should now be read to mean 'judges from any common law jurisdiction other than the United Kingdom' it would be difficult to see which the suggestion aims to scorn, Beijing or Hong Kong.

As far as Patten was concerned the danger lay in falling between two stools. Changing the 1991 agreement with China would alienate China. At the same time, it may still not be enough to forestall embarrassment if Hong Kong's Legislative Council were to reject the Government's bill on establishing the CFA.[12] In the end, fall he did. Jonathan Dimbleby's biography describes the assurances Michael Heseltine, then President of the Board of Trade and recently returned from Beijing, had received that China would be flexible, and that if only Patten would delay tabling the Government's disastrous bill some further accommodation could yet be reached. However, Patten considered that this would make the colonial Government look feeble.[13] Patten had the support of Douglas Hurd as Foreign Secretary, Kenneth Clarke as Chancellor of the Exchequer, against the Foreign Office and Heseltine. The solution was that Patten would have the authority to broker a deal but at the same time the bill had to get in in time for the Hong Kong legislature's 1995 summer recess. The general sense and atmosphere in late April 1995 was captured in an article in the New York Times:[14]

> 'There is a widely held view that despite the agreement in 1991', said a senior British official who asked not to be named, 'that the Chinese don't want a court set up until after 1997 when they'll have more control. They're dragging their feet but they want to blame us.'
>
> So sometime before June, whether or not the Chinese acquiesce, Mr. Patten will offer a bill to the legislature enshrining the secret agreement made in 1991 into law. But the bill is likely to meet stiff opposition and will be amended by Mr. Lee[15] to allow the presence of more than one foreign justice on the Court of Final Appeal.

---

[11] As we will discuss further below in Section VI.
[12] Dimbleby, *op. cit.*, 276.
[13] *Ibid.*, 282–3.
[14] Edward A. Gargan, 'Hong Kong Worries over Fate of Legal System under Chinese Rule', N.Y.T. (New York), 21 April 1995.
[15] Martin Lee QC, SC.

If the bill is passed with the amendment, and the British Government is lobbying hard to prevent that from happening, most colonial officials believe that Mr. Patten will withdraw the legislation and leave the matter to ... China and 1997. This very real possibility is what is generating a sudden wave of alarm.

The discussions in the Joint Liaison Group also reveal that the PRC's concern had to do with a question of timing; namely, that the CFA should not be established until the handover was done on 1 July 1997. It was clear that after that date, the UK would lose control of the issue. Timing had much to do then with substance. But as Patten saw it, it was to be either a compromise now, despite the Court not coming into operation before the handover in 1997, or losing control entirely of the issue. Crucially, Patten and Richard Hoare, Director of Administration in the Government Secretariat and acting head of the British team in the Joint Liaison Group, with Cabinet's blessing managed to secure two fundamental concessions from Beijing. The PRC, whose delegation in the Group was headed by Chen Zuo'er, agreed to drop its proposal that the Court's decisions could be reversed from Beijing, and that the Court should be prohibited from striking down laws on the basis of unconstitutionality. This left the proposal that 'acts of State' should be off-limits to the Court,[16] on which in exchange the UK side was to relent.[17] China's agreement to put the bill forward was secured on 7 June 1995.

In the public acrimony which followed Richard Hoare felt compelled to write a letter to the Independent newspaper:

> Sir ... You state that the agreement 'takes away the court's powers to rule on "acts of state"'. This is quite untrue. Nothing in the agreement or the CFA Bill takes away any powers from the court ... The formulation on 'acts of state' in the Basic Law will be the law of Hong Kong as from 1 July 1997, regardless of whether or not it is also included in the CFA Bill. And it will be for the courts of the SAR (Special Administrative Region of China) to interpret this formulation, save in exceptional cases which involve an interpretation of a provision of the Basic Law that relates to the powers of the central government, or the relationship between the central authorities and the region ... Both articles also quoted Martin Lee as attacking the agreement. But they failed to report the fact that it has been warmly welcomed by the Chief Justice of Hong Kong.[18]

---

[16] Chapter 6 of this book.
[17] Dimbleby, *op. cit.*, 284–5.
[18] R. J. F. Hoare, Letter: Court of Appeal in Hong Kong, *Independent* (London), 28 June 1995.

He goes on to assert acceptance of the agreement by other major nations, by industry and, on the basis of a poll, the people of Hong Kong. In any event, Patten went on to introduce the bill in the legislature without delay. Not only individual rights but property rights and contractual rights were at stake in this matter of having an independent, final adjudicative body that would be seen to be just as good as having the Privy Council.

By then the exchange of words between Patten and Martin Lee, the leader of the Democrats in Hong Kong, had bordered on the vituperative with Patten alleging that Lee's criticisms did a disservice to Hong Kong since the provision on acts of State reflected precisely what the Basic Law, which will govern Hong Kong after 1997, says. Article 19 of the Basic Law states that:

> The courts of the Hong Kong Special Administrative Region shall have no jurisdiction over acts of state such as defence and foreign affairs. The courts of the Region shall obtain a certificate from the Chief Executive on questions of fact concerning acts of state such as defence and foreign affairs whenever such questions arise in the adjudication of cases. This certificate shall be binding on the courts. Before issuing such a certificate, the Chief Executive shall obtain a certifying document from the Central People's Government.

Dimbleby cites Patten's (and China's) critics, not least Lee who declared the sun setting on the British Empire 'in shame', that British acceptance of acts of State was capitulation on an important issue of principle, but Patten's legal point was well founded. The Basic Law had been passed only five years ago, there were two years left before the 1997 Handover after which it would serve as the Hong Kong SAR's constitutional document. Convergence with the Basic Law was therefore not only inevitable, it was a pragmatic approach towards matters involving any final questions of fundamental legal principle. Britain had, as has been described earlier, no formal role in the Basic Law's drafting as such.[19]

In any event,[20] when the CFA did have to deal with acts of State after the handover,[21] there was hardly a murmur. It involved a 2011 case about whether the Democratic Republic of Congo could be subjected to the jurisdiction of the Hong Kong courts when Chinese foreign policy adopts the doctrine that

---

[19] It was Mr Lee who was a member of the BLDC from which he was later debarred, see Ming K. Chan, 'Democracy Derailed, Realpolitik in the Making of the Basic Law, 1985–90', in Ming K. Chan and David J. Clark, *The Hong Kong Basic Law* (Hong Kong: Hong Kong University, 1991), 3, 21–2.

[20] As will be discussed further in Chapter 6 of this book.

[21] In truth they were facts of State at common law and I will go on to explain what appears to be an evolution in the Anglo-Hong Kong common law of an Act of State doctrine which is rather different from that under the English common law.

foreign sovereigns ought to be immune from any legal process.[22] The CFA sought an interpretation from the Standing Committee of the National People's Congress (NPCSC).[23] In an earlier case, *Ma Wai Kwan*, occurring just after the 1997 handover, a challenge to the establishment of the Provisional Legislative Council had failed on the ground that its establishment was a sovereign act. That, however, was a bench of three judges sitting on Hong Kong's Court of Appeal. The case was critical on another front, the Court of Appeal albeit not the CFA, and albeit obiter, had confirmed that the courts could review and strike down local legislation.[24]

By a vote of thirty-eight to seventeen, the CFA bill was passed in July 1995.

III A MOST SOPHISTICATED BODY OF CONSTITUTIONAL RIGHTS

Although the preservation of the common law is often considered key to ensuring the rights of Hong Kongers, and to ensuring continued confidence in post-handover Hong Kong, the common law alone was seen from the British viewpoint to be insufficient after 1989. As it turned out it was the judicial fashioning of the Bill of Rights and Chapter III of the Basic Law,[25] by both Anglo-Hong Kong and other common law judges, which was to secure confidence in the years following immediately after the 1997 handover. The Joint Declaration had sought to accomplish three things – continuity of the common law, the establishment of Hong Kong's own CFA and the continued application of the provisions of the International Covenant on Civil and Political Rights. Yet it could not entirely have been foreseen that, rather than relying primarily or even solely upon external scrutiny through the periodic reporting mechanism under that Covenant, it was to be the judges

---

[22] See the trilogy of notes culminating in C. L. Lim, 'Beijing's "Congo" Interpretation, Commercial Implications' (2012) 128 *L.Q.R.* 6.

[23] Under article 158 of the Basic Law. See Interpretation of Paragraph 1, Article 13 and Article 19 of the Basic Law of the Hong Kong Special Administrative Region of the People's Republic of China by the Standing Committee of the National People's Congress (Adopted at the Twenty Second Session of the Standing Committee of the Eleventh National People's Congress on 26 August 2011). For a discussion of how the acts of State carve-out under article 19 compares to the matters on which the courts would first need to seek an interpretation of the NPCSC, see Byron S. J. Wang, 'Judicial Independence under the Basic Law', in Steven Tsang (ed.), *Judicial Independence and the Rule of Law in Hong Kong* (Hong Kong: Hong Kong University Press, 2001), 48, 66–7.

[24] *HKSAR v. Ma Wai Kwan* [1997] HKLRD 761. It was to be overruled by the CFA in the Ng Ka Ling case, *Ng Ka Ling v. Director of Immigration* (1999) 2 HKCFAR 4, discussed further below. See further, J. M. M. Chan and C. L. Lim (eds.), *Law of the Hong Kong Constitution*, 2nd ed. (Hong Kong: Sweet & Maxwell, 2015), 56.

[25] Discussed earlier in Chapter 3.

who were to develop within fifteen years what became the most sophisticated body of constitutional rights jurisprudence in the common law Far East.

In 1993, Peter Duffy in his evidence to Parliament was at pains to explain that although strictly speaking the Joint Declaration refers only to the Covenant's 'provisions', the entire procedural apparatus of reporting to the United Nations Human Rights Committee would also survive the handover.[26] As he had put it to the Committee:

> In relation to the position of Hong Kong itself, the language that is used in Article XIII might be the subject of divergent interpretations. One view of it would be to say that the provisions of the International Covenant remain in force in Hong Kong whether through the common law or the Bill of Rights or the Basic Law as the Foreign Office representative indicated, but that the 'provisions' do not necessarily include the procedures of the Covenant ... However, my view is that the restrictive interpretation of Article XIII, final sentence, does not give effect to what I would understand being the intention of that reference. The whole essence of International Covenants in the human rights field is not just to spell out a list of rights that are applied domestically. That is the function of domestic Bills of Rights, domestic constitutions. The essence of international human rights is the international procedure and the international mechanism. Thus, my interpretation of Article XIII – and that is a view that will be shared by other international lawyers – is that the reference to the provisions of the International Covenant should be understood as covering the mechanisms that had been in force in relation to Hong Kong (that is to say the reporting mechanism) should continue after 1997.[27]

As Duffy was also to point out, there were two mechanisms; the State reporting mechanism under which there is compulsory periodic reporting to the Human Rights Committee, and a further, optional, procedure which as Duffy explained to the Foreign Affairs Committee 'has not been applied to Hong Kong'. The UK had never applied the optional procedure under which individuals could also petition the Human Rights Committee while Hong Kong was under British colonial administration. This was a further procedure which would only apply in the case of States which also accepted and became party to the First Optional Protocol to the International Covenant on Civil and Political Rights. The United Kingdom was simply not a party to

---

[26] Minutes of Evidence, 3 November 1993, Foreign Affairs Committee, House of Commons, Sess. 1992–93, HC 842-ii, 1992/93 in *Relations between the United Kingdom and China in the Period Up to and Beyond 1997: First Report*, Great Britain, Parliament, House of Commons, Foreign Affairs Committee, vol. II (London: HMSO, 1994), 48, 53.
[27] Ibid.

the Optional Protocol. Perhaps in the ever hopeful vein of the international human rights lawyer, and probably the most distinguished international human rights lawyer in England, Duffy saw little difficulty in adopting what we might consider 'double standards' where at least there might be progress in enlarging the sphere of application of that procedure. The better view is possibly that he was suggesting that the UK too should accept individual petitions under the Optional Protocol. Here was how he put it:

> There is one issue which I ought to clarify in case any misunderstanding occurred as a result of my previous answer to your question. Currently the peoples of Hong Kong do not have access to an individual petition system. Such a system does exist under the International Covenant but it is contained in the optional protocol. Her Majesty's Government has not made the necessary declaration in order to bring that right of petition into play. As regards the obligation on the part of the Government of China by virtue of Article 13, final sentence of the first Annex, that obligation cannot therefore, as a matter of strict law, encompass an obligation to introduce something which previously did not exist, namely the right of individual access to the Human Rights Committee under the optional protocol. Currently, however, as a matter of international human rights protection ... it would be desirable for such a measure to be taken, but this is a measure that would have to be taken with the People's Republic of China and I am not aware that any such agreement has been made or would likely to be made.[28]

The PRC, perhaps remarkably, has followed Duffy's view to the letter. Hong Kong following the handover has not failed to submit periodic reports to the Human Rights Committee since. It does so as a part of the delegation of the PRC.[29] This is because, while the Hong Kong SAR has certain 'external affairs' powers so-called, the 'foreign affairs power' is vested in and belongs to the PRC.[30] What is also remarkable is that the PRC, at least as a whole, is not a party to the ICCPR. The PRC has signed the ICCPR but it has not ratified it. Instead it has to date ratified only the International Covenant on Economic, Social and Cultural Rights even if the two Covenants are in principle, or at least that is a broad opinion on the part of international lawyers, inter-related and interdependent. The question of the PRC assuming the duties under the ICCPR at least in respect of Hong Kong will be addressed in the next chapter, in the discussion on treaty succession; that is the idea that especially with

---

[28] Ibid., 54.
[29] See further, Chan and Lim, *op. cit.*, 559–62 (Chapter 6, 'Basic Law, Hong Kong Bill of Rights and the ICCPR', by Dinusha Panditaratne).
[30] Ibid., 89–94 (Chapter 3, 'External Affairs', by C. L. Lim and Roda Mushkat).

human rights treaties where there has been a change in sovereign authority prior human rights follow the people of the territory rather than the departing sovereign. The PRC it must also be mentioned rejects any occurrence of a succession event. As explained earlier,[31] China in its view never relinquished sovereignty in any lawful manner over Hong Kong. Putting this 'unjust treaties' issue aside, however, by 'treaty succession issue' one simply means that the application of prior treaties, and of treaties to which a 'successor' sovereign ascribes to, still needs to be resolved as a practical matter. In any case, as was mentioned just a moment ago, the PRC has upheld the application of the ICCPR's 'provisions' to Hong Kong voluntarily.

IV ADJUDICATION AND INTERPRETATION

The question that arises then is this. Absent the individual petitions procedure, would the reporting procedure under the ICCPR suffice? According to the Joint Declaration, the Hong Kong CFA will have the power of final adjudication. We have seen how the Bill of Rights Ordinance was passed by the colonial authorities in controversial circumstances, precisely because Chapter III of the Basic Law of the Hong Kong SAR contains its own fundamental rights provisions. In addition, the Basic Law already does in article 39 what the colonial administration's BORO aimed to do, which is to incorporate the provisions of the ICCPR as they had previously applied to Hong Kong into the domestic law of Hong Kong. In the case of article 39, this is accomplished at the constitutional level in Hong Kong. Article 39 of the Basic Law states in full:

> The provisions of the International Covenant on Civil and Political Rights, the International Covenant on Economic, Social and Cultural Rights, and international labour conventions as applied to Hong Kong shall remain in force and shall be implemented through the laws of the Hong Kong Special Administrative Region.
>
> The rights and freedoms enjoyed by Hong Kong residents shall not be restricted unless as prescribed by law. Such restrictions shall not contravene the provisions of the preceding paragraph of this Article.

In other words, the protection of fundamental rights is intended to be in the hands of the Hong Kong courts. Duffy, in giving evidence before Parliament's Foreign Affairs Committee, may not have considered it a matter which concerns the 'international' rather than the 'domestic' protection of human

---

[31] Chapter 1 of this book.

IV Adjudication and Interpretation

rights but, as can be seen, in Hong Kong's case there is a close and somewhat complex interaction between the two. In any event, our attention should be drawn to the role of Hong Kong's courts, in particular the CFA, in protecting individual rights as well as those of particular groups following the handover.

Declassified files show that following the release of the second draft of the Basic Law in February 1989, the UK proposed to the PRC through diplomatic channels that a 'new article is required that would make the Joint Declaration a reference point for interpreting, and for limiting amendments to the Basic Law'.[32] This is a re-emergence, in extended form,[33] of an earlier British objective which had faltered during the treaty negotiations; namely, to subject the Basic Law's amendment to the judgment of an 'international commission'. Geoffrey Howe had considered it a non-starter.[34] It is especially significant as a legal point when we consider that despite the Hong Kong SAR courts having the final power of 'adjudication' (1) the ultimate authority to interpret the Basic Law, as subsequent events have confirmed, rests not with the courts themselves but with the Standing Committee of the National People's Congress, and (2) this would include (although that power is yet to be exercised, other than in connection with democratic reform,[35] in connection with) the Basic Law's protection of individual rights in Chapter III. Article 158 of the Basic Law in its final form states in part, simply, that:

> The power of interpretation of this Law shall be vested in the Standing Committee of the National People's Congress.
>
> The Standing Committee of the National People's Congress shall authorize the courts of the Hong Kong Special Administrative Region to interpret on their own, in adjudicating cases, the provisions of this Law which are within the limits of the autonomy of the Region.
>
> The courts of the Hong Kong Special Administrative Region may also interpret other provisions of this Law in adjudicating cases. However, if the courts of the Region, in adjudicating cases, need to interpret the provisions of this Law concerning affairs which are the responsibility of the Central People's Government, or concerning the relationship between the Central Authorities and the Region, and if such interpretation will affect the judgments on the cases, the courts of the Region shall, before making their final judgments which are not appealable, seek an interpretation of the relevant

---

[32] Gary Cheung, 'Britain Proposed to Boost Hong Kong's Autonomy after Return to Chinese Rule in 1997 through De Facto Constitutional Court, Files Show', S.C.M.P. (Hong Kong), 6 January 2020.
[33] Amendment being one thing, interpretation another.
[34] See Chapter 2 of this book.
[35] Other, that is, in connection with the pace and nature of democratic reform, the right to vote and the right to political participation.

provisions from the Standing Committee of the National People's Congress through the Court of Final Appeal of the Region.

The 1990 UK proposal would have bound even the NPCSC to conform its interpretations to the Joint Declaration, and require the Hong Kong courts too to act accordingly. Article 159 of the Basic Law, which governs amendments, then goes on to state:

> The power of amendment of this Law shall be vested in the National People's Congress.
>
> The power to propose bills for amendments to this Law shall be vested in the Standing Committee of the National People's Congress, the State Council and the Hong Kong Special Administrative Region. Amendment bills from the Hong Kong Special Administrative Region shall be submitted to the National People's Congress by the delegation of the Region to the National People's Congress after obtaining the consent of two-thirds of the deputies of the Region to the National People's Congress, two-thirds of all the members of the Legislative Council of the Region, and the Chief Executive of the Region.
>
> Before a bill for amendment to this Law is put on the agenda of the National People's Congress, the Committee for the Basic Law of the Hong Kong Special Administrative Region shall study it and submit its views.
>
> No amendment to this Law shall contravene the established basic policies of the People's Republic of China regarding Hong Kong.

The last paragraph's reference to the 'established basic policies of the People's Republic of China regarding Hong Kong' is a clear reference to Annex I of the Joint Declaration. It had remained unchanged from its original form as what previously was article 170 of the first (1988) and article 158 of the second (1989) drafts of the Basic Law.[36]

In any event, the difficulty that was to arise subsequently following Hong Kong's handover involved the demarcation of the respective roles of the NPCSC in having the final word on a question of the interpretation of the Basic Law, and the final power of adjudication of the Hong Kong courts. Apart from some minor instances,[37] the Basic Law has hardly altered.

---

[36] Ming K. Chan and David J. Clark, *The Hong Kong Basic Law* (Hong Kong: Hong Kong University, 1991), 85, 145, 160.

[37] A 2010 amendment to Annex I which in essence enlarged the pool of electors of the Chief Executive, and to the list in Annex III of national laws that are to be applied in the Hong Kong SAR. In the latter case, it did not require any formal amendment since under article 18 of the Basic Law the NPCSC may add to or delete from the list following consultation of the Basic Law Committee of the Hong Kong SAR and the Hong Kong SAR Government.

The question of a demarcation between the respective roles of the NPCSC and the Hong Kong courts arises because common law courts do not distinguish between adjudication and interpretation, unlike their civilian counterparts in China.

V IN JUDICIAL HANDS

That difficulty has received particular attention in recent years but it was to arise almost at the very inception of the Hong Kong SAR just two years following the 1997 handover.[38] Andrew Li had become the first Chief Justice of the new Hong Kong SAR, succeeding Sir T. L. Yang against the background of the controversy described earlier over the appointment of non-permanent judges. Sitting on the Li Court was another judge in particular, Kemal Bokhary, with whom the Chief Justice once shared a room in chambers when they had first started out at the Bar. Bokhary would go on to record the highest number of dissenting opinions of which there have not been a great number on the Court, putting aside his capacity for the formidable deployment of the device of the separate concurring opinion. Bokhary's impact particularly in the public law sphere has been immense.[39] Between 1997 and 2012 Li and Bokhary played a prominent role in shaping the CFA's approach after which events in Hong Kong were to create new pressures in place of that period of relative calm and quiet constitutional development as confidence in the Hong Kong SAR soared.

The CFA, still testing its powers of judicial review in the new climate following *Ma Wai Kwan*, had been confronted with the question of whether Hong Kong should admit an estimated 300,000 people from the Chinese Mainland. At issue too was the status of Mainland children born of Hong Kong permanent residents. There were a number of such cases but the most famous was *Ng Ka Ling*. That case had concerned the requirement of an exit approval from the Chinese authorities in order for a Mainland person to travel to and to settle in Hong Kong. The CFA's decision, construing the right of abode under the Basic Law generously, sparked a profound social controversy fuelled by fears of unrestricted immigration and that Hong Kong's public services would be overwhelmed.

---

[38] The account in this section is drawn, with permission from Cambridge University Press, from C. L. Lim, 'Judicial Rhetoric of a Liberal Polity: Hong Kong, 1997–2012', in Rehan Abeyratne and Iddo Porat (eds.), *Towering Judges* (Cambridge: Cambridge University Press, 2021), ch. 7.
[39] Jill Cottrell and Yash Ghai, 'Concurring and Dissenting in the Hong Kong Court of Final Appeal', in Young and Ghai, *op. cit.*, 283, 313–21, and generally.

The Court considered that it had the power to decline to refer a question concerning the interpretation of the Basic Law to the NPCSC at all. Article 158 of the Basic Law, unlike article 19 which concerns acts of State such as defence and foreign affairs and which had caused such pre-handover controversy, states in its relevant parts that:

> The power of interpretation of this Law shall be vested in the Standing Committee of the National People's Congress.
>
> The Standing Committee of the National People's Congress shall authorize the courts of the Hong Kong Special Administrative Region to interpret on their own, in adjudicating cases, the provisions of this Law which are within the limits of the autonomy of the Region.
>
> The courts of the Hong Kong Special Administrative Region may also interpret other provisions of this Law in adjudicating cases. However, if the courts of the Region, in adjudicating cases, need to interpret the provisions of this Law concerning affairs which are the responsibility of the Central People's Government, or concerning the relationship between the Central Authorities and the Region, and if such interpretation will affect the judgments on the cases, the courts of the Region shall, before making their final judgments which are not appealable, seek an interpretation of the relevant provisions from the Standing Committee of the National People's Congress through the Court of Final Appeal of the Region. When the Standing Committee makes an interpretation of the provisions concerned, the courts of the Region, in applying those provisions, shall follow the interpretation of the Standing Committee. However, judgments previously rendered shall not be affected.

Rather than referring the question of whether the issue concerns 'the responsibility of the Central People's Government, or ... the relationship between the Central Authorities and the Region', the Court took the view that it should instead ask itself if the Basic Law provision to be interpreted is one which is excluded in the first place from the Court's purview. Since if it were not such an 'excluded provision' it would not then be necessary to refer it to the NPCSC.[40] One passage was to spark alarm, if not outrage, in certain quarters: 'It is therefore for the courts of the Region to determine whether an act of the National People's

---

[40] Where as in that case more than one constitutional provision needed to be read together, the Court proceeded to ask which of the provisions was 'predominant'. If that which is the 'predominant provision' is no itself an 'excluded provision' then it would follow that no referral would be necessary; see Chan and Lim, *op. cit.*, 58–60; 66–7.

Congress or its Standing Committee is inconsistent with the Basic Law, subject of course to the provisions of the Basic Law itself.'[41]

The newly established Tung Chee-hwa Government, relying upon Article 158 of the Basic Law, proceeded to seek to overturn the Court's reading by itself claiming and exercising the authority to refer the whole question to Beijing. It was at the time unclear whether the Government – rather than the Courts – had also the power of referral. The Government's argument, which ultimately was successful, was that having been entrusted with law enforcement it too possessed the power of referral.[42] Predictably there arose concern about encroachment. Following Beijing's interpretation, given in response to the Government's request,[43] the CFA was widely seen to have backed down. It issued a 'clarification' in *Ng Ka Ling (No. 2)*, purporting as it were to 'clarify' its own earlier judgment.[44] This drew predictable criticism.

In other words, the stage had been set for a frontal conflict between the Chinese and common law systems. Under the Chinese legal system the final power of interpretation lay with the NPCSC. However, from a common law viewpoint that power is bound up with the power of adjudication. Hence the second judgment in *Ng Ka Ling (No. 2)*, 'clarifying' the CFA's judgment in *Ng Ka Ling (No. 1)*.[45] Arguably it clarified nothing which may have been the intent but in any case it would have been important to hear the Court acknowledge it. So long as what the Court said amounted also to an admission of Beijing's authority then a legal crisis will have been to that extent averted.[46]

The precariousness of the line between socialist legality and the common law was evident,[47] even if it was unavoidable under 'one country, two systems'. Still, *Ng Ka Ling (No. 1)* showed that Hong Kong's CFA cannot be faulted for

---

[41] *Ng Ka Ling v. Director of Immigration* (1999) 2 HKCFAR 4, 25–6. It was, in legal terms, a resort to a doctrine of *acte claire*, on which see e.g. *Srl CILFIT v. Ministry of Health* (1982) Case 283/81.

[42] The Government's referral concerned two cases, *Ng Ka Ling* and another case, *Chan Kam Nga v. Dir. of Immigration* (1999) 2 HKCFAR 82, the question there involving the child's entitlement to the right of abode despite being born before the fact of its parent's acquisition of the status of a permanent resident.

[43] Which considered that children born outside the Hong Kong SAR must at the time of birth have at least one parent who was permanently resident.

[44] See further Johannes Chan, 'What the Court of Final Appeal Has Not Clarified in Its Clarification: Jurisdiction and the Amicus Intervention', in Johannes M. M. Chan, H. L. Fu and Yash Ghai (eds.), *Hong Kong's Constitutional Debate: Conflict Over Interpretation* (Hong Kong: Hong Kong University Press, 2001), 171.

[45] See Chan and Lim, *op. cit.*, 60; Chan, 'What the Court of Final Appeal Has Not Clarified', *op. cit.*, at 180–1.

[46] Chan, 'What the Court of Final Appeal Has Not Clarified', *op. cit.*, 180–1.

[47] At the time the most important textbook, by Yash Ghai, had already pointed out the difficulty of cocooning a common law system within a socialist legal order but that was at best

want of trying and the Court did subsequently go on to construe the scope of that NPCSC Interpretation narrowly.[48] Thus, even today, it is still asked which part of *Ng Ka Ling (No. 1)* remains. On this subject Justice Kemal Bokhary has remarked, extrajudicially, that:

> Article 158 of the Basic Law vests the power of interpretation in the Standing Committee of the National People's Congress. But then – and vitally to the 'one country, two systems' principle – the Standing Committee, by the same article, authorises the Hong Kong courts to interpret on their own the provisions of the Basic Law which are within Hong Kong's autonomy. That means the whole of the Basic Law excluding only a limited category of provisions: those that concern affairs that are the Mainland Government's responsibility or that concern the relationship between the Mainland authorities and Hong Kong. Also according to Article 158, the Hong Kong courts are required to seek an interpretation from the Standing Committee if they need to interpret any excluded provision. That requirement, it is to be stressed, applies only to excluded provisions. And the Court of Final Appeal did not consider any such provision to be involved in either of the two cases out of which the Reinterpretation arose.[49]

That may be true, however there is no question that the NPCSC decides ultimately, and in a related case the CFA went on, clearly, to accept that the NPCSC's power is plenary – that is, absolute, and unqualified.[50]

This halting start did not prevent the CFA from going on to fashion a most sophisticated and successful body of rights jurisprudence in the coming years. In *Leung Kwok Hung*, a 2005 freedom of assembly case, Li CJ's majority judgment referred to the freedoms of speech and assembly as those freedoms which 'lie at the foundation of a democratic society'.[51] That judgment recalled an earlier 1999 flag desecration case where free speech had been extolled in lyric form just as quickly as the Court had refused the application to strike down a law protecting the Hong Kong and Chinese national flags and emblems. Yet lyricism tends to survive the particular constitutional outcome. In the flag

---

a theoretical concern which may have only occupied the imagination of teachers at the University of Hong Kong where Ghai and his colleagues struggled with such issues.

[48] Kemal Bokhary, 'The Rule of Law in Hong Kong Fifteen Years after the Handover' (2013) 51 *Columbia Jo Transn'tl L* 287, 292, discussing *Lau Kong Yung*, and *Chong Fung Yuen v. Dir. of Immigration* (2001) 4 HKCFAR 211. See further, Chan and Lim, *op. cit.*, 66–70.

[49] Bokhary, *op. cit.*, 291.

[50] *Lau Kong Yung v. Director of Immigration* (1999) 2 HKCFAR 300.

[51] *Leung Kwok Hung v. HKSAR* (2005) 8 HKCFAR 229, at [1] (Li CJ, Chan PJ, Ribeiro PJ, Mason NPJ).

case, *Ng Kung Siu*, Li CJ had considered '[f]reedom of expression … a fundamental freedom in a democratic society', and that:

> It lies at the heart of a civil society and of Hong Kong's system and way of life. The Courts must give a generous interpretation to its constitutional guarantee. This freedom includes the freedom to express ideas which the majority may find disagreeable or offensive and the freedom to criticise governmental institutions and the conduct of public officials.[52]

In the later 2005 peaceful assembly case Li was to add that: 'The freedom of peaceful assembly is a fundamental right. It is closely associated with the fundamental right of the freedom of speech. The freedom of speech and the freedom of peaceful assembly are precious and lie at the foundation of a democratic society.'[53]

A democratic society? According to Li, '[t]olerance is the hallmark of a pluralistic society'.[54] This was to become perhaps the key *motif* in Li's more notable constitutional judgments. But what was his aim? To improve our ideas about governance by ensuring the 'vigour' of democratic debate? Or was it instead to allow minorities to be heard? According to Li:

> These freedoms are of cardinal importance for the stability and progress of society for a number of inter-related reasons. The resolution of conflicts, tensions and problems through open dialogue and debate is of the essence of a democratic society. These freedoms enable such dialogue and debate to take place and ensure their vigour. A democratic society is one where the market place of ideas must thrive. These freedoms enable citizens to voice criticisms, air grievances and seek redress. This is relevant not only to institutions exercising powers of government but also to organisations outside the public sector which in modern times have tremendous influence over the lives of citizens. Minority views may be disagreeable, unpopular, distasteful or even offensive to others. But tolerance is a hallmark of a pluralistic society. Through the exercise of these freedoms minority views can be properly ventilated.[55]

Still, the Court was again to reject the constitutional challenge and the convictions were upheld. But this time, unlike in the flag case, Bokhary broke ranks and uttered dissent.

---

[52] *HKSAR v. Ng Kung Siu* (1999) 2 HKCFAR 422 (*per* Li CJ).
[53] *Leung Kwok Hung*, at [1]–[2].
[54] Ibid.
[55] Ibid.

In the earlier flag case he had gone along – or perhaps had been persuaded to go along – with the Chief Justice and the majority, adding however that:

> In the course of her powerful address, counsel for the 2nd respondent posed a rhetorical question. If these restrictions are permissible, where does it stop? It is a perfectly legitimate question. And the answer, as I see it, is that it stops where these restrictions are located. For they lie just within the outer limits of constitutionality. Beneath the national and regional flags and emblems, all persons in Hong Kong are – and can be confident that they will remain – equally free under our law to express their views on all matters whether political or non-political: saying what they like, how they like.[56]

It seems true to say that some of the Li Court's most notably elegiac moments were when those who had pressed their rights failed before the Court. Putting that aside, Li's message was constant – that a democratic society is a society tolerant of diverse opinions, their articulation and their expression. The protection of minority groups and opinion became thus a noticeable preoccupation for him.

At times the entire lesson consisted of a pithy phrase – homosexuals 'constitute a minority in the community'.[57] Yet readers of the Hong Kong Law Reports understood his concerns about post-handover Hong Kong's civic health and his use of the Basic Law to instil a constitutional conscience. In contrast, Bokhary went beyond liberal tolerance and the inculcation of civic virtues. Outcomes mattered when construing and applying constitutional rights. He seemed to dislike paying homage only to principle and spoke directly to the preservation of Hong Kongers' freedoms. In the flag case Bokhary said:

> ... I am of the view that it is possible – even if by no means easy – for a society to protect its flags and emblems while at the same time maintaining its freedom of expression ... This is possible if its flag and emblem protection laws are specific, do not affect the substance of expression, and touch upon the mode of expression only to the extent of keeping flags and emblems impartially beyond politics and strife. In my view, our laws protecting the national and regional flags and emblems from public and willful desecration meet such criteria. They place no restriction at all on what people may express. Even in regard to how people may express themselves, the only restriction placed is against the desecration of objects which hardly anyone would dream of desecrating even if there was no law against it. No idea would be suppressed by the restriction. Neither political outspokenness nor any other form of outspokenness would be inhibited.[58]

---

[56] *Ng Kung Siu*, at [98] (Bokhary PJ, concurring).
[57] *Secretary for Justice v. Yau Yuk Lung* (2007) 10 HKCFAR 335, at [29].
[58] *Ng Kung Siu*, at [96]–[97] (*per* Bokhary PJ).

But why single out – if indeed that is what he did – political outspokenness? Is he what American constitutionalists might call a 'Brandeisian', one who grades the relative value of different forms of speech and expression before singling out political speech as deserving of the highest protection? If so, he is then unlike Andrew Li who in American constitutional terms is more of a Holmes than a Brandeis.[59] Still, all of this is to be done only under the respective national and regional flags and emblems – the very symbols of 'one country, two systems'. Without the flags and emblems there is no Hong Kong SAR.

The result may be the same but there always were clues to entirely different judicial philosophies. Bokhary's voice reflected closely Hong Kong's perennial fear of tyranny, Li spoke instead, indeed consistently, to a democratic nature and the abjuration of Hong Kong's own tyrannous sentiments. What is the significance of these two judges? What might we say, if anything, of their legacy today? Following, most notably, Bokhary's parting shot when, upon leaving the bench as a Permanent Justice, he had warned of 'clouds heralding a "storm of unprecedented ferocity" gathering over the rule of law in Hong Kong'.[60]

Two strands of judicial philosophy in the field of individual rights protection had emerged. The first emphasised a 'democratic' tolerance of diversity. The second brought the Basic Law's guarantees of political rights and freedoms to the fore. It might be asked whether some of the Court's judgments would have been so forcefully liberal without Bokhary's influence. The constitutional imagination of a society is a construct of the mind. In Hong Kong's case, it was in a significant sense a product of the court on which Andrew Li presided. There was much which had occurred in the preceding years – the Sino-British talks which led to the Sino-British Joint Declaration, the drafting of the Basic Law, the enactment by the colonial authorities of the Bill of Rights Ordinance. These, as the preceding chapters and this chapter have shown, were tumultuous years. Yet treaties and legislation do not themselves create the constitutional imagination of a society. Here judicial voices mattered, in their tone, their timbre, their persuasiveness or otherwise.

In a sense the boundaries have been tested, when attention turned inwards to fundamental questions about the nature of Hong Kong's society and its way of life. This was not a matter simply of differences from such ways on the

---

[59] A Holmesian being a believer in an entirely free market place of ideas. See *Leung Kwok Hung*, at [2].
[60] Austin Chiu, 'Retiring Court of Final Appeal Judge Warns of Legal Turmoil', *South China Morning Post*, 25 October 2012.

Chinese Mainland. One might suggest that Hong Kong grew to legal maturity by attending to its own immediate domestic concerns.

In any event, the Li Court restored an approach, discussed further below in Section VI, which aims to give a generous and purposive interpretation to rights. One judge placed great weight on the virtue of tolerance in a democratic, cosmopolitan and multicultural modern society, the other on the architectural design of a democratic polity defined by rights. Whatever public fears lurk now, we gained a better appreciation of what 'a high degree of autonomy' might mean. The view that the Basic Law, or any other constitutional document, can simply be followed ignores the fact that in the common law mind constitutional documents need first to be explained.[61] None can accuse Andrew Li or Kemal Bokhary of shying from this task of explaining how a liberal, rights-based constitutional arrangement emanating from a socialist legislative act should function.

VI HOW WE REASON ABOUT RIGHTS

In terms of its formal reasoning the CFA's approach to the interpretation of fundamental rights and liberties owes much to certain pre-handover beginnings, when the Hong Kong Bill of Rights first required judicial interpretation. This was before the handover and the late Mr Justice Silke as Vice-President of the colonial Court of Appeal was to set the tone and overall approach. He was a member of the Irish Bar whose career took him to Borneo thence to Hong Kong. That Borneo connection as was common in the day was apparently maintained with Silke serving subsequently as a Commissioner of the Supreme Court of Brunei Darussalam. It was 1991. A drug case had concerned the reverse onus of proof. According to Silke V-P:

> In my judgment, the glass through which we view the interpretation of the Hong Kong Bill is a glass provided by the Covenant. We are no longer guided by the ordinary cannons of construction of statutes nor with the dicta of the common law inherent in our training. We must look, in our interpretation of the Hong Kong Bill, at the aims of the Covenant and give 'full recognition and effect' to the statement which commences that Covenant. From this stems the entirely new jurisprudential approach to which I have already referred.[62]

While that view did not find favour with the Judicial Committee of the Privy Council, Mr Justice Silke's 'generous and purposive approach' was to find its

---

[61] Cass R. Sunstein, 'Of Snakes and Butterflies' (2006) 106 *Columbia L. Rev.* 2234, 2234.
[62] *R v. Sin Yau Ming* (1991) 1 HKPLR 88, 107 (Silke VP).

place after the handover, in the post-handover CFA judgments subsequently. In 1995, in the flag desecration case, Li CJ wrote: 'The Courts must give a generous interpretation to its constitutional guarantee.'[63] Again, in the seminal freedom of assembly judgment discussed earlier, the CFA held by a majority, with Li writing the main opinion and Bokhary PJ dissenting, that:

> It is well established in our jurisprudence that the courts must give such a fundamental right [to freedom of peaceful assembly] a generous interpretation so as to give individuals its full measure. On the other hand, restrictions on such a fundamental right must be narrowly interpreted. Plainly, the burden is on the Government to justify any restriction ... Needless to say, in a society governed by the rule of law, the courts must be vigilant in the protection of fundamental rights and must rigorously examine any restriction that may be placed on them.[64]

The CFA's approach was in one sense different from Silke's balancing approach, rather it involved the more familiar 'structured' approach or proportionality test. That involves asking, first, whether the legislative measure pursues a legitimate aim and what that aim is before, second, asking if the measure is in fact connected to that aim, whether it advances or fits that aim, and then asking, finally, if the measure is proportionate in light of that aim in that it restricts a fundamental right in a way that is no more than is strictly necessary. It is at this juncture that we also see the deep Anglo-European influence upon the reasoning of Hong Kong's post-handover courts, which in turn is derived from the House of Lords' and subsequently the UK Supreme Court's reception of European human rights jurisprudence, if not derived more directly from the Strasbourg court itself.

More recently however we have witnessed a fourth step in the analysis which is to ask if a sufficient margin of appreciation – *marge d'appréciation* – has been granted to the Government, or to the Hong Kong legislature, in the same manner as the Strasbourg court would accord a margin of appreciation. In the Strasbourg context an international court would not as with a local court be as well-placed to understand local needs or conditions, or perceivable differences in the various national laws of the Contracting States in respect of their reception of the European Convention on Human Rights. The seminal case in the European human rights context was the *Lawless* case concerning the detention without trial of an Irish Republican Army suspect and a derogation under article 15 from article 5 of the Convention concerning

---

[63] *HKSAR v. Ng Kung Siu* (1999) 2 HKCFAR 422 (*per* Li CJ).
[64] *Leung Kwok Hung v. HKSAR* (2005) 8 HKCFAR 229, at [1] (Li CJ, Chan PJ, Ribeiro PJ, Mason NPJ).

the right to liberty and security,[65] in which Sir Humphrey Waldock (C. H. M. Waldock, as he was then)[66] in his testimony supporting the Commission's judgment as its President had said:

> The concept behind [the doctrine in respect of article 15] is that Article 15 has to be read in the context of the rather special subject matter with which it deals: The responsibilities of a government for maintaining law and order in a time of war or other public emergency threatening the life of the nation. The concept of the margin of appreciation is that a government's discharge of these responsibilities is essentially a delicate problem of appreciating complex factors and of balancing conflicting considerations of the public interest; and that, once the Commission or Court is satisfied that the government's appreciation is at least on the margin of the powers conferred by Article 15, then the interest which the public itself has in effective government and in the maintenance of order justifies and requires a decision in favour of the legality of the Government's appreciation.[67]

That doctrine was to expand beyond the confines of article 15 of the European Convention in the Convention's jurisprudence. Nonetheless, its application has been questioned (also by this author)[68] for in Hong Kong's case the courts would be dealing solely with Hong Kong's own local measures. Still the leading text on the subject does take the position that application of the doctrine by domestic courts is not precluded:

> Just as there are circumstances in which an international court will recognize that national institutions are better placed to assess the needs of society, and to make difficult choices between competing considerations, so national courts will accept that there are circumstances in which the legislature and the executive ate better placed to perform those functions.[69]

In any event, there has been every suggestion that, rather than to look towards the views or formal interpretations of the Human Rights Committee, the CFA

---

[65] *Lawless v. Republic of Ireland* (No. 3), No. 332/57, Judgment of 1 July 1961 (No. 3), 1 E.H.R.R. 15.

[66] Waldock was supposed to have informed Professor Brian Simpson that international law was but diplomacy by another name, and that all business was conducted 'in the corridors'; A. W. B. Simpson, *Human Rights and the End of Empire: Britain and the Genesis of the European Convention* (Oxford: Oxford University Press, 2001), 966.

[67] Clovis C. Morrisson, *The Developing European Law om Human Rights* (Leiden: Sijthoff, 1967), 150, n. 170; also J. Christoffersen, *Fair Balance: Proportionality, Subsidiarity and Primarity in the European Convention on Human Rights* (Leiden: Brill, 2009) at 244, citing the verbatim record of the hearing of 8 April 1961.

[68] Chan and Lim, *op. cit.*, 602.

[69] Anthony Lester and David Pannick, *Human Rights Law and Practice* (London: Butterworths, 1999), 74.

has over time developed a very recognisably European body of human rights jurisprudence when viewed in terms of its formal reasoning. This has not precluded broader comparative influences, including the discernible influence at times even of the United States Supreme Court. Thus, in the flag desecration case there were very clear echoes of Justice Oliver Wendell Holmes Jr's 'free market of ideas'. Much will in practice depend upon the pleadings.

All of this, of course, is judge-made law, the common law, and assumes a judicial freedom to develop the Basic Law's and BORO's protection of fundamental rights, as well as to chart the course of Hong Kong's own rights regime.

VII 2020

In 2020, following the promulgation of a National Security Law in Hong Kong,[70] deliberate pressure was brought to bear on the UK Government to discontinue the practice of having British judges serve on Hong Kong's CFA as non-permanent judges. At the time the Lords Hoffman, Millett, Neuberger, Walker, Collins, Phillips, Reed, Sumption and Baroness Hale served in that capacity. Under the prevailing agreement two serving judges of the UK Supreme Court would occupy that role, but as of July 2020 there was only Lord Reed while a replacement for Baroness Hale was being sought.

Lord Reed, in a statement issued following the passage in Beijing and promulgation in Hong Kong on 30 June 2020 of the new law, has said:

> The new security law contains a number of provisions which give rise to concerns. Its effect will depend upon how it is applied in practice. That remains to be seen. Undoubtedly, the judges of the Court of Final Appeal will do their utmost to uphold the guarantee in Article 85 of the Hong Kong Basic Law that 'the Courts of the Hong Kong Special Administrative Region shall exercise judicial power independently, free from any interference'. As the Chief Justice of Hong Kong, the Hon Geoffrey Ma, recently said: 'The independence of the Judiciary and the rule of law are cornerstones of the Hong Kong community, and they are guaranteed under the Basic Law. It remains the mission and the constitutional duty of the Hong Kong Judiciary to maintain and protect them.'[71]

That statement was made following another widely reported statement by Mr Tugendhat, as chair of Parliament's Foreign Affairs Select Committee, who

---

[70] Discussed further in Chapter 10 of this book.
[71] Statement from the President of the UK Supreme Court, Lord Reed of Allermuir, 17 July 2020.

had said: 'How can they do that, how can they defend civil rights and commercial rights if they are being violated by the very law they are sent to uphold?'[72]

To the National Security Law's critics, its passage necessarily removes the duty of independence from which flows the duty of impartiality. Mr Tugendhat[73] does not say that, he implies it, but may not appreciate that a mere allegation that judicial independence has been removed should not lead automatically to judicial removal. In most circumstances that will be too convenient. In any event, it is difficult to discern his reasons for thinking that it will be helpful for the UK to remove Hong Kong's serving British judges, or to abolish an arrangement which has benefitted both Hong Kong and the UK since the handover.

Would Hong Kong's rights jurisprudence have developed so swiftly without the contribution of members of the House of Lords previously, and subsequently of the UK Supreme Court? Unless it can be shown that Hong Kong's highest court no longer acts independently according to article 85 of the Basic Law, there is, simply, no basis for concluding that judicial independence has vanished overnight in Hong Kong.

VIII UK JUDGES IN HONG KONG

It is in that connection that a development in 2014 was to spark public debate and an unusual intervention by a now former Chief Justice of the Hong Kong SAR. In 2014, following publication of the PRC State Council's White Paper on 'One Country, Two Systems' on 10 June, controversy centred on two notions; namely, that judges are expected to be patriotic, and that they were, at least as the word was translated into the English Language, 'administrators'. The suggestion that judges were a part of the administration was taken in other words, in some quarters at least, to mean that they were simply an arm of the Executive Branch. Andrew Li in an opinion piece in the South China Morning Post sought to dispel concern, writing that:

> The English version of the white paper included judges among 'those who administrate Hong Kong' (i.e. administer). In Hong Kong, with the

---

[72] 'Role of UK Judges in Hong Kong Appeal Court Comes under Scrutiny', *Guardian* (London), 2 July 2020.

[73] Who contrary to the Law Commission's views on the matter is advocating a revised treason law in the United Kingdom and thus cannot, one assumes, be taken to be against treason laws as such. See Richard Ekins, Patrick Hennessey, Khalid Mahmood MP and Tom Tugendhat MP, 'Aiding the Enemy', Policy Exchange, with a Foreword by Lord Judge, 2018, https://policyexchange.org.uk/publication/aiding-the-enemy/.

separation of powers, the executive, the legislature and the judiciary may be regarded as the three branches of government in the broad sense. The latter two are not part of the executive. Considering that the Chinese version of the white paper used the term zhi gang (which can be translated as the governance of Hong Kong), it would appear that this is what was intended.

Unfortunately, the English version used the word 'administrate'. This is unfortunate and is unsuitable. This word is usually understood in Hong Kong to refer to the executive authorities (for example, the Tung Chee-hwa, the Donald Tsang or the CY Leung administration). Clearly, the judiciary is not part of the executive. It would be best for this to be clarified. Any concern arising from the use of the word 'administrate' in English should be dispelled.[74]

However, that still leaves the second driving force in the controversy which had to do with where judicial fidelity ought to lie – in the Basic Law itself, or elsewhere. The Hong Kong understanding was perhaps expressed accurately by Li, according to whom patriotism is too vague but that in any case the judicial oath is to uphold the Basic Law, no more and certainly no less. Insofar as the Basic Law is concerned then, the Hong Kong SAR is an inalienable part of China,[75] and judicial independence is preserved through a separation of powers. Thus, there is no question of judges favouring the Hong Kong Government where that conflicts with their duty of impartiality. That simply is a deliberate misunderstanding of the issue. Li viewed the duty of impartiality as something which is subsumed by a duty of independence. As he put it: 'under the principle of judicial independence, judges should not be pro or anti anyone or anything. They should be fair and impartial. Judges have no master, political or otherwise.'[76]

It was a rare intervention. Some scholarly commentary has sought to make more of the issue however by linking the controversy to broader changes in China,[77] particularly in the strengthened role of the Communist Party of China (or CPC) resulting from an amendment to the first article of the 1982 PRC Constitution by the Thirteenth National People's Congress in 2018. That Congress had taken place following the Nineteenth CPC Congress in 2017.[78]

---

[74] Andrew Li, 'Under Rule of Law, an Independent Judiciary Answers to No Political Masters', S.C.M.P. (Hong Kong), 14 August 2014.
[75] Basic Law, article 1.
[76] Ibid.
[77] Johannes Chan, 'A Storm of Unprecedented Ferocity: The Shrinking Space of the Right to Political Participation, Peaceful Demonstration, and Judicial Independence in Hong Kong' (2018) 16 I.Con. 373, 375.
[78] See e.g. Yunbi Zhang, 'NPC Passes Constitution Update', China Daily (Beijing), 12 March 2018.

Still, the amendment to the PRC Constitution suggesting an expanded role for the CPC in China's governance should in principle have no relevance to the Joint Declaration insofar as it has no legal effect on what the Hong Kong Basic Law prescribes. As far as the Joint Declaration is concerned, the Basic Law is the focal document whose interpretation and application could, under the prevailing rules of international treaty interpretation, yet shape the Joint Declaration's proper interpretation; specifically if it establishes a subsequent agreement between the parties as to its meaning. In other words even absent any subsequent agreement, a 'subsequent practice' establishing the parties' agreement could shape the proper interpretation of a prior treaty obligation.[79]

However in Hong Kong and indeed under PRC law too the Basic Law itself has a constitutional status. That is because when the Basic Law was passed there was as well a Decision of the National People's Congress, adopted at the same session. It states that:

> Article 31 of the Constitution of the People's Republic of China provides: 'The State may establish special administrative regions when necessary. The systems to be instituted in special administrative regions shall be prescribed by law enacted by the National People's Congress in the light of the specific conditions.' The Basic Law of the Hong Kong Special Administrative Region is constitutional as it is enacted in accordance with the Constitution of the People's Republic of China and in the light of the specific conditions of Hong Kong. The systems, policies and laws to be instituted after the establishment of the Hong Kong Special Administrative Region shall be based on the Basic Law of the Hong Kong Special Administrative Region.[80]

Chinese scholars who argue that 'one country, two systems' does not logically preclude, and in fact must include, the application of the PRC Constitution to Hong Kong accept at the same time that the PRC Constitution cannot apply in its entirety to Hong Kong. Various aspects are pertinent to and relate only specifically to the operation of the socialist system in China.[81] Still, there is

---

[79] See C. L. Lim, 'Britain's Treaty Rights in Hong Kong' (2015) 131 *L.Q.R.* 348, but see Ewan Smith who disagrees, 'Constitutional Treaties in Hong Kong' (1 February 2017). Available at SSRN: https://ssrn.com/abstract=2942748>https://dx.doi.org/10.2139/ssrn.2942748>t (last accessed: 6 April 2021). See further Chapter 9 of this book.

[80] Decision of the National People's Congress on the Basic Law of the Hong Kong Special Administrative Region of the People's Republic of China, Adopted at the Third Session of the Seventh National People's Congress on 4 April 1990.

[81] See Zhenmin Wang, *Relationship between the Chinese Central Authorities and Regional Governments of Hong Kong and Macao: A Legal Perspective* (Singapore: Springer, 2019), 96.

a necessary element of overlap. In October 1989, Pamela Major of the Hong Kong Desk at the UKFCO wrote, in recently declassified files, of the:

> [C]onsequences as regards the PRC Constitution and the extent to which its structural provisions (as distinct from its ideological or policy provisions) have relevance in relation to, if not directly to, the SAR, that attracts indirectly those structural provisions of Chapter Three of the Constitution which regulate the NPC. At least, it cannot be said that such provisions have no relevance to the SAR.[82]

This must be correct. That a country is bound together by a singular constitution can hardly be controversial. At the same time, if a constitution prescribes two systems then these ought to be kept distinct and separate. There is no suggestion as a matter of legal rule or principle that socialist principles have already been applied to Hong Kong, or that there is any intention to do so. Indeed, the PRC's position is to the contrary. Who is to say whether public opinion, overwrought and proclaiming otherwise, could nonetheless be proven to be correct? Time will tell, but the suggestion that the socialist system now somehow applies is not presently one that is based upon the application of any legal principle. In the words of the FCO telegram just quoted, a distinction should be drawn between the 1982 PRC Constitution's 'ideological' or 'policy' aspects on the one hand, and its 'structural' aspects on the other. The suggestion, if there is such a suggestion, that the 'Chinese system' is not constructed of legal principle, or that it cannot be, would entail the view that the whole exercise of establishing such principles was pointless from the outset. That way madness lies.

As for whether British judges should continue to serve in Hong Kong the issue is current, and while the events below occur in 2021 and 2022 they are dealt with more expediently here. Lord David Neuberger put it this way in May 2021 following a speech which he delivered in 2017[83] and in which he had spoken of the role of non-permanent judges as canaries in the coalmine: 'To me the oxygen is still there enough for me to sing rather than to droop.'[84] Here too is his response to Guy Featherstonehaugh QC before an audience at the Inner Temple:

> [G. F.:] David can I just ask my last question which probably goes to the crux of the difference between you. You, with respect and admiration David, are

---

[82] TNA, FCO 40/2643, FM FCO to Deskby 190100Z Hong Kong, Telno. 2125, October 1989.
[83] 'Judges, Access to Justice, the Rule of Law and the Court of Final Appeal under "One Country, Two Systems"', University of Hong Kong, 13 September 2017.
[84] Reported first by @legalhackette on Twitter, 13 May 2021.

not a canary but if you were a canary you would have the most striking remarkable yellow plumage of anybody in the legal firmament ... what do foreign serving judges bring to Hong Kong and what would be lost through their removal given that people of your caliber can still sit there.

...

[D. N.:] ... it would send a bad message and it may lead to the walls crumbling. I don't now ... But I think the logic of my argument and the logic which seems to be in line with what Lord Reed said ... his message seems to be we are monitoring the situation, there are causes for concern and to that extent I entirely agree with Charlie, there are causes for concern ... but insofar as it is acceptable we shall continue. If that's right for one canary then it is right for all canaries ... When we handed Hong Kong back to the People's Republic of China we achieved a very significant benefit for the people of Hong Kong, in that we ensured that they had the Basic Law which was going to be enforced by an independent judiciary buttressed and supported by the canaries in the coalmine, by UK judges serving and retired, and this was not just supporting the rule of law as an abstract exercise but it was supporting individuals' rights and businesses' rights in Hong Kong for the benefit of the Hong Kong people and the benefit of the Hong Kong economy. The Basic Law is still there, the judges are still independent ... and as I said the canaries should still be singing.[85]

However, on 30 March 2022 Lord Reed and Lord Hodge, who still serve as judges of the UK Supreme Court, announced their resignation from Hong Kong's Court of Final Appeal. The other British overseas judges, Lord

---

[85] Lord David Neuberger and Lord Charlie Falconer, 'Should UK Judges and ex-Judges Be Sitting in Hong Kong', Inner Temple, Social Context of the Law Lecture, 6 May 2021, available in a video recording on the Inner Temple website. As this book was due to the Press, Lady Hale's intention not to renew her term on Hong Kong's final court of appeal was announced formally. At a talk given shortly afterwards at the kind invitation of the Statute Law Society, 'Hong Kong National Security Law', 15 June 2021, the present author was prompted to respond to the question of British judges, demonstrating perhaps the importance of the issue in the public mind. There was little reason to repeat Lord Sumption's arguments in the press, but the answer ought to be that it is entirely a matter for the judges alone. Lord Neuberger, for his part, had put it poignantly and he is quoted here. Lord Falconer takes a different view, and the event which is available in the public domain should be watched on video in its entirety in order that it be done proper justice. Lord Neuberger's arguments are in a way similar, at least to my mind, to the Foreign Office position quoted earlier – that Hong Kong's courts are regional, their jurisdiction is limited therefore, and the UK knew this in connection with the handover, the resumption of Chinese sovereignty and the arrangement so many years ago to have British judges sit in Hong Kong. The difference between Lords Neuberger and Falconer centred on article 55 of the National Security Law, which concerns where Hong Kong's autonomy ends, but this is a provision which has not so far been carried out. See further Chapter 9 of this book where its focus, however, is on article 4 of the National Security Law which receives too little attention.

Phillips, Lord Hoffman, Lord Neuberger, Lord Collins, Lord Sumption and Lord Walker, remain in place. Here then is the application of a distinction Lord Falconer would have had us draw in his debate with Lord Neuberger in May 2021. The Chinese Central Government and the Hong Kong SAR Government have responded to these judicial resignations by accusing the UK of interfering in the independence of the judiciary and the administration of justice in Hong Kong.[86] Hong Kong's Secretary for Justice wrote, in a letter to the international press, that there is the suggestion of political interference,[87] citing Lord Reed's statement that the decision that judges of the UK Supreme Court can no longer sit in Hong Kong was made 'in agreement with the government'. For his part, Lord Reed had explained to the House of Lords' constitution committee that any suggestion that there was interference would be 'mistaken', that 'I actually sought the meeting at which we took a decision because of my own concerns and found that ministers were of the same view'. Adding that it would have been 'rich irony' had it been otherwise.[88] Still, both members of the UK Supreme Court would have been aware of the UK Government's position and we might imagine a serving judge feeling that one cannot in good conscience continue if the PRC and the UK have conflicting political imperatives. It was the reference in Lord Reed's statement to a deteriorating situation in Hong Kong which has caused criticism, particularly where Lord Reed had explained that British judges would be seen to be endorsing an administration 'which has departed from values of political freedom, and freedom of expression, to which the Justices of the Supreme Court are deeply committed'.[89] The reply on the part of Hong Kong's Chief Executive was that it is not the job of judges in Hong Kong to endorse her administration.[90]

---

[86] Farah Master and Kirsty Needham, 'China Decries UK Judges Quitting HK Court, London Says Democracy at Stake', *Reuters*, 1 April 2022.

[87] Secretary of Justice's letter to the editor of the Wall Street Journal, 6 April 2022, www.doj.gov.hk/en/community_engagement/speeches/20220406_letter1.html (last accessed 10 April 2022).

[88] Sam Tobin, 'Reed Denies Political "Pressure" over Departure from Hong Kong', *Law Society Gazette*, 6 April 2022.

[89] A Statement from Lord Reed, President of the Supreme Court, The Right Hon. Lord Reed of Allermuir, 30 March 2022, www.supremecourt.uk/news/role-of-uk-judges-on-the-hong-kong-court-of-final-appeal-update-march-2022.html (last accessed 10 April 2022).

[90] Quoted in Master and Needham, 'China Decries', *op. cit.*; 'Britain Has Damaged HK's Judiciary: Carrie Lam', *R.T.H.K.*, 31 March 2022.

5

Foreign Treaty Relations

I THE CASE FROM MACAO

The Hong Kong SAR enjoys delegated treaty powers and relations and has in this sense 'its own' treaty regime; it retains on top of that certain colonial treaty features which were present before the handover, such as the continued application of the provisions of the International Covenant on Civil and Political Rights or 'ICCPR' notwithstanding that the PRC is not party to the ICCPR; finally, certain PRC treaties nonetheless apply to Hong Kong while Hong Kong is at the same time exempt or excluded from other PRC treaties. That at least was what the PRC and the UK agreed. Insofar as the application of PRC multilateral treaties to Hong Kong is concerned, these have been notified to third countries through a letter by the PRC to the United Nations Secretary-General as treaty depository.

The following case did not involve Hong Kong but rather Macao.[1] However it illustrates the difficulty in third countries in understanding and applying the bespoke approach taken in the Joint Declaration, and under the Basic Law, to Hong Kong's participation in international treaties. This can have commercial and other consequences. A company incorporated in Macao, Sanum Investments Limited, had invested in an integrated resort in the Lao People's Democratic Republic. The dispute which arose out of taxes imposed on the Laotian operation went to arbitration, with its seat in Singapore. Typical of investment treaty arbitration where often there is a treaty clause purporting to consent to the submission of disputes with investors to international arbitration, the State in the arbitration will object first to the tribunal's jurisdiction. In this case the tribunal decided that it had jurisdiction under the

---

[1] For a more detailed treatment, see C. L. Lim, 'Fragrant Harbour and Oyster Mirror: Beijing's Investment Treaty Policy towards Hong Kong and Macao', in L. E. Sachs and L. J. Johnson (eds.), *2015–2016 Yearbook of International Investment Law & Policy* (Oxford: Oxford University Press, 2018), 375.

1993 PRC-Lao PDR bilateral investment treaty. The tribunal's decision was in turn challenged on the usual procedural grounds contained in Singapore legislation (under Singapore's International Arbitration Act) before a Singapore High Court judge. One of Sanum's two principal arguments was that under 'one country, two systems' PRC treaties do not apply to the territory of Macao, and therefore did not apply to the benefit of Sanum, which was Macanese. The High Court judge agreed, applying the 1987 Sino-Portuguese Joint Declaration which bears a remarkable resemblance to the 1984 Sino-British Joint Declaration. The learned High Court judge also referred to the Sino-British Joint Declaration and the comparable case of Hong Kong.[2]

On appeal to the Singapore Court of Appeal things were to go awry.[3] Unlike the court below as well as an earlier Singapore High Court judgment, the Court of Appeal rejected the Sino-Portuguese Joint Declaration on grounds which if applied to its Sino-British counterpart would render the Joint-Declaration's treaty succession arrangements for Hong Kong into disarray. The PRC Foreign Ministry was to criticise this decision by Singapore's Court of Appeal. According to the court the general, customary, rule was that a territory coming under a 'new sovereign' would become subject to that new sovereign's treaties, and cease to be subject to the previous sovereign's treaties.[4]

Even assuming, first, that this 'moving treaty frontiers' rule is a general customary rule, which the court did, one would still need to be mindful of its exceptions. Second, and this was the more important legal policy issue, it was precisely because the moving frontiers rule would be unsuited to the Hong Kong and Macanese situations that a bespoke solution had been adopted in the Sino-British and Sino-Portuguese Joint Declarations. China's treaties would apply only exceptionally, the UK's treaties would exceptionally still apply, and in other limited cases such as with Hong Kong's own participation in the WTO, Hong Kong would have its own treaties.

Thus, the principal underlying issue at least from a PRC viewpoint was that the Singapore Court of Appeal sought a general rule to apply in an area of international law in which a rule of general application has always been uncertain, and where the principal treaty, the 1978 Vienna Convention on Succession of

---

[2] *The Government of the Lao People's Democratic Republic v. Sanum Investments Ltd.* [2015] SGHC 15.
[3] *Sanum Investments Ltd. v. The Government of the Lao People's Democratic Republic* [2016] SGCA 57.
[4] [2016] S.G.C.A. 57, para. 47, observing also that the moving treaty frontiers rule was common ground between the parties.

States in respect of Treaties or 'Vienna Treaty Succession Convention', has had little support and even fewer adherents. It was only the break-up of the former Yugoslavia which finally garnered sufficient Eastern European support for that treaty's entry finally into force.[5] The court sought to apply this supposed general rule to the highly specific case of Macao, which is governed by the Sino-Portuguese Joint Declaration. The real difficulty with searching for general rules in succession matters is that they are unsuited to where particular histories or geographical features are key, and where increasingly the modern approach is to have bespoke solutions rather than to leave these matters to supposed general rules of international law. In any case, widespread resort to negotiated succession arrangements has by now cast serious doubt on the moving treaty frontiers rule.[6]

International law can be viewed and applied with an inflated pretence towards universality, or it can be seen more modestly perhaps as no more than an attempt to make legal sense of complex individual histories and particular geographies. The door wherein the Singapore Court went was the former where the drafters of the Sino-Portuguese Joint Declaration, modelled closely on the Sino-British Joint Declaration, had chosen the latter.[7]

II A PROCEDURAL RABBIT HOLE

The attention of Singapore's Court of Appeal was drawn to the fact that the PRC had, as with the case of the Sino-British Joint Declaration, notified the United Nations (UN) Secretary-General of the treaty by way of letters, in which the PRC sought as well to have the diplomatic missions of the various UN Member States in New York notified of the new treaty arrangements. In the case of the Sino-British Joint Declaration, Mr Qin Huasun, wrote on 20 June 1997 to the UN Secretary-General, stating that the 'provisions' of the Covenant 'as applied to Hong Kong shall remain in force beginning from

---

[5] See Anthony Aust, *Modern Treaty Law and Practice*, 3rd ed. (Cambridge: Cambridge University Press, 2013), 321.

[6] See Roda Mushkat, *One Country, Two International Legal Personalities: The Case of Hong Kong* (Hong Kong: Hong Kong University Press, 1997), 27; J. M. M. Chan and C. L. Lim (eds.), *Law of the Hong Kong Constitution*, 2nd. ed. (Hong Kong: Sweet & Maxwell, 2015), para. 3.110. For the background to article 15 of the Vienna Treaty Succession Convention, see also Tai-heng Cheng, *State Succession and Commercial Obligations* (New York: Transnational, 2006), 104.

[7] See Mr Ma of the PRC Foreign Ministry; Xinmin Ma, 'The Application, Conclusion and Implementation of International Treaties in Hong Kong' (2012) *Chinese Yearbook of International Law* 121, 138 (in Chinese), citing this author and Professor Roda Mushkat writing in the first edition of J. M. M. Chan and C. L. Lim (eds.), *Law of the Hong Kong Constitution* (Hong Kong: Sweet & Maxwell, 2011), 83, 108.

1 July 1997'.[8] The letter appended also a list of PRC treaties which will apply. Treaties which are not on that list will not apply to post-handover Hong Kong.

However, the Singapore Court of Appeal reasoned that since a similar notification in the case of Macao complied with a procedure applying to the notification to the UN of multilateral rather than bilateral treaties, in the present case that notification does not therefore preclude the bilateral investment treaty between the PRC and the Lao PDR from applying to Macao. With only the greatest respect which this author feels towards the Singapore court, it was misled by an argument which upon close reflection was misconceived. This was no mere procedural point. At issue was a question of treaty intent involving a broader point of construction. Was it not Jessel MR who once was supposed to have said 'I am seldom wrong but never in doubt, except perhaps on a point of construction'? The story is almost certainly apocryphal,[9] but he did say: 'I am not, as I consider, to decide cases in favour of fools or idiots, but in favour of ordinary English people, who understand English when they see it, and are not deceived by any difference in type, but who have before them a very plain statement.'[10]

The Singapore court was correct that, strictly speaking, the 'UNSG letter' concerned only the application of multilateral treaties, but was it not also evidence of a wider Chinese treaty intent? That further question did not feature. In any event, the PRC's position appears to be that A-L-L, all, treaties which are not on the list will not apply to Macao and to Hong Kong, even if the origin of the letter to the UN in Hong Kong's case almost certainly was the difficulty, discussed in the Sino-British Joint Liaison Group, of the application of 214 multilateral treaties to Hong Kong. To be sure both the court below and the arbitration tribunal had also taken the same view as Singapore's Court of Appeal:

> as was noted by the Judge (at [95] of the Judgment), and indeed by the Tribunal as well (at [209]–[210] of the Award), the 1999 UNSG Note applies only to multilateral treaties for which the UN Secretary-General acts as depository. In fact, the UN Document No. ST/LEG/SER.E/26 in which the 1999 UNSG Note is recorded expressly states that the treaties covered by the publication pertain only to multilateral treaties, the UN Charter and certain pre-UN treaties. The absence of the PRC-Laos BIT from the annexes therefore says nothing of the applicability of the BIT to Macau. Accordingly,

---

[8] See (1997) 36 I.L.M. 1675.
[9] It was told to the author by Mr Lee Aitken. Jessel said in fact to Lord Coleridge: 'I may be wrong, and often am, but I never doubt'; Robert Q. Kelly and Frederic D. Donnelly, *The Law Library: Proceedings, Sixth Biennial A.A.L.L.* Institute for Law Librarians (1964), 51.
[10] *Singer Manufacturing Co. v. Wilson* (1876) L.R. 2 C.D. 447.

we are satisfied that the Judge was correct to ascribe no weight to this piece of evidence.[11]

The Singapore Court of Appeal was therefore not alone. Yet the negative conclusion, that bilateral treaties apply, is insufficiently supported if the evidence should consist only of the nature of the procedure applying to China's letter to the UN. Rather the matter is also inseparable from a broader set of facts about the bespoke arrangements for Macao (and Hong Kong), including the attempt to notify the world in order to secure the broadest recognition of and acquiescence to these arrangements.

Singapore's Court of Appeal, having adopted the moving treaty frontiers rule, as it was in any case common ground between the parties, then narrowed the question down to whether an exception to that rule applied. Or, an exception to the rule that a treaty applies to the whole territory of the State under Article 29, Vienna Convention on the Law of Treaties 1969 (VCLT). In other words, to the whole of Chinese territory. Let us call it the 'whole territory' clause for simplicity.

Even if we were to assume, against the Singapore court, that the moving treaty frontiers rule does not apply, which is the PRC's position since it is not in fact a generally accepted rule, because there was no succession event, or because any question of succession was resolved by a bespoke arrangement which under whatever procedure was notified to the whole world and was widely accepted and recognised, one would still have to contend with the VCLT's whole territory clause, that is, VCLT, article 29. And so the question was this, put simply, was there, in the first exception to article 29, a contrary intent on the part of China or Lao to exclude the application of the investment treaty to Macao? Or, applying the second exception to article 29 of the VCLT, can it be established in some other way that the investment treaty does not apply to Macao? The Singapore court answered 'no' to both; even when the Lao PDR had furnished various diplomatic notes from the PRC, both at the first instance trial and on appeal, in seeking to establish that restrictive reading to be the intent of both countries.

Instead the court was taken down a rabbit hole; which involved deciding whether the subsequent conduct of the parties could establish a mutual treaty intent and, relatedly, the appropriate cut-off date for such evidence to be placed before it.[12] In sum, a procedural point about the UN Secretary-General's function as depository had now led to another procedural question about late evidence. In the course of all this an article in the 2013 volume of the

---

[11] [2016] S.G.C.A. 57, para. 94.
[12] Discussed further in Lim, 'Fragrant Harbour', *op. cit.*, 401–3, 404–8.

Chinese Yearbook of International Law seems not to have been brought to the court's attention. In it Mr Ma Xinmin had explained the PRC view that (as there was no lawful cession in the nineteenth century) there was no succession to territory in respect of the handover of Hong Kong, and similarly we might add of Macao. China has asserted the view through various successive governments since at least the 1920s that the Treaty of Nanking of 1842 ceding Hong Kong, the Peking Convention of 1860 ceding the Kowloon Peninsula as a Hong Kong dependency, and the Second Peking Convention of 1868 leasing the New Territories to Britain for ninety-nine years, and likewise with the Sino-Portuguese Treaty of Peking of 1887 (the Lisbon Protocol) and the Sino-Portuguese Treaty of Friendship and Commerce of 1888 which ceded sovereignty over Macao to Portugal, were all 'unequal treaties'.[13]

Here is a fuller statement than that of Huang Hua, referred to earlier in this book, if only to convey a more ample sense of successive Chinese positions. In the Chinese Foreign Minister's report to the National People's Congress dated 6 November 1984 following the conclusion of the Sino-British Joint Declaration, referring to the three nineteenth-century treaties regarding Hong Kong, Mr Wu Xueqian (Wu Xue Qian) declared them to be 'all the product of armed aggression', and that:

> The Chinese people has [*sic.*] never recognized these unequal treaties. The successive Chinese Governments have never recognized the above-mentioned unequal treaties. After the founding of the PRC, our Government has repeatedly expounded the position of our country toward the problem of Hong Kong, that is, Hong Kong is Chinese territory and China does not recognize the three unequal treaties imposed on China by the imperialists. In regard to this question which was left over by history, the Chinese Government consistently held that it should be peacefully settled through negotiation on an appropriate occasion and, pending settlement, the status quo should be temporarily maintained.[14]

---

[13] See Ingrid Detter, 'The Problem of Unequal Treaties' (1966) 15 I.C.L.Q. 1070; Hungdah Chiu, 'Comparison of the Nationalist and Communist Chinese View of Unequal Treaties', in Jerome A. Cohen (ed.), *China's Practice of International Law: Some Case Studies* (Cambridge, MA: Harvard University Press, 1972), 239; Peter Wesley-Smith, *Unequal Treaties 1989–1997: China, Great Britain and Hong Kong's New Territories* (Hong Kong: Oxford University Press, 1983), 184–7; Tieya Wang, 'International Law in China: Historical and Contemporary Perspectives' (1990-II) 221 *Recueil des cours* (1990-II), 237 *et seq.*; Yash Ghai, *Hong Kong's New Constitutional Order*, 2nd ed. (Hong Kong: Hong Kong University Press, 1999), 9–12.

[14] Wang, *op. cit.*, 343.

Mr Ma and also Mr Anthony Aust, formerly of the UK Foreign and Commonwealth Office,[15] have both also explained that the moving treaty frontiers rule, as formulated under the Vienna Treaty Succession Convention, is not in their view at least a customary rule. Ma pointed out that the Convention had garnered the signatures of only nineteen countries in the world. Although we should also add, that at the last count there were twenty-two parties being themselves the result largely of splintering and succession. The Vienna Treaty Succession Convention, as Ma stresses, is not in itself applicable to China since the PRC never became a party to it.[16] Beijing's diplomatic and legal position is thus plain. There is no moving treaty frontiers rule. There is too no succession situation to which such a rule – even supposing that there is such a rule – could apply. There is, rather, the unequal treaties doctrine.

I do not mean to defend the Chinese viewpoint unnecessarily on this point, but it at least explains the PRC's surprise upon hearing the Singapore court declare that the former must have all along been aware of the moving treaty frontiers rule,[17] and that, therefore, its treaties must necessarily all apply to Macao and by extension Hong Kong.

III HONG KONG'S TREATIES, THE PRC'S TREATY REGIME AND RESIDUAL COLONIAL-ERA AGREEMENTS

So, applying all this to the Hong Kong SAR, what external treaty and other powers of its own does it, in Beijing's view, possess? Under point seven of the 'Twelve Points',[18] Hong Kong shall have the freedom to conduct its own external economic and cultural relations. This is now contained in paragraph 3(9) and (10), and in Annex I, Article XI of the Joint Declaration which states in paragraph 3 that:

> (9) The Hong Kong Special Administrative Region may establish mutually beneficial economic relations with the United Kingdom and other countries, whose economic interests in Hong Kong will be given due regard.
>
> (10) Using the name of 'Hong Kong, China', the Hong Kong Special Administrative Region may on its own maintain and develop economic and

---

[15] Aust, *op. cit.*, 321.
[16] Ma, *op. cit.*, 138 (in Chinese).
[17] [2016] S.G.C.A. 57, paras. 57–8. For the PRC's reaction, see Hong Xu, 'The Application of Treaties to the Hong Kong and Macao Special Administrative Regions', *Legal Daily*, 22 October 2016 (in Chinese); *China Daily*, 21 October 2016 (in Chinese and English).
[18] See Chapter 2 of this book.

cultural relations and conclude relevant agreements with states, regions and relevant international organisations.

The Government of the Hong Kong Special Administrative Region may on its own issue travel documents for entry into and exit from Hong Kong.

Annex I ('Elaboration by the Government of the People's Republic of China of Its Basic Policies Regarding Hong Kong'), putting aside the passages on consular relations, goes on to state that:

General
Subject to the principle that foreign affairs are the responsibility of the Central People's Government, representatives of the Hong Kong Special Administrative Region Government may participate, as members of delegations of the Government of the People's Republic of China, in negotiations at the diplomatic level directly affecting the Hong Kong Special Administrative Region conducted by the Central People's Government. The Hong Kong Special Administrative Region may on its own, using the name 'Hong Kong, China', maintain and develop relations and conclude and implement agreements with states, regions and relevant international organisations in the appropriate fields, including the economic, trade, financial and monetary, shipping, communications, touristic, cultural and sporting fields. Representatives of the Hong Kong Special Administrative Region Government may participate, as members of delegations of the Government of the People's Republic of China, in international organisations or conferences in appropriate fields limited to states and affecting the Hong Kong Special Administrative Region, or may attend in such other capacity as may be permitted by the Central People's Government and the organisation or conference concerned, and may express their views in the name of 'Hong Kong, China'. The Hong Kong Special Administrative Region may, using the name 'Hong Kong, China', participate in international organisations and conferences not limited to states.

International agreements
The application to the Hong Kong Special Administrative Region of international agreements to which the People's Republic of China is or becomes a party shall be decided by the Central People's Government, in accordance with the circumstances and needs of the Hong Kong Special Administrative Region, and after seeking the views of the Hong Kong Special Administrative Region Government. International agreements to which the People's Republic of China is not a party but which are implemented in Hong Kong may remain implemented in the Hong Kong Special Administrative Region. The Central People's Government shall, as necessary, authorise or assist the Hong Kong Special Administrative Region Government to make appropriate arrangements for the application to the Hong Kong Special Administrative Region of other relevant international

agreements. The Central People's Government shall take the necessary steps to ensure that the Hong Kong Special Administrative Region shall continue to retain its status in an appropriate capacity in those international organisations of which the People's Republic of China is a member and in which Hong Kong participates in one capacity or another. The Central People's Government shall, where necessary, facilitate the continued participation of the Hong Kong Special Administrative Region in an appropriate capacity in those international organisations in which Hong Kong is a participant in one capacity or another, but of which the People's Republic of China is not a member.

All of it bears careful reading.[19] Hong Kong does not have or possess the foreign affairs power of the PRC. The authority to 'develop relations and conclude and implement agreements with states, regions and relevant international organisations in the appropriate fields, including the economic, trade, financial and monetary, shipping, communications, touristic, cultural and sporting fields' is today exemplified in the Hong Kong SAR's separate membership of the World Trade Organization (WTO) where the WTO, as with its predecessor the General Agreement on Tariffs and Trade 1947, does not limit participation only to States. This last is now being tested with the Trump Administration's recent actions under the United States' Hong Kong Autonomy Act.[20] Hong Kong-made goods are to be labelled 'Made in China'. Hong Kong however is a separate customs territory,[21] and a WTO member in its own right. The Hong Kong SAR Government has at the time of writing declared that it will pursue WTO dispute settlement.[22] It has little choice but to do so as it has its own standing before the WTO to preserve. Were an international organisation to admit only States Hong Kong may instead be represented as a part of the PRC delegation. This is put into practice as a matter of routine.

However, the PRC's treaties do not apply, contrary to the view of the Singapore court in *Sanum*, before, first, consulting Hong Kong while, at the same time, some previous treaties extended by the UK to Hong Kong will continue to apply, most notably the provisions of the ICCPR, the International Covenant on Civil and Political Rights, notwithstanding that the PRC itself is not a party to the ICCPR in its own right, having only signed but not ratified the Covenant. In short the bespoke treaty arrangements for post-handover Hong Kong are complex, involving Hong Kong's own treaty

---

[19] In the company of articles 150–3 of Chapter VII (External Affairs) of the Basic Law.
[20] Presidential Executive Order – 'Country of Origin Marking of Products in Hong Kong', Federal Register, 11 August 2020; United States' Hong Kong Autonomy Act Pub. L. 116-149.
[21] For which see also Basic Law arts. 116 and 151.
[22] Finbarr Bermingham, 'Hong Kong's WTO Threat against US "Made in China" Ruling Puts City in Uncharted Waters', S.C.M.P. (Hong Kong), 21 August 2020.

regime, the application and disapplication of the PRC's regime and the residual elements of a previous colonial treaty regime.

In the case of the ICCPR, the late James Crawford who was entirely familiar with Hong Kong's arrangements had suggested that the PRC had itself become a party to the Human Rights Covenant albeit only in respect of Hong Kong.[23] However, as has previously been mentioned even independent experts such as Peter Duffy seemed to accept, apparently on the basis of the Foreign Office's own explanation,[24] the distinction between China's acceptance of only 'the provisions' of the ICCPR and accepting the ICCPR as a treaty party. As for Duffy's argument that this nonetheless would not preclude the need to report under the ICCPR's procedures (i.e. acceptance also of the 'procedures' as he called it) of the ICCPR, the PRC has duly complied with that periodic reporting procedure. That then raises the following question. How does Hong Kong which is not a State party to the ICCPR participate in the periodic reporting procedure? Several answers can be offered. One answer at least is unsatisfying, that Hong Kong itself is party to the ICCPR and that is because the ICCPR is open only to the participation of UN Member States. The truth is that it is the PRC which participates. But that only postpones the question, in what capacity does the PRC do so? There are at least three approaches.[25] The first involves saying that a human rights treaty 'follows the people not the place', and in this regard is unlike other types of treaty. The Human Rights Committee's Chairman once suggested this to the United Kingdom,[26] but it is a contentious proposition in an uncertain area of law. A second approach is also controversial and involves saying that Hong Kong itself has become party to the Covenant. This proposition relies upon the Covenant being open to members of a UN specialised agency. Hong Kong is a member of a number of such specialised agencies but it would need to be a 'State' nonetheless under article 48(1) of the ICCPR, a provision which is easily overlooked. A

---

[23] James Crawford, *Rights in One Country: Hong Kong and China*, The Hochelaga Lectures 2004 (Hong Kong: Hong Kong University Law Faculty, 2005), 29.

[24] HC 842-ii 1992–93 ('the language that is used in Article XIII might be the subject of divergent interpretations. One view ... would be to say that the provisions of the International Covenant remain in force in Hong Kong whether through the common law or the Bill of Rights or the Basic Law as the Foreign Office representative indicated, but that the "provisions" do not necessarily include the procedures of the Covenant ... However, my view is that ... the reference to the provisions ... should be understood as covering the mechanisms that had been in force in relation to Hong Kong (that is to say the reporting mechanism) should continue after 1997').

[25] On which see further, Johannes Chan, 'State Succession to Human Rights Treaties: Hong Kong and the International Covenant on Civil and Political Right' (1996) 45 *I.C.L.Q.* 928, 934, 939–40, 941–94.

[26] UN Doc. CCPR/C/79 Add.57, 3 November 1995.

third approach is Crawford's, just mentioned earlier. After all we have seen how China through its Permanent Representative, Mr Qin Huasun, had written on 20 June 1997 to the UN Secretary-General, stating that the 'provisions' of the Covenant 'as applied to Hong Kong' shall remain in force after the Handover.

Whatever that ultimate legal basis the continued application of certain UK treaties did become a prominent feature in the Sino-British Joint Liaison Group, even if the PRC was not itself a party to those treaties. The uncontroversial examples are the 1924 Hague Rules,[27] which strike a balance between ship owners' and cargo owners' interests by exempting the former's liability from certain excepted perils, including negligence in the navigation and management of the ship, to which the UK is but the PRC as a 'ship-owning' rather than traditionally 'cargo-owning' nation is not party.

This gets us to the 'authorise and assist' language above in the Joint Declaration and it can be illustrated with the example of bilateral investment treaties such as that in *Sanum*. It is often thought mistakenly that, because Hong Kong is generally authorised under the Joint Declaration and the Basic Law to conclude economic agreements,[28] it can therefore enter freely and on its own into bilateral investment treaties (BITs) as it does with free trade agreements (FTAs). This is a misconception. The UK practice was for colonial Hong Kong to enter into such investment treaties having been duly and specifically authorised to do so by the UK. A survey of colonial era BITs will soon reveal this when one observes the wording in their preambles. Hong Kong's post-handover practice was, simply, to continue in a similar vein to colonial Hong Kong's previous treaty practice. Thus the Hong Kong SAR enters into investment treaties having been duly authorised to do so by the Central People's Government of the PRC.

So how then are FTAs different? One answer is that the GATT and subsequently the WTO admitted customs territories but under article XXIV of the General Agreement on Tariffs and Trade (and article V of the General Agreement on Trade in Services) parties to the GATT and GATS are permitted or 'authorised' to depart from their obligations by entering into FTAs and customs unions. Thus FTAs are authorised under the GATT and GATS to which Hong Kong is party in its own right, and because these treaties do not require Statehood in the first place as a condition for Hong Kong's participation in them. A further complication arises when an FTA, a comprehensive FTA, contains within it an investment treaty. That part of it at least would

---

[27] International Convention for the Unification of Certain Rules of Law relating to Bills of Lading, and Protocol of Signature, 25 August 1924.
[28] Basic Law, art. 151.

require Beijing's specific authorisation. In granting its specific authorisation Beijing thereby 'authorises and assists' the Hong Kong SAR 'to make appropriate arrangements for the application to the Hong Kong Special Administrative Region of other relevant international agreements'. The 'authorise and assist' clause is therefore a fallback of great potential utility to the Hong Kong SAR.

Then come two final near identically worded clauses. The first deals with facilitating 'where necessary' Hong Kong's 'continued participation ... in an appropriate capacity in those international organisations in which Hong Kong is a participant in one capacity or another' and to which the PRC is a party. The second is similar but applies where the PRC is not a party to that international organisation.

Thus, if we were to take say the application of the UN Convention on the International Sale of Goods of 1979 (CISG) and the ICCPR as examples, we see in both cases that the PRC is a UN Member State, Hong Kong however is not a 'participating country', it is not a country at all, in the case of the CISG but participates in the ICCPR despite not being a country. The way in which the PRC facilitates the Hong Kong SAR's participation in the ICCPR has already been mentioned. Under the procedure for country reports to be submitted periodically to the Human Rights Committee which oversees compliance with the ICCPR, China submits Hong Kong's periodic report and thereby facilitates the latter's participation despite not being itself a party to the ICCPR. However the PRC represents China as a member, indeed as one of the Permanent Five in the Security Council, of the UN. In the case of the CISG too the PRC is a UN Member but while it is a CISG Contracting State, Hong Kong has until now not considered itself subject to the CISG. It is to this last which we now turn. The subject involves private international commercial relations, which is also discussed in the next chapter albeit in the context of China's carve-out of foreign affairs and defence from the sphere of Hong Kong's autonomy.

IV PRIVATE INTERNATIONAL COMMERCIAL RELATIONS

Assume that a European person, say an Italian, German, French or Swiss person, and a Hong Kong person choose PRC law to govern their contract for the international sale of goods. Their true intention however is to choose the application of the CISG. That is possibly because (1) the CISG is a compromise between choosing the Anglo-Hong Kong common law and the Italian, German, French or Swiss law of contracts, and (2) both parties are aware, or have been advised, that the CISG will not necessarily apply of itself automatically to their contract. Why is that, one might ask, for is it not true that under article 1(1)(a) of the CISG the CISG applies whenever two persons both of whom have their places of business in a CISG Contracting State enter into a contract for the international sale of goods? The Hong Kong person is from a CISG Contracting State, China, while Italy, Germany, France and Switzerland are all CISG Contracting States too. Some courts have taken just that view but others may not for they may be aware that the common law applies in Hong Kong, and that Hong Kong does not consider the CISG to be applicable.

The choice of PRC law will not work because the PRC has entered a treaty reservation (a declaration under article 95 of the CISG) which excludes the application of article 1(1)(b) of the CISG. That is the provision which would enforce a choice of law under private international law. It applies the CISG 'when the rules of private international law lead to the application of the law of a Contracting State', article 1(1)(b), CISG.

A more creative solution will have to be found if the parties seek the application of the rules contained in the CISG. All of that is so much legal detail; the larger question however is why it ought to be so difficult for a Hong Kong person who is in China to have a law on international sales which is the same law as that which would be applied between a person who has their place of business in the PRC, and another who has theirs in the United States, Canada, Singapore, South Korea, Italy, Germany, France, Switzerland and seventy-five other countries at the last count. All of these countries have in effect the same, in principle identical, law governing the international sale of goods. Put another way every one of these eighty-four countries will treat an international sales contract by the same law but Hong Kong will apply what in effect is English law on the international sale of goods.[29]

As of 2022, steps are being taken in the form of the Sale of Goods (United Nations Convention) Ordinance (Cap. 641), which has not yet entered into force, to address this apparent anomaly. No doubt the reason for thinking that Hong Kong should treat the international sale of goods differently was due to the preservation of its previous Anglo-Hong Kong common law regime but there is no necessary inconsistency between having a common law regime and applying the CISG as the examples of numerous other common law jurisdictions have demonstrated, from the United States and Canada to Singapore, Australia and New Zealand.

---

[29] In other words, the Sale of Goods Act 1979 in the case of English Law, but in Hong Kong its analogue would be the Sale of Goods Ordinance (Cap. 26).

V ECONOMIC RELATIONS WITH THE MAINLAND

The importance of commercial relations with Mainland China would tend to suggest a degree of convergence in the legal regulation of cross-border transactions. By and large that has been uncontroversial, albeit being sometimes a relatively neglected aspect of discussions about Hong Kong's autonomy. Between the Hong Kong SAR and the Mainland there exists the Closer Economic Partnership Arrangement, which in substance is an FTA but it is labelled an 'arrangement' rather than an agreement which may (though it certainly need not) denote a treaty between sovereigns. There is no international law issue involved in fact for as we have seen the GATT and the GATS authorise further FTAs between separate customs territories. Hong Kong and the Mainland are two quite separate customs territories.

Yet that deals only with questions of market access. Everyday commercial transactions face the usual difficulties not just in the fact that Chinese contract law and the common law are different (despite also having important similarities), but also in judicial approaches towards choice of law. In broad terms however there are similarities in the ways a judge on the Mainland and a judge in Hong Kong would approach the question 'what law governs this contract?'[30] They would look for an express agreement, the common law judge would go further to look for an implied agreement, and failing that what common lawyers call the proper law of the contract which is the law with which the transaction has its closest and most real connection. As to all this the Hong Kong CFA has said that the approach is in substance the same in Hong Kong and the Mainland,[31] notwithstanding the common lawyer's additional intermediate step of seeking an implied agreement on choice of law.

It is not always the same in substance. Imagine a Hong Kong person and a Mainland person choosing different laws to govern their contract which has to do with a commercial transaction on the Mainland. There is no express agreement between them but can it not be said that, by implication if neither choose PRC law, then there is an implied choice of 'anything but PRC contract law'? If on the Mainland judges were to look for an express choice of the parties where in Hong Kong a judge will look to an express choice as well as to an implied choice, then in Hong Kong it would be incorrect to say that PRC law

---

[30] As to its formation, validity, interpretation and performance.
[31] *First Laser Ltd v. Fujian Enterprises (Holdings) Co Ltd & Anor*, unrep., FACV 6/2011, 6 July 2012.

will apply even if PRC law is the system of law with which the transaction is most closely connected.[32]

Such problems have not been resolved by the Joint Declaration whose concern is with the preservation of Hong Kong's common law system where that has been written into existing constitutional arrangements. Yet nothing compares, as we will see,[33] with the difficulties which have arisen on the criminal law front, in relation to extradition.

That is unsurprising. The purpose of the Joint Declaration is only to keep even the commercial law systems of Hong Kong and the Mainland separate where that sometimes risked defying economic sense. The Joint Declaration does the opposite of the commerce clause in the United States Constitution '[t]o regulate Commerce with foreign Nations, and among the several States, and with the Indian Tribes', and the creation of a European Common Market in Europe where so much of Hong Kong's business now is with the Chinese Mainland.

VI NOT MOVING TREATY FRONTIERS BUT A BESPOKE SOLUTION

Thus, contrary to the moving frontiers rule which would simply have the PRC's treaties apply to post-handover Hong Kong and disapply the UK's treaties previously, the Joint Declaration creates a bespoke arrangement in foreign treaty relations. Some PRC treaties will in fact apply although these will be constrained by an underlying principle which is if they fall into the sphere of the conduct of the PRC's foreign affairs and defence.[34]

At the same time treaty provisions to which the UK is a party will continue to apply, even where the PRC is not a party to them. The exception is governed again by the principle that UK treaties which would intrude into the foreign affairs and defence powers of the PRC will not apply to Hong Kong. Examples of these include the optional protocols to the Vienna Convention on Diplomatic Relations of 1961 and the Vienna Convention on Consular Relations of 1963 for these contain compromissory clauses submitting disputes arising under them to the International Court of Justice, and the PRC is not a party to these protocols. Likewise with treaties governing nationality and statelessness to which the UK is a party but the PRC is not.[35]

---

[32] See Maisie Ooi, 'First Laser Ltd v. Fujian Enterprises (Holdings) Co Ltd: A Case of Uncommon Choice (of Law)?' (2013) 43 *H.K.L.J.* 553.
[33] Chapter 10 of this book.
[34] Wan Pun Lung, 'Application and Conclusion of Treaties in the Hong Kong Special Administrative Region of the People's Republic of China: Sixteen Years of Practice' (2013) 12 *Chinese J.I.L.* 589, 594.
[35] Ibid., 595.

VI Not Moving Treaty Frontiers But a Bespoke Solution

As for the Hong Kong SAR's power to enter into treaties some such as the covered agreements of the WTO are authorised generally, whereas the power to negotiate and agree BITs is by way of a more specific authorisation from the Chinese Central People's Government. Other examples where specific authority is required, because absent general authority the foreign affairs power vests in the Central People's Government, are mutual legal assistance and extradition agreements, agreements on the transfer of sentenced persons and visa abolition agreements.[36] In any case there is a variety of other treaties which Hong Kong negotiates and concludes routinely on its own, the most prominent of this perhaps being bilateral tax agreements. The principal provision on this matter is article 151 of the Basic Law:

> The Hong Kong Special Administrative Region may on its own, using the name 'Hong Kong, China', maintain and develop relations and conclude and implement agreements with foreign states and regions and relevant international organizations in the appropriate fields, including the economic, trade, financial and monetary, shipping, communications, tourism, cultural and sports fields.

Investment treaties have not been construed as falling into the 'economic and trade fields' clause in article 151 of the Basic Law in the same way that tax treaties are 'financial'. Rather it has been argued that specific authorisation to enter into BITs is based upon another catch-all Basic Law provision, article 20:

> The Hong Kong Special Administrative Region may enjoy other powers granted to it by the National People's Congress, the Standing Committee of the National People's Congress or the Central People's Government.

Air Services Agreements are more complex. Article 133(1) of the Basic Law states, that:

> Acting under specific authorizations from the Central People's Government, the Government of the Hong Kong Special Administrative Region may:
> (1) renew or amend air service agreements and arrangements previously in force;
> (2) negotiate and conclude new air service agreements providing routes for airlines incorporated in the Hong Kong Special Administrative Region and having their principal place of business in Hong Kong and providing rights for over-flights and technical stops; and
> (3) negotiate and conclude provisional arrangements with foreign states or regions with which no air service agreements have been concluded.

---

[36] Ibid., 602–3.

All scheduled air services to, from or through Hong Kong, which do not operate to, from or through the mainland of China shall be regulated by the air service agreements or provisional arrangements referred to in this Article.

This is an express provision granting a specific authorisation, rather than falling within the general authorisation of article 151 quoted earlier. Article 133(1) also applies only to 'All scheduled air services to, from or through Hong Kong, which do not operate to, from or through the mainland of China'. Thus where flights occur between other parts of China and foreign countries notwithstanding stops in Hong Kong, or where Hong Kong international flights stop in China, they fall outside article 133(1)'s specific authorisation.[37]

VII A PLAYTHING OF THIRD NATIONS

So much attention however has been paid to the preservation of UK treaties, particularly the 'first' of the two international human rights covenants, the ICCPR, where notably the PRC has accepted only that the 'provisions' of the ICCPR apply, that what often is ignored is that Hong Kong thrives not just on individual freedoms but also freedom of trade and commerce. Hong Kong's separate membership of the WTO, even its power to enter into other trade agreements and the specific authority to enter into investment treaties, or the power to conclude tax treaties or air services agreements, or at least those with no mainland flight connections, are important. But insufficient where within economic regions or even globally competition law regimes have converged, intellectual property regimes too, rules on contractual and other commercial laws, such as rules on what law governs a commercial contract, as well as rules on the recognition and enforcement of civil and commercial judgments have been harmonised if not unified.

As for third country acceptance of the Joint Declaration's complex tailored arrangements, the answer lies not in presumed general rules governing treaty succession. In the first place there was in the PRC's view no treaty succession question since there was no succession. China is not a successor sovereign, it always was Hong Kong's sovereign. On the Chinese view British colonial administration demonstrated no more than a hiatus in the exercise of Chinese sovereignty which, on the basis of an unjust treaties doctrine, was held in abeyance until the time was ripe for resolving the dispute with the UK. The UK's position has already been described,

---

[37] *Ibid.*, 601–3, and article 132(1) of the Basic Law.

VII A Plaything of Third Nations

Whatever a third country might think of the Chinese view, and of the unjust treaties doctrine, modern conditions, not least in the Hong Kong example, show how supposed general rules of 'treaty succession' are inapt. There is no substitute for a more searching analysis of the particular circumstances of the specific case. The question in respect of Hong Kong may have been complicated too by the fact that what was involved in *Sanum* was a treaty to which the forum State was not party. One way may be to ask whether courts in the position of the Singapore Court of Appeal are dealing with matters purely of foreign law, which at common law would raise questions of fact, or with the international customary rules of 'treaty succession'. There was an earlier case,[38] involving a defamation suit, in which service of the writ abroad was challenged for non-compliance with the Singapore-PRC treaty on judicial assistance in civil and commercial matters. The treaty had not been extended by the PRC to Hong Kong. It was common ground that the treaty, not being a defence or foreign affairs treaty, should be presumed to apply to Hong Kong. Relying on an opinion by Rimsky Yuen SC, sometime Hong Kong Secretary for Justice, as well as letters from the PRC and Singapore foreign ministries, the Judicial Commissioner, and subsequently the Chief Justice presiding in the Court of Appeal hearing in *Sanum* v. *Lao*, held that the presumption had been rebutted. Menon JC considered that the Sino-British Joint Declaration should be upheld instead. This, with respect, is the better approach rather than to treat the question as one involving whether the Joint Declaration is binding on third countries which in *Sanum* the Court of Appeal denied. It would also be in closer accord with the judgments of other third country courts.[39]

As we will see in Chapter 10, it is extradition and the criminal law however which now dominate discussion of Hong Kong's arrangements. Three issues should be kept apart in viewing Hong Kong's autonomous powers, the first discussed in the previous chapter has had to do with Beijing's power to construe the Basic Law definitively, the second, discussed in this chapter, consists of the two broad kinds of authorisations to Hong Kong to enter into treaties, while the third consists of the foreign affairs and defence exceptions to Hong Kong's autonomy. The next chapter will discuss this last category in a way as a prelude to discussion in Chapters 10 and 11[40] of more recent events concerning the passage of the National Security Law for Hong Kong. These three broad exceptions mark the limits of Hong Kong's autonomy not just in

---

[38] *Lee Hsien Loong* v. *Review Publishing Co. Ltd.* [2007] 2 S.L.R.(R.) 273.
[39] *Edwards* v. *Canada* [2003] FCJ No 1508 (Can. Ct. App. 2003); *Edwards* v. *Canada* 2002 ACWSJ 4959 (Can. Tax. Ct. 2002).
[40] Article 55 of the National Security Law of 2020 is also discussed in Chapter 6 of this book.

foreign treaty relations but also in Hong Kong's exercise of its independent judicial functions and preservation of the common law.

The more other nations, including third country nations such as the United States, Australia, New Zealand and the European Union, react to current events in Hong Kong with the suspension of their Hong Kong extradition agreements, which Hong Kong has specifically been authorised to enter into, the larger becomes the sphere of PRC foreign affairs and consequently the narrower the sphere of Hong Kong's autonomy. Such interventions, rather than recognising the terms of the Joint Declaration, now threaten to disrupt the balance struck between London and Beijing. It is counterproductive and it is Hong Kong which bears the consequence of becoming a plaything of third nations.

6

Acts of State, Foreign Affairs, Defence

I HIGH MATTERS OF STATE

The PRC's foreign affairs power had, briefly, been described in the previous chapter, together with the power in the realm of defence. These powers impose together important and at times anxious limitations on Hong Kong's autonomy, not just on Hong Kong's external affairs and foreign treaty relations but also on the judicial function of the courts. In the 'Twelve Points' which became the Joint Declaration, the sixth was that Hong Kong would manage its own affairs except in defence and foreign affairs. That qualification is often forgotten or dismissed, but it cannot be so easily brushed aside. It now is found in paragraph 3(2) of the Joint Declaration and in its Annex I, Article I. Article 3(2) states that:

> The Hong Kong Special Administrative Region will be directly under the authority of the Central People's Government of the People's Republic of China. The Hong Kong Special Administrative Region will enjoy a high degree of autonomy, except in foreign and defence affairs which are the responsibilities of the Central People's Government.

Article I of the first annex to the Joint Declaration then elaborates upon China's basic policies in the relevant part:

> The Hong Kong Special Administrative Region shall be directly under the authority of the Central People's Government of the People's Republic of China and shall enjoy a high degree of autonomy. Except for foreign and defence affairs which are the responsibilities of the Central People's Government, the Hong Kong Special Administrative Region shall be vested with executive, legislative and independent judicial power, including that of final adjudication. The Central People's Government shall authorise the Hong Kong Special Administrative Region to conduct on its own those external affairs specified in Article XI of this Annex.

In the Basic Law,[1] the analogue provisions are the following. Article 13 states that:

> The Central People's Government shall be responsible for the foreign affairs relating to the Hong Kong Special Administrative Region.
>
> The Ministry of Foreign Affairs of the People's Republic of China shall establish an office in Hong Kong to deal with foreign affairs.
>
> The Central People's Government authorizes the Hong Kong Special Administrative Region to conduct relevant external affairs on its own in accordance with this Law.

Article 19 of that law then states, in part, that:

> The courts of the Hong Kong Special Administrative Region shall have no jurisdiction over acts of state such as defence and foreign affairs. The courts of the Region shall obtain a certificate from the Chief Executive on questions of fact concerning acts of state such as defence and foreign affairs whenever such questions arise in the adjudication of cases. This certificate shall be binding on the courts. Before issuing such a certificate, the Chief Executive shall obtain a certifying document from the Central People's Government.

Article 48 of Section 1 (The Chief Executive) in Chapter IV of the Basic Law reads:

> The Chief Executive of the Hong Kong Special Administrative Region shall exercise the following powers and functions:
>
> ...
>
> (9) To conduct, on behalf of the Government of the Hong Kong Special Administrative Region, external affairs and other affairs as authorized by the Central Authorities ...

Section 2 of that Chapter, Chapter IV, dealing with the Executive Authorities, goes on to state in a corresponding article, article 62, that:

> The Government of the Hong Kong Special Administrative Region shall exercise the following powers and functions:
>
> ...
>
> (3) To conduct external affairs as authorized by the Central People's Government under this Law ...

Notice that the references are to 'external affairs' rather than to foreign affairs. Such external affairs powers, particularly as they relate to Hong Kong's treaty

---

[1] See further J. M. M. Chan and C. L. Lim (eds.), *Law of the Hong Kong Constitution*, 2nd ed. (Hong Kong: Sweet & Maxwell, 2015), ch. 3.

relations have already been discussed.[2] They are contained in Chapter VII of the Basic Law.

In the next Chapter of the Basic Law, Chapter VIII (Interpretation and Amendment of the Basic Law), a well-known provision about interpretation, article 158, states in part that:

> The Standing Committee of the National People's Congress shall authorize the courts of the Hong Kong Special Administrative Region to interpret on their own, in adjudicating cases, the provisions of this Law which are within the limits of the autonomy of the Region.
>
> The courts of the Hong Kong Special Administrative Region may also interpret other provisions of this Law in adjudicating cases. However, if the courts of the Region, in adjudicating cases, need to interpret the provisions of this Law concerning affairs which are the responsibility of the Central People's Government, or concerning the relationship between the Central Authorities and the Region, and if such interpretation will affect the judgments on the cases, the courts of the Region shall, before making their final judgments which are not appealable, seek an interpretation of the relevant provisions from the Standing Committee of the National People's Congress through the Court of Final Appeal of the Region.

Thus, insofar as the courts are concerned there are in fact two kinds of broad limitations. First, acts of State including those relating to foreign affairs and defence are out of bounds for Hong Kong's government and courts. Secondly, 'affairs which are the responsibility of the Central People's Government, or concerning the relationship between the Central Authorities and the Region' are beyond the authority of, more precisely the authorisation given to, the Hong Kong courts to interpret the Basic Law. Clearly 'affairs which are the responsibility of the Central People's Government' would include foreign affairs and defence as well.[3]

A near-identical formulation to 'affairs which are the responsibility of the Central People's Government or concerning the relationship between the Central Authorities and the Region' is also to be found as a limitation on the powers of the Hong Kong legislature. Article 17 of the Basic Law States that:

> Laws enacted by the legislature of the Hong Kong Special Administrative Region must be reported to the Standing Committee of the National People's

---

[2] Chapter 5 of this book.
[3] Byron S. J. Wang, 'Judicial Independence under the Basic Law', in Steven Tsang (ed.), *Judicial Independence and the Rule of Law in Hong Kong* (Hong Kong: Hong Kong University Press, 2001), 48, 66.

Congress for the record. The reporting for record shall not affect the entry into force of such laws.

If the Standing Committee of the National People's Congress, after consulting the Committee for the Basic Law of the Hong Kong Special Administrative Region under it, considers that any law enacted by the legislature of the Region is not in conformity with the provisions of this Law regarding affairs within the responsibility of the Central Authorities or regarding the relationship between the Central Authorities and the Region, the Standing Committee may return the law in question but shall not amend it. Any law returned by the Standing Committee of the National People's Congress shall immediately be invalidated. This invalidation shall not have retroactive effect, unless otherwise provided for in the laws of the Region.

II ACTS OF STATE AT COMMON LAW

In respect of the Joint Declaration's and Basic Law's foreign affairs and defence exceptions, these are therefore subsumed under 'acts of State'. The PRC's exclusion of acts of State from the reach of the post-handover courts drew attention in 1995, five years after the passage of the Basic Law, with the PRC's insistence that such acts are beyond the jurisdiction of the Hong Kong courts. This exception had been conceded by the UK during the discussions in the Sino-British Joint Liaison Group (the JLG), paving the way for the establishment of the Court of Final Appeal (CFA).[4]

Where the line lies between the State's foreign affairs and defence powers and the limits of Hong Kong's autonomy is still being defined today but it has become an issue of increasing importance. Lord Patten, as discussed earlier,[5] questioned what acts of State are. At the least, they are not unknown to the common law under which there is the idea that some matters are non-justiciable before the courts. Where non-justiciability is applied to the situation where the courts are called upon to adjudicate upon the acts of foreign States, particularly in their own territory, it goes by the special name of the Act of State doctrine.[6]

In contrast with the prerogative powers of the English Crown in certain situations, in the face of a public law suit,[7] non-justiciability does not at

---

[4] Chapter 4 of this book.
[5] Chapter 5 of this book.
[6] See further, Ewan Smith, 'Acts of State in Belhaj and Rahmatullah' (2018) 134 L.Q.R. 20, discussing *Belhaj v. Straw* [2017] UKSC 3; [2017] 3 All E.R. 337 and *Rahmatullah v. Ministry of Defence* [2017] UKSC 1; [2017] 3 All E.R. 179.
[7] As will be discussed immediately below.

common law denote however a lack of jurisdiction unlike how Hong Kong's Basic Law conceives of an 'act of State', but instead is a reason to refrain from exercising such jurisdiction. Thus, a key difference is that in the Basic Law for Hong Kong the Hong Kong courts are deprived of jurisdiction altogether, whereas in England and Wales the courts have jurisdiction but have in the past treated certain matters of foreign affairs as being beyond the realm within which there are applicable judicial standards.[8] The position under the English Common Law developed over the last forty or so years bears recounting, albeit only briefly, in order to understand how the Anglo-Hong Kong common law at the very least sees it; particularly as the Hong Kong Department of Justice had at least once sought to interpret 'acts of State' in common law terms.

In England, Lord Wilberforce had defined the Act of State doctrine broadly in a seminal judgment in *Buttes Gas* v. *Hammer*:[9] 'the courts will not adjudicate upon the transactions of foreign sovereign States'.[10] This was an unusual oil dispute in which Buttes Gas had emerged victorious against Occidental Petroleum following years of litigation in the United States but where at a press conference subsequently Occidental's flamboyant owner Armand Hammer claimed improper methods and collusion between Buttes and the Ruler of Sharjah, was sued for libel by Buttes, and therefore found a way for the whole case to be retried before the English courts.[11] In any event Lord Wilberforce's judgment made it plain that in England too acts of State concern matters of foreign affairs.

Subsequently, in the *International Tin Council Case*,[12] the appellants had obtained an arbitration award against the Council which they sought to enforce against the Department of Trade and Industry as the representative of the United Kingdom, claiming amongst other things that member states of the Council were jointly and severally liable in respect of unsatisfied arbitral awards. The House of Lords held that the English courts lacked competence in respect of international transactions entered into by independent sovereigns, and that in that case the transaction had involved a treaty not incorporated into English Law.

A refinement was subsequently introduced when in the subsequent *Kuwait Airways Case*,[13] concerning the expropriation of Kuwaiti aircraft by the Iraqi

---

[8] It is not at present a settled point and the jurisprudence in England is moving.
[9] *Buttes Gas & Oil co.* v. *Hammer (No. 3)* [1982] A.C. 888.
[10] Ibid., 931G–932A.
[11] I. A. E. Insley and Frank Wooldridge, 'The Buttes Case: The Final Chapter in the Litigation' (1983) 32 I.C.L.Q. 62.
[12] *J. H. Rayner Ltd.* v. *Dept. of Trade* [1990] 2 A.C. 418 (H.L.).
[13] *Kuwait Airways Corporation* v. *Iraqi Airways Company (Nos. 4 and 5)* [2002] 2 AC 883.

Government following Iraq's unlawful invasion and occupation of Kuwait, in which the House of Lords held that – the principle in *Buttes Gas* notwithstanding – the dispute over the aircraft was justiciable. Distinguishing *Buttes Gas*, in *Kuwait Airways* there were at least clear and manageable international law standards to be applied. A plain breach of the UN Charter had occurred, unlike in *Buttes Gas* in which a dispute over an oil concession granted by Umm al Quwain (UAQ) to Buttes saw the Ruler of Sharjah backdate a decree in order to expand Sharjah's claim to territorial waters to twelve nautical miles measured from the baselines, a claim not recognised by the UK which was responsible for Sharjah's foreign affairs until 1971. There was a response from the Government of Iran which laid claim to Abu Musa nine miles from which oil had been discovered. Instructions were given by the British political agent to the ruler of UAQ not to permit operations in the area by rival Occidental, owned by Armand Hammer. British naval, air and military operations ensued in a show of force in May 1970, and, again, Iran intervened. Following a settlement between Sharjah and Iran in November 1971 the Ruler of Sharjah was assassinated in 1972 after which Occidental's concession was terminated by UAQ in 1973. In these circumstances, Lord Wilberforce held, famously, that:

> these are not issues upon which a municipal court can pass. ... [T]here are ... no judicial or manageable standards by which to judge these issues, or to adopt another phrase ... the court would be in a judicial no-man's land: the court would be asked to review transactions in which four sovereign states were involved, which they had brought to a precarious settlement, after diplomacy and the use of force, and to say that at least part of these were 'unlawful' under international law. I would just add ... that it is not to be assumed that these matters have now passed into history, so that they now can be examined with safe detachment.[14]

In *Buttes* events rather than having passed into history were unsettled, whereas in *Kuwait Airways* the outcome was clear.[15]

At the domestic level, at least historically, as was explained in *International Tin Council*, there was an analogue to the Act of State doctrine in the form of the Crown's prerogative power in foreign affairs. The courts traditionally would not interfere with the exercise of the foreign affairs prerogative save where rights under law were at issue, in which case in England an Act of

---

[14] *Buttes Gas v. Hammer (No. 3), op. cit.*, 938 per Lord Wilberforce.
[15] *Kuwait Airways v. Iraqi Airways (Nos. 4 and 5), op. cit.*, paras 25, 113, 125 and 146 per Lords Nicholls, Steyn, Hoffmann and Hope; cited in *Occidental Exploration and Production Co. v. Republic of Ecuador* [2005] E.W.C.A. Civ. 1116, para. 25 per Mance LJ.

Parliament would be required if the exercise of the prerogative were to purport to alter common law rights.[16]

All this in what constitutes still a moving area of law in England[17] affects how we might view the most recent events in Hong Kong. Insofar as rights under Hong Kong law may be affected by the latest 2020 National Security Law,[18] the Basic Law has always envisaged a decision by the Standing Committee of the National People's Congress (NPCSC) to add to the list of laws to be extended to Hong Kong to be promulgated by way of entry in the Government Gazette in Hong Kong. It might be said to be, it is, the equivalent of a UK legislative act.[19]

III THE HONG KONG DEPARTMENT OF JUSTICE'S VIEW IN 2002

Acts of State are therefore typically understood in the Hong Kong context, at least in its bare essentials from a common law viewpoint. In 2002 in connection with the Government of Hong Kong's proposed national security law under Basic Law article 23,[20] a precursor to the later 2020 National Security Law controversy,[21] questions regarding acts of State had arisen but were dismissed by Hong Kong's Department of Justice (HKDOJ).[22] However, the definition of acts of State also involves, at least potentially, an interface between PRC Law and the Hong Kong common law. From the Hong Kong viewpoint it can be viewed only in common law terms subject to any contrary meaning which is to be given in the Basic Law by the NPCSC under article 158 of the Basic Law.

The Hong Kong Department of Justice's (DOJ's) position, in a paper submitted in 2002 to the legislature's Panel on Security and Panel on Administration of Justice and Legal Services, discussed (only) acts of State under the common law along the lines discussed in the preceding section. To put it in its full context that paper was written in 2002, seven years after the 1995 pre-handover Sino-British compromise leading to the establishment of the CFA.[23] In it, DOJ first cited the definition in *Halsbury's Laws of England* of an

---

[16] See further, Ewan Smith, 'Is Foreign Policy Special?', O.J.L.S., published online 9 May 2021, discussing as well in addition to *Belhaj* and *Rahmatullah* cited earlier, *R (Miller & Dos Santos) v. Secretary of State for Exiting the European Union* [2017] UKSC 1.
[17] Ibid.
[18] Chapter 10 of this book.
[19] See further, Chapter 10 of this book.
[20] Ibid.
[21] Ibid.
[22] L.C. Paper No. CB(2)86/02–03(02).
[23] Chapter 4 of this book.

act of State as: 'a prerogative act of policy in the field of foreign affairs performed by the Crown in the course of its relationship with another state or its subjects'.[24] DOJ then cited as well the late E. C. S. Wade: 'an act of the executive as a matter of policy performed in the course of its relations with another state, including its relations with subjects of that state, unless they are temporarily within the allegiance of the Crown'.[25]

It might be thought instead that DOJ should have spelt out more fully in stating 'the position under the common law' that 'assuming the position under PRC Law is the same as that under the common law, the common law position is as follows'. But, that the common law view of the Act of State doctrine was irrelevant unless it had been a foreign affairs matter, which in respect of the 2002 national security law debate at least it was not. However, that was not DOJ's view, that is, to assimilate the Act of State doctrine at common law with its meaning under the Basic Law, at least in this instance. At issue was whether the proscription of a body on the Mainland by the Central Authorities, under PRC Law, would have been reviewable by the Hong Kong courts. The simple answer was no, unlike the reviewability of the proscription of such bodies by Hong Kong's Secretary for Security. The Act of State doctrine simply does not come into it but that in any case on the common law understanding of acts of State, which concerns 'relations between Governments' (i.e. foreign affairs), no such acts were involved at all.

As for the defence exception, a similar explanation could perhaps also be applied, analogous to English law's recognition of the prerogative of defence in England.[26] So, it is English law's or the common law's, or the traditional Anglo-Hong Kong common law's, 'recognition' of prerogatives that in reality is involved for a prerogative power is simply what the common law recognises rather than produces.[27]

IV HONG KONG PRACTICE

Two examples of practice as it has developed in Hong Kong may be mentioned, and they illustrate different scenarios or situations. The first, occurring in 2019, concerned Bona Mugabe, daughter of the then Zimbabwean

---

[24] L.C. Paper No. CB(2)86/02–03(02), citing *Halsbury's Laws of England* (4th ed., reissue), vol. 18(2), para. 613.
[25] 'Act of State in English Law: Its Relation with International Law' (1934) 15 B.Y.B. I.L. 98, 103.
[26] Chapter 10 of this book.
[27] See Sebastian Payne, 'The Royal Prerogative', in Maurice Sunkin and Sebastian Payne (eds.), *The Nature of the Crown* (Oxford: Oxford University Press, 1999), 77, 106.

President Robert Mugabe.[28] It demonstrates that matters of foreign affairs may be governed by Hong Kong law simply by extending the relevant rules of PRC foreign relations law to the territory of Hong Kong. Ms Mugabe was then a student at the City University, the former colonial City Polytechnic of Hong Kong. In January 2019 her bodyguards were alleged to have assaulted two *Sunday Times* photographers. DOJ had declined to prosecute them, and subsequently they left Hong Kong. Earlier in January Mrs Grace Mugabe, the late President Mugabe's wife, was alleged also to have 'attacked' another photographer. A legislative council panel enquiry was formed. The Secretary of Justice Mr Wong Yan Lung said:

> OCMFA advised that in accordance with customary international law and Chinese diplomatic practice, the Central People's Government in general confers diplomatic privileges and immunities to spouses of foreign heads of states during their stay in China, including Hong Kong, and requested the HKSARG [the Government of the HKSAR] to handle the case in accordance with Article 22.1(3) of the Regulations of the People's Republic of China Concerning Diplomatic Privileges and Immunities (the Regulations).

He went on to add an explanation of post-handover Hong Kong practice:

> The ... persons [who] shall enjoy immunity and inviolability necessary for their transit through or sojourn in China [include] other visiting foreigners to whom the Chinese Government has granted the privileges and immunities specified in the present Article.
>
> OCMFA further advised that the privileges and immunities that Mrs Mugabe enjoyed included the immunity from criminal jurisdiction equivalent to that enjoyed by diplomatic agents under Article 14 of the Regulations, irrespective of whether the relevant act was performed in the exercise of official functions.
>
> The issue of privileges and immunities is a matter of foreign affairs, which is the sole responsibility of the Central People's Government under Article 13.1 of the Basic Law. It is further specifically governed by the Regulations, which apply to Hong Kong by virtue of Article 18.2 and their inclusion in Annex III of the Basic Law upon their promulgation by the Promulgation of National Laws Notice 1997.
>
> This case has been handled strictly in accordance with the Regulations and the relevant customary international law and practice. In fact, apart from China, several states grant immunities to spouses of foreign heads of state.[29]

---

[28] See further, Chan and Lim, *op. cit.*, 3.075–3.082.
[29] Secretary for Justice's Opening Remarks at Meeting of LegCo Panel on Administration of Justice and Legal Services, 30 March 2009.

Coming to the second example, what if a matter is claimed to involve foreign affairs but no PRC rule had been extended to Hong Kong; in other words, what if there were a potential conflict between Hong Kong law and PRC foreign relations law? Or a conflict between Hong Kong law and a defence matter? In the widely known 'Congo Case', two ICC arbitration awards against the Democratic Republic of Congo (DRC), which had concerned previous financing arrangements, had remained unpaid and the awards were purchased as distressed debt by a vulture fund, FG Hemisphere. Separately a number of Chinese parties including the China Railway Group obtained mining concessions in Congo in exchange for which payment of an access fee was to be made to the DRC. The fees were transferred to Hong Kong and disclosed, it appears, under Hong Kong's stock exchange rules. FG Hemisphere having discovered this information applied to the Hong Kong courts for an interim injunction to restrain payment of the monies to the DRC while it commenced garnishee proceedings for the monies to be paid to FG Hemisphere instead. The DRC argued that it was immune from any suit before the courts. The question was whether this was true under post-handover Hong Kong law. Prior to the handover Hong Kong law had recognised a commercial exception to the immunity of foreign sovereigns, in other words it applied the restrictive rather than absolute immunity rule. Thus if the nature of a transaction was commercial then immunity will not attach. However the application of what in effect was the UK State Immunity Act of 1978 to Hong Kong had lapsed with the handover on 1 July 1997. Lawyers in Hong Kong perhaps assumed the correct position to be that since the commercial exception is applied at common law the post-handover continuation of the common law would mean that the restrictive immunity doctrine will continue to be applied.

At first instance the High Court judge Mr Justice Reyes considered that even if the commercial exception did apply the DRC would not be immune,[30] but the test the learned High Court judge applied in this regard was held by the Court of Appeal in a robust decision to be incorrect. The Court of Appeal upheld the commercial exception at common law and held that it applied to remove the DRC's immunity on these facts.[31] However, the Court of Final Appeal then over-ruled the Court of Appeal by a 3:2 majority with strong dissenting opinions by Justices Bokhary PJ and Mortimer NPJ who also opposed referring the question to the NPCSC. A majority of the court (Chan PJ, Ribeiro PJ and Mason NPJ) not only considered that the position

---

[30] *FG Hemisphere Associates LLC v. Democratic Republic of Congo* [2009] 1 H.K.L.R.D. 410.
[31] *FG Hemisphere Associates LLC v. Democratic Republic of the Congo* [2010] 2 H.K.L.R.D. 66. See also C. L. Lim, 'State Immunity in Post-Handover Hong Kong' (2011) 127 *L.Q.R.* 159.

under PRC law should apply but that it also required Beijing to confirm that interpretation.[32] The importance of the matter was that there had been no extension of the relevant PRC legal position to Hong Kong as such, there being no PRC law on foreign state immunities. However, absolute immunity is recognised in the PRC and the matter fell within foreign affairs and involved an act of State. It was, according to the NPCSC, therefore outside the autonomy of the Hong Kong SAR.[33]

The Vice-Chairman of the NPCSC's Legislative Affairs Commission, Mr Li Fei, explained to the NPCSC that,[34] first, it is 'a legal issue as well as a policy issue'; second, the Hong Kong SAR must 'apply and give effect to the rules or policies on state immunity' which the PRC 'has determined to adopt and must not depart from such rules or policies nor ... adopt rules that are inconsistent with them'; third, the Hong Kong SAR's courts 'have no jurisdiction over acts of state involving foreign affairs'; fourth, the Hong Kong courts 'have no jurisdiction over the act of the Central People's Government in determining the rules or policies on state immunity'; and finally 'if Hong Kong were to apply any 'inconsistent' rule that would 'contravene' the Basic Law for the Hong Kong SAR. For its part, the NPCSC went on to answer the questions put by the CFA by confirming that, first, it is Beijing which should decide China's rule or policy on state immunity; second, the Hong Kong courts are bound to apply and give effect to that rule or policy; third, the matter falls within the meaning of 'acts of state such as defence and foreign affairs'; and finally, that the Anglo-Hong Kong common law rule of restrictive immunity has since changed to a rule of absolute immunity in post-handover Hong Kong.[35]

V THE 'CONGO' CASE

The *Congo* case is important precisely because, unlike the Mugabe incident, it had not involved an extension of PRC law to Hong Kong and is closest to being a true example of how the Act of State doctrine operates, at least in

---

[32] See C. L. Lim, 'Absolute Immunity for Sovereign Debtors in Hong Kong' (2011) 127 *L.Q.R.* 495; C. L. Lim, 'Worldwide Litigation over Foreign Sovereign Assets' (2016) 10 *Dispute Resolution International* 145, 150 *et seq.*
[33] *Democratic Republic of the Congo v. FG Hemisphere Associates LLC (No. 1)* (2011) 14 H.K.C.F. A.R. 95 for the CFA's 'provisional' judgment. As for the confirmation of that judgment and the NPCSC interpretation in Annex I to that judgment, see *Democratic Republic of the Congo v. FG Hemisphere Associates LLC (No. 2)* (2011) 14 HKCFAR 395. See further, C. L. Lim, 'Beijing's "Congo" Interpretation: Commercial Implications' (2012) 128 *L.Q.R.* 6.
[34] See (2011) 14 H.K.C.F.A.R. 39 (Annex I).
[35] *Ibid.*

Hong Kong. Earlier, in 2002 DOJ had managed to avoid the question of how the doctrine is to be defined, and how it should properly be construed. It did so by showing that the question involved only whether the Hong Kong courts could review an act of the Mainland authorities under PRC law carried out on the Mainland. Plainly the Hong Kong courts have no authority over such matters, which by themselves do not necessarily involve any act of State at all. In the Mugabe incident that had, as has been mentioned, involved a Mainland law extended to Hong Kong which the Government gave due effect to as Hong Kong law.

However, in the *Congo* case, what arguably was Hong Kong common law yielded to the foreign affairs exception. It is only close to being an illustration of a true application of the foreign affairs exception. That is because, in the end, the CFA requested an interpretation from the NPCSC which in turn invoked the Act of State doctrine and the foreign affairs exception, and that was for all intents and purposes the end of the matter. Carefully viewed, the application of the exception was bolstered by that act of interpretation under article 158 of the Basic Law. That said is it not simply to be expected that controversial cases will be sent to the NPCSC by the courts? If the answer is 'yes', then that is the modality which we might expect will be adopted in future cases as well. Had there been no NPCSC interpretation in *Congo*, certain questions would have lingered. For example, in the Court of Appeal in that case, Stock V-P had said of the argument that an act of State was involved:

> I cannot think that a purposive interpretation of art.19 of the Basic Law, read in full legislative and historical context, could sensibly lead to the conclusion to which Mr. Barlow would take us ... It would be otherwise were this Court asked to pronounce upon the legality under international or national law of the Central People Government's stated position as to sovereign immunity or upon the legality of an act of the Central Government in exercise of its stated position. But we are not asked to do so. In that the Central Government has stated its principled position both in letters to this Court and, historically, in other circumstances to which I shall later advert, we are asked to determine the common law in Hong Kong on the question of sovereign immunity from jurisdiction taking into account the stated position of the Central Government and, in that regard, noting the principle discussed below that, where it is possible to do so, the courts and the executive should on such issues not speak with two voices.[36]

---

[36] [2010] 2 H.K.L.R.D. 66, [40]–[41].

V The 'Congo' Case   141

The point which emerges is that the issue is otherwise to be viewed, usually, in common law terms by a common law judge. Madam Justice Yuen in her concurrence had said:

> state immunity should not be regarded as solely executive-driven, as simply an act in a State's conduct of its *relations* with foreign States, but as a matter of *law* which falls to be decided by the courts of the forum State. This underlying legal nature of state immunity should inform and be applied consistently in relation to the issues in this appeal.[37]

Indeed the practice in the United Kingdom is that if it involves a matter of law rather than fact then that is a question reserved for the courts not the executive branch and no certificate will be issued.[38] In the CFA the three appellate judges in the majority were to see it all rather differently:

> The Office of the Commissioner is the 'office in Hong Kong' established to deal with foreign affairs under Article 13(2) of the Basic Law. Its letters therefore authoritatively establish what the PRC's foreign affairs policy on state immunity is and what prejudice is likely to flow from the HKSAR courts taking a deviating position. It is common ground among the parties that China's policy on state immunity is that the immunity is absolute. As indicated above, those letters should be taken to have the status of declarations of facts of state, which the HKSAR courts (even without any Article 19(3) certificate) accept as authoritative statements of facts within the peculiar cognizance of the executive organ of government having charge of the nation's foreign policy. It falls to the courts to determine on the basis of those facts whether an act of state exists and if so, what its nature and extent is, attaching the legal consequence of non-justiciability if and insofar as appropriate. As we have indicated, the Court's provisional conclusion in the present case is that the CPG's determination of the PRC's policy of absolute state immunity comes within the phrase 'acts of state such as defence and foreign affairs' in Article 19(3), a conclusion which is sufficiently supported by the undisputed and authoritative facts of state declared in the OCMFA Letters, without need for a certificate.[39]

Their view, seen from a common law viewpoint, was confirmed by the NPCSC in the latter's interpretation.[40] That is the Anglo-Hong Kong

---

[37] Ibid., [249].
[38] Elizabeth Wilmshurst, 'Executive Certificates in Foreign Affairs: The United Kingdom' (1986) 35 I.C.L.Q. 157, at 165 and 168.
[39] FG Hemisphere Associates LLC v. Democratic Republic of the Congo (No 1) (2011) 14 H.K.C.F.A.R. 95, [363].
[40] At common law in England, as distinct from the Anglo-Hong Kong law of today, things may be very different. Put bluntly there would be a great deal of difference between facts of State and

common law and it has ramifications, perhaps even wide ramifications, for commercial contracts and disputes.[41]

In the *Congo* case there had been a series of letters from the PRC Foreign Ministry. The first two were issued before the Court of First Instance and the Court of Appeal judgments stating, respectively, the PRC's position on the absolute immunity rule, and continued adherence to that rule since the PRC had signed but to date has not ratified the UN Convention on the Jurisdictional Immunities of States. It was a third letter, put before the CFA, and it was this letter which stated that the matter was one involving the PRC's foreign policy. One question which emerged was why the procedure under article 19 of the Basic Law does not appear to have been adhered to:

> The courts of the Region shall obtain a certificate from the Chief Executive on questions of fact concerning acts of state such as defence and foreign affairs whenever such questions arise in the adjudication of cases. This certificate shall be binding on the courts. Before issuing such a certificate, the Chief Executive shall obtain a certifying document from the Central People's Government.[42]

The *Congo* case notwithstanding it appears that article 19 has never been applied. It should at least have raised questions about whether such certificates being confined to the attestation of questions only of fact would necessarily have achieved the same result as an article 158 interpretation under the Basic Law by the NPCSC. Therein probably lies the answer to the question why article 19 was not resorted to but we do not know.

VI THE PREROGATIVE POWERS AT COMMON LAW

At common law the prerogative powers of the Crown are residual. These are powers recognised by the courts to repose in the Crown, by which one means the Government of the State, in the absence of any legislative authority at all. The exercise of prerogative powers may attract civil liability, originally in England under the Crown Proceedings Act 1947 and in Hong Kong under the Crown Proceedings Ordinance,[43] but the prerogative orders so-called most

---

acts of State. On facts of State, see, more recently, *Al-Juffali* v. *Estrada* [2016] EWCA Civ 176. It would appear that the distinction is receding from the Anglo-Hong Kong common law.

[41] Particularly in light of the Court of Appeal's view, which the CFA did not pronounce upon, that contractual waivers would be ineffectual in the Anglo-Hong Kong Common Law's reception of English Law. *Cf.* Lim, 'Worldwide Litigation', *op. cit.*, 153, citing *NML Capital* v. *Republic of Argentina* [2011] UKSC 31 (per Lord Collins).

[42] (2011) 14 H.K.C.F.A.R. 95, [363]. I have also discussed all this previously at greater length in Chan and Lim, *op. cit.*, paras. 3.052–3.072.

[43] Crown Proceedings Ordinance (Cap. 300).

notably of certiorari, mandamus and prohibition which would quash governmental action, or mandate, or prohibit such action,[44] would not lie against the Crown.[45] Despite modern inroads into this bar to judicial review of the Crown's actions that remains largely the case and comes probably closest to a common law conception of 'State' action lying outside the jurisdiction of the courts, where at the same time the common law in contrast to civilian legal thought does not contemplate 'the State' very often but rather 'the Crown'.[46]

Strictly speaking, as we have seen, the Act of State doctrine concerns principally inter-State relations including foreign affairs where the Basic Law in article 19 adds 'defence' which as will be discussed immediately below overlaps with the prerogative power to protect the Realm. Recall too *Buttes* in which Lord Wilberforce referred to 'transactions in which four sovereign states were involved, which they had brought to a precarious settlement, after diplomacy and the use of force'. It is likely however that, read in its proper context, the reference to the use of force – which then could implicate defence – is only a reference to the existence of 'unmanageable standards' as a reason for the courts to decline to exercise their jurisdiction.[47]

As for the prerogative to protect the Realm, Lord Justice Purchas once said:

> the prerogative power which indisputably resides in the Crown is to 'protect the Realm', 'keep the Queen's peace', 'to make treaties', etc. . . . Whether the prerogative powers variously described are merely various aspects of the same fundamental power to protect the Realm, or are separate individual powers may be more important academically than in the resolution of the issues raised in the appeal.[48]

It might be asked whether a 2020 National Security Law passed by Beijing and extended to Hong Kong under the Basic Law is an 'act of State' at all. This is when one views it through the lens of the English common law. Yet the provision on acts of State, namely article 19 which excludes the jurisdiction of the courts, is not where the problem lies, unlike in 1995 when the scope of the jurisdiction of the courts became a principal issue in Sino-British Joint

---

[44] Following the Civil Procedure Rules 1998, which replaced the Rules of the Supreme Court in England and Wales, quashing orders, mandatory orders and prohibiting orders.
[45] See Martin Laughlin, 'The State, the Crown and the Law', in Sunkin and Payne, *op. cit.*, 33, 71.
[46] *Ibid.*, 74.
[47] *Buttes Gas v. Hammer (No. 3)*, *op. cit.*, 938 *per* Lord Wilberforce.
[48] *R v. Secretary of State for the Home Department, ex parte Northumbria Police Authority* [1989] 1 Q.B. 26 (C.A.), 46.

Liaison Group discussions. Particular prominence has been paid to article 55 of the 2020 National Security Law, which states:

> The Office for Safeguarding National Security of the Central People's Government in the Hong Kong Special Administrative Region shall, upon approval by the Central People's Government of a request made by the Government of the Hong Kong Special Administrative Region or by the Office itself, exercise jurisdiction over a case concerning offence endangering national security under this Law, if: (1) the case is complex due to the involvement of a foreign country or external elements, thus making it difficult for the Region to exercise jurisdiction over the case; (2) a serious situation occurs where the Government of the Region is unable to effectively enforce this Law; or (3) a major and imminent threat to national security has occurred.[49]

While accepting that this has been especially controversial, categories (1) to (3) above are also in fairness extremely limited categories. The objection is ultimately that letting the executive authorities decide when alleged subversives may be engaged with foreign elements is fraught. With regard to the 2020 law a key issue lies then in what 'defence' means. In this respect the Hong Kong Act of State doctrine,[50] let alone any analogy with prerogative powers recognised at common law, is superseded by more precise provisions which refer to 'defence' without requiring the intervention of a further notion of an 'act of State'.

Article 18 of the Basic Law states, in part, that:

> National laws shall not be applied in the Hong Kong Special Administrative Region except for those listed in Annex III to this Law. The laws listed therein shall be applied locally by way of promulgation or legislation by the Region.
>
> The Standing Committee of the National People's Congress may add to or delete from the list of laws in Annex III after consulting its Committee for the Basic Law of the Hong Kong Special Administrative Region and the government of the Region. Laws listed in Annex III to this Law shall be confined to those relating to defence and foreign affairs as well as other matters outside the limits of the autonomy of the Region as specified by this Law.

Thus, it may be asked whether a National Security Law falls under this provision or if it, strictly, involves instead a policing matter within the autonomous powers of the Hong Kong SAR. Is national security defence or policing?

---

[49] G.N. (E.) 72 of 2020.
[50] As I have said this appears to be a development that is distinct from the English common law's use of the term.

That is only the position under the Basic Law. Paragraph 3 of the Sino-British Joint Declaration in turn states, that:

> (2) The Hong Kong Special Administrative Region will be directly under the authority of the Central People's Government of the People's Republic of China. The Hong Kong Special Administrative Region will enjoy a high degree of autonomy, except in foreign and defence affairs which are the responsibilities of the Central People's Government.

Paragraph 11 goes on to state, however, that:

> The maintenance of public order in the Hong Kong Special Administrative Region will be the responsibility of the Government of the Hong Kong Special Administrative Region.

Finally, Article XII in Annex I of the Joint Declaration states, that:

> The maintenance of public order in the Hong Kong Special Administrative Region shall be the responsibility of the Hong Kong Special Administrative Region Government. Military forces sent by the Central People's Government to be stationed in the Hong Kong Special Administrative Region for the purpose of defence shall not interfere in the internal affairs of the Hong Kong Special Administrative Region. Expenditure for these military forces shall be borne by the Central People's Government.

Mr Dominic Raab, the United Kingdom Foreign Secretary, has said, in respect of the 2020 National Security Law:

> We have very carefully now assessed the contents of this national security legislation since it was published last night. It constitutes a clear violation of the autonomy of Hong Kong, and a direct threat to the freedoms of its people, and therefore I'm afraid to say it is a clear and serious violation of the Joint Declaration treaty between the United Kingdom and China.[51]

The UK's position appears to be, and it is only apparent,[52] that the new 2020 National Security Law breaches paragraph 11, because national security is a public order matter rather than one involving the defence of the People's

---

[51] 'UK Says China's Security Law Is Serious Violation of Joint Declaration on Hong Kong', *Reuters*, 1 July 2020.

[52] The UK has not condescended to provide much further detail in its two six-monthly reports despite using the formula that there is a 'clear and serious' breach of the Joint Declaration; see UKFCO, The Six-Monthly Report on Hong Kong, 1 January to 30 June 2020, 23 November 2020, 14–15 (reproducing Raab's Parliamentary statement, which refers without much further detail to paragraph 3(3), (5) and (11) of the Joint Declaration); UKFCO, The Six-Monthly Report on Hong Kong, 1 July to 31 December 2020, 10 June 2021.

Republic.⁵³ In effect such an argument, if indeed it is the UK argument, would involve saying that the Sino-British Joint Declaration decides where the PRC's defence begins and where police powers end in a part of China, whereas the PRC considers this a legitimate extension of a defence-related law under article 18 of the Basic Law. As for whom should decide, Beijing or Hong Kong, the matter can be approached in the following way. Hong Kong's legislative autonomy is constrained not by the 'defence and foreign affairs' limitation but rather by the fact that under article 17 where a piece of legislation is one 'regarding affairs within the responsibility of the Central Authorities or regarding the relationship between the Central Authorities and the Region' (i.e. including foreign affairs and defence) then the NPCSC can invalidate it. The logical way to approach this, at least under the Basic Law, is that it is the NPCSC which decides where to draw the line in respect of Hong Kong's autonomy.

In short, in the latest controversy to which we shall return in Chapter 10, the PRC looks to its legislative and other powers in respect of defence matters, which are outside Hong Kong's competence, while the UK appears to have in mind Hong Kong's autonomous police powers in contrast to the PRC's defence powers. China and Britain lie in different beds, each haunted by a different nightmare. In one there is a charter for a special territory, in the other only a treaty for a lost city.

---

[53] The UK's position is explored more closely in Chapter 10. Still, it is gleaned only from parliamentary statements and such. It may be said that the UK hardly has the incentive to provide a more detailed legal position. One difficulty is that, equally, it may be difficult to take a view which is not more closely articulated in legal terms seriously, or as a treaty argument at all. Pressing on with that argument which is dressed loosely in legal garb by rounding up a limited number of allied Western capitals does not strengthen it, the audience being global.

7

Demos

I THE COLONIAL DEMOCRATIC CARVE-OUT

In the first place it is instructive to ask how a poet could meet the challenge of representing the population of a city on stage; in the second, this exercise is likely to shed light on the political function of Greek tragedy. More specifically it will shed light on the relationship between tragedy and democracy – a vexed question in recent years – for no consideration of democracy in drama can neglect the role of democracy's central player.[1]

The issue of having a fully fledged democratic system in Hong Kong goes close to the heart of the whole Hong Kong issue today.

It is often portrayed as a treaty issue. It is not, or at least not clearly so, and for the following reason: namely, that the 1984 Sino-British Joint Declaration failed to secure democratic reform either on its own, or through what often is referred to as the 'incorporation' of the International Covenant on Civil and Political Rights. This usually is (mis)taken to mean an incorporation of that human rights treaty itself, wholesale, rather than a recasting or transformation of albeit most, but not all of its provisions in the form of a local, domestic law. The UK had carved out the right to vote, and to political participation. For good reason for there was not then or now a fully elected legislature in Hong Kong, and certainly the colonial Governor was an unelected figure. These features were carried through into the post-handover period. 'Continuity', if one prefers to describe it thus, and it has been a sore issue ever since.

Prior to the 1997 handover the promise of an elected legislature in the 1984 Joint Declaration meant for the UK that work should start now, whilst the territory remained in British hands. In 1993 three international lawyers appeared before the Foreign Affairs Committee, supporting Lord Patten's

---

[1] D. M. Carter, 'The Demos in Greek Tragedy' (2010) 56 *The Cambridge Classical Journal* 47, 47.

proposal to push ahead with democratic reforms before handing Hong Kong over to China. Patten in his memoirs has cited this support with satisfaction, referring to 'three different teams' of international lawyers.[2]

During the course of those committee hearings in Parliament the committee chairman asked one of the experts, the late Peter Duffy, one of the most admired human rights lawyers in his day, if Duffy knew of any international law opinion which would consider the UK's actions or proposed actions unlawful. The answer according to Duffy 'in short' was 'no'.[3] Even if Duffy did not know them, presumably the Chinese lawyers would have thought otherwise, but let us put that aside.

Two years prior to that hearing, the 1991 Hong Kong Bill of Rights Ordinance (hereafter the BORO or the Ordinance)[4] had been enacted by the colonial legislature, seeking to incorporate as it were the provisions of the International Covenant on Civil and Political Rights (ICCPR, or Covenant) into Hong Kong law. It was ostensibly a response to well-known events on the Mainland. The 1991 Ordinance granted the colonial judges the power to strike down legislation which was incompatible with the Covenant's provisions. For all intents and purpose, and certainly as a matter of common law theory, a treaty incorporated by statute is statutory law, and no more. There is no such thing as a treaty applying under domestic law, no 'self-executing' treaty in the American parlance.[5] Saying that 'the ICCPR' is a part of Hong Kong law is a misnomer.

In any event, the Joint Declaration itself had made no mention of such incorporation although arguably at least does not prohibit it. Rather, Section XIII, Annex I had pinned the legal assurance of rights and freedoms to the then existing colonial common law,[6] with that same provision – Section XIII of Annex I of the Joint Declaration – stating three paragraphs on however that 'the provisions' – only 'the provisions' – of the Covenant 'as applied to Hong Kong shall remain in force'. 'To' rather than 'in' Hong Kong. In other words, these 'provisions' as they applied only as international but not domestic Hong Kong law would continue to be applied after the handover. They would

---

[2] Chris Patten, *East and West* (London: MacMillan, 1998), 66.
[3] Minutes of Evidence, 3 November 1993, Foreign Affairs Committee, House of Commons, Sess. 1992–93, HC 842-ii, 1992/93 in *Relations between the United Kingdom and China in the Period Up to and Beyond 1997: First Report*, Great Britain, Parliament, House of Commons, Foreign Affairs Committee, vol. II (London: HMSO, 1994), 48, 53.
[4] Bill of Rights Ordinance (Cap. 383).
[5] See James Crawford, *Brownlie's Principles of Public International Law*, 8th ed. (Oxford: Oxford University Press, 2012), 64.
[6] See Article XIII, Annex I, which speaks of 'rights and freedoms as provided for by the laws previously in force in Hong Kong'.

be applied as they had been under British colonial rule in 1984, at which point the only guarantee of rights which existed were those under the common law. The other side of the argument would be that the incorporation of the Covenant's provisions breached the assurance that these 'provisions' would continue to be applied the same way; as unincorporated rights under the Anglo-Hong Kong common law. This point, at least of treaty law, has never been resolved satisfactorily. Chinese objections to the Ordinance certainly did not prevent its passage or, curiously, its continuation after the handover. Until today the Ordinance remains in force almost in its entirety but for the repeal of inconsequential provisions.

At the same time, however, the UK had entered a carve-out, a treaty reservation, to Article 25 of the Covenant which grants the right to vote and to political participation.[7] That treaty reservation naturally was taken due account of in the drafting of Hong Kong's Bill of Rights Ordinance. In short, the Ordinance provided for no international rights to vote or to political participation, so long as colonial rule prevailed.

If one were to have asked 'would it violate the Joint Declaration if the Covenant were to be incorporated into Hong Kong law before handing the territory back to China?' a credible argument could be made for saying 'no', since the Joint Declaration says that the provisions of the Covenant would 'continue' to apply. But another way of viewing it would have restricted such provisions to their 'application' without assuming the treaty's incorporation as such. Still, regardless of China's status as a non-Contracting Party to the Covenant, it would have been fraught politically to argue that the UK, which is a Contracting Party, was prevented from in fact incorporating the Covenant into Hong Kong law; even if the Covenant never was incorporated under domestic law in the UK. Rather, the European Convention on Human Rights and Fundamental Freedoms 1950 is incorporated in the UK under the Human Rights Act of 1998; a fact which has in these strange times drawn its own controversy in the UK. Whatever the reasons, and which may one day yet come into full light, the BORO remains Hong Kong law and many of the Covenant's provisions are incorporated under Hong Kong domestic law. So too the carve-out of democratic rights and this, today, is a key issue.

---

[7] Adopted by United Nations General Assembly Resolution 2200A (XXI) on 16 December 1966, in force 23 March 1966. The UK added its signature on 16 September 1968 and ratified on 20 May 1976.

The position is more straightforward in some ways where the Hong Kong Basic Law itself also incorporates these provisions of the Covenant. Article 39 of which states that:

> The provisions of the International Covenant on Civil and Political Rights, the International Covenant on Economic, Social and Cultural Rights, and international labour conventions as applied to Hong Kong shall remain in force and shall be implemented through the laws of the Hong Kong Special Administrative Region.
>
> The rights and freedoms enjoyed by Hong Kong residents shall not be restricted unless as prescribed by law. Such restrictions shall not contravene the provisions of the preceding paragraph of this Article.

Notice that unlike the case with the UK's incorporation of the Covenant's provisions through the 1991 BORO, which may even be said to conflict with the Joint Declaration, the Hong Kong Basic Law itself requires such incorporation, which it terms 'implementation'. But what of the democratic carve-out? The leading case on the continued effect today of the UK treaty carve-outs to the International Covenant is one dealing with the UK's original immigration reservation rather than its democratic reservation – the Court of Final Appeal's decision in *Comilang Milagros Tecson v. Director of Immigration*.[8]

How was maintaining a carve-out of democratic rights, especially after having incorporated the rest of the Covenant under Hong Kong law, to be reconciled with the splendour and pageantry, and ultimately the bitter acrimony, of Patten's democratic reforms? To be fair, as Sir Percy Cradock pointed out, Britain's position had shifted under John Major.[9] Patten himself advocated, we should assume in good faith, that shift. 'Better late than never' became more than homespun wisdom. It had become a principled political stance which led to a spectacular diplomatic fallout between the two sides. Principled or not – no doubt, China had its own views – Patten's reforms were to become a catalyst for events which have now reached a climax in the recent political crisis, with post-handover Hong Kong now halfway through the fifty-year period.

Perhaps Patten had not much choice either, such was the clamour for reforms locally that despite his efforts he too had fallen foul of Hong Kong's democrats. Yet Lord Patten was no last Viceroy of India, content to deliver the last major colonial outpost to its rightful owners as swiftly as possible. Where

---

[8] (2019) 22 HKCFAR 59 [30]–[35], [40]–[42], [60]–[61], [63]–[65].
[9] Percy Craddock, *In Pursuit of British Interests* (London: John Murray, 1997), 205.

Mountbatten was to serve whatever policy direction, wittingly or not,[10] emanating from the Foreign and Commonwealth Office, Lord Patten was to make colonial policy never mind history.

Similar sentiments, of principle or expressed as such, have since led Mr Johnson, the current British Prime Minister, to proclaim a treaty breach and – as if history itself could be turned – embark upon another, larger attempt at restoring British honour in 2020. Britain is back, nearly twenty-five years after it had sailed and left. But to what end? Sparked by a debate over a proposed extradition bill in Hong Kong in 2019,[11] by 2020 violent street protests now involve advocacy of independence, the sort of demand which the colonial introduction of democratic rights and self-government was inextricably bound up with in so many parts of the globe during the course of the previous century. In response, Beijing passed the National Security Law in the summer of 2020.[12] By the autumn, under that law, five legislators who purportedly had encouraged or sought foreign intervention were disqualified from remaining on the legislature, triggering in turn a walk out by the entire opposition. The UK together with other countries of the 'Five Eyes' intelligence group, namely the United States and what historically were the White Dominions of Australia, Canada and New Zealand,[13] issued a declaration:

> The disqualification rules appear part of a concerted campaign to silence all critical voices following the postponement of September's Legislative Council elections, the imposition of charges against a number of elected legislators, and actions to undermine the freedom of Hong Kong's vibrant media.
>
> We call on China to stop undermining the rights of the people of Hong Kong to elect their representatives in keeping with the Joint Declaration and Basic Law. For the sake of Hong Kong's stability and prosperity, it is essential that China and the Hong Kong authorities respect the channels for the people of Hong Kong to express their legitimate concerns and opinions.
>
> As a leading member of the international community, we expect China to live up to its international commitments and its duty to the people of

---

[10] Unwittingly, according to one highly controversial popular account, Narendra Singh Sarila, *The Shadow of the Great Game: The Untold Story of India's Partition* (New York: Carroll & Graf, 2006).

[11] Chapter 9 of this book.

[12] Chapter 10.

[13] By the early part of the twentieth century Domiion status had been granted to Britain's white settlement colonies. Others such as India were granted Dominion status after the Second World War. The Five Eyes group was a Cold War creation with its roots in Anglo-American wartime signals intelligence cooperation.

Hong Kong. We urge the Chinese central authorities to re-consider their actions against Hong Kong's elected legislature and immediately reinstate the Legislative Council members.[14]

The Spokesperson for the Office of the Commissioner of the Ministry of Foreign Affairs in the Hong Kong SAR replied with what now has become a standard rebuke:

> No single word or clause in the document, which has altogether eight paragraphs and three annexes, grants the UK any responsibility to Hong Kong after the city's return, still less any right to meddle with Hong Kong affairs. The UK has no sovereignty, jurisdiction or the right to supervise Hong Kong, and likewise other countries are in no position to make unwarranted comments about Hong Kong affairs on the pretext of the Joint Declaration.[15]

The negotiating history of the Joint Declaration also does show this as a consistent view insisted upon by the PRC.[16] In addition, the UK's assertion that there is a Covenant right to democracy, to the right to vote and to political participation, and that the Joint Declaration guarantees such a right is contestable, and is in any event contested by the PRC. To this we now turn.[17]

II 'AS APPLIED TO HONG KONG'

Too little, if anything, is known presently about the Sino-British discussions on the UK's treaty reservation to the ICCPR. Since the 1997 handover, the PRC has maintained that earlier British reservation. Insofar as incorporation of the ICCPR's provisions were concerned, the hope or belief was that since the 1990 Basic Law, passed by the National People's Congress seven years before the handover, itself states in article 39 that 'the provisions' of the Covenant 'as they applied' before the handover will continue to do so, then that will serve to entrench – in other words, lock in – the incorporation of the Covenant by the 1991 BORO even after the handover. It was a piece of ingenuity behind the

---

[14] Hong Kong Joint Statement, 18 November 2020, www.gov.uk/government/news/joint-statement-on-hong-kong-november-2020 (last accessed 6 April 2021). This is not to say there were not others, for which see the German statement on behalf of thirty-nine countries in the Third Committee Debate in the United Nations, https://new-york-un.diplo.de/un-en/news-corner/201006-heusgen-china/2402648 (last accessed 20 August 2021). See further, Chapter 11, of this book.

[15] 'Any External Interference in Hong Kong Affairs Is Doomed to Fail', Office of the Commissioner of the Ministry of Foreign Affairs in the Hong Kong SAR, 19 November 2020, www.fmcoprc.gov.hk/eng/gsxw/t1833728.htm (last accessed 6 April 2021).

[16] See Chapter 2.

[17] In the case of the other 'Four Eyes' there is no treaty claim at all.

design and enactment of the Ordinance, that it will require Chinese law to entrench it.[18]

All of this had taken place only after the 1984 Joint Declaration where the Joint Declaration had been silent on any change to Hong Kong's colonial legal regime before the actual date of the 1997 handover.[19] The Provisional Legislature of the Hong Kong SAR (and the PRC which appointed its members) could of course have repealed BORO after the handover. But for the repeal of certain sundry provisions, however, (1) BORO was preserved alongside (2) the Basic Law's own incorporation of the ICCPR's provisions, in addition to (3) a separate chapter of its own in the Basic Law granting fundamental rights. It is this which has been referred to in Hong Kong as the 'triple entrenchment' of rights in post-handover Hong Kong.[20]

And yet the 'provisions' of the Covenant as they applied before the handover, both before and after the 1984 Joint Declaration, still excluded article 25(b) on the right to vote and to political participation. That provision states that:

> Every citizen shall have the right and the opportunity, without any of the distinctions mentioned in article 2 and without unreasonable restrictions:
> . . .
> (b) To vote and to be elected at genuine periodic elections which shall be by universal and equal suffrage and shall be held by secret ballot, guaranteeing the free expression of the will of the electors . . .

The UK reservation had stated, originally, that:[21]

> The Government of the United Kingdom reserves the right not to apply sub-paragraph (b) of article 25 in so far as it may require the establishment of an elected Executive or Legislative Council in Hong Kong . . .

In his letter to the UN Secretary-General,[22] China's Permanent Representative had stated that the ICCPR, as applied to Hong Kong, shall continue to apply

---

[18] See Andrew Byrnes, 'And Some Have Bills of Rights Thrust upon Them: Hong Kong's Bill of Rights', in Philip Alston (ed.), *Promoting Human Rights through Bills of Rights* (New York: Oxford University Press, 2000), 318, 334.

[19] For researchers on the history of the Basic Law, it is a question of the greatest interest. Viewed with an understanding of the Vienna Convention on the Law of Treaties, see art. 31(3)(b), Sino-British diplomatic exchanges and practice during the Basic Law's drafting could 'establish' subsequent Sino-British agreements which in turn affect the proper interpretation of the 1984 Joint Declaration.

[20] The phrase is Professor Albert Chen's.

[21] UN Treaty Database, at www.treaties.un.org.

[22] Letter from the Permanent Representative of the PRC to the UN, H.E. Mr Qin Huasun to the Secretary-General of the United Nations, H.E. Mr Kofi Annan, 20 June 1997, (1997) 36 *ILM* 1675.

after 1997. The words 'as applied' import, and no doubt are intended to import, the UK's own reservation.[23] What is left, in short, is only what the Basic Law says about that right.[24]

What about the Joint Declaration? It does not speak, at least expressly, of a 'right' to vote although it speaks of other rights. Paragraph 3(5), which Mr Raab cited to Parliament in 2020 and which the UK's Six-Monthly Report covering that period faithfully reproduced, states that:

> The current social and economic systems in Hong Kong will remain unchanged, and so will the life-style. Rights and freedoms, including those of the person, of speech, of the press, of assembly, of association, of travel, of movement, of correspondence, of strike, of choice of occupation, of academic research and of religious belief will be ensured by law in the Hong Kong Special Administrative Region.

Article XIII of Annex I to the Joint Declaration then states:

> The Hong Kong Special Administrative Region Government shall maintain the rights and freedoms as provided for by the laws previously in force in Hong Kong, including freedom of the person, of speech, of the press, of assembly, of association, to form and join trade unions, of correspondence, of travel, of movement, of strike, of demonstration, of choice of occupation, of academic research, of belief, inviolability of the home, the freedom to marry and the right to raise a family freely.

True, the PRC itself would not have wanted the UK to move in the direction of a democratised, let alone fully democratised, Hong Kong. A long letter to Geoffrey Howe, just as Cradock was to leave his post as ambassador to Beijing in December 1983, from the British Ambassador to Peking now casts some light on the UK's official deliberations:

> There is ... one feature of Chinese policy that could be helpful. This is that they seem to envisage a development of self-rule in Hong Kong in the period between now and 1997, perhaps based on elections. Hitherto, we have avoided this, the normal development in dependent territories,[25] because of a well-based belief that the Chinese would think we were guiding Hong Kong towards independence and the fear that there would be a clash between

---

[23] For the Human Rights Committee's view, see J. M. M. Chan and C. L. Lim, *Law of the Hong Kong Constitution*, 2nd ed. (Hong Kong: Sweet & Maxwell, 2015), 1018 *et seq.*

[24] See C. L. Lim, 'The Green Paper from a Constitutional Perspective' (2007) 37 *H.K.L.J.* 741.

[25] From the perspective of United Nations law however, rather than English law, it can well be said as this book also argues that Hong Kong was no longer even if it ever were a 'British dependent territory' strictly speaking. See Chapter 3's discussion of the Committee of Twenty-Four at the United Nations.

KNT[26] [sic.] and Communist supporters. Although the Chinese are, no doubt, thinking only in terms of a situation where the ultimate fate of Hong Kong as a Special Administrative Region is settled, there are advantages in this for us. The more Hong Kong has representative institutions, the more these institutions can share the burden of representing the wishes of the people of Hong Kong to Peking; and the more difficult it will be for Peking to represent any failure of policy there as being a plot by HMG.[27]

In two further telegrams, Cradock first reported a dinner conversation with Ji Pengfei:

> Ji went on to speak about the larger question of democracy. He said that the first Government of the SAR might be produced by consultation rather than election. But there would have to be a stipulation in the Basic Law that an electoral system would be introduced. I said that we did not see any great difficulty in holding elections in Hong Kong. It could be done before 1997. Ji interjected immediately that this would not do (*na bu xing*). In answer to my question he said that this was because the time was not yet ripe. It would create confusion.[28]

He goes on to observe that:

> On the negative side were some of his [Ji Pengfei's] comments on the development of full democracy in Hong Kong before 1997. It rather looks as if the Chinese do not wish to see a fully democratic system in place before they are in a position to oversee it. This, however, is no reason not to pursue the theme. The Chinese will be on pretty weak ground, having themselves said that democracy is the ultimate aim in the SAR.[29]

Any suggestion today that China is somehow to be held responsible for any lack of progress in establishing a fully democratic system risks ignoring a number of points. Chiefly, there is the question of what the Joint Declaration means by a 'legislature ... constituted by elections'.[30] Is what China meant originally by the term 'elections' necessarily the same as, say, the straightforwardly Parliamentary sense in which that term usually is understood in the UK? Lord Patten as we have seen chose to interpret the term in the sense

---

[26] KMT, Kuomintang.
[27] TNA/PREM 19/1059 (Pt. 10 – Future of Hong Kong, New Territorial [sic.] Leases), Percy Cradock to Geoffrey Howe, 12 December 1983, para. 17.
[28] TNA/PREM 19/1057 (Pt. 10), FM Peking 200730Z Dec 83 to Immediate FCO, Telno. 1378 of 20 Dec 1983, Info Immediate Hong Kong.
[29] TNA/PREM 19/1057 (Pt. 10), FM Peking 200705Z Dec 83 to Immediate FCO, Telno. 1380 of 20 Dec 1983, Info Immediate Hong Kong.
[30] Annex I, art. 1.

of direct elections in the British sense, the justification given being not much more than that the arguments against pushing forward with democratic reforms were groundless – 'What anyway of realpolitik?', he asked.[31] That, if it can be put so strongly, even if the UK itself never necessarily understood an election in the sense used in the Joint Declaration to mean an elected Parliamentary system, it was still not too late to advance along a semblance of that interpretation.[32] As will be discussed below, this was not entirely without foundation since the Chinese side must at least be taken to have understood what the UK intended, but at the same time there was a sense that the way the colonial authorities intended to approach the matter, even as early as the tenure of Sir Edward Youde as Governor, risked a breach of the Joint Declaration.

The colonial government some two months before the conclusion of the 1984 Joint Declaration had already issued a green paper, proposing LegCo elections by experimenting with a form of electoral college. It would comprise urban and regional council members, district board members and a well as functional constituencies. In other words, by electoral college and the old merchant guilds, the latter being reminiscent of the medieval European guilds of old. There was also the suggestion of 'unofficial' (i.e. non-governmental) Executive Council and LegCo members holding ministerial rank, even the possibility of their electing the Governor. This was self-government in the making, as one might imagine under the sort of model which previously used to be introduced as a prelude to colonial independence elsewhere from India to Malaya; and it was, precisely, what China had no doubt intended to avoid by removing Hong Kong from the UN decolonisation committee's list of non-self-governing territories in 1972. By such removal, unlike other colonies, Hong Kong was to be recovered by China rather than to be prepared for any form of self-government.[33] That, at least, would be the position under international law, and the Joint Declaration itself provides no basis for thinking it should have changed.

However, two months after the Joint Declaration was initialled and published in September 1984 but before it was signed in December, a white paper

---

[31] Patten, *East and West, op. cit.*, 37.
[32] Except that one of Patten's first acts was to keep the Executive Council, his de facto 'cabinet' separate and distinct from an increasingly unruly partially elected legislature.
[33] UNGA resolution 2908 approved the report of the decolonisation committee, the 'Committee of Twenty-Four' established by UNGA resolution 1654 in the aftermath of UNGA resolution 1514, recommending the removal of Hong Kong from the list of non-self-governing territories to which the UK had included Hong Kong in 1946. For a critical view, *cf.* Patricia A. Dagati, 'Hong Kong's Lost Right to Self-determination: A Denial of Due Process in the United Nations (1992) 13 *N.Y.L. Sch. J. Int'l & Comp. L.* 153.

followed, instituting the colony's new system. The 1984 White Paper envisaged the possibility of introducing direct elections in 1987. Clearly the UK while seeking to make the Joint Declaration more palatable ('not just handing Hong Kong over to communist China after all') must have known that, having lost Hong Kong, it would be laying the seeds for a demand for full democracy.[34] A columnist in one of the Hong Kong papers described as 'communist' in a telegram from the Governor to the FCO had suggested that the UK was seeking to present a *fait accompli*, arguing that Hong Kong's political future was not for the UK to decide upon, and that it was too early to say whether that would be in keeping with the Basic Law which was yet to be drafted. The 'independent' press called it a 'farewell show'.[35] Whatever the UK's motivations, it is significant that the publication of the White Paper occurred between initialling and signature. In international law terms doing so after signature but before ratification would not be unlike tearing out the fittings after completion on a property. In any event, it would risk a breach of the doctrine of good faith in international law which allows one State to rely upon a unilateral public declaration by another of its position,[36] or where a State exercises its rights without regard for the rights of another.[37] Doing so once it is confirmed, through the initialling of the negotiated text, that Hong Kong was lost to the UK would at least allow one to say that there was as yet no signed treaty.

Recent research has shown that a little more than a year after the ratification of the Joint Declaration in May 1985, in December 1985, Youde had reported to the FCO on his meeting with Ji Pengfei, the Second Director of the

---

[34] See Albert Chen's chapter, in Chan and Lim, *Law of the Hong Kong Constitution, op. cit.*, 253–6.

[35] TNA/PREM 19/1530 (Pt. 18, Future of Hong Kong, New Territorial [sic.] Leases), Deskby 261200Z, FM Hong Kong 261000Z Nov 84 to Immediate FCO, Telno. 3611 of 26 November 1984.

[36] See e.g. *Nuclear Tests Case (Australia v. France)* (Merits) [1974] ICJ Rep. 253, para. 46. The same principle that would apply if it were said that even a unilateral Chinese statement could create a binding legal obligation. As I have mentioned, applied to Annex I of the Sino-British Joint Declaration it would mean that even if something is couched as a unilateral statement that would not prevent it necessarily from becoming legally binding. Yet that is not the issue, the Annex clearly is a part of a legally binding treaty. Rather, the question has to do with its content rather than its legal nature. What does it mean to have a dispute with a State about the true meaning or precise content of its own policies? Particularly when these policies have been transcribed into a piece of implementing legislation (the Basic Law) which states clearly that it is for the Chinese central authorities to provide an authoritative interpretation of the meaning of that legislation, and where the treaty which is sought to be implemented also envisages the Chinese side (and only the Chinese side) passing such detailed Chinese legislation?

[37] Bin Cheng, *General Principles of Law as Applied by International Courts and Tribunals* (Cambridge: Grotius, 1987), 130.

Hong Kong and Macau Affairs Office of the PRC State Council, in which Youde explained to Ji that the colonial government was committed to the '1987 Review' as promised in that 1984 White Paper, concerning the development of the political system in 1988.[38] Ji, according to Youde's report, replied that the PRC had no objections since legislative 'elections' were envisaged in the Joint Declaration, however '[a] fully directly elected system was not necessarily right' and more 'time was needed' in order to 'judge whether there should be direct, indirect or some other form of election'.[39] This was no different from what Ji had said to Cradock almost two years before, in December 1983. During Youde's visit to Beijing from August to September the following year, in 1986, the Chinese view was again reaffirmed; that the colonial authorities 'should take no decision on direct elections before the publication of the Basic Law in 1988'.[40] In other words, all roads should lead to, and converge with, the Basic Law. Meeting Ji in Beijing in October 1986, Tim Renton, Minister of State for Foreign and Commonwealth Affairs, sought to assure Ji Pengfei that the 1987 review would only discuss 'a limited matter only: a proportion of seats perhaps being filled by direct election'.[41] Ultimately, a compromise was struck; that if direct elections were not introduced until after the enactment of the Basic Law (which ultimately was adopted by the Seventh National People's Congress on 4 April 1990), then the PRC side would see to it 'that there was appropriate provision for it in the Basic Law'.[42] The long and short of it, so far as these records appear to show, is that the Joint Declaration would defer to the Basic Law in the matter of electoral reform; and so it was that the Basic Law was to provide for gradual reform beginning in 1991;[43] only to unravel following Lord Patten's subsequent arrival and in the lead-up to the 1997 handover. For China, the Joint Declaration's reference to legislative elections was something to be worked out gradually and it certainly did not in itself entail

---

[38] TNA/PREM19/1796, Youde to FCO, Telno. 2804, 11 Dec. 1985, cited and discussed in Albert H.Y. Chen and Michael Ng, 'Sino-British Diplomacy in the Making of the Constitutional Order of the Hong Kong SAR: Historical Investigations into the Drafting of the Basic Law (1984–1990)', m/s on file with the author. The author is indebted to Professor Chen and Dr Ng for sharing their work in advance.

[39] Youde to FCO, also quoted and discussed in Chen and Ng, *op. cit.*

[40] The reference is to the 1988 Draft; TNA, PREM 19/1796, letter enclosing a briefing to the Prime Minister (PM) for the call from R. N. Culshaw of the FCO to Charles Powell, Private Secretary to PM, 8 Sept. 1986; Chen and Ng, *op. cit.*

[41] TNA, PREM, 19/1796, Evans from Peking to FCO, Telno. 1989, 14 Oct. 1986; Chen and Ng, *op. cit.*

[42] Ibid.

[43] Discussed in Section IV below.

any promise of a fully elected legislature even if subsequently, purely as a domestic matter, this was to be promised following the 1997 handover and the demise of colonial rule. It is for that reason that the PRC bodes no interference in this regard.

There is a further dimension to all of this, which cannot be confined to the issue of political reform as if that issue stood on its own. Was all this not just the UK seemingly taking a previous decolonisation template and applying it to the circumstances of Hong Kong? Self-government or self-rule, replete with democratic reform, then followed by independence. That at least was the standard British template applied to numerous colonies previously. Not only that, imperial policy was and is still, today, presented as having always intended the self-government of the coloured colonies, and thus no colony was ever lost but only came to fruition. One contemporary writer puts it thus, in writing about the present-day Commonwealth of Nations: 'The Commonwealth in British and international history has undoubtedly suffered from the whiggish myth that self-government had always been the objective of British policy, that a smooth, almost seamless and effortless transfer of powers occurred between the British and the colonial political elite.'[44]

Doing the same with Hong Kong would have been unsuited to the very ideas of self-determination and territorial integrity which had emerged during the negotiations leading to the establishment of Woodrow Wilson's League of Nations. Then, China was to be disappointed when Shandong (Shantung) was to remain in Japan's possession,[45] with at best an uncertain date for its return. Subsequently the Manchuria crisis was to render the League asunder. Following the Second World War there was again to be disappointment where there were hopes that colonial territories such as Hong Kong would be restored to China. After Japan's defeat British control was regained on 30 August 1945 with the arrival of H.M.S. Swiftsure. The United States President pushed for the restoration of Hong Kong to China but Churchill had held firm.[46] The very suggestion that Hong Kong was therefore to be returned to a communist State was in this sense anathema to the portrayal of a colonial civilising mission.

---

[44] Mélanie Torrent, 'A Commonwealth Approach to Decolonisation' (2012) 65 (3) Études Anglaises 347, 348.

[45] That Woodrow Wilson who had promoted China's case could not accept, and refused, the Japanese delegation's condition – recognition of a principle of racial equality – was a factor. For an accessible account, see e.g. Paul French, *Betrayal in Paris* (London: Penguin, 2014), 38, 50.

[46] Walter La Feber, 'Roosevelt, Churchill and Indochina: 1942–45' (1975) 80 *Am. Hist. Rev.* 1277. As with Versailles when the Chinese side pressed for Shandong to be regained, and failed, again Britain was to guard jealously its imperial possessions.

In any case, none of this was necessarily what the Joint Declaration meant by 'elections'. From the PRC viewpoint the Joint Declaration as such almost certainly does not mean a fully elected legislature necessarily, '[a] fully directly elected system was not necessarily right' as Ji had put it,[47] but that – to Patten, who subsequently came onto the scene – was where the three independent international law opinions to the Foreign and Commonwealth Affairs Select Committee, referred to earlier, were to come in useful. They 'confirmed' the 'legality' of proceeding with Patten's proposal to enlarge the franchise before the 1997 handover, and Duffy as we saw testified to Parliament that he knew of no other legal opinion that would consider this a breach of the Joint Declaration.

The subsequent adverse reaction on the PRC's part is now a matter of record.[48] It is interesting to compare, too, the UN Human Rights Committee's view, that body entrusted with surveillance of compliance with the International Covenant on Civil and Political Rights. The view of that committee, first expressed before the handover, is that while the original British treaty reservation is in place, there is no obligation to move towards greater democratisation but that if there were progress on such reforms then at that point the reservation would be extinguished.[49] This view was only to emerge after the 1993 Parliamentary committee hearing but in an important sense it contradicts the notion that simply because the Joint Declaration speaks of an elected legislature it therefore permits the UK to push ahead with its own interpretation before the handover. That view offered before Parliament's Foreign Affairs Committee was always open to question as a matter of treaty law. One could put it more strongly. It was, possibly, a treaty breach by the UK.

III 'ACCOUNTABILITY'

Aside from electoral reform there is a related issue. Not only is an independent judiciary indispensable – no one had questioned this, not even the 2014 PRC State Council's white paper which had stirred such controversy in Hong Kong[50] – but ought there to be a 'separation of powers'? One that, specifically, would have the executive account to an elected legislature. Advocacy of this view came to the fore in September 2020 when the term

---

[47] Youde to FCO, *op. cit.*
[48] Chapter 4 of this book.
[49] UN Doc. CCPR/C/HKG/CO/2, 21 April 2006, para. 18, reiterating its view in UN Doc. CCPR/C/79/Add.57, 9 November 1995, para. 19.
[50] At least in the author's view. The White Paper is discussed further in Chapter 8 of this book.

'separation of powers' was removed by the Hong Kong SAR's Education Bureau from school textbooks on the basis that it was nowhere to be found expressed in the Basic Law. The controversy led ultimately to the Secretary for Justice intervening publicly to explain the Hong Kong SAR Government's position.[51]

The colonial system had been executive-led and the incorporation of the ICCPR's provisions under the 1991 BORO had carved out the right to vote and to political participation until 1997, even while Patten had at the same time initiated reforms in anticipation of a democratic post-handover Hong Kong. Yet the overall aim of the Joint Declaration was not to democratise rather than to ensure continuation of the previous system in Hong Kong. It was to guarantee that the socialist system of government would not be imposed for fifty years. Except, for the words 'the legislature of the Hong Kong Special Administrative Region shall be constituted by elections' having been included in Article I of Annex I. Article I also states, importantly, that '[t]he chief executive will be appointed by the Central People's Government on the basis of the results of elections or consultations to be held locally'. Notice the ambiguity. There is no suggestion of executive accountability to the legislature in the Westminster sense. On 3 September 1984, towards the end of the end of the negotiations, Youde wrote in a telegram explaining the outstanding issues from the UK's viewpoint, one of which was that:[52]

> On constitutional matters it is already our agreed objective to allow nothing to appear in the constitutional annex which rules out an elected Chief Executive both before and after 1997, and to specify that there will be an elected legislature.

So what then might we mean by 'elections'? The Chinese consider the President of the PRC to be 'elected'. It would be different if Hong Kong had been handed over to the UK by the PRC, rather than to have been handed over by the UK. One might then say 'elected' means what it means in the UK. The truth is that the Joint Declaration as with any treaty is a disagreement reduced to writing. In the case of the Joint Declaration that disagreement, not least over

---

[51] See 'Constitutional Order Clarified'; 5 September 2020, available on the Government news portal at www.news. gov.hk; Gary Cheung and Natalie Wong, 'Separation of Powers Has No Place in the City', S.C.M.P. (Hong Kong), 9 September 2020.

[52] TNA/PREM 19/1267 (Pt. 17, Future of Hong Kong, New Territorial [sic.] Leases), Deskby FCO 031300Z, Deskby Peking 040100Z, FM Hong Kong 031130Z September 1984 to Immediate FCO, Telno. 2624 of 3 September 1984. Immediately after the words quoted, the Governor states that: 'We ought also to aim to have it recorded that the Executive will be accountable to the Legislature.' This became the final sentence of the third paragraph of Article I of Annex I of the Joint Declaration, and the issue is discussed further below.

democratic reform in Hong Kong, and which caused the derailment of the 'through-train', in that the partially elected pre-1997 legislature ultimately was dissolved,[53] has continued after the handover; culminating in widespread unrest in the 2019 violent protests. Cradock as we have seen was more pointed about the origins of the current political crisis. Britain had simply changed course after concluding the Joint Declaration. Still, public expectations of democratic reform run high, and regardless of the Joint Declaration, the Basic Law promises it.

IV THE BASIC LAW

Under the Basic Law, eighteen out of sixty legislators were to be elected in 1991 by universal suffrage, twenty-one were to be returned under the functional constituencies system,[54] another eighteen were to be appointed, and this combination would then be rounded off with three further government members. The colonial Government had been prompted to increase the number of elected members following the events of 4 June 1989.[55] That elected number would rise again to twenty in 1995, and the number of elected legislators in 2000 and 2004 would further increase under the Basic Law of the Hong Kong SAR to twenty-four and thirty respectively,[56] thus making the legislature more representative over time. The 'through train' so-called would have had an elected legislature in 1995 serve its full term until 1999.[57] But Patten having initiated his reforms against China's protestations, would every elected legislator now do so? China was against it,[58] resulting in derailment of the 'through train' and a Provisional Legislative Council being also elected after the handover by a Selection Committee which had been established by Beijing for electing the Chief Executive. To some Lord Patten was the wrong choice in the wrong place at the wrong time, even if he would have been the right person perhaps in another place or in another time. Percy Cradock was critical but had, together with Sir David Wilson, been removed, purged might be a better word, by John Major who favoured Patten. For his part Patten was as unsparing in his denunciations of the former British ambassador as Cradock

---

[53] See Chapter 4 of this book.
[54] First introduced by the colonial government in 1985 in order to increase political representation.
[55] See Chan and Lim, *Law of the Hong Kong Constitution, op. cit.*, 258 (chapter by Albert. H. Y. Chen).
[56] Basic Law, Annex II.
[57] See Decision of the National People's Congress on the Formation of the First Government and First Legislative Council of the HKSAR, April 1990.
[58] Patten, *East and West, op. cit.*, 76.

was unstinting in his own remarks. Responding to a question from Mr Henry Tang in the colonial Legislative Council about what the Governor proposed to do to strengthen the rule of law, which in fact was a question about the controversy concerning the agreement the UK had reached with China regarding the Court of Final Appeal, Patten said:

> I think that we suffer in Hong Kong from an epidemic of what we call at home, Craddockitis, and it is something which affects not just dyspeptic retired ambassadors; it clearly goes wider than that. And there are a number of ingredients to the disease, a number of symptoms. There is a belief that one has a monopoly of virtue, a belief that one has a monopoly of wisdom about what is right for Hong Kong, a belief that one has a monopoly of concern about the things which have made Hong Kong so special and a belief that unless everybody else agrees with you and follows your own analysis, that, as far as Hong Kong is concerned, is the end of the road. Hong Kong is doomed unless people always agree with you. Those are some of the symptoms of this epidemic.[59]

No doubt that played well in Hong Kong which in any event was to return its first legislature a year after the handover, in 1998, with the number of legislators elected by universal suffrage staying at twenty. Subsequent elections followed Annex II of the Basic Law, that number increasing to twenty-four and thirty for the 2000 and 2004 LegCo elections consequently.

In the 2008 legislative elections, the number of directly elected members on the basis of universal suffrage remained at thirty (out of a sixty-seat LegCo). This was achieved with a 2004 interpretation by the Standing Committee of the National People's Congress (NPCSC).[60] It was the second time that the NPCSC had issued an interpretation under article 158 of Hong Kong's Basic Law.[61] Amongst other things the interpretation construed the method of elections 'after 2007' to include any elections held in 2007. But its most notable feature was that the Basic Law's requirement that any reform should be endorsed by two-thirds of LegCo was to be construed to require that the Government's reform proposal, if any, should first be reported to the NPCSC for approval before being tabled before LegCo. Following the 2004 interpretation, the Chief Executive, Mr C. H. Tung, had submitted his report.[62] In it, he had recommended amendment of the method for selecting

---

[59] Hong Kong Legislative Council, Official Record of Proceedings, 13 July 1995, 5424, in which 'Craddockitis' is spelled with a double 'd'.
[60] NPCSC Interpretation of 6 April 2004.
[61] See Chan and Lim, *Law of the Hong Kong Constitution*, op. cit., 1028 et seq.
[62] Ibid., 1029 et seq.

the Chief Executive in 2007 and for LegCo elections the following year. The NPCSC responded with a 2004 Decision which concluded that absent a broad consensus in Hong Kong the 2007 and 2008 Chief Executive and LegCo elections would not be by way of the introduction of universal suffrage.[63] In other words, things were to remain in a holding pattern; the existing system would remain unchanged until further notice and the ratio of LegCo members returned by direct election on the basis of universal suffrage to those returned by functional constituency seats would remain at 50:50.

This is not to say that there was not some progress afterwards within the constraints presented. Under Mr Donald Tsang's subsequent tenure as Chief Executive his reforms led to an expanded seventy-seat LegCo for the next 2012 LegCo elections which while returning thirty-five members – half of the total number of legislators – by direct election saw a further five functional constituency seats which were to be returned by 3.2 million voters who previously had enjoyed no voting rights in connection with any functional constituency seat. The significance of these reforms was that the arrangements for the 2012 LegCo elections reflected Beijing's own endorsement of the Democrats' earlier 2010 reform proposal.[64]

But things were about to take a dramatic turn. Whether the widespread and largely peaceful protests of 2014 marked the beginning of the end, as some observers are wont to suggest, or simply the end of a new beginning in the post-handover period remains presently unclear. The 2014 protests did not originate from public dissatisfaction with LegCo reform but rather from dissatisfaction with the proposal for reforming the method for selecting Hong Kong's Chief Executive in 2017.

V 2014

A new Chief Executive, Mr C. Y. Leung, had been chosen earlier in 2012 by a 1,193 member Election Committee; the number of members of that committee having previously been increased by way of a limited reform measure from 800 to 1,200 in 2010.[65] By 2014 public attention, and impatience, had become focused on the selection of the next Chief Executive by universal

---

[63] Decision of the Standing Committee of the National People's Congress on the Chief Executive's Report on whether there is a need to amend the methods for selecting the Chief Executive of the Hong Kong Special Administrative Region in 2007 and for forming the Legislative Council of the Hong Kong Special Administrative Region in 2008, April 2004.
[64] Chan and Lim, *Law of the Hong Kong Constitution, op. cit.*, 1017.
[65] Its roots lay in an earlier 2005 proposal by Mr Tsang but which was defeated by LegCo; *ibid.*, 1036 *et seq.*

suffrage. In the popular imagination this was what Beijing had promised. Article 45 of the Basic Law states, that:

> The chief executive of the Hong Kong Special Administrative Region shall be selected by election or through consultations held locally and be appointed by the Central People's Government.
>
> The method for selecting the chief executive shall be specified in the light of the actual situation in the Hong Kong Special Administrative Region and in accordance with the principle of gradual and orderly progress. The ultimate aim is the selection of the Chief Executive by universal suffrage upon nomination by a broadly representative nominating committee in accordance with democratic procedures.

In this regard, the language of the first paragraph of Article 45 mirrors the language of the Joint Declaration: 'The chief executive of the Hong Kong Special Administrative Region shall be selected by election or through consultations held locally and be appointed by the Central People's Government.'[66]

Soon after the 2014 Hong Kong protests (dubbed variously 'Occupy' or the 'Umbrella Movement') were a reaction to a further 2014 NPCSC Decision.[67] The NPCSC had decided that while Hong Kong was now ready to elect its Chief Executive, the candidates were themselves to be nominated by what essentially was the limited body of roughly 1,200 persons which until that point had elected the Chief Executive of the Hong Kong SAR. This 'Election Committee' according to the 2014 Decision would be transformed into a 'Nominating Committee'. Moreover, no more than two or three candidates would be nominated. At a glance, this is not inconsistent with Article 45, which states as an 'ultimate aim' the 'selection of the Chief Executive by universal suffrage upon nomination by a broadly representative nominating committee'. Would it be 'in accordance with democratic procedures'? Quite arguably, yes, if the comparison is with the degree to which the voter gets freely to choose the leadership in the UK of the Tory Party, the Labour Party or the LibDems. The critic says 'no', if it is to be a PRC-style election. Yet the truth may be that neither is the benchmark. In Hong Kong's case, it would have yielded transparency at least in terms of the candidates vying for nomination.

---

[66] Joint Declaration, article I.
[67] Decision of the Standing Committee of the National People's Congress on Issues Relating to the Selection of the Chief Executive of the Hong Kong Special Administrative Region by Universal Suffrage and on the Method for Forming the Legislative Council of the Hong Kong Special Administrative Region in the Year 2016, 31 August 2014.

Had all of this been accepted perhaps some sort of step forward could yet have been taken towards democratic reform in Hong Kong, even if some readers might baulk at this suggestion. In any case, that question became itself the subject of public controversy. The protesters in 2014 decided to adopt an unyielding approach which drew public sympathy and gained international public attention by paralysing central Hong Kong for a continuous seventy-nine days.

VI THE ORIGINS OF PUBLIC IMPATIENCE

The origins of public impatience may perhaps be traced in part to the establishment of a timetable for reform in 2007. The Government had issued a Green Paper on Constitutional Development that year, which had led in turn to a 2007 NPCSC Decision.[68] Professor Albert Chen, a member of the NPCSC's Basic Law Committee, had described the Chief Executive's 2007 report to the NPCSC as having signified a (positive) turn from focusing on, in the words of Article 45, the 'actual situation' (the objective social and political conditions in Hong Kong) to the subjective expectations of the populace.[69] Be that so the 2007 Decision preserved the status quo, effectively extending the NPCSC's earlier 2004 Decision.

Following the 2012 Chief Executive election, the new Chief Executive, Mr Leung, in his report to the NPCSC on constitutional reform, recommended that universal suffrage should be introduced in the Chief Executive election but that there should be no (further) change to the system for the 2016 legislative elections.[70] According to his radio broadcast: 'Politics is the art of the possible. Universal suffrage is now within reach. Hong Kong does not have to stand still. Constitutional reform should move forward, whatever the pace.'[71]

Yet the politics was to prove insurmountable. The 2014 Hong Kong protests in response to the NPCSC's Decision on a restricted pool of nominees put

---

[68] The Decision of the Standing Committee of the National People's Congress on Issues Relating to the Methods for Selecting the Chief Executive of the Hong Kong Special Administrative Region and for Forming the Legislative Council of the Hong Kong Special Administrative Region in the Year 2012 and on Issues Relating to Universal Suffrage, 29 December 2007.

[69] Albert Chen, 'A New Era in Hong Kong's Constitutional History' (2008) 38 *H.K.L.J.* 1, 6.

[70] 'Letter to Hong Kong' by the Chief Executive, Mr C. Y. Leung, broadcast on Radio Television Hong Kong, Press Release, HKSAR Government, 14 September 2014; see further, Chan and Lim, *Law of the Hong Kong Constitution, op. cit.*, 1040.

[71] Press Release, 14 September 2014, above.

paid to the Chief Executive's proposal. At the present time the democratic reform process has come to a complete standstill.

VII THE SILENT DECLARATION

A fundamental issue concerns the essentially domestic nature of the democratic reform process. The Joint Declaration as we have seen has little to say beyond the stipulation that the legislature shall 'be constituted by elections'. It says nothing at all about electing the Chief Executive. The UN Human Rights Committee in exercising its surveillance function under the ICCPR does not agree and has taken a consistent view that once democratic elections are established the right to universal suffrage will have been triggered notwithstanding the original UK reservation to article 25(b) of the ICCPR. That view has been questioned for in effect supplying a disincentive to move towards establishing an elected legislature. Whether that body has the power to pronounce upon and, in effect, to dismiss a party's treaty reservation has also been questioned by the United States and the United Kingdom.[72] Perhaps most importantly, no such right is mentioned in the Joint Declaration itself.

As for the Chinese and British positions, it would appear that the latter is holding China to the promise of democratic reform. Still, that promise can only be what is found in the Basic Law but as such the Basic Law grants the power to Beijing to interpret what its terms mean. If it were argued instead that the Basic Law's promise is also a promise to the United Kingdom then that is what the Sino-British Joint Declaration was for, not the Basic Law. The argument is untenable. The Basic Law is a piece of Chinese legislation and the idea that it is subject to anyone else's interpretation, or that its interpretation is not solely a domestic matter, is unsustainable without evidence of some treaty agreement to that effect. That is the only possible issue today with the phrase a 'legislature ... constituted by elections' in the Joint Declaration.[73] As for the Chief Executive, she or he 'shall be selected by election or through consultations held locally'.[74] The Joint Declaration states clearly that having an election is only one option.

---

[72] Observations of the United States of America and of the United Kingdom on General Comment No 24, GAOR, UN Doc A/50/40, Annex VI (1995); (1995) 16 *Hum. Rts. L. J.* 422, 424. The International Law Commission has taken the position, however, that treaty monitoring bodies possess the power to comment at least, and to make recommendations, in this regard. See Report of the ILC on the Work of its 49th Session (1997), GAOR, 52nd Sess., Supp No. 10 (A/52/10) paras. 5, 6 and 8.
[73] Article I, Annex I.
[74] Basic Law, art. 45. This, as we have seen, mirrors the language of Art. I of the Joint Declaration.

All this brings us to the period in the run-up to the 2017 elections, and the ensuing chapters in this book propose to discuss events after the 2014 protests up to 2020; beginning with controversy over the State Council's 2014 white paper. These were to be six long years during which everything was to change.

In the meantime, however, democratic reform remains a potent issue. In January 2021, following a mass walkout by the pan-democrats in protest over the latest disqualifications of November 2020,[75] over fifty people were arrested over a plan to take control of the legislature with the apparent principal aim of removing the Chief Executive by defeating the Government's budget.[76] On its face the intention appears only to mount a possible no-confidence vote. For their part, the Hong Kong authorities commenced investigations into what they consider to be a broader plan to paralyse and ultimately to topple the Hong Kong Government. The UK Secretary of State denounced this action, again as a treaty breach. However draconian to the liberal sensibility, and to the alliance of Western democracies which the UK sought to rally behind the cause, it is after all a British bilateral treaty. Is it a treaty breach? Even accepting a right to vote and to political participation,[77] are these international treaty rights? These are salient questions if the treaty is to have anything to do with the matter.

Subversion poses its own issues. Imagine a plan to remove the colonial Governor. Could that have been sedition at common law?[78] Simply mounting

---

[75] There had been earlier disqualifications. One source of additional controversy was the NPCSC which, wielding its plenary authority to interpret the Basic Law, had issued an interpretation of article 104 of the Basic Law while the matter of disqualification of candidatures was still before the Hong Kong courts. Art. 104 concerns the oath-taking requirement for legislators. The NPCSC had interpreted the oath taking requirement to require compliance 'with the legal requirements in respect of … form and content. An oath taker must take the oath sincerely and solemnly, and must accurately, completely and solemnly read out the oath prescribed by law' and that '[a]n oath taker is disqualified forthwith from assuming the public office specified in the Article if he or she declines to take the oath. An oath taker who intentionally reads out words which do not accord with the wording of the oath prescribed by law, or takes the oath in a manner which is not sincere or not solemn, shall be treated as declining to take the oath. The oath so taken is invalid and the oath taker is disqualified forthwith from assuming the public office specified in the Article.' See 'Interpretation of Article 104 of the Basic Law of the Hong Kong Special Administrative Region of the People's Republic of China by the Standing Committee of the National People's Congress', adopted by the Standing Committee of the Twelfth National People's Congress at its Twenty-fourth Session on 7 November 2016).

[76] Basic Law, art. 52.

[77] Chan and Lim, *Law of the Hong Kong Constitution*, op. cit., chapter 29.

[78] 'Subversion' being a separate offence introduced by the 2020 National Security Law, on which see further Chapter 10 of this book. The latest offence of subversion is though not unknown rarely known at common law. For the offence of sedition in Hong Kong, see ss. 9, 10 of the Crimes Ordinance (Cap. 200) in Hong Kong. It has a long common law history, finding its

a no-confidence vote cannot of course be considered so under a Westminster model of parliamentary government.[79] The Hong Kong authorities, for their part, claim that there is more than that. In any case a Westminster system of parliamentary government is not what the Sino-British Joint Declaration, and subsequently the Basic Law, have provided for.[80] Rather, what we have had is an executive-led colonial model and thereafter a vague promise in the Basic Law that there will be continued democratic improvements.

way too into Hong Kong's pre-handover laws. For the sixteenth-century roots of sedition at common law, see R. B. Manning, 'The Origins of the Doctrine of Sedition' (1980) 12 *Albion* 99. For the history of the offence of sedition in colonial Hong Kong, see Bob Allcock, 'National Security Law in a Common Law Framework', Speech, Basic Law, Institute, 2002 and Albert H. Y. Chen who discusses the unsuccessful attempt in 1997 to restrict its scope in the Crime Ordinance. See also the non-binding 'Johannesburg' Principles on National Security, Freedom of Expression and Access to Information, which requires seditious speech and expression to be linked to the incitement of imminent violence; 'Treason, Secession, Subversion, Sedition And Proscribed Organizations: Submission to LegCo on the Consultation Document', L.C. Paper No. CB(2)413/02-03(01).

[79] Nor would holding an unofficial primary election, which the latest miscreants did hold, necessarily amount to a crime; see 'Holding primaries can't be illegal, says Ronny Tong', *R.T. H.K.*, 6 January 2021.

[80] The issue is linked to a suggestion of a separation of powers involving, it is also suggested, the Chief Executive's broad 'accountability' to LegCo. There is nothing in the Basic Law which provides for any such broad accountability. What there is the budget clause in art. 52(3) of the Basic Law under which if the Government's budget or any other important bill is twice rejected following LegCo's dissolution then the Chief Executive must resign and more widely art. 64 which states that in addition to abiding by the law and obtaining approval for expenditure, the Government of the Hong Kong SAR 'shall present regular policy addresses to the Council' and that 'it shall answer questions raised by members of the Council'. Whether one might choose to call that 'accountability' does not a Westminster system make. Declassified records show the UK's awareness that the PRC's draft of the Basic Law implements the previous executive-led system. During the drafting of the Basic Law, the UK had proposed, following a legal opinion by Sir William Wade (H.W.R. Wade) and Sir Zelman Cowen, for which see TNA, FCO 40/2643, D.H. Anderson to E.S. Wilshurst, 8 November 1989, attaching a memorandum dated the same day from Paul Fifoot, that what is now art. 64 should consist instead of a 'shorter and more comprehensive formulation': 'The Government of the Hong Kong Special Administrative Region shall abide by the law and shall be accountable to the Legislative Council of the Region for matters which the Hong Kong Special Administrative Region administers on its own in accordance with this Law.' See TNA, FCO 40/2643, Paul Fifoot to Shao Tianren, 9 November 1989. This was in response to the PRC's draft which stated that 'accountability' shall be limited to four matters – implementing laws, presenting reports of its work, answering questions and obtaining approval for expenditure. The UK's formulation was not adopted by the PRC. What we have now is art. 64 of the Basic Law which after stating, as it did in the original PRC draft, the Government of the Hong Kong Special Administrative Region's 'accountability' to LegCo, goes on to insert a colon which is then followed by the four matters mentioned strictly. The present Government for its part has taken its own position, on which see Teresa Cheng SC, 'An Executive-led System, with the Executive, Legislature and Judiciary Performing Constitutionally Designated Roles', *S.C.M.P.*, 9 September 2020.

There is a wider aspect. Some attempt had been made in the 1990s to steer the international law of self-determination, which grew out of the twentieth-century UN decolonisation era,[81] towards support for a right to democracy following the end of the Cold War.[82] This was in part encouraged by a push for third generation human rights, the rights of groups and peoples,[83] and in part also by a renewed interest amongst some in the community of international lawyers in self-determination following the breakup of the former Socialist Federal Republic of Yugoslavia. The UK appears to have chosen to emphasise civil rights, not least the freedoms of speech and of assembly, rather than a right under any law to democratic governance.[84] In any event, Hong Kong has become one of the latest arenas in which the co-optation of the global human rights movement towards diplomatic and geostrategic ends has been manifest.[85] It has the UK and the PRC at odds with each other geostrategically against an even broader backdrop of an increasingly rivalrous Sino-US international relationship. The issue of democratic reform is caught up in a new and evolving global environment, and in that regard foreign policy, defence and national security considerations have entered, however unwelcome that may be, into the mix.[86] The UK's reaction to the 2021 mass arrests ought to be viewed too in that light. The Foreign Secretary, Mr Raab's statement reads, in part: 'The mass arrest of politicians and activists in Hong Kong is a grievous attack on Hong Kong's rights and freedoms as

---

[81] See A. Rigo Sureda, *The Evolution of the Right to Self-determination – A Study of United Nations Practice* (Leiden: Sijthoff, 1973); Michla Pomerance, *Self-determination in Law and Practice – The New Doctrine in the United Nations* (The Hague: Nijhoff, 1982); John Dugard, *Recognition and the United Nations* (Cambridge: Grotius, 1987).

[82] See Thomas M. Franck, 'The Emerging Right to Democratic Governance' (1992) 86 *A.J.I.L.* 46; James Crawford, 'Democracy and International Law' (1993) 64 *B.Y. B. I. L.*113. For a nuanced contemporary study, warning also against 'one size fits all' views about democratic systems, see Professor Hilary Charlesworth's 'International Legal Encounters with Democracy' (2017) 8 *Global Policy* 34.

[83] James Crawford (ed.), *The Rights of Peoples* (Oxford: Clarendon, 1988); Antonio Cassese, *Self-determination of Peoples – A Legal Appraisal* (Cambridge: Grotius and Cambridge University Press, 1995), 302.

[84] See e,g., UKFCO, The Six-Monthly Report on Hong Kong, 1 January to 30 June 2020, 23 November 2020, 14–15 (reproducing Raab's Parliamentary statement, citing paragraph 3(3), (5) and (11) of the Joint Declaration.

[85] See e.g. David W. Kennedy, 'The International Human Rights Regime: Still Part of the Problem?', in Rob Dickinson, Elena Katselli, Colin Murray, Ole W. Pedersen (eds.), *Examining Critical Perspective on Human Rights* (Cambridge: Cambridge University Press, 2012), 19.

[86] See Chapters 10 and 11 of this book.

VII *The Silent Declaration*   171

protected under the Joint Declaration.'[87] The Spokesperson in the PRC's London Embassy has replied in the following terms:

> Subversion of state power is a crime that no country would tolerate. China upholds the rule of law. Hong Kong is a society under the rule of law. We firmly support the Hong Kong police in taking the relevant actions in accordance with law. The statement of the UK side contains groundless accusations against China, shows no respect for facts and blatantly interferes in the affairs of Hong Kong SAR. The Chinese side expresses its grave concern and strong opposition.[88]

He went on to add that:

> The Chinese Government remains unwavering in its determination to safeguard national sovereignty, security and development interests, fully and accurately implement 'One Country, Two Systems', and oppose any external interference in Hong Kong affairs. Attempts to interfere or mount pressure will not succeed. The Chinese side urges the UK side to recognize the fact that Hong Kong is now part of China, view the National Security Law and the lawful enforcement by Hong Kong police in an objective and fair manner, right its wrongs immediately and stop taking the Sino-British Joint Declaration as an excuse to interfere in the affairs of Hong Kong SAR, which are China's internal affairs.[89]

The plan to remove the Chief Executive of Hong Kong and thereby trigger a reaction by Beijing which ultimately causes an adverse international reaction, albeit by leveraging on a right to vote and a right to political participation, and also the rights to free speech and association, has an additional feature in the local Hong Kong context. It could have been to force democratic reform. However, its stated aim at least by its author was to provoke Beijing into a series of actions in the hope that it would lead in the end to international sanctions against the Chinese Government.[90] The matter is now before the courts and no more can be said.

---

[87] 'Hong Kong Pro-democracy Arrests: Foreign Secretary statement'; UK FCO Press Release, 6 January 2021.
[88] 'Embassy Spokesperson's Remarks on the Wrong Remarks by the UK Secretary of State for Foreign, Commonwealth and Development Affairs', Embassy of the People's Republic of China in the United Kingdom of Great Britain and Northern Ireland, Press and Media Service, 7 January 2022.
[89] *Ibid.*
[90] ' Explainer: What Is Benny Tai's "10 Steps to Burn with Us?"', *The Standard* (Hong Kong), 6 January 2021. This newspaper article refers to the author of that strategy who together with some fifty others were arrested in 2021.

Does the Sino-British Joint Declaration provide for democratic political rights in Hong Kong, by itself or through the operation of the ICCPR, that are broad enough to justify the latest statement by the UK Secretary of State that the mass arrests of those who participated in 'Burn with Us' involve a treaty breach? There is too little in the Joint Declaration itself, which the UK had negotiated with the PRC.[91] Mr Raab's January 2021 statement could also be premised, simply, upon the UK's view that by merely having the National Security Law that amounts to a treaty breach. If so that would be a constraint which cannot be said to have been envisaged by the Joint Declaration as it is written. Be that all as it may, these latest events bode ill for democratic reform in Hong Kong, be it in changing the current method of electing the Chief Executive, or for reform of the Hong Kong legislature in turning it ultimately into a fully and freely elected chamber on the basis of universal equal suffrage.

---

[91] See Chapter 10 of this book, which discusses the 2020 National Security Law.

PART III

2014–2021

Introduction to Part III

Beginning in 2014 there was a series of controversies before violent protests erupted in connection with the Hong Kong Government's 2019 Extradition Bill, which in turn led to the National Security Law of 2020. Often discrete events do not suggest a larger catastrophe until it is too late. The controversy over the State Council's 2014 white paper, even the 'Occupy' Protests of that year, the strange 'missing booksellers' controversy in late 2015 and the 2017 West Kowloon Terminus issue each did not in themselves suggest the sweeping legislative changes that would take place by 2020. The legislative bombshell was a response to the violence of 2019 amidst also official allegations of foreign interference. Inevitably, the Joint Declaration was to feature in the UK's response. There had been a prior British allegation of a 'serious' treaty breach in February 2016 with respect to the 'missing booksellers' incident, where the then Secretary of State claimed reliance on publicly undisclosed contemporaneous sources of information. It was an early illustration of the diplomatic and legal difficulties surrounding 'dual nationality'. In 2020, there were to be more dramatic allegations of a 'clear and serious' treaty breach, and a dramatic Sino-British fallout in respect of British Nationals (Overseas) passports.

There is also liberal international opinion, about the infringement of liberal rights. First, treaty-based liberal values, including those of free speech and association, had not been incorporated into Hong Kong law by or before the Joint Declaration. As was seen in Part II, liberal rights were to be stipulated in Chinese law, written by the Chinese side without the UK's participation. Second, this could not have been in ignorance of long-standing international diplomatic disagreements, and the fact that China has not ratified the International Covenant on Civil and Political Rights, indeed all this was done by way of the Joint Declaration despite and because of these known facts. One need not be an educated Sinophile, however, to see that treating a treaty for the resumption of Chinese sovereignty as one that might also allow

British treaty intervention in the name of liberal democratic rights would be extremely delicate. Third, the 2020 National Security law states expressly the preservation of individual rights according to international standards, using a very precise form of words found in Annex I of the Joint Declaration and the Basic Law. That Western democracies have joined in a chorus of criticism about the erosion of rights is unsurprising but it is important to understand that all this is distinct from the treaty issue. In contrast, sanctions and the move by the United States to require Hong Kong products to be labelled 'Made in China' touch upon Hong Kong's autonomy as an international financial and trading hub.

There are broader geopolitical considerations involved. China's homogeneity does not extend to regions in its periphery and these have, unsurprisingly, become the focus of intense human rights diplomacy in conditions now virtually indistinguishable from the Cold War. That aspect cannot be ignored in any explanation of the descent into unilateral sanctions, retorsion and countermeasures following passage of the 2020 law.

8

Patriotism, Comprehensive Jurisdiction, Formal Allegiance: 2014–2017

I A RAPID SEQUENCE OF EVENTS

Something of an introduction may be helpful. There was, first of all, the PRC State Council's 2014 white paper, which is said to have contributed in turn to the 2014 protests,[1] then there was the peculiar 'missing booksellers' affair in late 2015, and after that the extension of Mainland Chinese Law, in 2017, to the Kowloon terminus of a newly constructed rail link.[2] In addition, there was the 'article 22' issue and it may on reflection be best to begin with that.

Article 22 of the Basic Law states that: 'No department of the Central People's Government and no province, autonomous region, or municipality directly under the Central Government may interfere in the affairs which the Hong Kong Special Administrative Region administers on its own in accordance with this Law.' That provision was brought into acute public focus in April 2020. The Liaison Office and the Hong Kong and Macao Office had criticised the HKSAR's Legislative Council (LegCo) for its dysfunctionality.[3] LegCo was dysfunctional but that was not the point, which concerned instead allegations of an 'interference' with Hong Kong's affairs. That summer attention on article 22, now bordering upon fixation in the press, was again triggered, this time in connection with the Central People's Government's Office for Safeguarding National Security in the Hong Kong SAR, a newly established entity under the

---

[1] 'The Practice of the 'One Country, Two Systems' Policy in the Hong Kong Special Administrative Region, white paper, State Council of the PRC, 10 June 2014, hereafter cited as the '2014 white paper', http://english.www.gov.cn/archive/white_paper/2014/08/23/content_281474982986578.htm (last accessed 6 April 2021).
[2] This is a part of an initiative to integrate Hong Kong economically with the economy of Southern China, known as the Guangzhou–Shenzhen–Hong Kong Express Rail Link ('Guangshengang XRL', or simply 'the XRL', for short).
[3] See e.g. Johannes Chan, 'A Strained Interpretation of Article 22 of the Basic Law' (2020) 50 H.K. L.J. 7.

2020 National Security Law.[4] By then it had become an entirely different matter, a national security matter, but even before the passage of the 2020 National Security Law article 22 had, together with the 2014 white paper, come to embody a sense of Hong Kong's autonomy being eroded as a special administrative region. Accompanying that, however, was a risk of overstating the importance of that provision in construing 'no department of the Central People's Government' to mean that Hong Kong is off-limits to the Central Government itself rather than any 'department' of it.

In fact all this was only the culmination of years of increased popular anxiety. A key issue which the State Council's 2014 white paper had highlighted six years before was that 'one country, two systems' ought to be considered to be a work in progress:

> A summary of the policy's [i.e. one country, two system's] implementation in the HKSAR, and a comprehensive and correct understanding and implementation of the policy will prove useful for safeguarding China's sovereignty, security and development interests, for maintaining long-term prosperity and stability in Hong Kong, and for further promoting the 'one country, two systems' practice along the correct track of development.[5]

It seemed, however, to have had the opposite effect. The 'Occupy' protests in Hong Kong, an expression of defiance against the NPCSC's decision to curtail the number of candidates who may be elected to the position of Chief Executive,[6] showed that as early as 2014 contesting visions of 'one country, two systems' had already come to a head.

At the same time, what occurred in 2014 would have only confirmed the Chinese sovereign authorities' and Mainland commentators' view that 'one country, two systems' had somehow over time become widely misunderstood. The 2014 protests were aimed at the NPCSC's decision that the candidates who may stand for election to the post of Chief Executive ought to be limited to two or three persons who would first have to be nominated by what currently is the body of 1.200 persons entrusted to elect the Chief Executive. That 'Election Committee' as it is styled presently would become instead a new 'Nomination Committee'. This at any rate was the NPCSC's decision on reforming the method for the election of Hong Kong's Chief Executive. Unlike various proposals for reform which previously had been

---

[4] Chapter 10 of this book.
[5] Foreword, 2014 white paper, *op. cit.*
[6] See the previous chapter of this book.

I A Rapid Sequence of Events

rejected,[7] this however was no mere proposal but an authoritative decision. In the words of the 2014 white paper:

> The NPC Standing Committee has the power of interpretation regarding the Basic Law of the HKSAR, the power of decision on revising the selection methods of the chief executive and the Legislative Council of the HKSAR, the power of supervision over the laws formulated by the legislative organs of the HKSAR, the power of decision on the HKSAR entering a state of emergency, and the power of making new authorization [*sic.*] for the HKSAR.[8]

As has already been mentioned in the previous chapter, this would seem unobjectionable under the Basic Law, at least on its face. Article 45 of which states that: 'The ultimate aim is the selection of the Chief Executive by universal suffrage upon nomination by a broadly representative nominating committee in accordance with democratic procedures.' There is nothing in the Joint Declaration which would require an elected Chief Executive at all, referring only to a Chief Executive who will be selected through election or 'consultation'.[9] That the Election Committee or Nomination Committee would reflect Beijing having a substantive influence is likewise not a legal objection, either under the Basic Law or indeed the Joint Declaration.

Subsequently, in 2015, there was the dramatic and disturbing allegation that certain persons may have been 'abducted' by Mainland authorities in violation of Hong Kong's autonomy. In these circumstances, in midst of such a rapid sequence of events, extending Mainland laws albeit only to the 'Mainland side' of the joint immigration control point at the Kowloon terminus of the newly constructed XRL in 2017 was bound to trigger further consternation. The whole terminus was located within the territory of Hong Kong, specifically in Kowloon. An interesting question which emerged was this. Even accepting that Mainland laws could be applied in Hong Kong, which no doubt they can within the limits of the Basic Law, can they however be applied in the same manner as on the Mainland in light of Hong Kong's own guarantee of fundamental rights? The principled answer is 'no' for Hong Kong rights will still need to be upheld within the territory of the Hong Kong SAR.

All these events formed in turn a prelude to the controversy in 2019 over the Hong Kong Government's proposed bill which would have allowed extradition worldwide, including to the Chinese Mainland.[10] The violent protests

---

[7] See the previous chapter.
[8] 2014 white paper, *op. cit.*, Pt. II.
[9] Joint Declaration, art. 1.
[10] Chapter 9 of this book.

which ensued became a watershed moment for the post-handover arrangements, leading directly to the National Security Law of 2020. Nearly halfway through the fifty years of autonomy assured under the Sino-British Joint Declaration the Hong Kong SAR enters now a new phase.

II OVERALL JURISDICTION AND JUDICIAL PATRIOTISM

Unsurprisingly, the Sino-British Joint Declaration is chiefly of historical interest only in the 2014 white paper.[11] Following a recital of the return of Hong Kong and the establishment of the Hong Kong SAR under 'one country, two systems' it goes on to state that:

> The system of the special administrative region, as prescribed in the Constitution of the People's Republic of China and the Basic Law of the HKSAR, is a special administrative system developed by the state for certain regions. Under this system, the central government exercises overall jurisdiction over the HKSAR, including the powers directly exercised by the central government, and the powers delegated to the HKSAR by the central government to enable it to exercise a high degree of autonomy in accordance with the law. The central government has the power of oversight over the exercise of a high degree of autonomy in the HKSAR.[12]

The emphasis is on the fact that autonomy is but a creature of delegation from the central authority. Controversy triggered by the white paper concentrated narrowly upon this assertion that the Central People's Government exercises 'overall jurisdiction' over Hong Kong, and what was presumed to be a declaration that Hong Kong's judges were only 'administrators' – an unfortunate translation from the Chinese original according to Andrew Li, the former Chief Justice, and Professor Shigong Jiang whose views I will go on to discuss below – and that therefore they too should be 'patriotic'. To the casual observer these are anodyne statements while to others they will not be at

---

[11] 'Deng Xiaoping made clear [to Margaret Thatcher] the Chinese government's position on the question of Hong Kong, pointing out that sovereignty was not a matter for discussion and that China would take back Hong Kong in 1997. It was under this premise that China and Britain would negotiate ... [The] Joint Declaration [confirmed] that the government of the PRC would resume its exercise of sovereignty over Hong Kong with effect from July 1, 1997. The Chinese government also made clear in the Joint Declaration its basic policies regarding Hong Kong based on the "12 Principles". The signing of the Sino-British Joint Declaration marked the entry of Hong Kong into a 13-year transition period before its return to China. During this period, the Chinese government unswervingly followed the "one country, two systems" policy ... and resolutely held off interference to promote the preparation work for Hong Kong's return'; 2014 white paper, *op. cit.*, Pt. I.
[12] *Ibid.*, Pt. II.

all, and it might also have been a reflection of the nervous state of affairs that they were to cause the controversy which they did. In any event, the incident prompted Andrew Li to say that:

> what is of great concern is the requirement in the white paper that judges should be patriotic. There is no universal definition of patriotism ... A person may be regarded as patriotic by some but not by others ... Under the principle of judicial independence, judges should not be pro or anti anyone or anything. They should be fair and impartial. Judges have no master, political or otherwise.[13]

That last sentence, put starkly, went to the heart of public disquiet. Li's piece in the press had also come in the wake of a suggestion that the Hong Kong Bar had been misdirected in its criticisms.[14]

Perhaps nowhere is the difference between the common law and Chinese socialist legality better illustrated than by the fact that no disloyalty is attributed to Her Majesty's judges when limiting the prerogative powers in the exercise of their judicial function. Under socialist legality the matter is viewed in an entirely different light. There is no distinction to be drawn, such as under the common law, between pronouncing upon the legality of a request by the Prime Minister for Parliament to be prorogued, and a pronouncement made in the exercise of the Monarch's sole prerogative.[15] Mr Li's statement verges however upon the suggestion that only a 'disloyal' judge will avoid the charge of partiality, and this strikes a discordant note perhaps even to the common law ear.

Still, loyalty or patriotism does not come into it precisely because that can safely and not inconsistently be assumed on the part of the common law judge, and that in essence was the view taken by Professor Jiang Shigong of Peking University who had served previously in the liaison office in Hong Kong. He is also thought to have been involved in drafting the white paper and we will return to that. No doubt, we are in an age of public criticism of judges, even in

---

[13] Andrew Li, 'Under Rule of Law, an Independent Judiciary Answers to No Political Masters', Opinion, S.C.M.P. (Hong Kong), 15 August 2014; see further Peter So, 'Judges Don't Need to Be Patriots, Says Former Top Judge Andrew Li', S.C.M.P. (Hong Kong), 15 August 2014.
[14] See 'White Paper on the Practice of "One Country, Two Systems" Policy in the Hong Kong Special Administrative Region', Response of the Hong Kong Bar Association, 11 June 2014. For criticism by Professor Shigong Jiang, see 'Professor Qiang Shigong Exercises "Patriotic Powers" to Defend the System, Using Unorthodox Arguments to Counter the Bar Association', 19 June 2014, published in Chinese on the online news site www.post852.com (on file), hereafter 'Shigong Jiang's Views'.
[15] R (on the application of Miller) v. The Prime Minister [2019] UKSC 41, hereinafter 'Miller (No. 2)'.

England, even from official quarters. In Hong Kong there is as yet no hint of any requirement of 'patriotism' leading as such to the erosion of judicial independence or direction being given to judges by political decision-makers, but Mr Li's successor, Geoffrey Ma CJ – who was himself to retire in January 2021 – was compelled to respond to a spate of public criticism of Hong Kong's judges.[16] A key issue is that any attack on the judges goes beyond even robust criticism of court judgments and instead to the motivations of individual judges. There the common law draws the line.[17] But be that all as it may it was however the issue of Beijing's 'overall jurisdiction' which was to foretell the future course of events.

III SOVEREIGNTY, DELEGATED AUTHORITY, TREATY

Hong Kong has autonomy and jurisdiction over only particular affairs as laid out originally in the Sino-British Joint Declaration. This is a delegated authority – what else could it be but delegated and subordinate? Any other view and Chinese sovereignty would be lost. For example, if it were suggested that the PRC were somehow accountable through a treaty to the UK in the way that it manages Hong Kong. This is different from saying that treaty obligations impose an impermissible constraint upon sovereignty. Treaties impose various forms of constraint, international law imposes various constraints, but accountability to any other for the management of one's own territory is, in Chinese eyes, at least inconsistent with the Joint Declaration whose principal purpose was to register the UK's acceptance of the resumption of Chinese sovereignty.

Equally, suggestions that in some respects Hong Kong would possess characteristics that approximate to Statehood[18] was never a position which could in the Chinese view sit well with Chinese sovereignty either. Sovereignty was during the negotiations considered to be wholly indivisible. Who decides the scope of those delegated powers was what the UK had sought to address and pin down in treaty form. But here two different designs which were entirely at odds continue to influence how things are viewed today.

---

[16] Chris Lau et al., 'Judicial Reforms Should Not Be Based on Unhappiness over Court Rulings, Hong Kong's Retiring Top Judge Warns in Speech Reflecting on Decade-long Tenure', S.C. M.P. (Hong Kong), 5 January 2021.

[17] 'With the judgements we can be robustly critical. With the motives, we cannot', Hansard, vol. 664, 25 September 2019, Hon. Geoffrey Cox QC, addressing Parliament in the aftermath of Miller (No. 2), *op. cit.*

[18] Roda Mushkat, *One Country, Two International Legal Personalities: The Case of Hong Kong* (Hong Kong: Hong Kong University Press, 1997).

The first, discussed in the previous chapter, was the British 'colonial template' employed throughout Africa and Asia for initial self-governance as a prelude to independence from colonial rule. The second was Deng Xiaoping's 'one country, two systems' formula which to British ears was perhaps taken to mean self-governance without the final step of independence but self-governance nonetheless. And with it an elected, responsible government. From the Chinese viewpoint it is simply the age-old problem of administering the frontiers of the Chinese Empire. According to Professor Jiang Shigong, the PRC's 'twelve points' during the negotiations which led to the Joint Declaration, attributed to Deng Xiaoping, may be traced to Mao's approach to the governance of China's frontier regions. The twelve points rather than being unique, as Thatcher was to describe 'one country, two systems', reflected a well-settled approach to what China considered to be the difficulties of administering China's frontier lands and their respective populations. In this regard, we should view the twelve points as in connection with the 'Seventeen-Article Agreement' regarding Tibet,[19] and also the PRC's approach to Taiwan, rather than with Britain's past decolonisation policies. Indeed, since the Joint Declaration was to be implemented through the Basic Law – PRC legislation – one could say that the Chinese view is the more salient. What the UK might think of all this is quite another matter.

Yet therein lies the rub and it goes some way towards explaining the white paper's reference to Beijing's 'overall jurisdiction' and the public controversy which ensued in Hong Kong during the summer of 2014. Insofar as the white paper is concerned, this is a matter which concerns China's administration of its frontiers. The controversy had centred, as has been mentioned, on the perception that judges were being treated as a part of the administration, indistinguishable – according to that perception – from the executive branch, and that 'patriotism' or loyalty was to be expected from all such 'administrators', all of them, judges and civil servants alike. Yet, according to Jiang such criticism is misplaced if the suggestion is that – as it now is heard in so many quarters – it aims to undermine judicial independence. Jiang argues, at least as this author understands it, that all that is meant is allegiance in the manner that say a Queen's Counsel with republican sympathies (and this in fact is his example) would nonetheless be expected to be 'loyal' and demonstrate allegiance to the Monarch. By 'the Monarch' here one means a symbol of State.[20]

---

[19] Shigong Jiang, *China's Hong Kong* (Singapore: Springer, 2017), 87 *et seq.*
[20] There is no conception of 'the State' in common law thought, in the manner that there is no Kelsenian general theory of law and State. There is 'the Crown'. See further e.g. Cheryl Saunders, 'The Concept of the Crown' (2015) 38 *Melbourne L.R.* 873.

In other words, the point in the white paper concerns allegiance rather than judicial independence.[21]

IV CROWN AND STATE, ALLEGIANCE AND PATRIOTISM

Despite incredulity at the time, Mr Justice Stone (as he then was) in a well-known post-handover case on Crown Immunity in Hong Kong was, from a common law standpoint, entirely precise in having referred in His Lordship's judgment to 'the Chinese Crown'.[22] The 2014 controversy was perfectly illustrative of slippage in a mis-translation of the concept of 'the Crown' (in lieu of 'the State') where the term 'the Crown' always has at common law slipped between a reference to the Monarch in her public or personal capacity and, according to Lord Templeman, to the government of the day.[23] Also, it should be added, to Ministers and to parts of the administration.[24] Steeped in common law thought, it is not wholly surprising that in the Hong Kong Bar's view the treatment in the English version of the white paper of the broader question of allegiance to the Chinese Crown, in a manner of speaking, was to become conflated with the subordination of the judiciary to the executive authorities. The silent parade which ensued was no laughing matter: 'A record number of lawyers took to the streets yesterday to protest against Beijing's white paper that they say jeopardises judicial independence, a value that sets Hong Kong apart from the rest of the country.'[25] Reuters reported it in the following terms:

> Beijing raised alarm when it released a white paper this month, spelling out its interpretation of the one country, two systems model, in which it said being patriotic and "loving the country" is a basic requirement for the city's administrators, including lawyers.
>
> The Hong Kong government said in a statement the rule of law was the cornerstone upon which Hong Kong built its success, adding the white paper was not intended to interfere with that.[26]

---

[21] Shigong Jiang's Views, *op. cit.*
[22] *The Hua Tian Long* (No. 2) [2010] 3 H.K.L.R.D. 611.
[23] *M v. Home Office* [1994] 1 A.C. 377, 395; *Town Investments Ltd v. Department of the Environment* [1978] A.C. 359, 400.
[24] Saunders, *op. cit.*, 875, citing the New Zealand scholar Professor Janet McLean, in Janet McLean, *Searching for the State in British Legal Thought* (Cambridge: Cambridge University Press, 2012), 140–8.
[25] Stuart Lau *et al.*, 'Hong Kong Lawyers March to Defend Judiciary in Wake of Beijing's White Paper', *S.C.M.P.* (Hong Kong), 27 June 2014.
[26] Adam Rose and Nikki Sun, 'Hong Kong Lawyers March in Protest against Perceived China Meddling', *Reuters*, 27 June 2014.

Few probably paid attention to the Government's last statement above but by 2021 the question of allegiance had come to a head. Does not a Hong Konger owe allegiance to China as sovereign? During the Sino-British treaty negotiations the UK accepted that UK nationals in the civil service would owe their allegiance to the special administrative region,[27] but by 2021 there were those who would hold elected office declining to take an oath of allegiance which itself had become controversial.

An Exchange of Memoranda between the UK and the PRC had accompanied the Joint Declaration. That was to the effect that while three million or so Hong Kongers could have BN(O) passports, they would not be treated as passports strictly by China but as 'travel documents' instead except for the use of such documents for entry into China. The British Memorandum reads, in part:

> All persons who on 30 June 1997 are, by virtue of a connection with Hong Kong, British Dependent Territories Citizens (BDTCs) under the law in force in the United Kingdom will cease to be BDTCs with effect from 1 July 1997, but will be eligible to retain an appropriate status which, without conferring the right of abode in the United Kingdom, will entitle them to continue to use passports issued by the Government of the United Kingdom.[28]

The PRC Memorandum in turn reads:

> The Government of the People's Republic of China has received the memorandum from the Government of the United Kingdom of Great Britain and Northern Ireland dated 19 December 1984.
>
> Under the Nationality Law of the People's Republic of China, all Hong Kong Chinese compatriots, whether they are holders of the 'British Dependent Territories Citizens' Passport' or not, are Chinese nationals.
>
> Taking account of the historical background of Hong Kong and its realities, the competent authorities of the Government of the People's Republic of China will, with effect from 1 July 1997, permit Chinese nationals in Hong Kong who were previously called 'British Dependent Territories Citizens' to use travel documents issued by the Government of the United Kingdom for the purpose of travelling to other states and regions.[29]

Following the passage of the 2020 National Security Law for Hong Kong the UK now offers a 'pathway toward UK citizenship', citing the PRC's violation of

---

[27] One might add 'of the PRC'.
[28] Beijing, 19 December 1984.
[29] Ibid.

the Joint Declaration. China in turn treats this as a breach, and has threatened countermeasures as a legitimate response under international law. As of 31 January 2021, the PRC no longer recognises BN(O) passports even for the limited purposes just stated. By February, the Hong Kong Government announced that the single nationality requirement under China's nationality law would be enforced stringently.[30] The question of national allegiance which first had emerged in 2014 comes now also to a head.

A final issue also needs mention in connection with the State Council's white paper. It involved the question of the application of the 1982 Constitution of the People's Republic of China. That the Basic Law for Hong Kong and its ultimate legal basis lie in the 1982 PRC Constitution are not points that are in any serious legal doubt. That fact ensures the Basic Law's application to the Mainland authorities themselves. Its 'direct' application to Hong Kong however is another matter. In this regard, what two of the principal Chinese Mainland scholars have pointed out is that the more precise question is which? Which articles of the 1982 PRC Constitution must, logically, apply directly to Hong Kong?[31] Wang Zhenmin, formerly of the Hong Kong Liaison Office and now returned to teaching at Tsinghua University, takes the following view:

> The provisions of the Constitution with regard to China's highest organs of state power, state leaders, the state's highest administrative organs and the state's highest military institutions, the provisions with regard to the national flag, the national emblem and the capital city as well as other provisions with regard to national sovereignty, foreign diplomacy and national defense – all unquestionably apply to the SARs or should be acknowledged and respected by the SARs.[32]

He goes on to add that: 'the socialist system and local institutions of state power and local administrative institutions, the state judicial and procuratorial organs – are not appropriate for the SARs and have been revised or replaced in the relevant provisions of the SARs' Basic Laws'.[33]

This is in line with the October 1989 telegram from Pamela Major in the UKFCO.[34] Shigong Jiang has also sought to explain some of the origins of the

---

[30] Tony Cheung and Jeffie Lam, 'Carrie Lam Confirms Hong Kong "Strictly Enforcing" Policy of Not Recognising Dual Nationality', S.C.M.P. (Hong Kong), 9 February 2021. We will return to this issue in the concluding chapter.
[31] Zhenmin Wang, *Relationship between the Chinese Central Authorities and Regional Governments of Hong Kong and Macao: A Legal Perspective* (Singapore: Springer, 2019), 96; Jiang, *China's Hong Kong*, op. cit., 142–3.
[32] Wang, op. cit., 96.
[33] Ibid.
[34] TNA, FCO 40/2643, FM FCO to Deskby 190100Z Hong Kong, Telno. 2125, October 1989.

issue. During the drafting of the Basic Law a clause had been proposed to address the relationship between the two; the PRC Constitution on the one hand, and the Basic Law for the Hong Kong SAR on the other. This in turn led to Annex III of the Basic Law wherein those Mainland laws which apply to Hong Kong will be stated, and the fact that the PRC Constitution was not included therein is, according to Jiang, the reason why it is supposed, inaccurately, that the 1982 Constitution has no application at all.[35]

V BOOKSELLERS

Turning from patriotism to formal allegiance, the 'missing booksellers' affair as it is known[36] had raised questions which in some senses recall the post-war prosecution of the famous Nazi propaganda broadcaster, William Joyce.[37] Joyce was an American citizen who had acquired a British passport by then stating, be it by deliberate misrepresentation or simple mistake, that he had been born a British subject. Pleading his alien status was his strongest defence to a charge of treason committed outside the realm for it would then need to be asked how an alien could be guilty of treason in these circumstances. However, since he had for long lived within the realm and acquired a valid British passport, that defence did not save him. Lord Jowitt LC, who wrote for the majority in the House of Lords, considered that the true question was not where treason can be committed but by whom.[38] Their Lordships held that acquiring a British passport, by whatever means, entitled Joyce to the Crown's protection and thus having sought such protection he owed a reciprocal duty of allegiance. The majority of their Lordships considered that this duty of fidelity was owed for as long as the passport remained valid. However, Lord Porter dissented on the ground that it was for the jury to determine whether William Joyce had renounced British protection by that time, for, while it was assumed that he had entered Germany with it, the passport was never found, and Joyce himself claimed that by then he had decided to become a German citizen. The trial judge had instead directed the jury that the question of Joyce's continuing allegiance was an issue of law and because of that Lord

---

[35] Jiang, *China's Hong Kong*, op. cit., 142.
[36] The author acknowledges with gratitude both the *Law Quarterly Review* and Sweet & Maxwell for permission to re-use previously published material, see C. L. Lim, 'The Sino-British Treaty and the Hong Kong Booksellers Affair' (2016) 132 L.Q.R. 552–6. Revisions have been made to the following material for the purposes of the present book.
[37] *Joyce v. DPP* [1946] A.C. 347; [1946] 1 All E.R. 186.
[38] *Ibid.*, 357.

Porter would have allowed Joyce's appeal on the ground that the jury had been misdirected.[39]

A similar issue was to arise in 2016 in Hong Kong, under Chinese law, in respect of those Hong Kong Chinese residents whom China has for long considered 'Chinese Hong Kong compatriots'. In the 2016 booksellers affair, the police had received various reports during the previous year concerning an eventual total of five missing persons who apparently had disappeared in the period between October and December 2015. All five were connected to the same Hong Kong bookstore. Allegedly, three had disappeared while present on the Chinese mainland, one while in Thailand and, in the final case of Mr Lee Po, from Hong Kong itself. The whole affair received global press coverage amid ample public speculation that Mr Lee in particular had perhaps been unlawfully removed to the mainland by the Chinese authorities. Mr Lee denies this but his case culminated in the British Foreign Secretary's report to Parliament in February 2016 that, although 'the full facts of the case remain unclear', 'our current information indicates that Mr. Lee was removed to the mainland without any due process under HKSAR law'. Mr Hammond concluded that 'this constitutes a serious breach' of the Sino-British Joint Declaration.[40]

It was the first time the UK Government had publicly declared a treaty breach since the 1997 handover. The reader can imagine the public reaction at the time in Hong Kong. The proposition is straightforward – the Joint Declaration, containing the terms of China's commitments, is the very basis for a claim of 'British treaty rights' in Hong Kong until 2047.[41]

The Hong Kong bookstore itself was owned by a publishing company which apparently specialised in a thriving market for titillating, at times admittedly even blatantly fictional, works on the personal lives of China's political leaders. This is said without suggesting however the facts or true cause of the incident.[42] Be that as it may, things came to a head when Mr Lee Po, who holds a British passport, was alleged to have disappeared from Hong Kong on 30 December 2015, one week before Mr Hammond's visit to Beijing in early January 2016. China's Foreign Minister, Mr Wang Yi, responded to the press while speaking alongside Mr Hammond by stating that under both Chinese law and Hong Kong law Mr Lee was 'first and

---

[39] Ibid., 374–82.
[40] Secretary of State for Foreign and Commonwealth Affairs, Six Monthly Report on Hong Kong, July to December 2015, 11 February 2016, at 3.
[41] See further C. L. Lim, 'Britain's "Treaty Rights" in Hong Kong' (2015) 131 L.Q.R. 348.
[42] Common lawyers at least in England would, if this were the only cause, think of *Entick v. Carrington* (1765) 19 St. Tr. 1030. Colonial common law may have other examples.

foremost a Chinese citizen'.[43] The implication was that this matter, as with others in the past, should not trouble the UK. It recalls a more sweeping assertion by China just two years previously that the UK had no remaining rights left to press in respect of Hong Kong since all outstanding obligations had been honoured.[44]

However, the latest statement is more specific and it sits uneasily with any blanket denial of British treaty rights. It raises a real but thorny question, about the position of Sino-British dual nationals, whose existence the British and Chinese governments preferred not to admit until events in 2020/21 were to bring it to the fore.[45] That is the first aspect. There is however a second aspect which recalls the famous post-war case involving William Joyce. That case too had concerned penal authority over an 'alien' national in connection with a crime committed outside the territorial criminal jurisdiction of the claiming state.

Turning to the first, the aspect of dual nationality, the problem has partly to do with the Chinese view that Britain never was a legitimate sovereign power in Hong Kong. As such, it could never have possessed the authority to award British passports to the Hong Kong Chinese in that capacity. At the same time, Chinese law does not recognise dual nationality. Thus, during the Sino-British negotiations the fact that there were more than three million Hong Kong Chinese British Dependent Territories Citizens (BDTCs) under Britain's Nationality Act of 1981 had to be side-stepped. However, in order to preserve confidence in post-handover Hong Kong, they were to be granted the right to become British Nationals Overseas (BNOs) under the Hong Kong (British Nationality) Order of 1986. Others were granted the right to become British Overseas Citizens (BOCs), a new category for non-Chinese Hong Kong BDTCs instituted at the Hong Kong Indian community's behest. Since there could be no agreement between Britain and China on the question of nationality, the UK appended a memorandum to the 1984 Sino-British Joint Declaration, instituting the BNO scheme which entitles holders of British BN(O) passports to travel and to consular protection except for entry into and protection on the Chinese mainland.[46] At the same time, Beijing appended its

---

[43] Tom Phillips and Ilaria Maria Sala, 'Philip Hammond Presses China over UK Citizen Among Missing Booksellers', *Guardian* (London), 5 January 2016.
[44] On which, see also Lim, 'Britain's "Treaty Rights" in Hong Kong', *op. cit.*
[45] Chapter 11 of this book, on the National Security Law and its aftermath including retorsive measures and countermeasures in the strict sense taken by both the UK and PRC on the basis of allegations of breaches of the Sino-British Joint Declaration, and of the terms of a simultaneous Sino-British Exchange of Memoranda dated 19 December 1984.
[46] United Kingdom Memorandum, 19 December 1984, also reproduced in J. M. M. Chan and C. L. Lim (general eds.), *Law of the Hong Kong Constitution*, 1st ed. (Hong Kong: Sweet & Maxwell, 2011), at 993.

own separate memorandum declaring such BNOs to be Chinese nationals as of 1 July 1997 while still recognising British 'travel documents' (as opposed to 'passports') for third-country travel.[47] Neither memorandum forms a part of the main text and annexures of the Joint Declaration itself and this delicate compromise, of having Chinese nationality existing alongside BNO 'status', had worked until Lee Po's case.

That compromise leads us to the second, jurisdictional, dimension to the strange affair in 2016. Here the similarities with Joyce's case come into focus. In *Joyce v. DPP*, uncertainty too had surrounded William Joyce's British passport but, as the trial judge and the House of Lords had held, what mattered was that Joyce held a valid British passport in his own name at the time he committed the offence. He could therefore be charged with and convicted of treason. It did not matter that he was in fact an American citizen. As Lord Jowitt had put it, Joyce was 'claiming the continued protection of the Crown and thereby pledging the continuance of his fidelity'.[48] In Lee Po's case, China also claimed Mr Lee's allegiance, notwithstanding his 'British' nationality. Beijing's claim however was not founded apparently upon any act of Mr Lee in seeking Chinese protection, at least at the time, unlike in Joyce where William Joyce had applied for a British passport.[49] Rather that claim was supported by the Chinese Memorandum's statement that all Hong Kong Chinese compatriots are nationals of China.[50] The term 'Chinese compatriot' has at least a historical meaning. It is taken to refer to the Chinese overseas under the principle of *jus sanguinis*. Thus, 'Hong Kong Chinese compatriots' refer specifically to the 'Hong Kong overseas Chinese'. It is another way of saying that the Hong Kong Chinese have always been Chinese notwithstanding British rule. As in *Joyce*, the existence of a duty of allegiance is what truly matters. In Mr Lee's case, however, that allegiance exists not because of what he did but because of what he apparently had omitted to do, for he had chosen not to divest himself of Chinese nationality. The fact that Mr Lee holds a 'British passport' is considered by China to be an insufficient act of renunciation of his Chinese nationality. Presumably the reason would not be very different from the House of Lords' reason for holding that William Joyce's

---

[47] See J. M. M. Chan and C. L. Lim (general eds.), *Law of the Hong Kong Constitution*, 2nd ed. (Hong Kong, Sweet & Maxwell, 2015), 164–5 (Chapter 5, 'Nationality and Permanent Residence', by J. M. M. Chan); Yash Ghai, *Hong Kong's New Constitutional Order*, 2nd ed. (Hong Kong: Hong Kong University, 1999), at 157.
[48] *Joyce v. DPP*, *op. cit.*, 371.
[49] *Ibid.*, 369–71.
[50] Chinese Memorandum, 19 December 1984, second paragraph; reproduced in Chan and Lim, 1st ed., *op. cit.*, 994.

treason was insufficient to withdraw him from his allegiance to the UK.[51] Had Joyce sought British protection by using his passport, he would still have been entitled to it. Similarly, were Mr Lee to apply for a Hong Kong Chinese passport, as he subsequently apparently wished to do, he would still be entitled to it. Consequently, he would enjoy China's protection notwithstanding the fact that he held a UK passport. That is the whole purpose of the Chinese Memorandum referred to earlier, which states that Mr Lee's 'British passport' is only a 'travel document'.[52] From the Chinese viewpoint, Mr Lee's BN(O) passport had no bearing on his true nationality at all.

The whole affair highlighted the question of whether ordinary Hong Kong Chinese who hold British passports ever gave any real thought to this matter until now. Unlike William Joyce's case, there will be many who have never been resident on the mainland. Presumably, 'Chinese Hong Kong compatriots' hold British passports precisely because they do not wish to possess or possess only a Chinese passport, specifically a Chinese passport issued by the Hong Kong authorities to Chinese citizens who have the right of abode in Hong Kong.[53] Such Chinese Hong Kong residents cannot be expected to read diplomatic memoranda appended to an international treaty. Even if they should have done so they are unlikely to have considered it necessary as a practical matter formally to renounce their Chinese nationality, and even if they did attempt to do so such renunciation may yet be refused.[54]

But because they, like Mr Lee, are considered Chinese nationals 'first and foremost', a subtly ambiguous turn of phrase which only highlights the difficulty during the Sino-British negotiations and Chinese law's prohibition of dual nationality, the usual international law rule is that the UK cannot espouse a claim on behalf of such persons against China. In short, the Chinese Minister's recent statement was a textbook example of the treaty and customary international rule that in cases involving dual nationals one country of nationality cannot espouse a claim on behalf of that national against the person's other country of nationality.[55]

Mr Lee subsequently claimed that he wished to renounce his British nationality and there was a suggestion that he should be refused such

---

[51] Joyce v. DPP, op. cit., 371–2.
[52] Chinese Memorandum, 19 December 1984, third paragraph.
[53] Hong Kong Basic Law, art. 154.
[54] See PRC Nationality Law of 1980, art. 10; Hague Convention on Certain Questions Relating to the Conflict of Nationality Laws 1930, arts. 1 and 6.
[55] Hague Convention 1930, to which the UK and China are both party, art. 4; see further, Craig Forcese, 'The Capacity to Protect: Diplomatic Protection of Dual Nationals in the "War on Terror"' (2006) 17 E.J.I.L. 369, at 384–5.

renunciation by the UK authorities. Such refusal following the Foreign Secretary's assertion of a treaty breach would not only have mired the UK in deeper diplomatic controversy with China at the time, it would have threatened to unravel the delicate compromise reached during the Sino-British negotiations. A compromise which now, with the passing of the 2020 National Security Law, is in genuine danger of becoming unravelled.

The UK's position in respect of the Lee Po Affair in 2016 was likely to have been based upon practical necessity, principle or both. Passive British acceptance of the affair would have eroded any British authority left under the Joint Declaration. Amid a widespread public outcry, the UK could not have done less than it did. Lastly, it may be thought that the proper answer to any sweeping denial of British treaty rights lies in pointing to those very aspects of the Sino-British treaty which guarantee the rights of Hong Kong residents and Hong Kong's autonomy until 2047. This in fact the UK has now done, in addition to its controversial policy, which China denounces, of instituting a 'path to citizenship' for BN(O) passport holders and their dependents.

To be sure, nothing prevents China from extending its laws to Hong Kong residents so long as that is limited to mere prescription and does not stretch to actual enforcement action in Hong Kong in violation of a resident's rights under Hong Kong law. Unlike Joyce's case, the booksellers' alleged crime of selling banned books may also be easier to be proven to have occurred at least partly on the mainland. While the Sino-British Joint Declaration does require rights attending upon arrest or extradition to be observed, and it generally prohibits any hint of Chinese enforcement action in Hong Kong territory in breach of those rights, such rights hold good only in Hong Kong. But they do hold good in Hong Kong; hence the outcry caused by Lee Po's case.

As it turned out, it was unclear that Mr Lee was ever detained or charged with any crime on the mainland, and he was the only one of the five booksellers who was said to have been 'involuntarily removed' from Hong Kong. So where do we go from here?

International law advisors know that the ideal solution is almost always diplomatic. While there continued to be several twists to the story subsequently, involving the momentary return to Hong Kong of at least three of the booksellers, with Mr Lee himself having since returned at least twice, Mr Lee's claim that he had entered China voluntarily made a British treaty objection practically impossible to sustain. All that the Foreign Secretary was left with was this carefully worded statement to Parliament: 'The full facts of the case remain unclear, but our current information indicates that

Mr. Lee was involuntarily removed to the mainland without any due process under Hong Kong SAR law.'[56]

No international claim can be supported by instinct alone, and the UK appeared to have done all that it could. It had insisted on Hong Kong's autonomy, the exclusive powers of the Hong Kong authorities and the legal rights of Hong Kong residents within the territory. Beijing, for its part, did not disagree with any of this. As for consular access, the situation was at least complicated by the UK's own Memorandum to the 1984 Sino-British Joint Declaration, which states that BNOs shall (only) be entitled to 'consular services and protection' upon request 'when in third countries'.[57] With Mr Lee's return to Hong Kong, the question of British consular access on the mainland became moot. That question is governed by the two memoranda, with the Chinese Memorandum clearly forbidding it.[58] Having said all this, there is a separate consular agreement between China and the UK which may also have had some relevance. However, the short point is that there was no suggestion of any controversy there.

That was the diplomatic solution. Three decades of constructive ambiguity on the position of dual nationals, so carefully crafted in 1984, remained intact, at least in respect of the Lee Po Affair, and any advantage in pressing the argument further possibly was weighed against it.

By 2020, however, the issue could no longer be contained, accompanied by the low point reached in Sino-British relations. The UK announced that special visa rules would, as of January 2021, permit BN(O) passport holders long-term entry into the UK with what the UK Government has termed a 'pathway to citizenship'. By January 2021, Chinese 'countermeasures' had become a matter of public discussion, threatening to unravel the Sino-British Exchange of Memoranda of 1984. The Lee Po Affair had focused attention on the extension of Chinese nationality to Hong Kongers where on the one hand three million people prohibited from entering the UK would, in effect, have otherwise been rendered stateless, and where on the other hand China could hardly have been expected to absorb three million 'foreigners' overnight. The issue now turns to calls, in light of the new policy of the UK Government, to enforce the Chinese nationality law's prohibition of dual nationality and to withdraw the privileges of Chinese nationality with which the right of abode in Hong Kong is tied, if not such nationality itself entirely.

---

[56] Six Monthly Report, February 2016, at 3.
[57] United Kingdom Memorandum, para. (d).
[58] Chinese Memorandum, 19 December 1984, fourth paragraph.

However the question raised today of British jurisdiction over Chinese nationals was, during that 2016/2017 period, still some three years away in the future. What had drawn public attention was rather, and for the next three years, the issue of Beijing's jurisdictional reach in Hong Kong. It began with a statement in the 2014 white paper, which three years later was followed by what seemed a storm in a teacup; the extension of Mainland law to the West Kowloon terminus in 2017. By 2019 the proposed Hong Kong Extradition Bill was to lead to widespread violent protests amidst fears of the prescriptive jurisdictional reach of Mainland laws and its actual enforcement. By 2020, the protests themselves led the Standing Committee of the National People's Congress to pass the Law of the People's Republic of China on Safeguarding National Security in the Hong Kong Special Administrative Region, otherwise known as the 2020 National Security Law.

VI THE LAW IN A TRAIN STATION

In 2017, there was controversy over the application of PRC law wholesale at least on the 'Mainland side' to the area of the immigration checkpoint to be located in a new Kowloon rail terminus – the future West Kowloon terminus for the Guangzhou-Shenzhen-Hong Kong Express Rail Link, otherwise known as the 'XRL'.[59] Hong Kong's Secretary for Justice had suggested that since Hong Kong's Basic Law does not define Hong Kong territory expressly, it does not do so at all. As such, he reasoned, any part of Hong Kong may be 'leased' to the Mainland making it 'Mainland territory'. Accordingly, Hong Kong law, including such fundamental rights as are protected under the Basic Law, will not apply within such territory, indeed to any territory 'leased' to the Mainland.[60] This then was what the Government had suggested to be the proper legal position. The controversy concerned the operation of Mainland immigration controls in West Kowloon, and more specifically the application of Mainland laws in their entirety to the area of the proposed terminus. The Government's plan was to have a 'co-location' arrangement at the proposed terminus in Hong Kong's West Kowloon area, by which it meant a simultaneous exercise by both the Mainland and Hong Kong authorities of immigration and other legal controls.

Roughly a quarter of the terminal building area was to be (and presumably now is) leased to the Mainland authorities. The purpose itself is unexceptional enough, even desirable, involving the need to ease travel between Hong Kong

---

[59] L.C. Paper No. CB(2)1966/16–17(01), 'LegCo Paper'.
[60] RTHK (Radio Television Hong Kong), 25 July 2017.

and the Mainland. There was no apparent quarrel too with allowing Mainland immigration checks to be completed simultaneously with those of Hong Kong. Rather, it related to the legal means; namely, the alienation of Hong Kong territory and the cessation of Hong Kong laws and law enforcement together with it. What stirred public disquiet was perhaps the more basic assumption that there is no legal impediment at all to such alienation, or to the application and enforcement of Chinese Mainland laws; that this somehow is akin to the transfer of land for the United States' 1867 Alaska purchase, or in the Government's own example, the lease of a part of Shenzhen Bay Port to Hong Kong thereby constituting the Hong Kong Bay Port Area.[61]

The Shenzhen Bay analogy may have been inapposite as it did not raise the question of constitutionally protected rights, which was what was involved in the case of a lease by Hong Kong as lessor when that results in the application of Mainland penal laws in the territory in question.

The overall context may also have been important. Presumably the public mood was not improved, first, by the fact that the suggestion took place against repeated British allegations that the PRC had breached the 1984 Sino-British Joint Declaration in late 2015, in connection with Lee Po's case discussed earlier. Second, there was by now a broader difference that had emerged publicly between London and Beijing about the status of the 1984 Declaration.[62] Beijing claims that the 1984 treaty is fully performed. London takes the view that China's resumption of sovereignty was not the only function, perhaps not even the principal function, of the treaty. Instead, in the UK's view the 1984 treaty guarantees the rights and freedoms of Hong Kong's inhabitants, the continuation of Hong Kong's previous legal regime, and a high degree of autonomy for Hong Kong except in the spheres of the PRC's defence and foreign affairs.

Beijing doesn't disagree with the substance of the claims about autonomy but it is Hong Kong's Basic Law – an instrument which implements the treaty – which serves as the true guarantor of Hong Kong's high degree of autonomy (article 2), the continuation of laws previously in force, not least colonial Hong Kong's common law system (article 18), the system for safeguarding fundamental rights and freedoms (article 11) and crucially – under article 18 of the Basic Law – that Chinese Mainland 'laws' do not apply in Hong Kong unless extended to Hong Kong by way of promulgation or legislation, following consultation of the Basic Law Committee and the Hong Kong Government, and even so only if such Mainland laws should involve

[61] LegCo Paper, *op. cit.*, para. 29.
[62] C. L. Lim, 'Britain's "Treaty Rights" in Hong Kong' (2015) 131 L.Q.R. 348.

defence, foreign affairs or other matters which fall within Beijing's sphere of competence. Mainland laws which have been so extended to Hong Kong are or are then listed in Annex III to the Basic Law.

Not all Mainland laws will require this procedure in order to apply in Hong Kong. For example, when Hong Kong's Court of Final Appeal sought an interpretation from Beijing concerning the application in Hong Kong of the Mainland doctrine of absolute foreign sovereign immunity. That the doctrine applies was confirmed by both Beijing and the Court on the basis that Hong Kong's autonomy does not in any case extend to matters of foreign affairs.[63] However, immigration controls clearly fall within Hong Kong's sphere of autonomy.

Still, it is not any denial of Hong Kong's own border controls that was at issue but, on its face, the application and enforcement by Mainland officials of innominate Mainland laws in Hong Kong territory. Rather than to extend only defined Mainland 'immigration' laws to the area of the West Kowloon terminus, the Hong Kong Government explained that which Mainland laws might have to be applied could hardly be specified beforehand. Hence the proposal was that all Mainland laws should apply. To the extent that Hong Kong private as well as public laws – for example, health and safety laws – might also need to be applied to the area, and Hong Kong's jurisdiction preserved or reserved, these will be listed expressly.[64] That at least was the Government's proposal, subject to a 'co-operation agreement' being reached with Beijing, Beijing's final word on the matter and the passage of appropriate Hong Kong legislation.[65] At the time, construction of the new terminus was already 95 per cent complete and it was intended that the rail terminus should be functioning by the third quarter of 2018.

Could it have been the extension of Chinese law to Hong Kong which had caused controversy? Was it to do instead with Hong Kong having a power to lease land? After all, there is a clause in the Basic Law which was drafted precisely to allow the Mainland authorities to grant such additional powers to the Hong Kong Government as necessary. It is also difficult to believe that the controversy concerned how the new train station was to operate. That is hardly likely to amount to any large incursion upon the rights of Hong Kong's inhabitants. Instead, the whole difficulty seemed to have been psychological, prompted by anxiety about an opening of the floodgates should

---

[63] See e.g. C. L. Lim, 'Beijing's "Congo" Interpretation: Commercial Implications' (2012) 128 L. Q.R. 6, discussed in Chapter 5 of this book.
[64] LegCo Paper, *op. cit.*, paras. 42–5.
[65] *Ibid.*, para. 30.

it ever be admitted that rights assured under Hong Kong law can be evaded by the simple expedient of a lease.

So we turn to Hong Kong's rights regime. The guarantees under the 'provisions' of the International Covenant on Civil and Political Rights of 1966 are, as we have seen, incorporated into Hong Kong law by the Basic Law and also under the former colonial government's Bill of Rights Ordinance which in turn its architects imagined would be 'entrenched' by the Basic Law by the automatic operation of the clause incorporating those provisions of the Covenant 'as applied' to Hong Kong.[66] Here lies a most significant difference between the Hong Kong and Mainland legal regimes. Thus, even if Mainland law were to be extended to any part of Hong Kong, the protection of rights and freedoms will ordinarily have to be ensured. The well-known flag desecration case which once went before the courts in Hong Kong serves as illustration. The Chinese law protecting the Chinese national flag had been extended to Hong Kong but that law was challenged for violating the freedom of expression. Hong Kong's Court of Final Appeal granted the application for judicial review although the challenge was ultimately to fail.[67]

The Justice Secretary's view in 2018 that Hong Kong's territorial bounds are undefined under the Basic Law aims to circumvent this legal issue. If indeed Hong Kong's territorial limits are malleable no question can arise about the protection of civil rights under the Basic Law. There is the distant echo of nineteenth-century Western railway and territorial leases from China itself. These had avoided using the language of war occupation leases precisely to avoid scrutiny under the Hague Regulations.[68] The practical question as far as the West Kowloon terminus was concerned was whether the Hong Kong and Central Governments would, notwithstanding the lease, seek to preserve civil rights under Hong Kong law. If the wholesale application of Mainland laws to however narrowly defined an area can be brushed aside as a minor issue, it did involve an important underlying matter. Namely, the enjoyment of fundamental rights in Hong Kong. The leasehold theory would suggest that since such territory is no longer to be considered within Hong Kong's jurisdiction that question would not arise.

---

[66] Basic Law, art. 39.
[67] HKSAR v. Ng Kung-siu & Anor [1999] 3 H.K.L.R.D. 907, [2000] 1 HKC 117.
[68] Michael J. Strauss, *Territorial Leasing in Diplomacy and International Law* (Leiden: Brill-Nijhoff, 2015), 74.

Still, it fell to the Hong Kong SAR Government to state clearly which local laws it would like to see preserved. The better view arguably would have been to state the provisions of the Covenant as applied presently under Hong Kong law as being preserved, rather than to suggest that the Basic Law knows not where Hong Kong lies. Jurisdiction over questions which touch upon fundamental rights should, accordingly, remain with the Hong Kong courts. Mention has been made of the flag case, and to this one could add the Law of the People's Republic of China on the Garrisoning of the Hong Kong Special Administrative Region. Article 20 of that Law is also instructive on the allocation of jurisdictional powers between the Chinese military courts and the Hong Kong courts.

The whole discussion, in a sign perhaps of Beijing's growing impatience as well as of things to come, was then pre-empted by a decision of the Standing Committee of the National People's Congress. This question of the preservation of fundamental rights was to come to the fore in 2019. Attention shifted between 2015 and 2018 to reintroducing a national security law bill in Hong Kong and a law to protect the PRC national anthem, Tian Han'sand Nie Er's 'March of the Volunteers'.[69]

During this period much attention was to focus on what appeared to be an electoral matter; namely, the disqualifications of six LegCo members for what were considered to have been improprieties in taking their oath of office. These were fought out in court with several judgments handed down during the 2017 to 2019 period,[70] stoking grave disquiet. Having said that the issue was indissociable, in Beijing's view, from that of allegiance where Beijing had become increasingly wary of a stark absence of national allegiance in democratic participation. Thus patriotism which first had become in 2014 the subject of vociferous public debate had completed its course. That issue was to shift from thereon to the related

---

[69] In Hong Kong the anthem has been the focus of another controversy. To people on the Chinese Mainland it retains a deep significance having emerged as a part of the 1930s movement to liberate the Chinese people from foreign occupation. Prior to the Asian and African anti-colonialist movement(s) of the 1950s, 60s and 70s and the involvement of African American internationalism with it, the African-American polyglot, Paul Robeson, became known for an early 1940s rendition and for his translation of it into English with Liangmo Liu; Lira P. Lee, 'Paul Robeson: The People's Singer (1950)/Liu Liangmo – The Founding of McGhee Chinese School (1944)', in Judy Yung et al. (eds.), *Chinese American Voices: From the Gold Rush to the Present* (Berkeley: University of California Press, 2006); Robert Vitalis, 'The Midnight Ride of Kwame Nkrumah and Other Fables of Bandung (Ban-doong)' (2013) 4 *Humanity* 261.

[70] *Chief Executive and Secretary for Justice* v. *President of Legislative Council* [2017] 1 HKLRD 460; *Secretary for Justice* v. *Leung Kwok Hung* [2019] H.K.C.A. 173.

issue of formal allegiance, nationality in other words but it was the device of rendition to the Mainland from the Hong Kong SAR which in 2019 was to trigger a rapid chain of events. It has wrought genuine international consequences. Throughout this period Sino-British diplomatic statements and exchanges concerning the Joint Declaration grew louder.

9

Fundamental Rights and the 2019 Extradition Bill

I LEASE TO RENDITION

Central to the 'West Kowloon terminus' issue was whether Hong Kong's guarantee of rights would still apply, notwithstanding the application of Mainland law. Mr Rimsky Yuen, then Secretary for Justice, had adopted the legal position that a lease not of property but of territory would be involved and that apparently would have avoided the issue of Hong Kong rights superimposed upon the application of Mainland laws. A very similar issue was to emerge albeit in different guise, in 2019, in connection with the prospect of renditions to the Mainland. Would Hong Kong's rights regime apply to requests for rendition? Unlike the earlier 2014 protests, 2019 was marked by a degree of violence which initially the world outside was perhaps slow to recognise. The following very harsh characterisation of the events is from the journal *Asian Affairs* which criticised a Government 'paralysed by indecision', which 'failed to grasp the changed expectations of Hong Kong people' and was 'stunned by the realisation of the extent of discontent':

> In the summer of 2019 Hong Kong has been shaken by prolonged protests, ostensibly regarding the issue of amendments to the extradition law but with deeper roots in the discontent of large parts of the population. The initially peaceful protests, on several occasions numbering according to the organisers at least a million people, frequently deteriorated into violent clashes between protesters and the Police, creating a cycle of violence that proved beyond the capability of the government to break. The protesters grew more radical and more willing to engage in violence to achieve their aims, or indeed as a nihilistic expression of discontent.[1]

---

[1] Martin Purbrick, 'A Report of the 2019 Hong Kong Protests' (2019) 50 *Asian Affairs* 465, 465.

The essential legal issue, namely the prospect of the continued protection of fundamental rights, was probably mischaracterised as a question about the preservation of the Sino-British treaty.

It was not just that extradition to China and in this case rendition to the Mainland was, as it had proven elsewhere, bound to be politically controversial. It was not that the controversy had to do with the absence, necessarily, of the kinds of trial protections which in the West – and Hong Kong society is, in this sense, Western – would have been taken to be fundamental, inalienable rights. Nothing in the 2019 'Extradition Bill' itself which the Government had proposed would necessarily have foreclosed the enforcement of fundamental rights in extradition hearings. At any rate, allowing a proper debate on that issue, or simply entrusting rights protection to the Hong Kong courts, would have been preferable – from a rights viewpoint – to the 2020 National Security Law which in Beijing's view became necessary to quell further unrest, indeed what bordered upon insurrection. The BBC used the term 'anti-government protests'.[2] *The Guardian* and *Reuters* were perhaps a little closer with 'radical uprising' and 'revolt', respectively.[3]

Still, there were a number of key differences between the earlier West Kowloon issue and the 2019 protests. The 'leasehold theory' in the earlier West Kowloon context had circumvented the issue of the application of the Basic Law. However, even assuming that theory to be correct, and that the Interpretation and General Clauses Ordinance is just as easily overcome,[4] treaties such as the Joint Declaration also operate differently from the domestic Basic Law. Unlike a mini-constitution which essentially is what the Hong Kong Basic Law is, treaties may not as easily be confined to – they are not always contained by – the territory to which the treaty is intended to apply.[5] The 1969 Moon Treaty governs conduct on Earth as much as on the Moon. That then is one possible retort to the 'leasehold theory'. Unlike the Basic Law, the Joint Declaration defines 'the Hong Kong area' (stating, for example, that it includes Kowloon). This difference was to arise when the UK, notwithstanding the PRC's protestations, sought to intervene in the events of

---

[2] 'The Hong Kong Protests Explained in 100 and 500 Words', 28 November 2019, www.bbc.com/news/amp/world-asia-china-49317695 (last accessed 6 April 2021).

[3] Tania Branigan and Lily Kuo, 'How Hong Kong Caught Fire: The Story of a Radical Uprising', *Guardian* (Manchester), 9 June 2020; 'The Revolt of Hong Kong', *Reuters*, various dates, www.reuters.com/investigates/section/hongkong-protests/ (last accessed 6 April 2021).

[4] The Ordinance refers to a constitutional document, the PRC State Council's map promulgated by Order No. 221 on 1 July 1997.

[5] See further, S. Karagiannis, 'Article 29', in Olivier Corten and Pierre Klein (eds.), *The Vienna Convention on the Law of Treaties: A Commentary*, Vol. I (Oxford: Oxford University Press, 2011), 731, 732–5.

2019. However, we will need to recall how the UK and the Colonial Government had in fact viewed the issue of rights and their protection.

II TWO TREATIES DON'T MAKE ONE

Much ink has been spilt on how the guarantees in the International Covenant on Civil and Political Rights' provisions have somehow been 'entrenched' under colonial Hong Kong's Bill of Rights Ordinance, which led to amendment to the colonial Letters Patent, as well as under the Basic Law. The Colonial Government, faced with the prospect of the handover, passed the Bill of Rights Ordinance which implemented the provisions of the Covenant in the belief, or hope, that the Basic Law itself – which states that 'the provisions' of the Covenant 'as applied to Hong Kong shall remain in force and shall be implemented through the laws of the Hong Kong Special Administrative Region' (article 39) – will be sufficient to entrench the Bill itself post-handover.[6] Whatever one makes of hope a devolution treaty such as the Joint Declaration is, at least from the UK's viewpoint, better and it should come as no surprise that the UK should wish to claim treaty rights. It is not that one cannot imagine a sentence with the words 'Britain' and 'China' without the word 'treaty' being somewhere in it. But historic distrust of 'British treaties' is not what is likely to be the real cause of the PRC's rejection of any true substance contained in the Joint Declaration, rather it was the other way round; the PRC's position during Sino-British negotiations was that the Joint Declaration is intended primarily to assure Hong Kong which too is in China's interest that the current social and economic system and Hong Kong's way of life shall remain unchanged, while at the same time British 'interests' in the colony will be taken care of. The extent to which London recognised this to be true, though it must never admit to it, is a nice question. The manner, however, or instrumentality for realising that assurance is through the Basic Law, rather than by any treaty directly whose purpose in large part therefore becomes ornamental. The UK may indeed raise any diplomatic claim it might have against the PRC, but it is not in China's eyes to involve itself at all in how Hong Kong is run on a day-to-day basis. Notwithstanding the tensions and differences leading, ultimately, to necessary accommodations, compromises and two declarations conjoined, there in fact would be no 'British treaty' worth its name once the PRC 'resumes' its sovereignty over Hong Kong. That at any rate is for all intents and purposes the Chinese view.

---

[6] Andrew Byrnes, 'And Some Have Bills of Rights Thrust Upon Them: Hong Kong's Bill of Rights', in Philip Alston (ed.), *Promoting Human Rights through Bills of Rights* (Oxford: Oxford University Press, 2000), 318, 334.

II Two Treaties Don't Make One

The UK's view may be more complex. What was important was to avoid simply beating a hasty retreat, or for that matter to avoid walking off in a huff. Its negotiators were reminded when the talks threatened to fall apart to stay in the game, even when principle would be compromised, precisely in the hope of shaping the future of the former colony. Not least for public consumption, and as a part of the aim that the UK should leave with dignity. Whether, as I have mentioned, the Joint Declaration was simply ornamental, meaning that it was all – A-L-L, all – just for public consumption, is a question whose answer may not be altogether useful to have. There was at least also the need to secure actual British interests, and for Parliament to be satisfied that some genuine concessions had been obtained in what otherwise was a disaster. There would be no British administration and, as the UK had assured the PRC, no British 'links of authority'.[7] None.[8] The treaty however necessary, and in its own way remarkable,

---

[7] Discussed in Chapter 2 of this book.

[8] In any event, motive and meaning are distinct. It is not here suggested that from a legal view glimpses through the negotiation papers – and only, in fact, the contemporaneous British papers – need bring any great certainty in acquiring the true meaning of any treaty. During the Vienna Conference on the Law of Treaties held from 1968 to 1969 some delegates took the position that the meaning of a treaty is to be discovered by construing its words, much as one might interpret an English contract. Sir Gerald Fitzmaurice had perhaps the greatest influence during that period in advancing this textual view, which we attribute to the eighteenth-century Swiss international lawyer Emer de Vattel; see e.g. Francis G. Jacobs, 'Varieties of Approach to Treaty Interpretation: With Special Reference to the Draft Convention on the Law of Treaties before the Vienna Diplomatic Conference' (1969) 18 I.C.L.Q. 318, 322. Some other delegations however considered context to be the more important indicator of meaning. Eventually the provision in the Vienna Convention on the Law of Treaties which governs treaty interpretation would require, as a compromise, attention to both the treaty text and the treaty context, but what counts as context was closely circumscribed; see Vienna Convention on the Law of Treaties 1969, art. 31. Still, this theory of how treaties should be interpreted is one thing, it is a 'book law' view, how international lawyers deal in fact with treaty interpretation may be quite another. The use of the negotiating history or *travaux preparatoires*, evincing a more 'subjective' approach more closely associated with Fitzmaurice's predecessor as rapporteur at the International Law Commission, Sir Hersch Lauterpacht, is so widespread despite the Vienna Convention rule on its proper use and the reason, as usual, is forensic; Julian David Mortenson, 'The Travaux of Travaux: Is the Vienna Convention Hostile to Drafting History?' (2013) 107 A.J.I.L. 780. The International Law Commission's initial work product which had led to the Vienna Conference, with Sir Humphrey Waldock having succeeded Fitzmaurice as special rapporteur, had made room for that subjective approach as (only) a supplementary means of interpretation; Jacobs, *op. cit.*, 326–7. It is worth observing, even if only in passing, that the codification of the law of treaties reflected England's golden age in the field of international law. The end product, the Vienna Convention on the Law of Treaties, was to feature strongly as the basis of Sir Ian Sinclair's advice during the Sino-British negotiations on the Joint Declaration. One of the chief issues the PRC was concerned with was the express inclusion of a doctrine of unjust treaties, which failed to transpire. At least, as its preeminent international lawyer was to observe, as an express clause; Tieya Wang, 'International

would always prove insufficient when measured against the UK's original negotiating aims.

For sheer bluntness on this point, albeit as a passive observer, we have the diaries of Alan Clark, former member of Margaret Thatcher's cabinet, who wrote in his entry for Tuesday, 14 April 1997:

> Tim[9] explained to me, effectively, that Hong Kong had 'gone'. UK influence in matters of this kind was nil. Autonomy, 'LegCo', 'ExCo', Chinese susceptibilities all have 'to be taken carefully into consideration'.
>
> One more piece of wealth and real estate that has been allowed just to run through our fingers.[10]

That precisely is how the PRC too views it, and in 2019 there emerged the question whether a proposed rendition arrangement, in fact one which resembles the UK's own extradition legislation but allowing the transfer of fugitives from one part of the country to another part of the same country, should be thwarted by the UK's criticisms.

An almost equal amount of effort has gone into understanding the relevance of another treaty; into ascertaining whether it might be Hong Kong or the PRC which possibly could be considered a treaty party to the International Covenant on Civil and Political Rights. The whole debate is highly conjectural. The Covenant requires ratification or accession and the PRC has not ratified it, while in Oppenheim we find the statement that:

> It is difficult to establish that a State which has not formally acceded to a treaty to which it could have acceded has nevertheless in some way become a party to it by some informal procedure, such as a letter offering to apply the treaty on a basis of reciprocity or by mere conduct in conformity with the treaty.[11]

It should be observed as well that the International Covenant is not on the two lists of treaties appended to the PRC's 1997 letter to the UN Secretary General – either on the list of those treaties which will apply to Hong Kong where the PRC is a party to that treaty, or the list of those treaties which will continue to apply to Hong Kong after the handover despite the PRC not being a party. For Hong Kong's purposes, the Covenant is neither fish nor fowl. One might add nor good red herring.

Law in China: Historical and Contemporary Perspectives' (1990) 221 *Recueil des cours* 195, 333–44.
[9] Timothy Renton, Minister of State for Foreign and Commonwealth Affairs.
[10] Alan Clark, *Diaries* (London: Weidenfeld & Nicolson, 1993), 160.
[11] *Oppenheim's International Law*, 9th ed., vol. 1 (London: Longman, 2008), § 611.

III THE APPLE CART

The Joint Declaration, we saw, sought to preserve the continued application of at least 'the provisions' of the International Covenant on Civil and Political Rights in Hong Kong. The precise legal basis for such application may be somewhat precarious, but in practice it usually has raised no difficulty. In fact the PRC itself has signed the Covenant, though importantly it has yet to ratify it. When asked what lawful basis there is for Hong Kong's continued fulfilment of a reporting 'obligation' under the Covenant, a practice facilitated routinely by the PRC Foreign Ministry, one answer is that once China had notified the United Nations Secretary-General (who happens also to act as depository for the purpose of the Covenant) that the Covenant's 'provisions' as they applied previously will continue to be applied, China would have stood some risk of being accused of violating the principle of good faith under international law had it done otherwise.[12] Recall that Peter Duffy's evidence to the House of Commons Foreign Affairs Committee was that acceptance of human rights obligations should be considered to be an acceptance too of human rights procedures. This need not mean that the PRC or for that matter Hong Kong is a party to the Covenant but so long as the PRC is a signatory, and there is acceptance of the Covenant's provisions in respect of Hong Kong, the preservation of rights under the Covenant ought to commend itself. No-one's purpose is served in upsetting that particular apple cart.

The point is often only weakly understood, and this is not to mention the PRC view that there has been a resumption of sovereignty rather than a succession of States. As a reliable commentary had put it: 'The People's Republic of China has even explicitly succeeded to the ICCPR obligations of, respectively, the UK and Portugal in respect of territories that have been transferred from those countries to the PRC, Hong Kong, and Macao, even though the PRC as an entity is not a party to the ICCPR.'[13]

The late James Crawford,[14] in a talk delivered at the University of Hong Kong in 2004, considered that the PRC itself had therefore become a party to the Covenant even if only in respect of Hong Kong.[15] On

---

[12] See art. 18, Vienna Convention on the Law of Treaties 1969.
[13] Sarah Joseph and Melissa Castan, *The International Covenant on Civil and Political Rights: Cases, Materials, and Commentary*, 3rd ed. (Oxford: Oxford University Press, 2013), para. 26.47.
[14] Formerly Judge at the International Court of Justice, Whewell Professor of International law at Cambridge University 1948–2021.
[15] James Crawford, *Rights in One Country: Hong Kong and China* (Hong Kong: Hong Kong University Law Faculty, 2005), 29.

this point, there are at least three views.[16] The first relies upon saying that a human rights treaty unlike other sundry treaties 'follows the people not the place'. The Human Rights Committee's Chairman once suggested this very point to the United Kingdom,[17] but it is a contentious proposition in an uncertain legal area.

A second is related but probably untenable and involves saying that Hong Kong might itself have become party to the Covenant. Such a proposition relies on the Covenant being open not only to State participation but also by members of the United Nations Organisation and of any UN specialised agency. Hong Kong is an example of the latter, being a member of a number of such specialised agencies such as the World Health Organisation for example. Article 48 of the Covenant states that:

> 1. The present Covenant is open for signature by any State Member of the United Nations or member of any of its specialised agencies, by any State Party to the Statute of the International Court of Justice, and by any other State which has been invited by the General Assembly of the United Nations to become a party to the present Covenant.

So far so good but article 48 goes on to state that:

> 3. The present Covenant shall be open to accession by any State referred to in paragraph 1 of this article.

Which Hong Kong by any measure is not, it is not a 'State'.

A third approach is Crawford's – after all it was China which through its Permanent Representative, Qin Huasun, wrote on 20 June 1997 to the UN Secretary-General stating that the 'provisions' of the Covenant 'as applied to Hong Kong shall remain in force beginning from 1 July 1997'.[18] Mr Anthony Aust, formerly of the Foreign and Commonwealth Office, has written separately acknowledging that for its part Annex I, article XIII of the Sino-British Joint Declaration states only that 'the provisions' of the Covenant shall continue to apply to Hong Kong.[19] It fits the careful statement which Duffy had made to Parliament before the handover, and almost without a doubt is also the PRC's position.

---

[16] See further, Johannes Chan, 'State Succession to Human Rights Treaties: Hong Kong and the International Covenant on Civil and Political Rights' (1996) 45 I.C.L.Q. 928, 934, 939–40, 941–2.
[17] CCPR/C/79 Add.57 (3 November 1995).
[18] (1997) 36 I.L.M. 1675.
[19] Anthony Aust, *Modern Treaty Law and Practice*, 3rd ed. (Cambridge: Cambridge University Press, 2013), 338.

Insofar as the Sino-British Joint Declaration is concerned no question about PRC or Hong Kong membership of the Covenant therefore need arise. The precise legal basis does not matter as much as the actual, continued application of the guarantees of civil and political rights. A British promise that this was to be so had played a crucial role in reassuring Hong Kong's inhabitants during the period leading up to the 1997 handover. That it may not have the solid legal basis which it is widely assumed to have, had not been felt previously in real practical terms.

There is a final, separate, treaty law point to be made which concerns the operation, though not the validity, of the Joint Declaration. The promise of the continued application of the Covenant's provisions is contained in Annex I to the Sino-British Declaration, which although being a part of the treaty itself is – according to that Annex's title – the PRC's own 'elaboration' of its 'basic policies regarding Hong Kong'. The question thus presented is whether a British promise to Hong Kong had in fact become a Chinese treaty promise to the United Kingdom, as opposed to being a mere 'elaboration' of Chinese policy. This is possible as a matter of treaty interpretation but it is at best only a legal argument.[20]

It is here that Beijing's stance that China has already fulfilled all its promises to the United Kingdom, and that the Declaration is as a treaty fully executed, comes into sharp focus. For China's part – as Ewan Smith at Oxford (and formerly of the Foreign and Commonwealth Office) in an unpublished article has also discussed – the 1984 treaty applied to the thirteen-year period between its conclusion and entry into force and Hong Kong's handover in 1997. However the promise that in essence Hong Kong's way of life will remain unchanged for fifty years from 1997 (the date of Hong Kong's handover) need not mean that China undertakes any continuing treaty 'obligations' to the United Kingdom in respect of that promise. Dr Smith however sought to discern the PRC's meaning on this point from the 2014 State Council White Paper.[21]

Various press statements appearing from late 2014 have been more difficult to interpret. One could have taken some statements to suggest that, for Beijing, the Joint Declaration is fully executed. However the late Xu Hong[22]

---

[20] See further, C. L. Lim, 'Britain's "Treaty Rights" in Hong Kong' (2015) 131 L.Q.R. 348, but see Ewan Smith, 'Constitutional Treaties in Hong Kong' (1 February 2017). Available at SSRN: https://ssrn.com/abstract=2942748> or <http://dx.doi.org/10.2139/ssrn.2942748 (last accessed 6 April 2021).
[21] State Council Information Office, Beijing, 10 June 2014, Section I, para. 3.
[22] Hong Xu (1963–2021), Director-General of the Department of Treaty and Law in the Ministry of Foreign Affairs of the PRC, formerly Ambassador of China to the Netherlands.

of the Foreign Ministry's Department of Treaty and Law explained that China also distinguishes the Declaration's main body from Annex I's 'elaboration' of the PRC's 'basic policies' towards Hong Kong. These statements probably do overlap, but in any case it is hard to see how the Joint Declaration's provisions on civil and political rights, including in its first annex,[23] are not to last for the full fifty-year period, as opposed to twenty, twenty-five or even forty-nine years, even without prejudging the legal status of the promises contained in the Joint Declaration. In other words whether it is a PRC treaty promise to the UK or a Chinese promise to Hong Kong does not seem to matter in practical terms.

IV BEYOND THE JOINT DECLARATION[24]

We often fail to differentiate between the manifold rights regimes in Hong Kong, whether they derive from the International Bills of Rights,[25] from Beijing, or from the common law and Magna Carta. In respect of the 2019 Extradition Bill which triggered the most serious unrest the territory has witnessed in recent times, by all accounts at least since 1956 when pro-Nationalist and pro-Communist forces in Hong Kong had engaged in mutual provocation, it is the common law which arguably was key to understanding the potential limitations of the proposed extradition reforms.

The 2019 'Extradition Bill' affair concerned a rendition procedure between the Hong Kong SAR and the Chinese Mainland, contained in a Bill introduced by the Government in April 2019. The UK claimed that the Bill risked a breach of the Joint Declaration:

> We are concerned about the potential effect of these proposals on the large number of UK and Canadian citizens in Hong Kong, on business confidence and on Hong Kong's international reputation. Furthermore, we believe that there is a risk that the proposals could impact negatively on the rights and freedoms set down in the Sino-British Joint Declaration. It is vital that extradition arrangements in Hong Kong are in line with 'One

---

[23] Compare para. 3(e) of the main body of the Joint Declaration, in which arguably the rights referred to are rights at common law, and article 13 of Annex I which refers also to the 'provisions' of the International Covenant on Civil and Political Rights.

[24] The following section is a substantially revised version of original material previously published in the *Law Quarterly Review*, see C. L. Lim, 'The Hong Kong Extradition Bill' (2020) 136 L.Q.R. 19. The author is grateful for permission to reproduce it here.

[25] Comprising both the International Covenant on Civil and Political Rights 1966, and the International Covenant on Economic Social and Cultural Rights 1966.

IV Beyond the Joint Declaration

Country, Two Systems' and fully respect Hong Kong's high degree of autonomy.[26]

The PRC's view was not only that this was an unwelcome intrusion. There was open suspicion expressed about UK involvement, which the UK denied, in the subsequent widespread unrest. An opinion piece in the *China Daily* had put it in the following terms: 'Ideologues in Western governments never cease in their efforts to engineer unrest against governments that are not to their liking, even though their actions have caused misery and chaos in country after country in Latin America, Africa, the Middle East and Asia.'[27] Jeremy Hunt, then the British Foreign Secretary, replied: 'Let me be clear what I said. I said that I condemned, and we as the United Kingdom condemn, all violence and that people who supported the pro-democracy demonstrators would have been very dismayed by the scenes they saw.'[28] I use the term 'rendition' because this is how the authorities in Hong Kong refer to a fugitive transfer from Hong Kong to the Mainland. That is since, as with rendition between the nations of the British Commonwealth where no treaty relations are involved, there is no treaty – strictly speaking there cannot be – between Hong Kong as a special administrative region and the Central People's Government.

What the 2019 Bill had proposed instead was an ad hoc procedure which would then also include rendition to the Mainland. That rendition procedure would have refined a pre-existing case-based or ad hoc approach very similar to that first introduced under the UK's 1989 Extradition Act and which the UK Extradition Act 2003 retains. The UK's ad hoc procedure allows for surrender where there is no general arrangement or agreement, and it would apply to all countries with which the UK has no such arrangement or agreement. As with the Hong Kong analogue under the 2019 Bill that would include rendition to Mainland China. Prior cases involving surrender from Hong Kong to the Mainland following the handover had not raised the same heightened public concern. Mainland fugitives had simply been deported.[29] In 2019, it was the prospect of any Hong Kong resident being capable of being surrendered to the Mainland which proved too much.

The controversy caused by the Fugitive Offenders and Mutual Legal Assistance in Criminal Matters Legislation (Amendment) Bill, gazetted on

---

[26] 'Proposed Extradition Law Changes in Hong Kong: UK and Canada Joint Statement', Press Release, UKFCO, 30 May 2019.
[27] Costas Pitas and Ben Blanchard, 'Britain Denies Supporting Violent Hong Kong Protests as China Media Slam "Western Ideologues"', *Reuters*, 4 July 2019.
[28] Ibid.
[29] See Johannes Chan and C. L. Lim (eds.), *Law of the Hong Kong Constitution*, 2nd ed. (Hong Kong: Sweet & Maxwell, 2015), 113–15.

29 March and introduced on 3 April 2019, led to Hong Kong's most severe political crisis since 1997. An estimated one million people marched on the streets of Hong Kong in June 2019. In a dramatic twist young protesters broke subsequently into Hong Kong's legislative council (LegCo) building, vandalised the premises, defaced the Hong Kong emblem and planted the colonial Hong Kong flag.

It was difficult however to see how much more Hong Kong's Bill could have been improved, assuming that all the rights under the Basic Law would have applied anyway, and consequently where the UK's treaty concern would lie if in fact these rights would have been protected.

No doubt, the concern was that Hong Kong's occupants, including UK nationals, who are living in one part of China as Hong Kong residents would face rendition to another part of it. The Chinese criminal justice system, depending upon whom one asks, ranges from being not too different from Hong Kong's to being entirely inadequate in protecting the rights of the accused. Improvements to China's criminal justice process, as Grenville Cross SC, formerly Hong Kong's Director of Public Prosecutions, sought to explain, failed to impress critics.[30] Responding to an urgent question in Parliament, the UK's Minister for Asia and the Pacific said:

> Some Hong Kong lawmakers have proposed an array of alternative solutions, including that additional legally binding human rights safeguards be included in the proposed legislation. In my meeting in London on 20 May with Hong Kong Secretary for Commerce and Economic Development, Edward Yau, I made it clear that proper consideration must be given to all these suggestions as part of a wider and more comprehensive consultation. More time for consultation would allow for a more adequate consensus to be built.[31]

What was clear was that the UK did not seek to pre-empt the Hong Kong judiciary. Mr Hunt, the Foreign Secretary, explained that: 'Hong Kong has an independent judiciary and it's not for me as foreign secretary of the UK to second guess how that judiciary works. What I was saying was that there would be serious consequences if the legally binding international agreement between the UK and China, if that was violated.'[32]

Extradition to China from colonial Hong Kong was once known, but that had involved laws which predated the 1949 Communist Revolution and the

---

[30] Grenville Cross, 'Fugitive Surrender: Rights and Responsibilities', *China Daily* (Beijing), 12 June 2019.
[31] Hansard, H.C. Vol. 661, col. 416 (10 June 2019).
[32] Pitas and Blanchard, *op. cit.*

establishment of the PRC; namely, colonial Hong Kong's Chinese Extradition Ordinance 1889. In *Re Iu Ki-shing*,[33] Piggott CJ had avoided the question of whether the colonial legislature had the power to pass any such law in the first place. His Lordship reasoned however that as the King had not objected His Majesty must have approved it as an exercise of the royal prerogative. It was Republican China which then ceased to submit any extradition requests, the reason being that the Republican authorities had rejected the 1868 Treaty of Tianjin for being an 'unequal treaty' and the 1889 Ordinance contained a reference to that treaty.[34] As the Hong Kong Government views it now, the Joint Declaration states expressly that following the Handover the PRC Central Government will assist the Hong Kong SAR in concluding international – including extradition – agreements.[35] The UK position however appeared to have been that China as sovereign should have been more circumspect in facilitating rendition from Hong Kong to the Mainland itself.

Yet, and first, the principles which shall apply to any future Hong Kong-Mainland arrangement were set down not long after the 1997 Handover. The question of an arrangement with Mainland China had been raised in March 1997 during the second reading of the Bill which became the present Ordinance. These principles were proposed by the Government during discussions in LegCo's Security Panel in 1998.[36] They are, that:

(1) article 95 of the Basic Law requires juridical relations and assistance with other parts of the Mainland to comply with Hong Kong law, i.e. including the Basic Law which itself implements China's basic policies towards Hong Kong as annexed to the Joint Declaration and incorporates the provisions of the International Covenant on Civil and Political Rights;
(2) there shall be no surrender unless pursuant to legislation;
(3) any arrangement must be acceptable to the Mainland and to Hong Kong;
(4) any arrangement must take into account the differences between Hong Kong and the Mainland under 'one country, two systems';
(5) any arrangement must comply with article 19 of the Basic Law which guarantees the independence of the Hong Kong judiciary.

---

[33] (1908) 3 H.K.L.R. 20.
[34] Yash Ghai, *Hong Kong's New Constitutional Order*, 2nd ed. (Hong Kong: Hong Kong University Press, 1999), 354; Janice Brabyn, 'Extradition and the Hong Kong Special Administrative Region' (1988) 20 *Case W. Res. J. Int'l L.* 169, 183–5.
[35] See Joint Declaration, Annex I, art. XI.
[36] L.C. Paper No. CB(2) 449/18-19(01), 14 May 2019, para. 6 and Annex II.

In short, all rights envisaged under the Joint Declaration and protected under Hong Kong's Basic Law must be assured. It is difficult to see how, if indeed such a requirement is met, that any further assurance should be required. One would have reached the limit of the protections under the 1984 Sino-British Joint Declaration.

Second, Hong Kong's 2019 Bill reflects the current UK extradition model. An ad hoc, case-based procedure is precisely that. It involves, potentially at least, treatment of requests from anywhere other than from countries where a general extradition arrangement already exists. The UK's own procedure would in principle at least allow extradition even to China.[37] As with that procedure, in Hong Kong's proposed bill there would have had to be a committal hearing where the Basic Law contains guarantees of Hong Kong's own standards of human rights protection, as does Hong Kong's Bill of Rights Ordinance. In addition, the existing ordinance, the Fugitive Offenders Ordinance (Cap.503) contains all the usual guarantees – the double criminality rule (section 2(2)), the political offence exception (section 5(1)(a)), the rule against discrimination on grounds of race, religion, nationality or political opinion (section 5(1)(c) and (d)), the double jeopardy rule (section 5(1)(e)), the specialty rule (section 5(2)), restriction against re-surrender (section 5(5)) and the death penalty exception (section 13(5)).

Third, is the existence of some ambiguity over the extent or degree of the similarity between the UK and Hong Kong regimes fatal, necessarily, from a UK viewpoint? True, assuming an extradition request is rejected by the courts following committal hearings, Hong Kong's Chief Executive would nonetheless have been able to proceed, at least in principle, with a surrender. But the famous illustration of that in England was the *Pinochet* case which showed the importance of the committal stage under the UK's 1989 Act. An application for *habeas corpus* following the magistrate's committal order led to an appeal to the House of Lords.[38] The objective of the appeal was to tilt the Home Secretary's hand. Committal hearings, an application for *habeas corpus* with the possibility of appeal, a torture claim, an application for discharge in case of delay in the person's surrender as well as the possibility of an application for judicial review of the Chief Executive's own decision would all be there to be availed under the Ordinance.[39]

---

[37] Extradition Act 2003 s. 194, superseding the 1989 Extradition Act s. 3(3)(b) for which see Clive Stanbrook and Ivor Stanbrook, *Extradition Law and Practice*, 2nd ed. (Oxford: Oxford University Press, 2000), 336–7.
[38] R v. Bow Street Stipendiary Magistrates Ex p. Pinochet Ugarte (No. 3) [2000] 1 A.C. 147; [1999] 2 All E.R. 97.
[39] L.C. Paper No.CB(2) 449/18-19(03, February 2019, 4–5.

However, extradition law is less developed in Hong Kong than in the UK. We do not yet know how the line of authorities starting with *Soering v. United Kingdom*[40] and culminating recently in *Lord Advocate v. Dean*[41] will play out in Hong Kong.[42] Put simply, does Hong Kong's Basic Law guarantee that a Hong Kong resident's rights will be enforced in the place of request? In other words, on the Chinese Mainland. *Soering* confirms that breach of the human rights of a person extradited from the requested state will amount to breach of that requested state's own human rights obligations. This 'Soering' rule is now reflected in sections 21 and 87 of the UK's 2003 Act.[43] Section 21 of the 2003 Act which applies to Part 1 territories which are subject to a European arrest warrant, in respect of which section 87 – which applies to Part 2 territories that are covered by multilateral and bilateral treaties – is in similar terms, states that the judge must decide whether extradition would be compatible with the person's Convention rights, and that discharge must be ordered in the case of incompatibility. However, such a provision does not exist, at least in express terms, in Hong Kong's proposed Bill. Little help came when some of Hong Kong's judges were reported to have said that they would feel unable to fulfil their judicial role in the face of Mainland Chinese pressure. According to the Reuters report this claim was made anonymously to the press by three senior members of the Hong Kong judiciary.[44] Even assuming it to be true, one might have expected only judicial resignations had the Bill been passed. So be it. It should not preclude any future development of Hong Kong's extradition law by its judiciary, including a future need to address *Soering* in this context.

If recent British statements say no more than that civil liberties should be upheld, that should cause no difficulty. Where these statements refer to the liberties guaranteed in the Annex to the Joint Declaration, they may appear to touch upon a Sino-British treaty controversy. Is the 1984 Sino-British Joint Declaration fully executed, as the PRC says in explaining its position? That treaty issue had emerged in public by 2015.[45] Beijing appears to claim that the 1984 Treaty is an executed albeit still valid treaty while London takes the view that China's resumption of sovereignty is not the only, perhaps not even the

---

[40] [1989] E.C.H.R. 14; (1989) 11 E.H.R.R. 439
[41] [2017] U.K.S.C. 44; [2017] 1 W.L.R. 2721.
[42] Christopher Gane, paper delivered at the International Symposium on Cross-border Criminal Justice under the Basic Law, The Chinese University of Hong Kong, 31 May 2019.
[43] John R. W. D. Jones, *Extradition and Mutual Legal Assistance Handbook*, rev. ed. (Oxford: Oxford University Press, 2011), 77–8.
[44] Greg Torode and James Pomfret, 'Hong Kong Judges See Risks in Proposed Extradition Changes', *Reuters*, 28 May 2019.
[45] Lim, 'Britain's 'Treaty Rights'', *op. cit.*, 348.

principal, function of the Sino-British Joint Declaration but that this treaty guarantees the rights and freedoms of Hong Kong's inhabitants, the continuation of Hong Kong's previous legal regime, and a high degree of autonomy for Hong Kong except in the spheres of China's defence and foreign affairs, for all of fifty years.

Yet the Joint Declaration's status is not necessarily the point, and for the present purposes it can be put aside. Why should one turn, immediately, to the Joint Declaration?[46] After all, it is the Basic Law which implements the Joint Declaration, guaranteeing Hong Kong a high degree of autonomy (article 2), the continuation of laws previously in force, not least colonial Hong Kong's common law system (article 18), the system for safeguarding fundamental rights and freedoms (article 11) and crucially – under article 18 of the Basic Law – that Chinese Mainland 'laws' do not apply in Hong Kong. The trouble is that the Basic Law has long been taken silently as a piece of Chinese law which is interpreted in the Chinese way.[47]

As I wrote previously, some years ago, the Basic Law's interpretation could have treaty significance; for, under the 1969 Vienna Convention on the Law of Treaties, subsequent British 'acceptance' of – rather than a need for express agreement to – practice under the Basic Law ought to be taken into account as a matter of treaty interpretation.[48] That at least is to look at it strictly from the viewpoint of an established principle of treaty interpretation. Dr Ewan Smith has criticised this view, urging instead that Hong Kong judges should look to the Joint Declaration when interpreting the Basic Law.[49] But be that all as it may, if an assertion of treaty rights is now intended to bolster the UK's involvement a political or diplomatic statement which claims such involvement would, ordinarily, have sufficed. That is all that legal principle might require. It is quite another thing to risk the suggestion that the long-standing arrangements under one country, two systems are now, somehow, inadequate; or that Hong Kong extradition law should be identical to that in the UK; rather than being similar and possibly even convergent. It is this which China objects to, the idea that beyond the four corners of the Joint Declaration the UK should have any continuing involvement of any kind.

In sum, the application of rights under the provisions of the Covenant is guaranteed under the Basic Law. Any lingering doubts could have been addressed by making the *Soering* rule explicit in the Bill, by having

---

[46] If it might seem strange to say this in a book about the Joint Declaration it should not. The Joint Declaration does not have to do with everything, and not everything has to do with it.
[47] Chan and Lim, *Law of the Hong Kong Constitution*, *op. cit.*, 66–72.
[48] Lim, 'Britain's "Treaty Rights"', *op. cit.*
[49] Smith, 'Constitutional Treaties in Hong Kong', *op. cit.*

a provision like sections 21 or 87 of the UK Act of 2003. Still, it may be cause for discomfort that, under article 158 of Hong Kong's Basic Law, the Standing Committee of the National People's Congress, which to some might stir an allergic reaction in recollection of Lord Atkin's reference to Lewis Carroll,[50] has the power to declare what the Basic Law means, including what its rights guarantees mean. Similarly, under section 24 of the proposed Bill, the Central People's Government can issue a directive to the Chief Executive declaring that a request for surrender has a serious impact on China's foreign affairs or defence.[51] Section 24, in turn, accords with the Basic Law's and Joint Declaration's exclusion of matters concerning foreign affairs and defence from the scope of Hong Kong's autonomy.[52] Article 158 of the Basic Law and section 24 of the Bill supply credence to the popular fear that anybody in Hong Kong could be surrendered to the Mainland with unpredictable consequences. The point, however, is that the Joint Declaration provides for its implementation by the Basic Law.[53] That is what the Joint Declaration says.

Yet all of these legal questions, including whether or not they are all or any of them within the terms of UK treaty 'acceptance' of Hong Kong's Basic Law, would have involved questions of legal principle. The protesters in Hong Kong rejected not the scheme of the Bill but the very idea of extradition to Mainland China. That involved not a question of legal principle, but politics. On 4 September 2019, the Chief Executive of Hong Kong declared the Government's Bill to have been withdrawn.

---

[50] *Liversidge* v. *Anderson* [1942] A.C. 206; [1941] 3 All E.R. 338.
[51] *Cf.* C. L. Lim, 'Beijing's "Congo" Interpretation: Commercial Implications' 128 *L.Q.R.* 6 for judicial recognition of the foreign affairs exception in the 'Congo' case (*Democratic Republic of the Congo* v. *FG Hemisphere Associates LLC (No. 2)* (2011) 14 H.K.C.F.A.R. 395.
[52] Basic Law, arts. 13 and 14; Joint Declaration, para. 3(b).
[53] Joint Declaration, para. 3(l).

10

The 2020 National Security Law

I HONG KONG'S NEW LAW

The repercussions of the passage and promulgation in Hong Kong of the 2020 National Security Law (NSL) have been global in reach.[1] Hong Kong featured prominently as the Trump Administration in the United States and Beijing teetered on the brink of a new Cold War.[2] The National Security Law marked also a downward spiral in Sino-British relations amidst a wider backlash from, amongst others, the 'Five Eyes' alliance nations, comprising the US, the UK, Canada, Australia and New Zealand. This chapter describes the controversy over the 2020 law and the Sino-British exchanges which took place around it, both before and after its passage.

A range of international actions, at times loosely and misleadingly described as 'countermeasures', followed, and these will be discussed in the next and concluding chapter. Such international acts involved not only the PRC, the US and the UK, but also the other countries of the Five Eyes Alliance, and the European Union. While the focus of the preceding chapters has been on the UK the period following the passage of the National Security Law coincided not only with a shift in the UK's diplomatic position away from the 'Golden Age' of Sino-British relations touted by London and Beijing during the Cameron years and towards the US, but also with a post-Trump emphasis in Washington on rebuilding US Western alliances. The latter is relevant such that coordinated action could suggest dexterity and a division of labour in the reaction of certain governments in the West. However by far the most

---

[1] An earlier version of the following was previously published in the Law Quarterly Review; C. L. Lim, 'Hong Kong's New Law' (2021) 137 L.Q.R. 11. It is reproduced here in revised and vastly expanded form, with permission.
[2] By October 2020 the *Financial Times* was publishing a series of articles on this theme. The BBC had in the previous month asked – 'Is the world entering a new Cold War?' Until then discussion of a Cold War was confined largely to foreign policy specialists and academics.

important development has been the UK's offer of what the Johnson Government terms a 'path to citizenship' for holders of British National (Overseas) – BN(O) – passports, and this too will be discussed in the next chapter against the framework of the international law rules governing – to give it its full technical nomenclature – 'countermeasures against perceived internationally wrongful acts'. That is the last issue which this book will need to address.

But, first, to the UK's initial reaction to Beijing's passing of the National Security Law. The UK proceeded to measure the passage of that law against the terms of the Sino-British Joint Declaration, leading it to claim a 'clear and serious' breach of the treaty, a claim which Beijing just as emphatically refutes.

II CATCHING THE GREASED PIG

Like catching a greased pig. That was how Lord Patten in his 1998 memoirs described arguing over what the Sino-British Joint Declaration of 1984 meant, during the run-up to 1997, the date of Hong Kong's 'handover'. As we have seen, China since the 1920s through successive governments has taken the view that Chinese sovereignty was never lost under its nineteenth century treaties with Great Britain. Its basis for saying so is that might does not make right. In 1983 the PRC's assertion of this 'unequal treaties' doctrine threatened to bring a halt to Sino-British negotiations. Recognition of Chinese sovereignty became, for Beijing, a prerequisite to holding any talks, which would in turn be limited strictly to how Hong Kong's future prosperity could be assured. That at least was how the PRC saw it. Mrs Thatcher, when she travelled to Beijing in September of 1982, cited the two nineteenth-century treaties whose express terms ceded Hong Kong Island and the territory of Kowloon in perpetuity to the UK. The UK's view was that these treaties were valid and binding and that as such they would require amendment if China's claim were even to be accepted. Beijing as we saw responded by threatening to announce, unilaterally, its intention of recovering Hong Kong within one or two years, that is, by 1984. It was Sir Percy Cradock, the British Ambassador to Beijing, who had avoided an impasse by drafting a letter for the British Prime Minister in terms which accepted that the latter could still recommend acceptance of Chinese sovereignty to Parliament, provided, however, that Hong Kong's inhabitants were also satisfied with the outcome of negotiations.[3]

That was how Sino-British negotiations were commenced formally, leading ultimately to the Joint Declaration. Things could have gone differently.

[3] Robert C. Cottrell, *The End of Hong Kong* (London: John Murray, 1993), at 102–3.

Speaking in Hong Kong during the return leg of her Beijing trip in 1982, Mrs Thatcher had strayed from her script and asked how China could be trusted if solemn treaties could be broken easily. An unnamed British official was quoted as having said 'stick to the facts, which are that the treaties are valid under international law, while the Chinese position, that they are invalid because unequal, is incorrect ... But going on to talk about questions of trustworthiness was to add a gratuitous statement of opinion.'[4]

History repeated itself in 2020. On 30 June, the Standing Committee of the National People's Congress (NPCSC) passed the new National Security Law for Hong Kong – to give it its full name, 'The Law of the People's Republic of China on Safeguarding National Security in the Hong Kong Special Administrative Region'.[5] It came into effect in Hong Kong on the same day through promulgation by the Hong Kong SAR Government. Critics allege that it is an incursion into rights and freedoms that is so substantial as to threaten to disrupt the arrangements under Hong Kong's Basic Law and violate the Sino-British Joint Declaration. Mr Johnson, the British Prime Minister, in a letter published more than three weeks earlier in *The Times* had written that: 'It is precisely because we welcome China as a leading member of the world community that we expect it to abide by international agreements.'[6] The day after the National Security Law was passed, the Foreign Secretary, Mr Raab, told the BBC:

> We have very carefully now assessed the contents of this national security legislation since it was published last night. It constitutes a clear violation of the autonomy of Hong Kong, and a direct threat to the freedoms of its people, and therefore I'm afraid to say it is a clear and serious violation of the Joint Declaration treaty between the United Kingdom and China.[7]

This time there was no Sino-British quarrel over nineteenth-century treaties, but a quarrel in respect of the 1984 Joint Declaration, and, while there is no issue of the Joint Declaration being unjust, the PRC appears to consider the Joint Declaration to have been completely executed following Hong Kong's handover, a view which the UK naturally denies. As we have seen however the existence of a threat to freedoms is not necessarily a treaty matter, and however important it was to portray such freedoms to have been preserved by treaty

---

[4] Ibid., at 93.
[5] G.N. (E.) 72 of 2020 (hereafter, 'NSL').
[6] *The Times* (London), 3 June 2020. Available also at www.gov.uk/government/speeches/pm-boris-johnson-article-on-hong-kong-3-june-2020 (last accessed 27 February 2020).
[7] Reported also in William James, 'UK Says China's Security Law Is Serious Violation of Hong Kong Treaty', *Reuters*, 1 July 2020.

both before the handover and now. In the end it comes down to the common law and to the Hong Kong Basic Law.[8] Whatever the proper answer in the philosophy of the common law, whether if 'reason is the life of the law'[9] this should, as Coke suggests, then be taken to mean the common law's reasons[10] or whether it should be instead the sovereign's reasons,[11] where a written constitution exists – albeit a 'mini constitution' in the case of Hong Kong – that should be the end of it.

Two further points were noteworthy, first that Mr Raab declared the 2020 National Security Law to be in violation of Hong Kong's Basic Law.[12] This reference to the Basic Law was repeated in the Prime Minister's response to a question from the Member of Parliament for Bracknell.[13] It may be advantageous to portray the National Security Law to be a breach not just of the Joint Declaration as the UK claims but also of the Basic Law itself, but it is at least curious that the UK would seek to decide what the Basic Law means, properly construed. As the Basic Law says, it is for the Standing Committee of the PRC's National People's Congress to have the authority in China to say what that Chinese law means. The accuracy of these British pronouncements on Chinese law is therefore also an issue, and this is discussed further below in Sections IV and V. More simply, one does not usually go around saying what an entirely foreign law should mean.

Declassified records now show a failure during the negotiations in the 1980s to have a 'constitutional court' which would also have had the Basic Law interpreted against the Sino-British Joint Declaration. The UK's proposals were threefold:

(1) That the Basic Law Committee be turned into a constitutional court.
(2) That a proclamation of any emergency be issued from Hong Kong not Beijing (and we will see the significance of this in the context of the UK

---

[8] Discussed earlier in Chapters 7 and 9.
[9] Coke upon Littleton, 97b ('reason is the life of the law, nay the common law itself is nothing but reason, which is to be understood of an Artificial perfection of reason, gotten by long study, observation, and experience, and not of every man's natural reason').
[10] *Bonham's Case*, 8 Co. Rep. at 118a, 77 Eng. Rep. at 65 ('the common law will control Acts of Parliament, and sometimes adjudge them to be utterly void; for when an Act of Parliament is against common right and reason, or repugnant, or impossible to be performed, the common law will control it and adjudge such Act to be void'); R. H. Helmholz, 'Bonham's Case, Judicial Review, and the Law of Nature' (2009) 1 *Jo Leg Analysis* 325.
[11] Thomas Hobbes, *A Dialogue between a Philosopher & a Student of the Common Laws of England*, J. Cropsey (ed.) (Chicago: University of Chicago Press, 1971) 55–7; Gerald J. Postema, 'Classical Common Law Jurisprudence (Part II)' (2003) 3 O.U.C.L.J. 1, 2–3.
[12] Foreign Secretary's statement in Parliament, Hansard, HC Vol. 678, col. 329 (1 July 2020).
[13] Prime Minister's Oral Answers, Hansard, HC Vol. 678, col. 322 (1 July 2020).

Foreign Secretary's statement to Parliament on the compatibility of the 2020 National Security Law with the Joint Declaration, below Sections IV and V).

(3) That, rather than vesting the final power of interpretation in the NPCSC as article 158 of the Basic Law now does, any interpretation or amendment should conform to the Sino-British Joint Declaration.

All of these proposals failed[14] but it would appear from recent Sino-UK exchanges four decades later that the UK still adheres to them, especially the last. The reader is asked to forgive this attempt to convey a flavour of the pertinent declassified material. They tell the story of why it may be that the Joint Declaration sometimes is thought of still in terms of what it might have been. The declassified records show attention in the FCO being paid instead to reports of a meeting of the Basic Law Drafting Committee in October 1989 where its members had expressed the view that the Draft Basic Law should not undergo any major changes thereafter. The relevant telegram summarises the issue as reported in the China Daily of 16 October 1989: 'Views that China should not station troops in Hong Kong after 1997, and that the right to declare a "state of emergency" and to "explain" the Basic Law should rest with the HKSAR, violated China's sovereignty.'[15]

Second, there was the curious incident following a letter from the Vice-Chairman of the British Conservatives in Paris, Christopher Mitchell-Heggs,[16] suggesting the creation of a constitutional court in which the power to interpret the Basic Law will be vested, rather than in the NPCSC in Beijing. That letter was addressed to Francis Maude, following an earlier letter in the same vein to Sir Geoffrey Howe.[17] Maude's reply to Mitchel-Heggs was diplomatic:

> I was interested in this idea, which, as you may know, appears in broadly similar form as one of the recommendations in the Report on Hong Kong of the House of Commons Select Committee on Foreign Affairs ... As you rightly say there is already a provision for a Committee of the Basic Law (Articles 17, 18, 157 and 158) ... you imply that it might be relatively

---

[14] Gary Cheung, 'Britain Proposed to Boost Hong Kong's Autonomy after Return to Chinese Rule in 1997 through De Facto Constitutional Court, Files Show', S.C.M.P. (Hong Kong), 6 January 2020. The author is grateful to Mr Cheung of the *South China Morning Post* for providing him with the declassified files which would have been sealed until 2049 were it not for the *Post*'s freedom of information request.
[15] TNA, FCO 40/2643, FM Peking to Priority FCO, Telno. 1841, October 1989.
[16] Inner Temple Barrister and French avocat.
[17] TNA, FCO 40/2643, Christopher K. Mitchell-Heggs to Geoffrey Howe, 19 May 1989.

straightforward to build on these articles to bring about the creation of a Joint Constitutional Court along the lines you propose. I am not so sure.[18]

What followed, in response to Maude's reply,[19] was an offer of assistance by the French lawyer and politician and subsequent chairman of the famous Badinter Commission which had been established by the European Communities as a result of the Conference on Yugoslavia,[20] Monsieur Robert Badinter. Monsieur Badinter had apparently offered to draft the terms of reference for the establishment of such a court.[21] Mitchell-Heggs wrote: 'What I would like to suggest, since Monsieur Badinter is a longstanding friend of mine, is that he might be requested, jointly by the Government in Peking and yourself, to provide a general guideline as to the way that such a constitutional court would be appropriate in the current circumstances.'[22] The ensuing recommendation to Maude from the Hong Kong Department with the backing of concurring legal advice was clear, even blunt:

> It is quite clear that the idea of a constitutional court is a non-starter. We put such an idea to the Chinese last year and they rejected it firmly. They believe that such a Court would only be suitable in a federal state, and that it could become an organ of power superior to the Central Government.[23]

So there is no greater judicial organ empowered to hold the Basic Law to the Joint Declaration's terms. Rather, there is a thorny issue which persists until today. The Joint Declaration says that the Basic Law – which Beijing interprets – implements the Declaration,[24] such that were it to be shown that the Joint Declaration has been breached it may in some cases have to be shown also that there has been a violation of the Basic Law. We will see how this features in the latest controversy, discussed below in Section III, concerning the 2020 National Security Law, but there is a notion which prevails in some quarters, the notion of a higher authority, which has become a persistent legal myth even if by then it was simply a century too late for anything resembling treaty extraterritoriality.

---

[18] TNA, FCO 40/2643, Francis Maude to Christopher K. Mitchell-Heggs, 21 August 1989.
[19] Then Minister of State, FCO.
[20] That is, of the Arbitration Commission of the Peace Conference on Yugoslavia.
[21] TNA, FCO 40/2643, Christopher K. Mitchell-Heggs to Francis Maude, 7 September 1989.
[22] Ibid.
[23] TNA, FCO 40/2643, A. R. Paul to P. S./Mr Maude, 17 October 1989. Maude's Private Secretary was Mark Lyall Grant.
[24] Joint Declaration, para. 3(l), and Annex I, art. I.

III THE NATIONAL SECURITY LAW AND THE PREORDAINED LIMITS OF AUTONOMY

A larger issue lurks now, having to do with where the high degree of autonomy for post-handover Hong Kong ends and Beijing's power begins. That broader issue was put in this way at least as early as an FCO draft reply of October 1989. It had been drafted in response to a submission from the Unofficial Members of the Executive and Legislative Councils (OMELCO):

> clearly the first we have to consider are matters which give rise to the consistency of the Draft Basic Law with the Joint Declaration. In this category fall ... Other categories of issues are those that relate to the relationship of the SAR to the Central Authorities, and the workability of the provisions designed to give effect to the high degree of autonomy which ... the SAR is to enjoy. To a certain extent these issues are connected: the greater the extent of the autonomy, the more restricted the scope of the inter-relationship between the authorities of the SAR and the centre. But the constitutive power of the centre ... and the reservations to the centre of foreign affairs and defence are factors which must, inevitably, be reflected in a Basic Law of this kind. This has consequences for the power of amendment, the extent of legislative autonomy and interpretation. It also has consequences as regard the PRC Constitution and the extent to which its structural provisions (as distinct from its ideological or policy provisions) have relevance in relation to, if not directly to, the SAR.[25]

The draft reply, prepared by Pamela Major, puts it exactly.

On 11 March 2021, thirty-two years later, the National People's Congress in Beijing was to decide to enlarge the Election Committee which selects the Chief Executive of the Hong Kong SAR and also the number of seats in LegCo amidst an emphasis on 'patriots ruling Hong Kong'.[26] Notably, these changes were to be effected though the unprecedented act of amending the Basic Law.[27] However, the more frequent practice since the handover had involved the

---

[25] TNA, FCO 40/2643, FM FCO to Deskby 190100Z Hong Kong, Telno 2125, October 1989.

[26] 'China NPC: Beijing to Overhaul Hong Kong Electoral System', *B.B.C.* (London), 5 March 2021; Lun Tian Yew and Marius Zaharia, 'Beijing Moves to Overhaul Hong Kong Politics, Squeezing Democratic Opposition', *Reuters*, 11 March 2021; Siu-kai Lau, 'Hong Kong Electoral Reform Will Facilitate Virtuous Politics', *China Daily* (Beijing), 16 March 2021; 'We Even Listened to the Pan-Dems: Zhang Xiaoming', *R.T.H.K.* (Hong Kong), 17 March 2021.

[27] And there was concomitant criticism that these bodies were being stacked. The UK has responded with the allegation that the PRC is 'in a state of on-going non-compliance' with the Joint Declaration, continuing that is from the alleged breaches described further below in this chapter. See George Parker et al., 'UK Declares China in Breach of 1984 Joint Declaration', *F.T.* (London), 13 March 2021. On 17 March 2021, the US imposed sanctions on a further twenty-four officials in retaliation for this latest development; just as Beijing and Washington were preparing for the first meeting in Alaska between their officials following the

exercise of the NPCSC's final power of interpretation. This final interpretative power includes the power to decide upon the compatibility of various actions and measures, not least the compatibility of laws such as the 2020 National Security Law. In a memorandum of 8 November 1989 enclosed in a request from the FCO to the Attorney-General's Chambers for advice on Draft Basic Law article 157 (now article 158) concerning the power of interpretation, Paul Fifoot who was Deputy Legal Adviser at the FCO wrote:

> There are a number of difficult issues as regards article 157, but it has to be remembered that the BL is the law of Mainland China as well as the HKSAR and in that respect falls under what passes for constitutional law in China. China, like all Communist countries provides for the interpretation of its principal laws by a high political organ of power. As a law of China, the BL is no exception. Further, it can hardly be expected that any sovereign state will be prepared to allocate the power to decide differences between itself and a component region to an organ of the region or indeed other than to an organ of the centre. If it were allocated to a judicial organ, it would hardly be possible to raise a question as to the aptness of a provision that the power of interpretation should rest with the centre.[28]

He appended an article by the Chinese jurist Xiao Weiyun, formerly Deputy Dean of the Law Department at Peking University, who had been involved in drafting the Basic Law. In it, Xiao explained that the HKSAR courts' powers of final adjudication 'does not mean that the SAR courts have the last word on interpretation questions', leading Fifoot to conclude that '[t]his appears to us to be a cogent response to the argument that Article 157 is not consistent with the JD'.[29] Following the failure of the British proposals described earlier, and the Basic Law having gone on to vest the authority to interpret that document in the NPCSC, it should have been the end of it. Certainly insofar as Chinese law and Hong Kong law are concerned.

It was not until 2016 that the UK declared, for the first time publicly, that the PRC had violated the 1984 Joint Declaration but there was at that time and quite correctly no mention of a breach of the Basic Law in British eyes. Putting aside for a moment the fact that the PRC appears to consider the Joint Declaration to have already been fully executed, a short note in the 2015 volume of the Law Quarterly Review had asked during the previous year if it was not already nearly too late for the UK to assert its treaty rights. This had

---

US Presidential Election. See James Griffiths, 'US Sanctions 24 Hong Kong and Chinese Officials Ahead of Blinken Meeting with Beijing', C.N.N. (Atlanta), 17 March 2021.

[28] TNA, FCO 40/2643, D. H. Anderson to E. Wilmshurst, 8 November 1989.
[29] Ibid.

been in respect of certain statements in the UK, by Lord Patten, about the issue of democratic reform in Hong Kong.[30] In the following year Mr Hammond, then the Foreign Secretary, was to conclude that the booksellers affair[31] 'constitutes a serious breach' of the Sino-British Joint Declaration.[32]

Though that hardly was merely of academic interest, it was not, however, until 2020 that the treaty question became a prominent feature[33] in the grave deterioration in Sino-British relations. In 2020 following Beijing's passage of the new National Security Law and its adoption in Hong Kong the UK has now, once again, alleged a breach of the Sino-British Joint Declaration. A key issue involves the absence of an explicit provision in the Joint Declaration or for that matter the Hong Kong Basic Law forbidding Beijing from legislating a national security law for Hong Kong. It would have been a confusion to treat a requirement under the Basic Law that Hong Kong should enact national security legislation with a prohibition preventing Beijing from doing so, and in fact the 2020 National Security Law requires explicitly that Hong Kong should do so 'as early as possible'.[34] Rather, Beijing is expressly permitted to extend Chinese national laws to Hong Kong. This is a grave point of contention and it relates to the proper interpretation of the Basic Law.[35]

IV THE 'SPIRIT'

The British Prime Minister Mr Johnson's opinion article in *The Times* during the summer of 2020 provides a good starting-point. Johnson wrote:[36]

> [T]he National People's Congress in Beijing [has] decided to impose a national security law on Hong Kong that would curtail its freedoms and

---

[30] C. L. Lim, 'Britain's Treaty Rights in Hong Kong' (2015) 131 *L.Q.R.* 348.
[31] Discussed in the previous chapter of this book.
[32] Secretary of State for Foreign and Commonwealth Affairs, Six Monthly Report on Hong Kong, July to December 2015, 11 February 2016, 3; C. L. Lim, 'The Sino-British Treaty and the Hong Kong Booksellers Affair' (2016) 132 *L.Q.R.* 552.
[33] What sort of feature becomes the next question, but a secondary question, for our purposes, in the context of the UK's alignment with the US amid the intensified rivalry between Beijing and Washington.
[34] NSL, art. 7.
[35] Within Hong Kong, published legal commentary had up to that point been prepared for what appears to have surprised the UK; that national security legislation would be passed with or without the intervention of the Hong Kong legislature. Such commentary tended to concentrate on constitutional strategies going forward and the resilience of liberal values. See Cora Chan and Fiona de Londras (eds.), *China's National Security: Endangering Hong Kong's Rule of Law?* (Oxford: Hart, 2020), in particular the chapter by Hualing Fu, 41–60, discussing the possibility of a national security law being imposed by Beijing.
[36] Johnson, *The Times, op. cit.*

dramatically erode its autonomy. If China proceeds, this would be in direct conflict with its obligations under the joint declaration, a legally binding treaty registered with the United Nations.

Following that law's passage by Beijing, Mr Johnson said this to Parliament:

> We stand for rules and obligations, and think that they are the soundest basis for our international relations. The enactment and imposition of this national security law constitutes a clear and serious breach of the Sino-British joint declaration. It violates Hong Kong's high degree of autonomy and is in direct conflict with Hong Kong Basic Law. The national security law also threatens the freedoms and rights protected by the joint declaration. We made it clear that if China continued down this path, we would introduce a new route for those with British national overseas status to enter the UK, granting them limited leave to remain with the ability to live and work in the UK, and thereafter to apply for citizenship; and that is precisely what we will do now.[37]

The British claim at the very least is that the PRC has violated the 'spirit' of the Joint Declaration, and indeed one can pick at elements in the new law. However, the notion of a 'clear' breach of the Joint Declaration and of a 'direct conflict' with the Basic Law should be viewed with genuine scepticism.

Had last year's Hong Kong Extradition Bill been passed such extradition would have been subjected to Hong Kong's rights regime.[38] But because the 2020 National Security Law originates from the Mainland authorities there is doubt whether the Hong Kong courts will, for example, have or exercise the power to modify or strike down any or all parts of it for being overly broad or vague or interpret rights and freedoms generously and compatibly with international standards. These all remain open questions. In 1999 the Court of Final Appeal in Hong Kong, in similar circumstances, had considered whether what was in effect the Mainland law protecting flags and emblems – which as with the present National Security Law had been extended by the Mainland authorities to Hong Kong – was constitutional in light of Hong Kong's guarantee of freedom of expression.[39] As it turned out the law was upheld but it could in principle have gone the other way. So it is not clear that Hong Kong's rights regime will have no role at all. The difference however between the flag law in 1999 and the latest law is that the latter may be said to concern also questions of defence and foreign affairs, a claim which

---

[37] Prime Minister's Questions, Hansard, HC Vol. 678, col. 322 (1 July 2020).
[38] C. L. Lim, 'The Hong Kong Extradition Bill' (2020) 136 L.Q.R. 19.
[39] *HKSAR v. Ng Kung Siu* (1999) 2 HKCFAR 422.

the UK disputes together with its consistency in the PRC's view with the Basic Law which is, as has already been mentioned, a piece of Chinese legislation.

We will return to the issue of Chinese legislation. What is noteworthy, insofar as the question of fundamental liberties is concerned, is that the new National Security Law states expressly that it is subject to Hong Kong's rights regime. Article 4 states, in part, that:

> The rights and freedoms, including the freedoms of speech, of the press, of publication, of association, of assembly, of procession and of demonstration, which the residents of the Region enjoy under the Basic Law of the Hong Kong Special Administrative Region and the provisions of the International Covenant on Civil and Political Rights and the International Covenant on Economic, Social and Cultural Rights as applied to Hong Kong shall be protected in accordance with the law.

Mr Raab's more ample statement to Parliament is useful, where, however, he has declared the UK's position that the new law 'cannot credibly' be reconciled with China's 'international obligations or indeed its responsibilities as a leading member of the international community'.[40] He should be quoted more fully:

> [T]he national security legislation contains a slew of measures that directly threaten the freedoms and rights protected by the joint declaration. The House will be particularly concerned by the potentially wide-ranging ability of the mainland authorities to take jurisdiction over certain cases without any independent oversight, and to try those cases in the Chinese courts. That measure violates paragraphs 3(3) and 3(5) of the joint declaration, and directly threatens the rights set out in the United Nations international covenant on civil and political rights, which, under the joint declaration, are to be protected in Hong Kong. That in particular represents a flagrant assault on freedom of speech and the right to peaceful protest for the people of Hong Kong.[41]

Paragraph 3(3) of the Joint Declaration states, in part, that:

> The laws currently in force in Hong Kong will remain basically unchanged.

Whereas paragraph 3(5) states in part that:

> Rights and freedoms, including those of the person, of speech, of the press, of assembly, of association, of travel, of movement, of correspondence, of strike,

---

[40] Foreign Secretary's statement in Parliament, Hansard, HC Vol. 678, col. 330 (1 July 2020).
[41] Foreign Secretary's statement in Parliament, Hansard, HC Vol. 678, col. 329 (1 July 2020).

of choice of occupation, of academic research and of religious belief will be ensured by law in the Hong Kong Special Administrative Region.

In the case of paragraph 3(3) it cannot, it does not, mean that Hong Kong cannot amend its laws or that Hong Kong cannot have new laws, whatever else it might mean. In the case of paragraph 3(5) what then might 'ensured by law' mean? By Hong Kong law, including the common law, but also the Basic Law as determined by the NPCSC in Beijing? Or by some treaty standard?

Let us say the suggestion is of some external treaty standard, what previously has been referred to in this chapter as a persistent legal myth, in other words that the UK did leave Hong Kongers with internationally assured rights as the royal yacht sailed out of Hong Kong Harbour in July 1997. Let us, first, keep two things separate. The human rights treaties – the International Covenant on Civil and Political Rights, and the International Covenant on Economic, Social and Cultural Rights which the Basic Law also refers to – these are one thing, while breach of the Joint Declaration is another despite the Declaration's preservation of individual rights and freedoms in Hong Kong.[42] The parts just mentioned in the Joint Declaration peg these protections to 'law' and 'the law previously in force in Hong Kong', rather than to the International Covenant on Civil and Political Rights. The Bill of Rights Ordinance (Cap.383), which the colonial authorities had passed subsequently, incorporates only the 'provisions' of the Covenant and was enacted only in 1991,[43] seven years after the Joint Declaration itself.

The essential point is that, on the one hand, the main text of the Joint Declaration's assurance of individual rights and freedoms, at least under Hong Kong law, is restricted to the colonial common law as it stood in 1984, at which point the UK had not incorporated either human rights treaty into Hong Kong law.[44] On the other hand, the references in the Basic Law, and now also the National Security Law, are likewise confined to 'the provisions' of the two human rights treaties 'as applied in Hong Kong'. As with Annex I of the Joint Declaration which contains also a separate Chinese reference to the

---

[42] Joint Declaration, para. 3(5); Annex I, art. XIII.
[43] In a talk which this author delivered at the invitation of the Statute Law Society, I described the UK's approach as having a blank cheque. Since the Chinese annex (Annex I) to the Joint Declaration referred to the International Covenant on Civil and Political Rights 'as it applied to Hong Kong', in 1984, in 1991 the UK sought to fill in what it considered to have been akin to a blank cheque in anticipation of the 1997 handover; incorporating the Covenant rights into Hong Kong law where previously it had not applied in Hong Kong domestic law under British colonial rule. It is a nice question what the 1990 Basic Law and the 2020 National Security Law mean by 'as applied to Hong Kong'. When? In 1984, 1990, 1997 or 2020?
[44] Joint Declaration, para. 3(e).

'provisions' of the two human rights treaties 'as they applied' to Hong Kong previously.[45] The more compelling view is – perhaps it always has been if we go back to Peter Duffy's testimony to Parliament in London during the Patten years – that the PRC accepts 'the provisions' of the Covenant, as they had applied to Hong Kong at the time, and the only true issue, at least then, was whether the PRC should not also accept concomitant human rights reporting. Here, again, is Duffy's original statement to the Parliamentary committee:

> [T]he language that is used in Article XIII might be the subject of divergent interpretations. One view ... would be to say that the provisions of the International Covenant remain in force in Hong Kong whether through the common law or the Bill of Rights or the Basic Law as the Foreign Office representative indicated, but that the 'provisions' do not necessarily include the procedures of the Covenant ... However, my view is that ... the reference to the provisions ... should be understood as covering the mechanisms that had been in force in relation to Hong Kong (that is to say the reporting mechanism) should continue after 1997.[46]

On his view human rights 'law' and human rights 'procedures' should go together in construing what had been accepted in the Sino-British Joint Declaration. A report has in fact been submitted periodically by the PRC since the handover under the Covenant's procedures.

However, the question now is how the 2020 National Security Law might be applied compatibly with these 'provisions' of the Covenant. There is also in this regard a connection between the issue of rights protection and the continued role of UK judges as foreign members ('non-permanent judges' so-called) of Hong Kong's highest court. Mr Tugendhat, the Chairman of the Foreign Affairs Committee in Parliament, has expressed the view that it is clear that rights[47] will not be upheld under the new law, and he has in any event become a forceful voice for the view that British judges should therefore have no part in it.[48] Lord Reed, however, struck a more cautious note in apparent response: 'The new security law contains a number of provisions which give rise to concerns. Its effect will depend upon how it is applied in practice.'[49] Mention has also been made previously of Lord Sumption's and

---

[45] Joint Declaration, Annex I, art. XIII.
[46] Peter Duffy, H.C. 842-ii 1992–3.
[47] 'International treaty rights, or merely Hong Kong rights?' one might ask.
[48] Owen Boycott, 'Role of UK Judges in Hong Kong Appeal Court Comes under Scrutiny', *The Guardian* (London), 2 July 2020.
[49] Statement from the President of the UK Supreme Court, 17 July 2020.

Lord Neuberger's views, albeit that in 2021 Lady Hale decided not to renew her term as a non-permanent judge.

In other words, let us wait and see. However, that careful attitude has not prevented the suggestion, even considerable pressure being brought, not just on judges but also on British lawyers, that they should not involve themselves in any Hong Kong work. It is related to the felt need to uphold and to be seen to uphold fundamental liberties. To the extent that it might have anything to do with any internationally assured treaty rights the point is, as has been explained, likely however to have been misconceived or at the very least great complexity has been glossed over with political statements of 'a clear breach'.

The UK left far less in treaty terms, certainly in terms of the protection of individual rights, than we would all like to admit.[50] Mr Raab as a member of the Government labelled a senior member of the legal profession a 'mercenary' for accepting, initially, instructions to represent the Hong Kong SAR Government in a prosecution unrelated to the National Security Law. Notably, notwithstanding the Bar Council's silence, some barristers – Baroness Kennedy, for example, who is well-known in human rights circles but who is also a founding member of the pressure group, the Inter-Parliamentary Alliance on China – have joined in the chorus of criticism. In the face of such pressure and citing the travel restrictions caused by the Covid-19 worldwide pandemic, David Perry QC withdrew.[51] Whether this is premised upon a sound understanding of the actual framework the UK had agreed to after the handover, it is difficult to see how any of it might help to sustain the rule of law and the common law in Hong Kong.[52]

---

[50] There were very good reasons, following the 1997 handover and the uncertainty hanging over the Hong Kong experiment, never to admit it too loudly.

[51] For reporting which went on to criticise the Bar Council for its studious silence, see Matthew Scott, 'The Legal Profession's Troubling Relationship with China', *Spectator* (London), 20 January 2021. Less consideration seems to have been given to the role of the bar in promoting the common law abroad. *Cf.* Lord Sumption in Jonathan Sumption, 'Britain Should Avoid Undermining the Hong Kong Judiciary', *Times* (London), 18 March 2021.

[52] There was confusion and much attention given to the applicability of the cab-rank rule to instructions from foreign clients. The short answer is that the rule now only applies to instructions that are domestic in nature, following an amendment in recent years. However, the reason for the rule had always been that if one were accused of something in England one might expect a barrister to defend her client, rather than to judge him. That reason should apply as well abroad, and to the need to foster international confidence in an independent bar; certainly one which will resist pressure including (if not especially) pressure from the government of the day. Before ss. 21–23 of the Anti-terrorism, Crime and Security Act of 2001 were repealed, thankfully, would it have done for barristers to refuse to represent the UK Government? The fact is that the National Security Law in Hong Kong seeks at least to

I have already mentioned the resignations of Lord Reed and Lord Hodge at the end of March 2022.

V FOREIGN AFFAIRS AND DEFENCE

Mr Johnson declared a violation of Hong Kong's autonomy.[53] Yet according to the Joint Declaration autonomy also ends where China's foreign and defence affairs begin, that much paragraph 3(2) of the Joint Declaration says. Mr Raab, in his statement to Parliament, offered some clarity about the UK's position on this point. He rejected the view that the foreign affairs or defence exceptions in the Joint Declaration could possibly apply, saying:

> Today I have the depressing but necessary duty to report to the House that the enactment of this legislation, imposed by the authorities in Beijing on the people of Hong Kong, constitutes a clear and serious breach of the joint declaration. Let me explain to the House the grounds for this sobering conclusion.
>
> First, the legislation violates the high degree of autonomy over executive and legislative powers and the independent judicial authority provided for in paragraph 3 of the joint declaration. The imposition of this legislation by the Government in Beijing, rather than it being left to Hong Kong's own institutions to adopt it, is also, it should be noted, in direct conflict with article 23 of China's own Basic Law for Hong Kong, which affirms that Hong Kong should bring forward its own national security legislation.[54]

Mr Raab's interpretation of Chinese law is not free of considerable difficulty, and it would appear that, barring what he has said about article 3 of the Joint Declaration, a large part of his argument that an unlawful incursion into Hong Kong's sphere of autonomy has occurred rests upon this statement about what Hong Kong's Basic Law means. Doubtless, article 23 of the Basic Law requires the Hong Kong SAR to enact its own national security legislation. It does not however prohibit Beijing from extending a national security law to Hong Kong. In fact a separate rule in article 18 states that Beijing may extend national laws (and the National Security Law is a national law) to

---

preserve the existing liberties of Hong Kongers in article 4, and one will just have to leave it to the judges and wait and see. Whereas the 2001 Act in the UK before the repeal of those provisions was only the latest example of the indefinite deprivation of liberty without trial in the tawdry history of preventive detention under English law. Under those provisions, which one hopes never to see again in any future guise, a s. 21 certificate by the Minister of State was excluded from review by the courts.

[53] Hansard, H.C. Vol.678, col.329 (1 July 2020).
[54] Ibid.

Hong Kong in matters of defence or foreign affairs. That rule reflects the more basic principle that both of these spheres lie outside the sphere of Hong Kong's autonomy. That was by the deliberate design of the Joint Declaration, and as for the application of PRC laws article 18 of the Basic Law reads:

> The Standing Committee of the National People's Congress may add to or delete from the list of laws in Annex III after consulting its Committee for the Basic Law of the Hong Kong Special Administrative Region and the government of the Region. Laws listed in Annex III to this Law shall be confined to those relating to defence and foreign affairs as well as other matters outside the limits of the autonomy of the Region as specified by this Law.

Article 18 was no mere Chinese invention afterwards. It reflects the language in the first paragraph of Annex I of the Joint Declaration:

> The Hong Kong Special Administrative Region shall be directly under the authority of the Central People's Government of the People's Republic of China and shall enjoy a high degree of autonomy. Except for foreign and defence affairs which are the responsibilities of the Central People's Government, the Hong Kong Special Administrative Region shall be vested with executive, legislative and independent judicial power, including that of final adjudication.

Turning then to these defence and foreign affairs exceptions so-called, it might be asked, first, what is national security if not defence? We have nothing too explicit but the UK appears to have it in mind that this is a matter of police powers rather than of foreign affairs or defence.[55] Indeed, Mr Raab had said in his Commons statement,[56] that:

> Fourthly, the legislation provides for the establishment in Hong Kong by the Chinese Government of a new office for safeguarding national security, run by and reporting to the mainland authorities ... directly intruding on the responsibility of the Hong Kong authorities to maintain public order. Again, that is directly in breach of the joint declaration – this time, paragraph 3(11).[57]

However, that would face the argument that the Joint Declaration's true concern was simply that no troops should be used for policing. Paragraph 3(11) is elaborated upon in article XII in Annex I of the Joint Declaration:

> The maintenance of public order in the Hong Kong Special Administrative Region shall be the responsibility of the Hong Kong Special Administrative

---

[55] Joint Declaration, Annex I arts. XI and XII.
[56] Mr Raab's 'fourth' point.
[57] Hansard, H.C. Vol. 678, col.330 (1 July 2020).

Region Government. Military forces sent by the Central People's Government to be stationed in the Hong Kong Special Administrative Region for the purpose of defence shall not interfere in the internal affairs of the Hong Kong Special Administrative Region.

In other words 'no troops', and there were no troops. None.

As for the second, foreign affairs, the surrounding events at the time did at least appear to suggest (they still do) that foreign affairs are closely involved, particularly in respect of the situation with the United States which has been fraught and certainly will continue to be so in the years ahead. Not least in respect of the Hong Kong issue.[58] The UK itself has since become a part – potentially an integral part – of that shift in the overall Sino-US relationship as it devises its own foreign policy strategy towards the lucrative Far East.[59] Be that so, Mr Raab has expressed the UK's position in the following way:

> In fact, the Basic Law ... allows Beijing to impose laws directly only in a very limited number of cases, such as for the purposes of defence and foreign affairs, or in the exceptional event of the National People's Congress declaring a state of war or a state of emergency. None of those exceptions applies here, nor has the National People's Congress sought to justify the law on any such ground.[60]

Whereas it would follow from the PRC's apparent position – that the treaty has already been fully performed – that no treaty justification was in fact required as the PRC would not be answerable to London. Indeed it was the very purpose of the Joint Declaration that any practice of treaty extraterritoriality of that kind should be brought to an end, and that this chapter in history is now closed. That being the case there would have been no need in Beijing's view to justify to the UK the passage of a Chinese law which in their view conforms to the Basic Law, and which is also PRC legislation. That, it would seem, is the basis for their rejection of any UK involvement in the issue. That there now is a British claim to some three million Hong Kongers as 'British nationals' raises a separate and potentially serious issue for the Sino-British treaty.[61]

VI THE OFFENCES UNDER THE NATIONAL SECURITY LAW

Yet it is the question of fundamental rights and liberties which has been the principal source of anxiety. The new law for Hong Kong covers four broad

---

[58] United States' Hong Kong Autonomy Act Pub.L. 116–49.
[59] See Robert Shrimsley, 'UK Policy towards China Is Riddled with Contradictions', *F.T.* (London), 11 March 2021.
[60] Hansard, H.C. Vol. 678, col. 329 (1 July 2020).
[61] This issue will be reserved for discussion in the next chapter.

points: (1) secession (NSL articles 20–21); (2) subversion (articles 22–23); (3) terrorism (articles 24–28); and (4) collusion with a foreign country or external elements (articles 29–30). Hong Kong law knows only laws on treason, sedition and the protection of official secrets. In drafting article 23 of Hong Kong's Basic Law, which requires Hong Kong to pass its own national security laws, it was thought initially that subversion would be superfluous to treason for which Hong Kong law already provides. However, a requirement that Hong Kong shall enact its own subversion laws was reinserted into the draft language of what subsequently became article 23.[62]

Treason is known to the common law and from which Hong Kong derives its own treason law, while subversion may be lesser known although – contrary to popular belief – it is not unknown.[63] Secessionist acts, including advocating secession, have no true equivalent as common law offences other than if, for example, a secessionist act were to fall within treason. Levying war may be an example. As for collusion with foreign governments or other foreign persons, that too could fall within treason in certain circumstances.

But whatever may be said about the strangeness of some of these categories, it cannot be assumed simply that they cannot fall within defence and foreign affairs. Whether they should fall into these categories is another matter. The National Security Law in prohibiting secessionist and subversive acts has now expanded the definition of these acts to include situations where they are unaccompanied by the use of force, adding 'whether or not by force or threat of force' in the case of the former, and the words 'or threat of force or other unlawful means' in the case of the latter. This is in contrast to the Hong Kong Government's concession in 2003 when it had attempted, and failed, to enact these laws amidst widespread protest, that is, that they would be limited to forcible acts. It is this too which, amongst others, is said now to impinge on individual rights, not least the freedom of expression in Hong Kong as well as of association and peaceful assembly. There is, moreover, concern as has been mentioned that these laws may be too broad or vague and so it is said the definitions of these offences as well as the imposition of mandatory minimum sentences violate international human rights guarantees.[64]

What has caused some incredulity also is that the National Security Law provides that it 'shall apply to offences under this Law committed against' the HKSAR 'from outside the Region by a person who is not a permanent resident

---

[62] Hualing Fu and Richard Cullen, 'National Security Law in Hong Kong: Quo Vadis – A Study of Article 23 of the the Basic Law of Hong Kong' (2002) 19 *Pacific Basin L.J.* 185 at 195–7.
[63] Bob Allcock, speech to the Basic Law Institute, 23 December 2002.
[64] See e.g., David O'Mahony, *BarTalk*, Issue No. 138, 9 July 2020, para. 8.

of the Region' (NSL article 38).[65] Taken at its broadest however the mere passage of any truly 'extraterritorial' assertion of jurisdiction[66] thus causes no offence under international law unless it is enforced in the territory of another sovereign. This is equally true under the 'protective principle', for example, where the state which prescribes the offence – typically where it needs to do so against non-nationals – lacks confidence in the laws of others to protect its own vital interests.[67] Thus, if there is to be any breach of international law it has, simply, not occurred. It may never occur. It should also be considered that any 'extraterritorial' assertion of jurisdiction could also be in respect of a crime which has occurred, at least in part, in Hong Kong and it is a commonplace thing to enforce the law within one's territory.

VII THAT HONG KONG SHALL ENACT ITS OWN LAW

A genuine misconception has had to do with article 23 of the Basic Law, previously mentioned, which requires Hong Kong to enact these laws 'on its own'. The UK says that Hong Kong's autonomy has been violated. The point is misconceived. Beijing says Hong Kong can still enact such laws; it should and in fact, it 'shall' (NSL article 7). But because Hong Kong has not done so for so many years, and in light of the tumultuous events in the past year, Beijing has adopted the view – whatever one's own opinion about its desirability – that it must do so with every lawful right. This may be unpopular in various quarters but it is not on its face, or 'clearly', a treaty breach. The Joint Declaration is many things but hardly a model of clarity. The greased pig will likely evade capture.

In addition, there has been the argument that under PRC and Hong Kong law, article 23 of the Basic Law restricts the Standing Committee of the NPCSC's power to enact the new law. There is no realistic prospect of such an argument being successful since the National People's Congress authorised the NPCSC to enact the law during the Third Session of the 13th Congress. Moreover, the NPCSC has the final authority to interpret the Basic Law,[68] and this the Hong Kong courts have long accepted.[69] One could not have

---

[65] In comparison with article 37 which is limited to the prescription of extraterritorial reach in relation to only nationals and Hong Kong SAR residents.
[66] Putting aside assertions in respect of crimes which may have occurred partly in Hong Kong, such as a conspiracy abroad to commit a Hong Kong offence in Hong Kong.
[67] Iain Cameron, 'International Criminal Jurisdiction, Protective Principle', *Max Planck Encyclopedia of Public International Law*, paras. 1 and 10.
[68] Art. 158 of the Basic Law.
[69] *Lau Kong Yung v. Director of Immigration* (1999) 2 H.K.C.F.A.R. 300.

imagined that the UK Government might now seek to step in and declare the Hong Kong courts to be wrong, but this in fact is what has happened. Indeed matters have gone further; it is today a commonplace thing to say, quite suddenly, that the Hong Kong courts are not good enough for British judges to sit on. It comes close, very close, to pre-empting events simply by declaring the end of the rule of law and threatening to withdraw British judges on whom the rule of law also depends.

A considerable part of the substantive legal aspects of the UK Foreign Secretary's Commons statement on the day the National Security Law entered into Hong Kong law – quite aside from Mr Raab's earlier point about who gets to pass such legislation, Beijing or Hong Kong, and whether Hong Kong's autonomy has been violated – was devoted to this question about the protection of individual liberties and fundamental freedoms. In his statement Mr Raab went on to say:

> Secondly, the national security legislation contains a slew of measures that directly threaten the freedoms and rights protected by the joint declaration. The House will be particularly concerned by the potentially wide-ranging ability of the mainland authorities to take jurisdiction over certain cases without any independent oversight, and to try those cases in the Chinese courts. That measure violates paragraphs 3(3) and 3(5) of the joint declaration, and directly threatens the rights set out in the United Nations international covenant on civil and political rights, which, under the joint declaration, are to be protected in Hong Kong. That in particular represents a flagrant assault on freedom of speech and the right to peaceful protest for the people of Hong Kong.
>
> Thirdly, the legislation provides that Hong Kong's Chief Executive, rather than its Chief Justice, will appoint judges to hear national security cases—a move that clearly risks undermining the independence of Hong Kong's judiciary, which is, again, protected by the joint declaration in paragraph 3(3).[70]

Care should be taken not to engage in speculating about Beijing's position, but the fact that it takes the view that the Joint Declaration has been fully performed is at least consistent with the absence of any article-by-article explanation of these points. However, this is not to say that there are not complexities which underlie the position which the UK appears to have taken. The UK's position appears to be that the defence and foreign exceptions do not

---

[70] Note: Mr Raab's 'first' point, concerning who has the authority to pass such laws, Hong Kong, Beijing or indeed both, and his 'fourth' point, concerning where responsibility to maintain public order lies, in Hong Kong or Beijing, were discussed earlier, in Section V.

apply, but that at the same time there was no declaration of an emergency. In any of those situations Beijing would be allowed under article 18 of the Basic Law to extend relevant national laws to Hong Kong SAR. The clause in article 18 reads:

> In the event that the Standing Committee of the National People's Congress decides to declare a state of war or, by reason of turmoil within the Hong Kong Special Administrative Region which endangers national unity or security and is beyond the control of the government of the Region, decides that the Region is in a state of emergency, the Central People's Government may issue an order applying the relevant national laws in the Region.

However, the provision which Mr Raab has cited, concerning the ability of the mainland authorities to take charge of certain cases, reflects the precise situations of war or other public emergency which article 18 describes. Article 5 of the National Security Law is worded as follows:

> The Office for Safeguarding National Security of the Central People's Government in the Hong Kong Special Administrative Region shall, upon approval by the Central People's Government of a request made by the Government of the Hong Kong Special Administrative Region or by the Office itself, exercise jurisdiction over a case concerning offence endangering national security under this Law, if:
>
> (1) the case is complex due to the involvement of a foreign country or external elements, thus making it difficult for the Region to exercise jurisdiction over the case;
> (2) a serious situation occurs where the Government of the Region is unable to effectively enforce this Law; or
> (3) a major and imminent threat to national security has occurred.

One possible conclusion is that the mainland authorities would exercise this reserve jurisdictional power precisely where an emergency will have been declared in the event of these three highly confined situations.

At the time of the events of 2020 there had been speculation about whether there would be an emergency, but it is not difficult to see why declaring a state of emergency could potentially have been disastrous in the context of a major global financial centre. Had there been such a declaration, there would lie an answer to all of Mr Raab's points above; for even if the International Covenant on Civil and Political Rights were to apply, article 4 of that Covenant allows for derogation in times of public emergency. One would not have carte blanche, there are non-derogable rights too such as in respect of the continued need to observe the rule prohibiting discrimination and torture, amongst others.[71] Rights to personal liberty and rule of law guarantees would however be derogable.[72]

Procedurally there would have to be a notification of the States Parties to the Covenant,[73] this in fact was a requirement inserted by the UK during the Covenant's drafting, but it would then raise an unresolved issue; namely, whether the PRC which has signed but not ratified the Covenant may be, somehow, a party to it at least in respect of Hong Kong. That is distinct from saying that the PRC already facilitates the fulfilment of Hong Kong's periodic reporting obligation to the Human Rights Committee (HRC) as a body established under the Covenant. The current theory appears to be that not only 'the provisions' of the Covenant as they were applied before the handover would continue to apply – that is, with the UK's pre-handover treaty reservation to the development of democratic politics in the city – but also the Covenant's 'human rights procedures', that is, the obligation to report to the HRC.

The short of it is that the PRC proclaiming a state of emergency would likely have opened Pandora's Box. Article 4 of the Covenant would in any case require the emergency to 'threaten the life of the nation' – *'menace l'existence de la nation'*.[74] Of course, not proclaiming an emergency also means that the requirements under the Covenant's rule do not apply; including the requirement that any measures shall be only temporary, or that they must be proportionate.[75] Finally, placing the emphasis on the absence of a declaration of a state of emergency assumes the correctness of the UK's claim that what is involved is not defence, or foreign affairs. That assumption too is open to question.

VIII MAKING A VIRTUE OUT OF NECESSITY

In sum, wherever else a violation of treaty rights may or may not be found, the case for saying that it lies in a breach of the Joint Declaration is open to some doubt. Beijing, for its part, has taken the view that the Joint Declaration is 'irrelevant', adding that 'other countries and organisations have no right to meddle in Hong Kong affairs on the grounds of the Joint Declaration'.[76] It has

---

[71] William A. Schabas, *Nowak's CCPR Commentary*, 3rd rev. ed. (Kehl: Engel, 2019), 87 *et seq.*
[72] Ibid., 97 discussing the defeat of a contrary Franco-American proposal during the negotiations.
[73] ICCPR, art. 4(3); *Nowak's Commentary, op. cit.*, 103.
[74] *Nowak's Commentary, op. cit.*, 93.
[75] ICCPR art. 4(1), *Nowak's Commentary, op. cit.*, 100 *et seq.*
[76] Matt Ho, 'Joint Declaration "Not Relevant" to National Security Law for Hong Kong, says Beijing', S.C.M.P. (Hong Kong), 11 June 2020.

been suggested that even implicit acceptance of Beijing's interpretations of the Basic Law, as the Joint Declaration's implementing instrument, could have treaty significance.[77] Such acceptance can amount to a subsequent practice in the application of the treaty which establishes the 'agreement' of the two parties, the UK and the PRC, regarding the Joint Declaration's proper interpretation.[78] It cannot be said, simply, and to leave it at that, that since the UK had no hand in drafting the Basic Law, therefore it cannot also be bound by anything said or done under that law.

So, when in doubt, protest and whether there is or not a 'clear breach' the better counsel may be to pretend that there is. It may be thought that the UK can hardly do less having promised so much. It is, however, a separate thing to embellish that by repeating Mrs. Thatcher's suggestion. There is a gap between how the Joint Declaration has been portrayed and how it is written, and there is little to gain substantively by pushing the argument too far, whatever the dispute over the interpretation, or even status, of the Sino-British Joint Declaration, whatever reason there may be to insist upon having a dispute.

---

[77] C. L. Lim 'Britain's "Treaty Rights" in Hong Kong' (2015) 131 L.Q.R. 348.
[78] Vienna Convention on the Law of Treaties 1969, art. 31(3)(b).

11

Aftermath

I THE IMMEDIATE REACTION

In the wake of the National Security Law, foreign nations reacted not just by way of criticism but also through a range of other actions, not all of which were always clear in respect of their nature or purpose. The press have dubbed these acts of 'retaliation' but that is not a term of art even where it may describe the motive. Reports such as the UK FCO's six-monthly reports or a similar process in the US under the 1992 Hong Kong Policy Act[1] have been regular and routine incidences since the handover, albeit objected to by China. However the 2019 Hong Kong Human Rights and Democracy Act in the US,[2] amending the earlier 1992 Act, was another matter. Still, 'retaliation' is too nebulous as a word.

The term 'international sanctions' is used very widely today, and confusingly, to refer to United Nations sanctions such as those imposed by the Security Council, which the founders of the UN Charter intended as a prelude to more forcible action, and also to 'unilateral sanctions' so-called or what international lawyers in a more clinical fashion prefer to call 'unilateral coercive measures'. This latter category – 'unilateral sanctions' – is contentious under international law. Aside, that is, from lawful countermeasures, what used to be called 'reprisals' when armed force was still a legitimate response. These are a known category, but they are lawful only within carefully prescribed bounds. Other, patently lawful, acts of 'retorsion' include the withdrawal of a foreign diplomat's credentials or even the expulsion of journalists whatever else one may think of that. So too are treaty terminations and suspensions within the bounds of the law of treaties. An example would be the lawful termination or suspension of an extradition treaty. Withdrawal of recognition, say of a foreign government, may also be entirely within the

[1] Pub. L. 102–383.
[2] Pub. L. 116–76.

prerogative of the withdrawing State but not where the rules of an international organisation requires the continued recognition of a particular status, such as that of a separate customs territory under the rules of the World Trade Organization (WTO) and/or of the General Agreement on Tariffs and Trade (GATT).

Between July and October 2020, the UK, Germany, Canada, New Zealand, the US, Finland and Ireland, in response to China's National Security Law, suspended their extradition treaties with Hong Kong. France stated that it would not be ratifying an extradition treaty with Hong Kong. These suspensions ostensibly were intended to safeguard the rights of nationals (and others) in the suspending States. In some cases such as the UK the same act could constitute retorsion, meaning that it could have been intended as a patently lawful (albeit less than friendly) reaction to the National Security Law. Thus, a foreign State – albeit apparently not the UK which, as a party to the Sino-British Joint Declaration, had declared a breach of the Sino-British treaty – could still treat the National Security Law as Beijing's lawful prerogative, or in any case may have no clear legal right to press, yet still react with a perfectly lawful act of its own to show its displeasure. That such suspensions are considered to be unfriendly would be the whole point, and the negative Chinese media coverage which followed showed that this was no exception. Having said all this, however, the UK's reaction could simply be an act of due diligence.[3]

In July, Beijing responded from its end with similar suspensions of Hong Kong's extradition treaties with the UK, Canada and Australia. The UK as I have mentioned presents a special case in light of its view as a party to the Joint Declaration. We do not know what goes on in diplomatic discussions and correspondence.[4] The UK's suspension of its extradition treaty with Hong Kong is however nothing more than a retorsive act. A countermeasure would be a measure which otherwise would be in itself unlawful.[5] The extradition treaty's suspension by the UK is not a countermeasure because it is in itself perfectly lawful. A more difficult question arises in relation to the UK's new 'visa policy' of providing a 'path to citizenship' for British Nationals (Overseas) passport holders, and we will come back to this below.

---

[3] For UK practice, see Neil McDonald, 'The Role of Due Diligence in International Law' (2019) 68 I.C.L.Q. 1041.
[4] 'UK Suspends Extradition Treaty with Hong Kong', BBC, 20 July 2020.
[5] If we were however to assume that the treaty suspension, which raises distinct legal questions of its own, is unlawful, the UK would still need to notify the PRC that it was imposing a countermeasure. No such notification has been reported publicly at least.

We will also come back to the Sino-British relationship. It is the US however which, albeit not party to the Joint Declaration, has been the most active in its response to the enactment of the National Security Law for Hong Kong. The US has imposed sanctions on individuals in Hong Kong and Mainland Chinese officials. It has also determined that Hong Kong goods should be labelled 'Made in China'. As we have seen a principle feature of Hong Kong's autonomy is its status as a separate customs territory, together with the power conferred under the Hong Kong Basic Law to exercise an external rather than foreign affairs power and participate in the GATT/WTO. The US reaction to the passage of the National Security Law was therefore tantamount to a denial of US recognition of Hong Kong's autonomy, but is it a lawful response? The 'Made in China' dispute also sheds light on the role of the Hong Kong SAR Government's delegated external affairs powers in defending the terms of Hong Kong's autonomy, notwithstanding a chorus of opinion in the press counselling against its exercise by bringing a formal dispute in Geneva.

In short, a curious feature in the aftermath of the National Security Law was that it was American action which stood out aside from the UK's offer of relaxed visa requirements for BN(O) passport holders. That UK reaction could be a countermeasure, but again is more likely in the absence of more specific evidence intended to be no more than a lawful act of retorsion. One which the UK considers to be entirely lawful and within its rights. But because the PRC clearly rejects its lawfulness that then raises a follow-on question about the interpretation, and status of the Sino-British Exchange of Memoranda on British Dependent Territory Citizenship (BDTC) dated the same day, 19 December 1984, as the date of signature of the Joint Declaration and which refers expressly to the Joint Declaration.

But, first, to US action where the US albeit a non-party, and not uncharacteristically,[6] claims nonetheless to be reacting to a breach of the Sino-British Joint Declaration. Much of what happened both before and after the passage of the National Security Law cannot also be divorced from Sino-American rivalry and a grave deterioration in the international situation which, but for the UK siding with the US, would have had no relevance strictly speaking to an understanding of Sino-British disagreements over the Joint Declaration. As it turned out the UK was – barring the controversy over BN(O) passports – otherwise restrained in its reactions at least until

---

[6] The US in respect of China had claimed a breach of the United Nations Convention on the Law of the Sea, a treaty to which again it is a non-party and which it had consistently refused to be a party to.

March 2021 when, having almost taken a back-seat to US action, it imposed UK sanctions not in respect of Hong Kong but curiously in tandem with the US approach of shifting the focus to Xinjiang. The Hong Kong situation is almost indissociable in the Chinese view from the involvement of certain Western nations in supporting, perhaps even in fomenting, secession in China. It is in any event inseparable from the rapidly deteriorating situation between the US and the PRC.

II MADE IN CHINA

What distinguishes the US requirement which was announced in July 2020 that Hong Kong goods should be re-labelled 'Made in China', notwithstanding any purpose that may have as an American unilateral sanction following the passage of the National Security Law for Hong Kong, is that the whole matter falls also under the scrutiny of WTO rules including under the GATT.[7] Despite the Trump Administration's efforts, which had continued the previous US policy of criticising the WTO dispute settlement system, the WTO still possesses the semblance of a compulsory third-party dispute settlement system.

On 14 July 2020, two weeks after the passage of the National Security Law and its promulgation in the Hong Kong SAR, the then US President signed into law the Hong Kong Autonomy Act[8] which Congress had passed and, pursuant to that Act, issued Executive Order 13936 – 'The President's Executive Order on Hong Kong Normalization'. That Executive Order aims to 'hold China accountable for its aggressive actions against the people of Hong Kong'. It states, further, that: 'It shall be the policy of the United States to suspend or eliminate different and preferential treatment for Hong Kong to the extent permitted by law and in the national security, foreign policy, and economic interest of the United States.'

On 10 August, US Customs and Border issued the following notice:

> In light of the President's Executive Order on Hong Kong Normalization, issued on July 14, 2020, suspending the application of section 201(a) of the United States-Hong Kong Policy Act of 1992 to the marking statute, section 304 of the Tariff Act of 1930, with respect to imported goods produced in

---

[7] The ensuing discussion draws from a talk which was given in Hong Kong following US customs' requirement that Hong Kong made goods be labelled 'Made in China' in which the present author argued for the initiation of WTO dispute settlement proceedings as a means of pacific settlement. See also Finnbarr Bermingham, 'Hong Kong's WTO Threat against US "Made in China" Ruling Puts City in Uncharted Waters', SCMP (Hong Kong), 21 August 2020.

[8] Pub.L. 116-49.

Hong Kong, such goods may no longer be marked to indicate 'Hong Kong' as their origin, but must be marked to indicate 'China'.[9]

The debate in Hong Kong itself turned to the prospects of initiating formal dispute proceedings against the US at the WTO and, on 23 February 2021, the Hong Kong delegation to the WTO went on to request the establishment of a WTO dispute settlement panel. The press in Hong Kong reported that GATT article 26.5(c) was the provision in question.[10] That is inaccurate. That provision states only that were a territory to acquire its own customs autonomy it may then seek to become a GATT contracting party, but colonial Hong Kong had become a GATT contracting party by 1986. It then took some eight years of negotiations, the Uruguay Round of negotiations, before the Marrakesh Agreement established the WTO. Article XI of the Marrakesh Agreement provides that a GATT contracting party at the time will automatically become an original founding WTO member. That is what the Hong Kong SAR is, a WTO founding member and the relevant provision is article XI. It was not until seven years later that the PRC itself became a WTO member, so that is something Hong Kong takes pride in. The governing clause is not a GATT provision but a provision of the Marrakesh Agreement.

A key issue in the Hong Kong SAR-US dispute involves the WTO's non-discrimination principle. What the US had decided was that the Hong Kong SAR, unlike other WTO members, should no longer be entitled to mark its goods as its own. That is where an argument now lies – that the US measure is discriminatory. Other WTO members will be able to mark their goods as their own but Hong Kong will not. In Hong Kong itself there was further confusion, with the suggestion in the press that Hong Kong cannot claim to be treated less favourably by being compared to China.[11] However, the unfavourable comparison is not with the PRC but rather with the differential treatment given to other fully fledged WTO members. The relevant provisions include GATT article I, paragraph 1, being the general non-discrimination rule, and GATT article IX.1 which forbids discrimination against a WTO member specifically in respect of the use of marks of origin. There also are other WTO agreements such as the Technical Barriers to Trade (TBT) Agreement which prohibits discrimination when imposing technical regulations on the importation of

---

[9] 85 FR 48551; also Presidential Executive Order – 'Country of Origin Marking of Products in Hong Kong', Federal Register, 11 August 2020; United States' Hong Kong Autonomy Act Pub. L. 116-49.
[10] See Bermingham, *op. cit.*
[11] See 'Analysing Hong Kong's WTO Challenge to Trump', *SCMP* (Hong Kong), Podcast, 21 August 2020.

goods originating from another WTO member, and considers marking and labelling regulations to be technical regulations in its Annex. So these are the sorts of provisions which impose stringent disciplines on any 'sanctioning', loosely speaking, of Hong Kong in this respect.

The US measure is also a reminder of what Kevin Hassett, Chairman of the White House Council of Economic Advisers, had threatened during a BBC interview in November 2018, that the PRC should be evicted from the WTO. There are however no WTO provisions for evicting or expelling any member. A WTO member can withdraw but there are no express provisions on expulsion. It no more than rhetoric. However, what the Executive Order on Hong Kong Normalisation tries to do is similar, not with the PRC but with the Hong Kong SAR. That is, to treat Hong Kong as if it were no longer a WTO member.

There is a further technical point. US Customs and Border Protection's (CBP's) statement reads:

> The change in marking requirement does not affect country of origin determinations. For purposes of assessing ordinary duties under Chapters 1 to 97 of the Harmonised Tariff Schedule of the United States, or temporary or additional duties under Chapter 99 of the Harmonised Tariff Schedule of the United States. Therefore goods that are products of Hong Kong, should continue to report International Organisation for Standardisation (ISO) country code 'HK' as the country of origin when required.

In other words, tariffs imposed on Chinese goods including the Trump Administration's punitive tariffs on the PRC will not after all be imposed. The US merely requires Hong Kong manufacturers to label Hong Kong goods as goods that are made in China, rather than to treat those goods as if they did come from the Chinese mainland rather than from the Hong Kong SAR as a separate customs territory. There is no question of differential duties or a change in US duties, there are no additional duties, there are no punitive duties such as those which are being applied to products from the mainland, there is no question about treating Hong Kong goods as goods that come from another WTO member. I put it in such a deliberate manner because it suggests the careful application of legal thought. This sanction is calibrated so precisely that no one should complain and perhaps more importantly, the US might succeed in removing the sanction from under the sheltering scope of something called the Rules of Origin Agreement. The US argument would be that all of this has nothing to do with rules of origin or where in fact the goods come from.

There has been criticism too of the Hong Kong SAR's decision to bring a WTO case that it will merely highlight controversy over Hong Kong's autonomy; that choosing to bring a case will just show that Hong Kong cannot do so without consulting Beijing. It is very difficult to understand the criticism, even assuming its underlying assumptions. The Basic Law, in Chapter 4, article 43 states that the Chief Executive, as the head of the Hong Kong SAR, is accountable to the Central People's Government (CPG) as well as being accountable to the SAR itself. Separately, there are at least two other relevant provisions in Chapters 5 and 7 of the Basic Law. In Chapter 5, which deals with the economy, article 116 states that the Hong Kong SAR 'shall' be a separate customs territory; and in Chapter 7 article 151 states that the Hong Kong SAR may, using the name 'Hong Kong, China', maintain and develop relations, conduct and implement agreements with foreign states, regions and international organisations. The word there is 'may' in article 151 unlike in article 116 where it is stated that the Hong Kong SAR 'shall' be a separate customs territory. Being its own customs territory has little to do with the fact that the Hong Kong SAR's Chief Executive is accountable to the CPG. She is but the two points are distinct. In any case, one should consider how the WTO works. WTO members consult each other regularly. The Hong Kong SAR consulting the PRC CPG would be no exception. Business is done in the WTO through informal groupings. During the Uruguay Round, there was the Beau Rivage Group. These were small, developing and developed nations which met to discuss common issues. Hong Kong was part of another informal grouping called the Buick Group. There was the Cairns Group dealing with agricultural issues, the West African Cotton Four, the Friends of Fish who met to discuss fisheries subsidies, the Friends of Geographical Indications, the Friends of the Development Box, and so on. In another called the Invisibles Group the members were senior officials who ordinarily were based in the various capitals rather than in Geneva. There was the Like-Minded Group and the Paradisus Group. How then can it be suggested that the Hong Kong SAR as a WTO member is prevented from consulting with the PRC CPG as a separate WTO member? Everyone consults when it comes to Geneva business, all of them.

As for whether there was a true choice in choosing to bring a WTO dispute in the circumstances, mention has already been made of article 116 and there are other provisions such as article 104 which requires the SAR Government to uphold the Basic Law which will include defending Hong Kong's status as a separate customs territory.

III INDIVIDUAL SANCTIONS

As for American sanctions on Hong Kong officials, a first tranche was imposed following the National Security Law's passage in 2020, and a second tranche in 2021 following the NPCSC's Decision of 11 March 2021 to reform Hong Kong's electoral laws. These reforms envisage an enlarged LegCo and an enlarged Election Committee to elect the Chief Executive. So-called smart sanctions are highly targeted. They are directed at specific persons be they natural or legal depriving them of the right to enter into transactions with US parties, including transactions routed through the US banking system, they freeze the assets of such parties and prohibit natural persons from entry into the US. They have become a mainstay of the array of diplomatic tools used following the passage of the Magnitsky Act, to give it its full name the Russia and Moldova Jackson–Vanik Repeal and Sergei Magnitsky Rule of Law Accountability Act of 2012.[12] Its expansion to target individuals globally deemed to be responsible for human rights violations was a result of the 2016 Global Magnitsky Human Rights Accountability Act,[13] In July 2020, the US President issued Executive Order 13936[14] which in turn led to the sanctioning in August of 11 Hong Kong and CPG officials following the passage of the National Security Law. They include the Chief Executive and the Secretary for Justice of the Hong Kong SAR. In late March, just before the first meeting held in Alaska between Chinese and American Officials since the Biden Administration entered the White House, in delivering an update to Congress under the Hong Kong Autonomy Act, the US Secretary of State announced sanctions imposed upon another twenty-four officials following the NPCSC's decision to reform Hong Kong's electoral laws.[15]

To the extent that unilateral sanctions claim to respond to human rights breaches they will take the form of countermeasures. Two aspects need to be observed. First, such measures are unilateral in the sense that the sanctioning country acts as judge, jury and prosecutor. This opens up the use of Magnitsky-style sanctions as a new human rights enforcement tool to the risk of abuse.

---

[12] Public Law No: 112–208 12/14/2012.
[13] Title XII, Subtitle F, ss. 1261 to 1265, National Defense Authorisation Act for Fiscal Year 2017, Pub. L. No. 114–328, 12/23/2016.
[14] Executive Order 13936, 14 July 2020.
[15] Pursuant to s. 5(a), Hong Kong Autonomy Act, H.R. 7440, Pub. L. No. 116–149. See 'Hong Kong Autonomy Act Update', Press Statement by Antony J. Blinken, Secretary of State, US State Department website at www.state.gov/hong-kong-autonomy-act-update/. For US sanctions in respect of Hong Kong generally, see https://home.treasury.gov/policy-issues/financial-sanctions/sanctions-programs-and-country-information/hong-kong-related-sanctions. (last accessed 26 August 2021).

III Individual Sanctions

Second, while unilateral sanctions are legally controversial the incompleteness of international law offers them a semblance of legal justification. The short of it is that international law permits self-help in the form of countermeasures. For its part, the International Law Commission has defined countermeasures[16] as acts which otherwise would be unlawful but are legally excusable (or justified) provided that they are only temporary, aimed at inducing compliance with international law, and are proportionate.[17]

There is however at least one genuine difficulty with this view which is that the taking of countermeasures:

> shall not affect:
> (a) the obligation to refrain from the threat or use of force as embodied in the Charter of the United Nations.[18]

There has been a persistent body of opinion that economic coercion too amounts to the use of force, that threat of economic coercion amounts to a threat to use force and that the words 'threat or use of force' in the Charter are not confined in their meaning to military force. It is not without controversy. The 'prevailing view', according to the writers, almost invariably from the Western Hemisphere, is that the relevant provision of the United Nations Charter only prohibits armed aggression. However, modern opinion would rest that conclusion purely upon an interpretation of article 2(4) of the Charter,[19] rather than the views of states. Notably, the General Assembly of the United Nations – representing the majority of nations – denounces unilateral sanctions ('unilateral coercive measures') regularly, doing so by resolution once every two years or so. However that ostensibly is justified upon the alternative basis that economic coercion would violate the principle

---

[16] International Law Commission, Articles on Responsibility of States for Internationally Wrongful Acts 2001, I.L.C. Ybk 2001/II(2), 26, arts. 22, 49; G.A.O.R., Fifty-Sixth Session, Supp. No. 10 (A/56/10), Ch. V; hereinafter 'ARSIWA'.
[17] ILC Draft Articles, arts. 49, 50.
[18] Ibid., art. 52.
[19] See James Crawford, *Brownlie's Principles of Public International Law*, 8th. ed. (Oxford: Oxford University Press, 2012), 747. The late Judge Crawford cites Professor Abrecht Randelzhofer of Berlin who in turn offers, aside from the citation of other writers, the view that otherwise art. 2(4) of the UN Charter, being the relevant clause, would not sit well with provisions such as art. 44 and, furthermore, that otherwise there would be no means for states to exert pressure upon other states to comply with international law. This is a fairly straightforward argument for the permissibility of unilateral coercive measures (i.e. sanctions) outside the framework of the United Nations Charter. See Abrecht Randelzhofer, 'Article 2(4)', in Bruno Simma (ed.), *The Charter of the United Nations: A Commentary*, 2nd ed. (Oxford: Oxford University Press, 2002), 112, 117.

of the sovereign equality of states.[20] Whatever its ultimate basis, the legality of unilateral economic coercion has routinely been denounced by the United Nations General Assembly.[21] Put bluntly, it is a reaction to the perception of larger or more powerful states coercing smaller, weaker and/or developing nations into compliance with what may involve only Western views of international law. There is a line which often lies unobserved between counter-terrorism action, or action against racial discrimination, on which there is consensus, and other forms of economic sanction on which there is not.

For its part, the PRC imposed retaliatory sanctions in August 2020 on Republican Party lawmakers in response to Trump Administration sanctions on Hong Kong and Chinese officials.[22] In March 2021, further retaliatory sanctions followed which were unconnected with Hong Kong. These were in response to US, EU and British sanctions in respect of the Xinjiang Autonomous Region.[23] There is a noticeable pattern of US policy's revolving focus and attention in respect of Tibet, Hong Kong, Xinjiang and Taiwan. On the Chinese side, there is a clear perception of a firm attempt to seek not only to delegitimise the PRC Government but also to destabilise and dismember China.[24]

The UK's statements and actions in respect of the Sino-British Joint Declaration take place, and should be viewed, in this broader context.

---

[20] UN Charter, art. 2(1).
[21] See further, however, Rebecca Barber, 'An Exploration of the General Assembly's Troubled Relationship with Unilateral Sanctions' (2021) 70 *I.C.L.Q.* 343.
[22] China imposes sanctions on Republican U.S. lawmakers over Hong Kong, *Reuters*, 10 August 2020.
[23] 'US and Canada Follow EU and UK in Sanctioning Chinese officials over Xinjiang', *Guardian* (London), 22 March 2021; Robin Emmott, 'EU, China Impose Tit-for-tat Sanctions over Xinjiang Abuses', *Reuters*, 22 March 2021; 'China Hits Back to Sanction UK Individuals and Entities Behind Smears of Xinjiang', *Global Times* (Beijing), 26 March 2021; 'China Sanctions US, Canadian Citizens in Xinjiang Row', *Agence-France-Presse/Voice of America*, 27 March 2021.
[24] The PRC highlights in its 2019 Defence White Paper the aims of deterring and resisting aggression; safeguarding national political security, the people's security and social stability; opposing and containing 'Taiwan independence', 'crack[ing] down on proponents of separatist movements', mentioning in this regard Tibet and Xinjiang ('the creation of "East Turkistan"'); safeguarding 'national sovereignty, unity, territorial integrity and security', amongst a total of nine items listed therein; 'China's National Defense in the New Era', State Council Information Office, PRC, July 2019. For official PRC statements drawing an analogy with the Boxer Protocol, see Kristin Huang, 'China-EU Relations: Beijing Ramps up the Rhetoric in dispute over Sanctions', *SCMP* (Hong Kong), 24 March 2021, quoting the PRC Foreign Ministry spokeswoman ('Their actions have reminded people of the history of the Eight-Nation Alliance'), albeit in the context of apparently coordinated sanctions.

IV THE UNITED KINGDOM

The UK had refrained from sanctions at least in respect of Hong Kong. Rather, Sino-British relations overall have been affected deeply by the offer of what the UK dubs 'a pathway to citizenship' for BN(O) passport holders who previously were limited to six months' visa-free entry into the UK; in effect, the UK's offer is that of a more flexible working visa arrangement which in turn could grant the right to apply for UK citizenship. It may be that by not treating BN(O) passport holders as UK citizens the UK is also hoping to avoid allegations of any treaty breach by the PRC. It is, on this view, to be presented as no more than an adjustment of visa arrangements. But this would be to enter into the realm of speculation. In any event, the UK Government has played up rather than played down the issue, and it has drawn a connection with its views in respect of Hong Kong. The PRC responded swiftly, stating that in its view the UK had violated the Sino-British Joint Declaration. In January, when the UK's new visa scheme was launched, the Xinhua news agency reported Tam Yiu-chung, a Hong Kong member of the NPCSC, saying that the UK had violated the Joint Declaration and that 'it was natural for the Chinese side to take countermeasures'. The report also cited the Hong Kong Secretary for Justice's views:[25]

> Cheng [Teresa Cheng, Secretary for Justice] said that at the signing of the Sino-British Joint Declaration, there was also an immediate exchange of memoranda between the two sides dealing with the issue of nationality. The British Memorandum stated that the British government will not confer the right of abode in Britain on holders of the BN(O) passport who are Chinese nationals in Hong Kong.[26]
>
> Cheng quoted former British officials as saying that Britain considered the provisions contained in the British Memorandum to be of binding effect. If BNO passport holders were given full British citizenship automatically, it would be a breach of the commitments made between China and Britain in the Sino-British Joint Declaration.

---

[25] 'Britain Betrays Trust over So-called BN(O) Passport: Various Sector in Hong Kong', *Xinhua*, 30 January 2021.
[26] This, it would appear, is an interpretation of the British Memorandum, para. (a) – that British Dependent Territories Citizens 'will be eligible to retain an appropriate status which, without conferring the right of abode in the United Kingdom, will entitle them to continue to use passports issue by the Government of the United Kingdom'.

The more strident *Global Times* of Beijing quoted the spokesperson of the Liaison Office of the Central Government in Hong Kong:

> Before Hong Kong returned to China in 1997, China and the UK had already reached a consensus on the BN(O) and exchanged MOUs, as the UK clearly promised that those who held BN(O) had no right of abode in the UK and China recognized it as a travel document.
>
> Twenty-four years later, the UK government has blatantly betrayed that trust and used the national security law for Hong Kong to manipulate the issue of BN(O) and expand its scope of application, trying to turn a large part of Hong Kong people into 'second-class citizens' and completely change the essence of the China-UK MOU on the issue, the liaison office spokesperson said.[27]

In response the PRC declared that it no longer would recognise the BN(O) passport as a travel document.[28] This precisely was the arrangement under the Exchange of Memoranda. Under the Chinese Memorandum; the PRC would recognise the BN(O) as a 'travel document' for travel 'to other States and regions'.[29] While under the UK Memorandum Hong Kong's British Dependent Territories Citizens will 'be eligible to retain an appropriate status which, without conferring the right of abode in the United Kingdom, will entitle them to continue to use passports issued by the Government of the United Kingdom'.[30] The UKFCO, for its part, expressed its 'disappointment' but said that it was not surprised.[31]

Where does all this leave the Joint-Declaration? In legal terms intact, despite the resultant consternation. Had the UK required 'recognition' of BN(O) passport holders in China in 1984, it would have meant that in 1997 the PRC would have had to absorb more than an estimated three million 'foreign' nationals, who at the time were also persons whom the UK would not have permitted to settle in the UK. They would in effect have been rendered Stateless. On this the two sides were in agreement, but that agreement has now for all intents and purposes broken down. It is interesting to compare Geoffrey Howe's speech to the House of Commons on 16 May 1984:

> I have to say that I do not believe that either this Parliament or a successor would favour changes which stimulated emigration from Hong Kong to the

---

[27] 'Chinese Central Government Agencies Blast UK for Betraying Trust over So-called BN(O) Passport for HK Residents', *Global Times* (Beijing), 31 January 2021.
[28] Whether this act is permanent is not an answer that can, at present, be answered.
[29] Chinese Memorandum, 19 December 1984.
[30] British Memorandum, 19 December 1984, para. (a).
[31] 'China Will No Longer Recognise British National Overseas Citizens', *Guardian* (London), 29 January 2021; 'UK Disappointed by Beijing BN(O) Stance', *RTHK* (Hong Kong), 30 January 2021.

UK or elsewhere. That is a further reason why we are looking for arrangements which would allow Hong Kong people to enter and leave the territory freely and, at the same time, provide a secure future for them there. That must remain a prime objective.[32]

Still, that was 1984, not now, but it would appear from this that the motivation for having China recognise BN(O) passports for travel outside China was linked to the need to prevent emigration to the UK, or indeed elsewhere. It was a UK demand in light of the UK's policy then. PRC de-recognition of BN(O) passports appears therefore to be a calibrated, direct response.

From an international legal viewpoint the questions which now arise are about whether the UK, having also chosen to treat the enactment of the National Security Law as a treaty breach, was imposing countermeasures in the strict legal sense. There seems to be less doubt, if any, that the PRC considers its de-recognition of BN(O) passports as a countermeasure.

Even so the PRC never recognised BN(O) 'passports' as more than 'travel documents' to all destinations other than China. The words 'other States and regions' in the Chinese Memorandum needs to be construed. If these words are taken to mean that BN(O) passport holders could still use them as travel documents to enter Hong Kong but not 'other regions' (such as the Macao SAR) then aside from any possible inconvenience the effects would still be limited. In March 2021 the Hong Kong SAR informed certain third-countries that it would no longer recognise BN(O) passports even as travel documents to other countries.[33] Be that so, it appears that these are countries with which the Hong Kong SAR – which also possesses its own delegated immigration powers – has signed so-called working holiday arrangements.[34] It remains to be seen, in the event that Hong Kong's request is ignored, what the legal consequences might be. What is clear is that the PRC and Hong Kong SAR governments no longer view the BN(O) as a valid travel document even to third countries, and that the PRC and the Hong Kong SAR consider this to be a legitimate countermeasure.

---

[32] TNA/PREM 19/1265 (Pt. 14, Future of Hong Kong, New Territorial [sic.] Leases); Speech by the Rt. Hon. Sir Geoffrey Howe QC MP Secretary of State for Foreign and Commonwealth Affairs Opening of the Debate on Hong Kong in the House of Commons: Wednesday, 16 May 1984.

[33] 'UK Defends Hong Kong Passport Rights against China', *Deutsche Welle* (Bonn, Berlin), 26 March 2021; Danny Mok, 'HK Tells 14 Countries to Stop Recognising BN(O) Passports', *SCMP* (Hong Kong), 26 March 2021; 'Hong Kong Tells Foreign Governments to Stop Accepting British Passports, *ABC News Online* (Sydney, Canberra), 26 March 2021.

[34] Art. 151, Basic Law.

Doubtless, the Sino-British Exchange of Memoranda inform the interpretation of the Joint Declaration,[35] and the British Memorandum states that it is presented 'in connection with' the Joint Declaration. However Memoranda of Understanding could, depending upon their proper construction, also impose obligations of their own. This appears to be the PRC's and the Hong Kong SAR's position; namely, that the UK had committed itself not to confer a right of abode through issuing BN(O) passports which the PRC and the Hong Kong SAR will then reciprocate by treating these as travel documents for travel to third countries. It has included acceptance of BN(O) passports at the Hong Kong SAR's immigration checkpoints and as proof of identity. That treatment has now been withdrawn as what China and the Hong Kong authorities consider to be a legitimate and proportionate countermeasure to the UK's breach of the British Memorandum's terms. Because that commitment, which itself is binding albeit in the form of a unilateral commitment, also informs China's and the UK's understanding of the Joint Declaration's nationality provisions breach of that commitment breaches also the Joint Declaration.[36] There may also be some evidence of the UK viewing the memoranda as being binding legally.[37]

Still, there the matter might have ended but for further UK claims of breach of the Joint Declaration following the NPCSC's January decision on electoral reform in Hong Kong. Since the passage of the National Security Law, the UK has cited a Joint Declaration breach in July 2020 because of that law, a second breach in November 2020 due to the disqualification of certain Hong Kong

---

[35] See art. 31(2)(a) of the Vienna Convention on the Law of Treaties 1969.

[36] The Hong Kong and Chinese perspective is stated, for example, in the Hong Kong Government News Service's report on the Hong Kong Secretary for Justice's views; 'S.J. Explains China-UK Pact', 30 January 2021, at www.news.gov.hk (last accessed 26 August 2021). In that report, Ms Cheng cites parliamentary statements by Sir Geoffrey Howe in 1985 and Lord Goldsmith in 2008 as evidence of the UK's own view that the UK is bound not to extend a right of citizenship to BN(O) passport holders.

[37] TNA/PREM 19/1265 (Pt. 14), 'Future of Hong Kong, Meetings with UMELCO Delegation: 15 May 1984', Hong Kong Department, 14 May 1984:

> **Nationality and other 'obligations' of HMG**
> 9. Not possible to give blanket assurances. Would not help confidence. Would be seen as anticipation of failure. Would reduce Chinese incentive to observe agreement if they could accuse HMG of underminging it . . .
>
> 10. Meanwhile will press Chinese hard in negotiation for a deal which will retain essentials of British nationality.
>
> **Precise Assurances in Agreement**
> 11. Have explained the main assurances would be the international agreement itself and Chinese self-interest.

legislators,[38] and a third breach in March 2021 due to the NPCSC decision to reform LegCo and the Election Committee. The UK's statements in respect of electoral matters while perhaps unremarkable are surprising from a treaty perspective because of the near complete absence of electoral provisions in the body of the Joint Declaration, rather than one line in Annex I, consisting of China's elaboration of its own policies, on having an elected legislature.[39] The references in the Joint Declaration to the selection of the Chief Executive are to selection by way of election 'or consultation'.[40] The promise of having as an ultimate aim the election by universal suffrage of the Chief Executive and of LegCo are found solely in the Basic Law, which is Chinese legislation.[41] For the UK to hold China to account on electoral reform would be not unlike the UK's position that Kenya should be responsible for the killing and torture of unarmed Mau Mau 'insurgents' since it had succeeded the Colonial Government rather than the United Kingdom having done so.[42] Lord Patten came according to his own account not too late, but he was too late for the UK, after its own silence in the Joint Declaration, to have any treaty basis now to gainsay Hong Kong's electoral arrangements. Hindsight is a poor guide to treaty practice. Dramatic analogies aside the more fundamental issue is that Sino-British negotiations, as we saw, came near to collapse on the issue of the severance of all and any links of British authority. This was due to the PRC's apprehension that sovereignty will be rendered meaningless by any claim of British authority in any guise, the validity and binding quality of the Joint Declaration and its annexes notwithstanding. Hence China's repeated assertion that Britain possesses no residual authority.

Be that all as it may, despite statements since July 2020 that the UK was contemplating sanctions, it has not taken a single countermeasure. This suggests great care on both sides in calibrating their physical rather than verbal responses precisely at least in respect of the Joint Declaration.

What neither party would want ideally, notwithstanding all these recent events, is to jeopardise the Joint Declaration. Connecting a measure, a new practice or policy, to the Joint Declaration is fraught. It leads to questions about whether that new policy or practice would otherwise be in itself a breach

---

[38] 'China Is Breaking the Treaty with Hong Kong Says Dominic Raab', *Guardian* (London), 12 November 2020.
[39] Art. 1, Annex I, Joint Declaration.
[40] Joint Declaration, para. 3(d), and art. 1 of Annex I.
[41] Arts. 45 and 68, Basic Law.
[42] *Mutua et al. v. The Foreign and Commonwealth Office* [2011] EWHC 1913 (Q.B.); [2012] EWHC 2678 (Q.B.) (unreported). See further, Ian Cobain and Richard Norton-Taylor, 'Mau Mau Massacre Cover-up Detailed in Newly-opened Secret Files', *Guardian*, 29 November 2012.

of the treaty but for the alleged breach to which it claims to respond.[43] Resort to self-help, a troubling privilege from the darker corners of an incomplete international legal order, could unravel the Joint Declaration.

At best the UK, it may be supposed, would prefer to treat its own new BN(O) policy as having nothing to do with law. The Exchange of Memoranda which the PRC treats as an integral part of the Sino-British Joint Declaration does not, from the UK's viewpoint, however contain any binding legal obligations of its own. It was a compromise because Thatcher was adamant, during the Sino-British treaty negotiations, that more than three million Chinese should not have the right to reside in the UK. Viewed in this way the UK's BN(O) policy at most amounts to retorsion – an unfriendly, albeit lawful, act. To the PRC it may appear as at the very least a countermeasure – an unlawful act which claims to be excused or justified by another breach, which the PRC denies. In answer to any UK allegation of breach, the PRC could also invoke one of the known defences under international law which would preclude wrongfulness – for example, that its response to recent events with the enactment of a National Security Law was necessary, leaving no choice of means.[44]

Countermeasures under the international law rules on State responsibility lead also to questions about treaty suspension. Such questions are, in turn, only an uncomfortable step away from those of treaty termination. Under article 65 of the Vienna Convention on the Law of Treaties a suspension or termination will need to be notified to the other party together with notification of the grounds upon which the notifying State relies.[45] Article 60 of the Vienna Convention allows termination or suspension only for a 'material' breach, rather than for a non-material breach on which the Vienna Convention says nothing explicit, and in this it is said resides the principle that such drastic action should keep within the bounds of proportionality.[46] A material breach consists, according to article 60(3), of:

(a) A repudiation of the treaty not sanctioned by the present Convention; or

---

[43] ARSIWA, *op. cit.*, arts. 22, 49.
[44] *Ibid.*, art. 25 but not limited thereto; see generally ARSIWA, Chapter V ('Circumstances Precluding Wrongfulness').
[45] Vienna Convention on the Law of Treaties 1969, art. 65(1).
[46] See further e.g. Malgosia Fitzmaurice, 'The Law of Treaties, the Law of State Responsibility and the Non-performance of Treaty Obligations: A View from the Case Law', in Michael J. Bowman and Dino Kritsiotis (eds.), *Conceptual and Contextual Perspectives on the Modern Law of Treaties* (Cambridge: Cambridge University Press, 2018), 748, esp. 750–3; for the interaction between the law of treaties and the international law of State responsibility, see also Christian J. Tams, 'Regulating Treaty Breaches', in Bowman and Kritsiotis, *ibid.*, 440, and also for an early discussion of the contemporary modern law, Shabtai Rosenne, *Developments in the Law of Treaties 1945–1986* (Cambridge: Cambridge University Press, 1989), 33 *et seq.*

(b) The violation of a provision essential to the accomplishment of the object or purpose of the treaty.

It is difficult to imagine the parties, quite aside from the questions of termination or suspension, to have intended through their silence[47] that the Joint Declaration could be subject to denunciation or withdrawal or that the Joint Declaration should imply a right to denounce or withdraw from it either in whole or in part.[48] For the reason that the Joint Declaration does not easily fall into the category of treaties which were 'not intended to set up an everlasting condition of things' to quote Lauterpacht's Oppenheim.[49] Assuming, however, that the present author is wrong there is at least respectable authority for saying that any such right would nonetheless have to fulfil the notification requirement set out in article 65 above even if the treaty does not say so expressly.[50] The matter is complicated a little further by the fact that commentators are in disagreement on an implied right to denounce or withdraw from a treaty.[51] The point is not entirely moot because of the suggestion, which has at least been made, that once Hong Kong had been handed over the Joint Declaration for all intents and purposes would have lost much of its practical importance.[52] That is consistent with saying that the territorial aspect, the handover, is 'an independent legal fact having a life of its own'.[53]

---

[47] The Joint Declaration is silent on denunciation/withdrawal.

[48] See Vienna Convention on the Law of Treaties 1969, art. 56; Theodore Christakis, 'Article 56', in Olivier Corten and Pierre Klein (eds.) *The Vienna Convention on the Law of Treaties: A Commentary* (Oxford: Oxford University Press, 2011), 1251 *et seq.*

[49] See Ian Sinclair, *The Vienna Convention on the Law of Treaties*, 2nd ed. (Manchester: Manchester University Press, 1984), 186, citing Fitzmaurice's 'Second Report on the Law of Treaties by Mr G. G. Fitzmaurice, Special Rapporteur', UN Doc. A/CN.4/107, 15 March 1957, [1957] ILC Ybk., vol. II, 16, 22, 52, and who in turn had cited the eighth edition of Oppenheim, L. Oppenheim, *International Law: A Treatise*, vol. 1, 'Peace', 8th ed., H. Lauterpacht ed. (London: Longmans, Green and Co., 1955), 938.

[50] Sinclair, *op. cit.*, 187.

[51] For example, Kolb rejects this possibility outright, Robert Kolb, *The Law of Treaties: An Introduction* (Cheltenham: Elgar, 2016), 217. Sinclair, whom I cited earlier, together with a string of eminent British commentators have long taken the contrary view, *op. cit.*, 186.

[52] It does not seem possible that desuetude or obsolescence could come into it, but denunciation or withdrawal would be another matter.

[53] See Kolb, *op. cit.*, 212–13. One possible difficulty, it is said, lies in article 62(2)(a) of the Vienna Convention on the Law of Treaties which concerns the application of the doctrine *rebus sic stantibus*. It has at least been read, supposedly, to prevent denunciation of or withdrawal also from a territorial boundary treaty. See Anthony Aust, *Modern Treaty Law and Practice*, 3rd ed. (Cambridge: Cambridge University Press, 2013), 256. This appears to reflect Waldock's view. See H. Waldock, 'Second Report on the Law of Treaties' [1963] ILC Ybk., vol. II, 36 (draft art. 17(4)); Laurence R. Helfer, 'Terminating Treaties', in Duncan B. Hollis (ed.), *The Oxford Guide to Treaties* (Oxford: Oxford University Press, 2012), 634, 638; Christakis, *op. cit.*, 1258–9, 1270–1. But Aust's statement in all likelihood conflates arts. 56 and 62. Waldock's proposal was

Whichever the case, a disagreement relating to a notification under the rule in article 65 of the Vienna Convention could in turn trigger larger and even more unpredictable consequences. A notifying party must wait three months and the suspension or termination can then take effect only in the absence of an objection.[54] But in the case where there is disagreement that could, at least in principle, trigger broader legal consequences – article 65(2) of the Vienna Convention on the Law of Treaties states that where there is an objection 'the parties shall seek a solution under the means indicated in article 33 of the Charter of the United Nations'. Article 33 of the Charter states, in turn, that:

> The parties to any dispute, the continuance of which is likely to endanger the maintenance of international peace and security, shall, first of all, seek a solution by negotiation, enquiry, mediation, conciliation, arbitration, judicial settlement, resort to regional agencies or arrangements, or other peaceful means of their own choice.
>
> The Security Council shall, when it deems necessary, call upon the parties to settle their dispute by such means.

That situation contemplated must be 'likely to endanger the maintenance of international peace and security'.

Whether the Joint-Declaration, rather than simply not containing a compromissory clause submitting any and all disputes to arbitration, could even be the subject of arbitral or judicial determination is an interesting question. Enough has been said of this aspect without belabouring the point. Suffice to say that there is a great deal of difference between accepting that something is a treaty, and accepting that its terms are necessarily capable of adjudication.[55]

V THERE IS LITTLE ADVANTAGE

Some of the key controversies today are only a symptom of the condition of the Sino-US relationship, which in turn has a broader impact, including its impact on Sino-British relations. At the same time Hong Kong has become caught up, indeed it has become one of the focal points, in a continued deterioration of the Sino-US relationship spanning territorial, trade and

---

not accepted by the ILC. See further, on art. 62, Malcolm N. Shaw and Caroline Fournet, 'Article 62', in Corten and Klein, *op. cit.*, 1411, 1421.

[54] Art. 65(2) of the Vienna Convention on the Law of Treaties.

[55] See e.g. J. E. S. Fawcett, 'The Legal Character of International Agreements', (1953) 30 *B.Y.B.I.L.* 381, 392, and who as a matter of minor curiosity was a relation of British Prime Minister Boris Johnson.

human rights controversies. In its larger aspect, the US which began as what Kissinger described as a revolutionary power continues to function as such in its advocacy of democratic rule everywhere, while the PRC asserts that the world order must remain true to the United Nations Charter model. Pressure on the Sino-British Joint Declaration is inevitable leading in the spate of twelve months between 2020 and 2021 in midst of a shift in British foreign policy to three public allegations by the UK of breaches of the Joint Declaration. These, as we have seen, are said to concern the enactment of the 2020 National Security Law for Hong Kong, disqualifications from political office and proposed reform of LegCo as well as of the Election Committee which elects Hong Kong's Chief Executive. The PRC has rejected these allegations in categorical terms.

The questions involved are controversial and contested within Hong Kong society. Matters of national security are especially jealously guarded by every nation. Article 4 of the National Security Law states that fundamental rights ought to be preserved and Article 5 states that so too should the rule of law. There has been, if comparisons from recent Anglo-American jurisprudence should be drawn, no indefinite deprivation of liberty without trial.[56] No military tribunals.[57] In respect of the electoral disqualifications it is very much an open question whether the freedoms of speech and belief should always prevail over a requirement that public office necessitates a solemn expression of allegiance to the Basic Law. Mr Justice Kemal Bokhary had put his finger on it, in his inimitable way, only two years after the 1997 handover:

> If these restrictions are permissible, where does it stop? It is a perfectly legitimate question. And the answer, as I see it, is that it stops where these restrictions are located. For they lie just within the outer limits of constitutionality. Beneath the national and regional flags and emblems, all persons in Hong Kong are – and can be confident that they will remain – equally free under our law to express their views on all matters whether political or non-political: saying what they like, how they like.[58]

The key word here is 'beneath', beneath the national and regional flags and emblems but while confidence may now be replaced by consternation the principle, the legal principle, remains unaltered. As for electoral reform, as

---

[56] In the UK, in recent times, see the Anti-terrorism, Crime and Security Act of 2001, ss. 21–23, now repealed. Under s. 21, the Secretary of State's certificate was not reviewable by the courts. This was only the latest episode in the long and tawdry history of preventive detention under English and Commonwealth laws.

[57] *Hamdan* v. *Rumsfeld* 548 US (2006), which allowed continued capture and detention without criminal charges or an ordinary trial in the context of the 'war on terror'.

[58] HKSAR v. *Ng Kung Siu* (1999) 2 HKCFAR 422 (*per* Bokhary PJ).

I have tried to show, the Joint Declaration has almost nothing to say. The Chief Executive is to be selected it says through election or consultations locally,[59] while LegCo should be constituted 'by election'.[60] The Declaration, valid though it is and binding, is thin gruel.

For the reasons I have tried to provide in the preceding pages, there is little that is clear about the latest allegations of treaty breach. In the circumstances, the UK's and PRC's actions, rather than some of their more robust statements, have also been justifiably and rightly circumspect. The PRC's de-recognition of BN(O) passports as valid travel documents is but a shot across the bow but there seems little likely advantage to the treaty parties in provoking the situation any further. Whatever moral satisfaction some might think could yet be obtained, or whatever interest on the part of others might still be served, in doing so.

VI THE HUNTER FROM THESPIAE

There were no meaningful democratic elections under colonial rule, and no suggestion had been made to incorporate into local law the international guarantees of rights which now are invoked so confidently in Westminster, or at least not until after the Joint Declaration had been concluded and the city was lost. At the same time, individual liberties, including free speech and association, have become a substitute way for urging democratic values. But it is precisely those certainties of international law in the Age of American Empire which now are being challenged, and in response defended through self-invocation, and self-reference. This turmoil in the current world order seems far removed from Hong Kong but its presence is felt keenly. Where one shouts that a million people in Hong Kong, in which the Gini co-efficient has risen dramatically between 1986 and 2020, had turned to the streets, little or no mention is made of the other six million inhabitants. It is in these circumstances that we should acknowledge the archival records, which show that both Hong Kong's institutional framework and its framework of rights were the result of hurried attempts at adaptation when the original negotiating aim of at least some form of continued British administration had to be abandoned. Claims to have established a complete constitutional order and framework of individual rights does not rest confidently upon the legal facts. The agreement which the UK left behind is more fragile and incomplete than one would like to think, however extraordinary its achievement. We have seen how the UK's

---

[59] Joint Declaration, para. 3(d), and art. 1 of Annex I.
[60] Art. 1, Annex I, Joint Declaration.

negotiators focused on having a detailed, long and binding treaty. Could the UK have secured more, or called Deng Xiaoping's bluff that if the negotiators failed to negotiate an agreement within two years China would have had to impose a unilateral solution? What we know from the archives is that British officials were working desperately to meet that timetable, and what was achieved was felt to be sufficient at the time. Did anyone suppose then that everything would always proceed smoothly for the next fifty years, such that if it did not one ought simply to proclaim the death of 'one country, two systems'?

And as for political liberalism, that cannot be a mere invention of foreign policy. Arguably where, or wherever, foreign policy has sought to institute political liberalism, that has failed far more often than it has succeeded. In a sense that is what Patten sought to achieve, which required the UK to take the view that since the Joint Declaration says that Hong Kong's way of life should remain unchanged, that way of life could yet be altered between the time the Joint Declaration was signed and came into force and the actual date of the handover. If there were to be any allegation that the goods were being tampered with before their delivery, international law could be relied upon to justify the move. In this case, three British international lawyers giving evidence before a parliamentary committee. And so the democratic experimentation with Hong Kong began in earnest, before its 1997 'handover' to a country whose system of government would be entirely different. The Indian example is much touted, insofar as Britain's own colonial legacy is concerned, as a great success. For every India, however, there have been numerous instances of failed democracies and corrupt, authoritarian and neglectful regimes. If the rule of law cannot exist without democratic and other civil and political rights then none of these have much by way of the rule of law. Whereas Hong Kong never has had any sort of parliamentary democracy. Still, its liberal way of life is a daily reality. There is for example a matter in the Hong Kong courts at the time of the writing of this book, an important test case on transgender rights in which the applicant is represented by a British barrister,[61] and which has its best chance of succeeding before Hong Kong's Court of Final Appeal. This is the Hong Kong court on which British and other judges sit, or at least former British judges, before which London barristers appear, capable of bringing their own direct experience and that of the common law elsewhere to bear.[62]

---

[61] Dinah Rose QC. See also the earlier landmark case of *QT* v. *Director of Immigration* [2018] HKCFA 28.
[62] Joshua Rosenberg, 'Hong Kong Gender Identity and Lord Reed', *Law Society Gazette*, 20 September 2021.

In these circumstances, the better approach is to make an imperfect treaty work rather than to proclaim, as some have done, that the treaty was perfect but that it simply has not worked. That, overnight, judges who continue to hear cases daily can now no longer be relied upon to be independent. That the common law has been a great gift which now should be returned, be that gift in the form of the participation of British judges or British barristers. That sentiment would be similar to Meiji Japan welcoming capitulary treaties because its laws were 'something sacred for the benefit of which foreigners were not worthy of enjoyment'.[63] That may have been a perfectly reasonable view, whereas any attempt today to sanction the common law in Hong Kong, in a fit of pique, would not be, for the following reasons.

Part of the difficulty is that the weaknesses, gaps and imperfections of the Joint Declaration have never been admitted openly. It would have been imprudent to do so, and so the popular public impression of a perfect constitutional arrangement was maintained, and Britain, the hunter from Thespiae, stared into the pool. Still, the argument had always been that 'one country, two systems' is the best solution for the city's inhabitants where the common law was to continue to matter in almost every sphere of life in the city. The Joint Declaration had been instrumental in achieving that solution. It was, and has been, implemented under Chinese law. People in Hong Kong were asked to invest their confidence in that arrangement in circumstances in which the UK would not accept them into the UK. To say now that Hong Kong's previous way of life has not been maintained and that a restrictive form of temporary residence has been instituted as a 'pathway to citizenship', whatever that will come to mean, involves a very sudden change of direction where the supposed triggering event may not have the ironclad treaty justification which it is said exists. The treaty is for all its other strengths akin to Swiss cheese, made in haste and only as an afterthought. The Hong Kong Secretary has cited paragraph 3(a) of the UK Memorandum, which states that

> British Dependent Territories citizens (BDTCs) under the law in force in the United Kingdom will cease to be BDTCs with effect from 1 July 1997, but will be eligible to retain an appropriate status which, without conferring the right of abode in the United Kingdom, will entitle them to continue to use passports issued by the Government of the United Kingdom.

The UK's interpretation, now, might be that the Memorandum promises only to grant eligibility for an appropriate status, without including any right to

---

[63] Cassese, *op. cit.*, 41, citing H. Otsuka, 'Japan's Early Encounter with the Concept of the Law of Nations' (1969) 13 *Japanese Annual of International Law* 56.

reside in the UK, but that this does not prevent the UK from granting that right. For example, it could be argued that the Memorandum ought not to preclude naturalisation by other means such as in the ordinary course of the daily application of UK immigration laws. However that is not the situation here. Instead, a broader linkage has been drawn with an allegation of treaty breach. Switching positions on BN(O) policy now, because of that allegation, goes against the purpose of having the Joint Declaration and preserving Hong Kong's institutional framework. A purpose which the UK had always maintained once the prospect of continued British administration had been lost.

VII CONCLUSION

As for making treaty arguments, a history of colonialism and its role in shaping modern international law are complicating factors which go some way towards explaining why appeals to international law can be heard very differently in different places, particularly where standards based upon civilisational values are invoked. In the current climate of Sino-American rivalry in which the UK plays a part, debate on civil and political rights, even dismissiveness towards a judge's duty of allegiance to the foreign place whose courts it is, begs the question, sometimes at any rate – whose international law, 'world' order, or worldview is it that is invoked as the proper measure? International law is a product of the perpetual struggles which, continually, define and redefine it over so many centuries, and which will continue to do so. Until the Renaissance there was the Christian humanist *jus gentium*. Then came Jean Bodin's sovereign princes who were answerable only to God,[64] by which time the modern age of Western colonialism was well on its way. Alberico Gentili, Regius Professor of Civil Law at Oxford and tutor to Elizabeth I, was to advocate a sharp divide between these sovereign princes of Europe and the barbarous tribes whose 'abominable lewdness', to use Gentili's own description,[65] rendered them 'savage and barbarous violators of the law of nature'.[66] By the nineteenth century, the world was considered by this new European Law of Nations to consist of civilised and uncivilised nations and the enslavement, for that is what colonialism was, of a large part of the uncivilised world could claim that it was justified under international law.

---

[64] Daragh Grant, 'Francisco de Vitoria and Alberico Gentili on the Juridical Status of Native American Polities' (2019) 72 *Renaissance Quarterly* 910, 911–12.
[65] Alberico Gentili, *De Iure Belli Libri Tres*, John C. Rolfe transl., vol. 2 (Oxford: Clarendon, 1933), 122; Grant, *op. cit.*, 911, quoting Gentili, above.
[66] Grant, *op. cit.*, 912.

Of these un-Christian, uncivilised parts, there were those which were not considered entirely barbarous but rather as sovereign kingdoms of a kind which nonetheless were thought only to be semi-civilised, to which category the Far Eastern kingdoms of China, Siam and Japan together with the Ottoman Empire belonged.[67] The instrument of their engagement, or subordination, was the capitulary treaty.[68] It is unsurprising then to find an Eastern sentiment, going beyond any peculiarly 'Chinese' viewpoint, even today, that national differences, including differences in choice of government, are too often considered by others to be foreign vulgarities which are claimed, sometimes falsely, to violate a universal international law.[69] After all, similar arguments have been used to justify extra-territorial European laws under capitulary treaties within Far Eastern borders. That is the context in which treaty claims are now heard, claims which are inextricably bound up with the contentious history of the European Law of Nations.[70]

As for socialism, international socialist resistance to colonialism is hardly new, and hardly new in Asia. From the time of the First International there has been a drawn-out ideological contest.[71] The Russian Revolution had created the first anti-imperialist state,[72] existing alongside more Wilsonian notions.[73] That contest led ultimately to United Nations General Assembly resolution 1514, subsequent resolutions, and the United Nations decolonisation process of the 1950s, 60s, 70s and 80s of which the removal of Hong Kong

[67] See R. P. Anand, *Studies in International Law and History* (Leiden: Nijhoff, 2004), 24–102.
[68] Antonio Cassese, *International Law in a Divided World* (Oxford: Clarendon, 1986), 40 *et seq*.
[69] See e.g. Yasuaki Onuma, *International Law in a Transcivilizational World* (Cambridge: Cambridge University Press, 2017).
[70] It is not as Ghai says merely a 'psychological' matter if by that is meant that it is irrational; Yash Ghai, *Hong Kong's New Constitutional Order: The Resumption of Chinese Sovereignty*, 2nd ed. (Hong Kong: Hong Kong University Press, 1999), 12; Peter Wesley-Smith, *Unequal Treaty, 1898–1997*, 2nd ed. (Oxford: Oxford University Press, 1998), 316–17.
[71] Talbot Imlay, 'International Socialism and Decolonization during the 1950s: Competing Rights and the Postcolonial Order' (2013) 118 *Am. Hist. Rev.* 1105.
[72] Robert J.C. Young, *Postcolonialism: An Historical Introduction, Anniversary Edition* (London: Wiley, 2016), 113–26.
[73] As Woodrow Wilson put it in his speech to Congress on 22 January 1917 'no peace can last or ought to last which does not recognize and accept the principle that governments derive all their powers from the consent of the governed, and that no right anywhere exists to hand peoples about sovereignty to sovereignty as if they were property'; 54.2 U.S. Congressional Record, 1742, quoted in W. Ofuatey-Kodjoe, *The Principle of Self-determination in International Law* (New York: Nellen Publishing Company, Inc., 1977), 79. Much of the rest of the twentieth century was to decide who would constitute 'a people', but insofar as Hong Kong was concerned, the key was to lie in the practice of the Committee of Twenty-Four, established by UNGA resolution 1654 in the aftermath of UNGA resolution 1514, that Hong Kong was to be recovered by China rather than to be prepared for any form of self-government. See Chapter 7 of this book.

from the list of non-self-governing territories – as I have said, as a means of achieving self-determination against colonial rule – forms only an aspect. Britain's international lawyers had pushed back against the new twentieth-century anti-colonialism as we have seen, in Sinclair's insistence for example that the fruits of conquest before 1928 were entirely legitimate.

Hong Kong has now arrived at the mid-point of the fifty-year period stipulated under the Joint Declaration and the Basic Law,[74] while many of these conflicts over international law have never been resolved.[75] That is what makes the Joint Declaration remarkable.

---

[74] Joint Declaration, para. 3(12); Basic Law, art. 5.
[75] The orthodox rule, it is said, is that a treaty is to be interpreted, and any question of its legality is to be determined also, according to the rules of international law which applied when the treaty was made. Some doubt crept in, aside from the subsequent opinions of developing and socialist countries, when a well-known arbitration award extended that view to include as well a need, based upon the facts of that dispute, to adhere to any evolving requirements of international law subsequently. In that case, Spanish discovery of the territory of the Island of Palmas was required to be supported by actual occupation as that had become a newly emergent requirement for proving title to territory. See *Island of Palmas (Netherlands v. USA)* (1928) 2 RIAA 829. One might dismiss that modification or extension of the orthodox rule as a confusion, particularly in support of the Western view that entitlements to territory would be thrown into disarray, i.e. if the twentieth century rule against forcible conquest were to be enforced retrospectively. See Anthony D'Amato, 'International Law, Intertemporal Problems', in Rudolf Bernhardt and Peter Macalister-Smith (eds.), *Encyclopedia of Public International Law* (Amsterdam: North-Holland, 1992), 1234–6. It involves a policy argument which today is being questioned increasingly in light of a felt need to confront international law's past as an instrument of colonialism. See Steven Wheatley, 'Revisiting the Doctrine of Intertemporal Law' (2021) 41 *O.J.L.S.* 484 discussing the recent *Chagos Archipelago Opinion* of the International Court of Justice, *Legal Consequences of the Separation of the Chagos Archipelago from Mauritius in 1965*, Opinion, 25 February 2019, and who is also critical of D'Amato's dismissal of the Palmas Island Award as a 'confusion'; also, more generally on grappling with colonialism, Carsten Stahn, 'Reckoning with Colonial Injustice: International Law as Culprit and as Remedy?' (2020) 33 *Leiden J.I.L.* 823. More directly, that policy argument was challenged by the PRC in the case of Hong Kong, which required a resolution in the form of the Joint Declaration in which neither side, British or Chinese, were to shift from their opposing positions. The Sino-British negotiations illustrated a serious difference over the intertemporal law doctrine. A doctrine which currently suggests that the continued enjoyment of international rights should conform to the subsequent post-colonial evolution of international law. It is that which explains the removal of Hong Kong from the list of non-self-governing territories; namely, the emergence of a principle of self-determination against colonial rule. Hong Kong was removed not because it had become self-governed but because China is.

APPENDIX

Joint Declaration of the Government of the United Kingdom of Great Britain and Northern Ireland and the Government of the People's Republic of China on the Question of Hong Kong

The Government of the United Kingdom of Great Britain and Northern Ireland and the Government of the People's Republic of China have reviewed with satisfaction the friendly relations existing between the two Governments and peoples in recent years and agreed that a proper negotiated settlement of the question of Hong Kong, which is left over from the past, is conducive to the maintenance of the prosperity and stability of Hong Kong and to the further strengthening and development of the relations between the two countries on a new basis. To this end, they have, after talks between the delegations of the two Governments, agreed to declare as follows:

1. The Government of the People's Republic of China declares that to recover the Hong Kong area (including Hong Kong Island, Kowloon and the New Territories, hereinafter referred to as Hong Kong) is the common aspiration of the entire Chinese people, and that it has decided to resume the exercise of sovereignty over Hong Kong with effect from 1 July 1997.
2. The Government of the United Kingdom declares that it will restore Hong Kong to the People's Republic of China with effect from 1 July 1997.
3. The Government of the People's Republic of China declares that the basic policies of the People's Republic of China regarding Hong Kong are as follows:
    (1) Upholding national unity and territorial integrity and taking account of the history of Hong Kong and its realities, the People's Republic of China has decided to establish, in accordance with the provisions of Article 31 of the Constitution of the People's Republic of China, a Hong Kong Special Administrative Region upon resuming the exercise of sovereignty over Hong Kong.

(2) The Hong Kong Special Administrative Region will be directly under the authority of the Central People's Government of the People's Republic of China. The Hong Kong Special Administrative Region will enjoy a high degree of autonomy, except in foreign and defence affairs which are the responsibilities of the Central People's Government.
(3) The Hong Kong Special Administrative Region will be vested with executive, legislative and independent judicial power, including that of final adjudication. The laws currently in force in Hong Kong will remain basically unchanged.
(4) The Government of the Hong Kong Special Administrative Region will be composed of local inhabitants. The chief executive will be appointed by the Central People's Government on the basis of the results of elections or consultations to be held locally. Principal officials will be nominated by the chief executive of the Hong Kong Special Administrative Region for appointment by the Central People's Government. Chinese and foreign nationals previously working in the public and police services in the government departments of Hong Kong may remain in employment. British and other foreign nationals may also be employed to serve as advisers or hold certain public posts in government departments of the Hong Kong Special Administrative Region.
(5) The current social and economic systems in Hong Kong will remain unchanged, and so will the life-style. Rights and freedoms, including those of the person, of speech, of the press, of assembly, of association, of travel, of movement, of correspondence, of strike, of choice of occupation, of academic research and of religious belief will be ensured by law in the Hong Kong Special Administrative Region. Private property, ownership of enterprises, legitimate right of inheritance and foreign investment will be protected by law.
(6) The Hong Kong Special Administrative Region will retain the status of a free port and a separate customs territory.
(7) The Hong Kong Special Administrative Region will retain the status of an international financial centre, and its markets for foreign exchange, gold, securities and futures will continue. There will be free flow of capital. The Hong Kong dollar will continue to circulate and remain freely convertible.
(8) The Hong Kong Special Administrative Region will have independent finances. The Central People's Government will not levy taxes on the Hong Kong Special Administrative Region.

(9) The Hong Kong Special Administrative Region may establish mutually beneficial economic relations with the United Kingdom and other countries, whose economic interests in Hong Kong will be given due regard.

(10) Using the name of 'Hong Kong, China', the Hong Kong Special Administrative Region may on its own maintain and develop economic and cultural relations and conclude relevant agreements with states, regions and relevant international organisations.

The Government of the Hong Kong Special Administrative Region may on its own issue travel documents for entry into and exit from Hong Kong.

(11) The maintenance of public order in the Hong Kong Special Administrative Region will be the responsibility of the Government of the Hong Kong Special Administrative Region.

(12) The above-stated basic policies of the People's Republic of China regarding Hong Kong and the elaboration of them in Annex I to this Joint Declaration will be stipulated, in a Basic Law of the Hong Kong Special Administrative Region of the People's Republic of China, by the National People's Congress of the People's Republic of China, and they will remain unchanged for 50 years.

4. The Government of the United Kingdom and the Government of the People's Republic of China declare that, during the transitional period between the date of the entry into force of this Joint Declaration and 30 June 1997, the Government of the United Kingdom will be responsible for the administration of Hong Kong with the object of maintaining and preserving its economic prosperity and social stability; and that the Government of the People's Republic of China will give its co-operation in this connection.

5. The Government of the United Kingdom and the Government of the People's Republic of China declare that, in order to ensure a smooth transfer of government in 1997, and with a view to the effective implementation of this Joint Declaration, a Sino-British Joint Liaison Group will be set up when this Joint Declaration enters into force; and that it will be established and will function in accordance with the provisions of Annex II to this Joint Declaration.

6. The Government of the United Kingdom and the Government of the People's Republic of China declare that land leases in Hong Kong and other related matters will be dealt with in accordance with the provisions of Annex III to this Joint Declaration.

7. The Government of the United Kingdom and the Government of the People's Republic of China agree to implement the preceding declarations and the Annexes to this Joint Declaration.
8. This Joint Declaration is subject to ratification and shall enter into force on the date of the exchange of instruments of ratification, which shall take place in Beijing before 30 June 1985. This Joint Declaration and its Annexes shall be equally binding.

Done in duplicate at Beijing on 19 December 1984 in the English and Chinese languages, both texts being equally authentic.

For the Government of the United Kingdom of Great Britain and Northern Ireland	For the Government of the People's Republic of China
Margaret Thatcher	Zhao Ziyang

ANNEX I

Elaboration by the Government of the People's Republic of China of its Basic Policies Regarding Hong Kong

The Government of the People's Republic of China elaborates the basic policies of the People's Republic of China regarding Hong Kong as set out in paragraph 3 of the Joint Declaration of the Government of the United Kingdom of Great Britain and Northern Ireland and the Government of the People's Republic of China on the Question of Hong Kong as follows:

I

The Constitution of the People's Republic of China stipulates in Article 31 that 'the state may establish special administrative regions when necessary. The systems to be instituted in special administrative regions shall be prescribed by laws enacted by the National People's Congress in the light of the specific conditions.' In accordance with this Article, the People's Republic of China shall, upon the resumption of the exercise of sovereignty over Hong Kong on 1 July 1997, establish the Hong Kong Special Administrative Region of the People's Republic of China. The National People's Congress of the People's Republic of China shall enact and promulgate a Basic Law of the Hong Kong Special Administrative Region of the People's Republic of China (hereinafter referred to as the Basic Law) in accordance with the Constitution of the People's Republic of China, stipulating that after the establishment of the Hong Kong Special Administrative Region the socialist system and socialist policies shall not be practised in the Hong Kong Special Administrative Region and that Hong Kong's previous capitalist system and life-style shall remain unchanged for 50 years.

The Hong Kong Special Administrative Region shall be directly under the authority of the Central People's Government of the People's Republic of China and shall enjoy a high degree of autonomy. Except for foreign and defence affairs which are the responsibilities of the Central People's Government, the Hong Kong Special Administrative Region shall be vested with executive, legislative and independent judicial power, including that of final adjudication. The Central People's Government shall authorise the Hong Kong Special Administrative Region to conduct on its own those external affairs specified in Section XI of this Annex.

The government and legislature of the Hong Kong Special Administrative Region shall be composed of local inhabitants. The chief executive of the Hong Kong Special Administrative Region shall be selected by election or through consultations held locally and be appointed by the Central People's Government. Principal officials (equivalent to Secretaries) shall be nominated by the chief executive of the Hong Kong Special Administrative Region and appointed by the Central People's Government. The legislature of the Hong Kong Special Administrative Region shall be constituted by elections. The executive authorities shall abide by the law and shall be accountable to the legislature.

In addition to Chinese, English may also be used in organs of government and in the courts in the Hong Kong Special Administrative Region.

Apart from displaying the national flag and national emblem of the People's Republic of China, the Hong Kong Special Administrative Region may use a regional flag and emblem of its own.

II

After the establishment of the Hong Kong Special Administrative Region, the laws previously in force in Hong Kong (i.e. the common law, rules of equity, ordinances, subordinate legislation and customary law) shall be maintained, save for any that contravene the Basic Law and subject to any amendment by the Hong Kong Special Administrative Region legislature.

The legislative power of the Hong Kong Special Administrative Region shall be vested in the legislature of the Hong Kong Special Administrative Region. The legislature may on its own authority enact laws in accordance with the provisions of the Basic Law and legal procedures, and report them to the Standing Committee of the National People's Congress for the record. Laws enacted by the legislature which are in accordance with the Basic Law and legal procedures shall be regarded as valid.

The laws of the Hong Kong Special Administrative Region shall be the Basic Law, and the laws previously in force in Hong Kong and laws enacted by the Hong Kong Special Administrative Region legislature as above.

III

After the establishment of the Hong Kong Special Administrative Region, the judicial system previously practised in Hong Kong shall be maintained except for those changes consequent upon the vesting in the courts of the Hong Kong Special Administrative Region of the power of final adjudication.

Judicial power in the Hong Kong Special Administrative Region shall be vested in the courts of the Hong Kong Special Administrative Region. The courts shall exercise judicial power independently and free from any interference. Members of the judiciary shall be immune from legal action in respect of their judicial functions. The courts shall decide cases in accordance with the laws of the Hong Kong Special Administrative Region and may refer to precedents in other common law jurisdictions.

Judges of the Hong Kong Special Administrative Region courts shall be appointed by the chief executive of the Hong Kong Special Administrative Region acting in accordance with the recommendation of an independent commission composed of local judges, persons from the legal profession and other eminent persons. Judges shall be chosen by reference to their judicial qualities and may be recruited from other common law jurisdictions. A judge may only be removed for inability to discharge the functions of his office, or for misbehaviour, by the chief executive of the Hong Kong Special Administrative Region acting in accordance with the recommendation of a tribunal appointed by the chief judge of the court of final appeal, consisting of not fewer than three local judges. Additionally, the appointment or removal of principal judges (i.e. those of the highest rank) shall be made by the chief executive with the endorsement of the Hong Kong Special Administrative Region legislature and reported to the Standing Committee of the National People's Congress for the record. The system of appointment and removal of judicial officers other than judges shall be maintained.

The power of final judgment of the Hong Kong Special Administrative Region shall be vested in the court of final appeal in the Hong Kong Special Administrative Region, which may as required invite judges from other common law jurisdictions to sit on the court of final appeal.

A prosecuting authority of the Hong Kong Special Administrative Region shall control criminal prosecutions free from any interference.

On the basis of the system previously operating in Hong Kong, the Hong Kong Special Administrative Region Government shall on its own make provision for local lawyers and lawyers from outside the Hong Kong Special Administrative Region to work and practise in the Hong Kong Special Administrative Region.

The Central People's Government shall assist or authorise the Hong Kong Special Administrative Region Government to make appropriate arrangements for reciprocal juridical assistance with foreign states.

IV

After the establishment of the Hong Kong Special Administrative Region, public servants previously serving in Hong Kong in all government departments, including the police department, and members of the judiciary may all remain in employment and continue their service with pay, allowances, benefits and conditions of service no less favourable than before. The Hong Kong Special Administrative Region Government shall pay to such persons who retire or complete their contracts, as well as to those who have retired before 1 July 1997, or to their dependants, all pensions, gratuities, allowances and benefits due to them on terms no less favourable than before, and irrespective of their nationality or place of residence.

The Hong Kong Special Administrative Region Government may employ British and other foreign nationals previously serving in the public service in Hong Kong, and may recruit British and other foreign nationals holding permanent identity cards of the Hong Kong Special Administrative Region to serve as public servants at all levels, except as heads of major government departments (corresponding to branches or departments at Secretary level) including the police department, and as deputy heads of some of those departments. The Hong Kong Special Administrative Region Government may also employ British and other foreign nationals as advisers to government departments and, when there is a need, may recruit qualified candidates from outside the Hong Kong Special Administrative Region to professional and technical posts in government departments. The above shall be employed only in their individual capacities and, like other public servants, shall be responsible to the Hong Kong Special Administrative Region Government.

The appointment and promotion of public servants shall be on the basis of qualifications, experience and ability. Hong Kong's previous system of recruitment, employment, assessment, discipline, training and management for the public service (including special bodies for appointment, pay and conditions of service) shall, save for any provisions providing privileged treatment for foreign nationals, be maintained.

V

The Hong Kong Special Administrative Region shall deal on its own with financial matters, including disposing of its financial resources and drawing up its budgets and its final accounts. The Hong Kong Special Administrative Region shall report its budgets and final accounts to the Central People's Government for the record.

The Central People's Government shall not levy taxes on the Hong Kong Special Administrative Region. The Hong Kong Special Administrative Region shall use its financial revenues exclusively for its own purposes and they shall not be handed over to the Central People's Government. The systems by which taxation and public expenditure must be approved by the legislature, and by which there is accountability to the legislature for all public expenditure, and the system for auditing public accounts shall be maintained.

VI

The Hong Kong Special Administrative Region shall maintain the capitalist economic and trade systems previously practised in Hong Kong. The Hong Kong Special Administrative Region Government shall decide its economic and trade policies on its own. Rights concerning the ownership of property, including those relating to acquisition, use, disposal, inheritance and compensation for lawful deprivation (corresponding to the real value of the property concerned, freely convertible and paid without undue delay) shall continue to be protected by law.

The Hong Kong Special Administrative Region shall retain the status of a free port and continue a free trade policy, including the free movement of goods and capital. The Hong Kong Special Administrative Region may on its own maintain and develop economic and trade relations with all states and regions.

The Hong Kong Special Administrative Region shall be a separate customs territory. It may participate in relevant international organisations and international trade agreements (including preferential trade arrangements), such as the General Agreement on Tariffs and Trade and arrangements regarding international trade in textiles. Export quotas, tariff preferences and other similar arrangements obtained by the Hong Kong Special Administrative Region shall be enjoyed exclusively by the Hong Kong Special Administrative Region. The Hong Kong Special Administrative

Region shall have authority to issue its own certificates of origin for products manufactured locally, in accordance with prevailing rules of origin.

The Hong Kong Special Administrative Region may, as necessary, establish official and semi-official economic and trade missions in foreign countries, reporting the establishment of such missions to the Central People's Government for the record.

VII

The Hong Kong Special Administrative Region shall retain the status of an international financial centre. The monetary and financial systems previously practised in Hong Kong, including the systems of regulation and supervision of deposit taking institutions and financial markets, shall be maintained.

The Hong Kong Special Administrative Region Government may decide its monetary and financial policies on its own. It shall safeguard the free operation of financial business and the free flow of capital within, into and out of the Hong Kong Special Administrative Region. No exchange control policy shall be applied in the Hong Kong Special Administrative Region. Markets for foreign exchange, gold, securities and futures shall continue.

The Hong Kong dollar, as the local legal tender, shall continue to circulate and remain freely convertible. The authority to issue Hong Kong currency shall be vested in the Hong Kong Special Administrative Region Government. The Hong Kong Special Administrative Region Government may authorise designated banks to issue or continue to issue Hong Kong currency under statutory authority, after satisfying itself that any issue of currency will be soundly based and that the arrangements for such issue are consistent with the object of maintaining the stability of the currency. Hong Kong currency bearing references inappropriate to the status of Hong Kong as a Special Administrative Region of the People's Republic of China shall be progressively replaced and withdrawn from circulation.

The Exchange Fund shall be managed and controlled by the Hong Kong Special Administrative Region Government, primarily for regulating the exchange value of the Hong Kong dollar.

VIII

The Hong Kong Special Administrative Region shall maintain Hong Kong's previous systems of shipping management and shipping regulation, including the system for regulating conditions of seamen. The specific functions and responsibilities of the Hong Kong Special Administrative Region Government in the field of shipping shall be defined by the Hong Kong Special Administrative Region Government on its own. Private shipping businesses and shipping-related businesses and private container terminals in Hong Kong may continue to operate freely.

The Hong Kong Special Administrative Region shall be authorised by the Central People's Government to continue to maintain a shipping register and issue related certificates under its own legislation in the name of 'Hong Kong, China'.

With the exception of foreign warships, access for which requires the permission of the Central People's Government, ships shall enjoy access to the ports of the Hong Kong Special Administrative Region in accordance with the laws of the Hong Kong Special Administrative Region.

IX

The Hong Kong Special Administrative Region shall maintain the status of Hong Kong as a centre of international and regional aviation. Airlines incorporated and having their principal place of business in Hong Kong and civil aviation related businesses may continue to operate. The Hong Kong Special Administrative Region shall continue the previous system of civil aviation management in Hong Kong, and keep its own aircraft register in accordance with provisions laid down by the Central People's Government concerning nationality marks and registration marks of aircraft. The Hong Kong Special Administrative Region shall be responsible on its own for matters of routine business and technical management of civil aviation, including the management of airports, the provision of air traffic services within the flight information region of the Hong Kong Special Administrative Region, and the discharge of other responsibilities allocated under the regional air navigation procedures of the International Civil Aviation Organisation.

The Central People's Government shall, in consultation with the Hong Kong Special Administrative Region Government, make arrangements providing for air services between the Hong Kong Special Administrative Region and other parts of the People's Republic of China for airlines incorporated and having their principal place of business in the Hong Kong Special Administrative Region and other airlines of the People's Republic of China. All Air Service Agreements providing for air services between other parts of the People's Republic of China and other states and regions with stops at the Hong Kong Special Administrative Region and air services between the Hong Kong Special Administrative Region and other states and regions with stops at other parts of the People's Republic of China shall be concluded by the Central People's Government. For this purpose, the Central People's Government shall take account of the special conditions and economic interests of the Hong Kong Special Administrative Region and consult the Hong Kong Special Administrative Region Government. Representatives of the Hong Kong Special Administrative Region Government may participate as members of delegations of the Government of the People's Republic of China in air service consultations with foreign governments concerning arrangements for such services.

Acting under specific authorisations from the Central People's Government, the Hong Kong Special Administrative Region Government may:

—renew or amend Air Service Agreements and arrangements previously in force; in principle, all such Agreements and arrangements may be renewed or amended with the rights contained in such previous Agreements and arrangements being as far as possible maintained;

—negotiate and conclude new Air Service Agreements providing routes for airlines incorporated and having their principal place of business in the Hong Kong Special Administrative Region and rights for overflights and technical stops; and

—negotiate and conclude provisional arrangements where no Air Service Agreement with a foreign state or other region is in force.

All scheduled air services to, from or through the Hong Kong Special Administrative Region which do not operate to, from or through the mainland of China shall be regulated by Air Service Agreements or provisional arrangements referred to in this paragraph.

The Central People's Government shall give the Hong Kong Special Administrative Region Government the authority to:

—negotiate and conclude with other authorities all arrangements concerning the implementation of the above Air Service Agreements and provisional arrangements;

—issue licences to airlines incorporated and having their principal place of business in the Hong Kong Special Administrative Region;

—designate such airlines under the above Air Service Agreements and provisional arrangements; and

—issue permits to foreign airlines for services other than those to, from or through the mainland of China.

X

The Hong Kong Special Administrative Region shall maintain the educational system previously practised in Hong Kong. The Hong Kong Special Administrative Region Government shall on its own decide policies in the fields of culture, education, science and technology, including policies regarding the educational system and its administration, the language of instruction, the allocation of funds, the examination system, the system of academic awards and the recognition of educational and technological qualifications. Institutions of all kinds, including those run by religious and community organisations, may retain their autonomy. They may continue to recruit staff and use teaching materials from outside the Hong Kong Special Administrative Region. Students shall enjoy freedom of choice of education and freedom to pursue their education outside the Hong Kong Special Administrative Region.

XI

Subject to the principle that foreign affairs are the responsibility of the Central People's Government, representatives of the Hong Kong Special Administrative Region Government may participate, as members of delegations of the Government of the People's Republic of China, in negotiations at the diplomatic level directly affecting the Hong Kong Special Administrative Region conducted by the Central People's Government. The Hong Kong Special Administrative Region may on its own, using the name 'Hong Kong, China', maintain and develop relations and conclude and implement agreements with states, regions and relevant international organisations in the appropriate fields, including the economic, trade, financial and monetary, shipping, communications, touristic, cultural and sporting fields. Representatives of the Hong Kong Special Administrative Region Government may participate, as members of delegations of the Government of the People's Republic of China, in international organisations or conferences in appropriate fields limited to states and affecting the Hong Kong Special Administrative Region, or may attend in such other capacity as may be permitted by the Central People's Government and the organisation or conference concerned, and may express their views in the name of 'Hong Kong, China'. The Hong Kong Special Administrative Region may, using the name 'Hong Kong, China', participate in international organisations and conferences not limited to states.

The application to the Hong Kong Special Administrative Region of international agreements to which the People's Republic of China is or becomes a party shall be decided by the Central People's Government, in accordance with the circumstances and needs of the Hong Kong Special Administrative Region, and after seeking the views of the Hong Kong Special Administrative Region Government. International agreements to which the People's Republic of China is not a party but which are implemented in Hong Kong may remain implemented in the Hong Kong Special Administrative Region. The Central People's Government shall, as necessary, authorise or assist the Hong Kong Special Administrative Region Government to make appropriate arrangements for the application to the Hong Kong Special Administrative Region of other relevant international agreements. The Central People's Government shall take the necessary steps to ensure that the Hong Kong Special Administrative Region shall continue to retain its status in an appropriate capacity in those international organisations of which the People's Republic of China is a member and in which Hong Kong participates in one capacity or another. The Central People's Government shall, where necessary, facilitate the continued participation of the Hong Kong Special Administrative Region in an appropriate capacity in those international organisations in which Hong Kong is a participant in one capacity or another, but of which the People's Republic of China is not a member.

Foreign consular and other official or semi-official missions may be established in the Hong Kong Special Administrative Region with the approval of the Central People's Government. Consular and other official missions established in Hong Kong by states which have established formal diplomatic relations with the People's Republic of China, may be maintained. According to the circumstances of each case, consular and other official missions of states having no formal diplomatic relations with the People's Republic of China may either be maintained or changed to semi-official missions. States not recognised by the People's Republic of China can only establish non-governmental institutions.

The United Kingdom may establish a Consulate-General in the Hong Kong Special Administrative Region.

XII

The maintenance of public order in the Hong Kong Special Administrative Region shall be the responsibility of the Hong Kong Special Administrative Region Government. Military forces sent by the Central People's Government to be stationed in the Hong Kong Special Administrative Region for the purpose of defence shall not interfere in the internal affairs of the Hong Kong Special Administrative Region. Expenditure for these military forces shall be borne by the Central People's Government.

XIII

The Hong Kong Special Administrative Region Government shall protect the rights and freedoms of inhabitants and other persons in the Hong Kong Special Administrative Region according to law. The Hong Kong Special Administrative Region Government shall maintain the rights and freedoms as provided for by the laws previously in force in Hong Kong, including freedom of the person, of speech, of the press, of assembly, of association, to form and join trade unions, of correspondence, of travel, of movement, of strike, of demonstration, of choice of occupation, of academic research, of belief, inviolability of the home, the freedom to marry and the right to raise a family freely.

Every person shall have the right to confidential legal advice, access to the courts, representation in the courts by lawyers of his choice, and to obtain judicial remedies. Every person shall have the right to challenge the actions of the executive in the courts.

Religious organisations and believers may maintain their relations with religious organisations and believers elsewhere, and schools, hospitals and welfare institutions run by religious organisations may be continued. The relationship between religious organisations in the Hong Kong Special Administrative Region and those in other parts of the People's Republic of China shall be based on the principles of non-subordination, non-interference and mutual respect.

The provisions of the International Covenant on Civil and Political Rights and the International Covenant on Economic, Social and Cultural Rights as applied to Hong Kong shall remain in force.

XIV

The following categories of persons shall have the right of abode in the Hong Kong Special Administrative Region, and, in accordance with the law of the Hong Kong Special Administrative Region, be qualified to obtain permanent identity cards issued by the Hong Kong Special Administrative Region Government, which state their right of abode:

—all Chinese nationals who were born or who have ordinarily resided in Hong Kong before or after the establishment of the Hong Kong Special

Administrative Region for a continuous period of 7 years or more, and persons of Chinese nationality born outside Hong Kong of such Chinese nationals;
— all other persons who have ordinarily resided in Hong Kong before or after the establishment of the Hong Kong Special Administrative Region for a continuous period of 7 years or more and who have taken Hong Kong as their place of permanent residence before or after the establishment of the Hong Kong Special Administrative Region, and persons under 21 years of age who were born of such persons in Hong Kong before or after the establishment of the Hong Kong Special Administrative Region;
— any other persons who had the right of abode only in Hong Kong before the establishment of the Hong Kong Special Administrative Region.

The Central People's Government shall authorise the Hong Kong Special Administrative Region Government to issue, in accordance with the law, passports of the Hong Kong Special Administrative Region of the People's Republic of China to all Chinese nationals who hold permanent identity cards of the Hong Kong Special Administrative Region, and travel documents of the Hong Kong Special Administrative Region of the People's Republic of China to all other persons lawfully residing in the Hong Kong Special Administrative Region. The above passports and documents shall be valid for all states and regions and shall record the holder's right to return to the Hong Kong Special Administrative Region.

For the purpose of travelling to and from the Hong Kong Special Administrative Region, residents of the Hong Kong Special Administrative Region may use travel documents issued by the Hong Kong Special Administrative Region Government, or by other competent authorities of the People's Republic of China, or of other states. Holders of permanent identity cards of the Hong Kong Special Administrative Region may have this fact stated in their travel documents as evidence that the holders have the right of abode in the Hong Kong Special Administrative Region.

Entry into the Hong Kong Special Administrative Region of persons from other parts of China shall continue to be regulated in accordance with the present practice.

The Hong Kong Special Administrative Region Government may apply immigration controls on entry, stay in and departure from the Hong Kong Special Administrative Region by persons from foreign states and regions.

Unless restrained by law, holders of valid travel documents shall be free to leave the Hong Kong Special Administrative Region without special authorisation.

The Central People's Government shall assist or authorise the Hong Kong Special Administrative Region Government to conclude visa abolition agreements with states or regions.

ANNEX II

Sino-British Joint Liaison Group

1. In furtherance of their common aim and in order to ensure a smooth transfer of government in 1997, the Government of the United Kingdom and the Government of the People's Republic of China have agreed to continue their discussions in a friendly spirit and to develop the co-operative relationship which already exists between the two Governments over Hong Kong with a view to the effective implementation of the Joint Declaration.
2. In order to meet the requirements for liaison, consultation and the exchange of information, the two Governments have agreed to set up a Joint Liaison Group.
3. The functions of the Joint Liaison Group shall be:
   (a) to conduct consultations on the implementation of the Joint Declaration;
   (b) to discuss matters relating to the smooth transfer of government in 1997;
   (c) to exchange information and conduct consultations on such subjects as may be agreed by the two sides.
   Matters on which there is disagreement in the Joint Liaison Group shall be referred to the two Governments for solution through consultations.
4. Matters for consideration during the first half of the period between the establishment of the Joint Liaison Group and 1 July 1997 shall include:
   (a) action to be taken by the two Governments to enable the Hong Kong Special Administrative Region to maintain its economic relations as a separate customs territory, and in particular to ensure the maintenance of Hong Kong's participation in the General Agreement on Tariffs and Trade, the Multifibre Arrangement and other international arrangements; and
   (b) action to be taken by the two Governments to ensure the continued application of international rights and obligations affecting Hong Kong.
5. The two Governments have agreed that in the second half of the period between the establishment of the Joint Liaison Group and 1 July 1997 there will be need for closer co-operation, which will therefore be intensified

during that period. Matters for consideration during this second period shall include:
(a) procedures to be adopted for the smooth transition in 1997;
(b) action to assist the Hong Kong Special Administrative Region to maintain and develop economic and cultural relations and conclude agreements on these matters with states, regions and relevant international organisations.

6. The Joint Liaison Group shall be an organ for liaison and not an organ of power. It shall play no part in the administration of Hong Kong or the Hong Kong Special Administrative Region. Nor shall it have any supervisory role over that administration. The members and supporting staff of the Joint Liaison Group shall only conduct activities with the scope of the functions of the Joint Liaison Group.

7. Each side shall designate a senior representative, who shall be of Ambassadorial rank, and four other members of the group. Each side may send up to 20 supporting staff.

8. The Joint Liaison Group shall be established on the entry into force of the Joint Declaration. From 1 July 1988 the Joint Liaison Group shall have its principal base in Hong Kong. The Joint Liaison Group shall continue its work until 1 January 2000.

9. The Joint Liaison Group shall meet in Beijing, London and Hong Kong. It shall meet at least once in each of the three locations in each year. The venue for each meeting shall be agreed between the two sides.

10. Members of the Joint Liaison Group shall enjoy diplomatic privileges and immunities as appropriate when in the three locations. Proceedings of the Joint Liaison Group shall remain confidential unless otherwise agreed between the two sides.

11. The Joint Liaison Group may by agreement between the two sides decide to set up specialist sub-groups to deal with particular subjects requiring expert assistance.

12. Meetings of the Joint Liaison Group and sub-groups may be attended by experts other than the members of the Joint Liaison Group. Each side shall determine the composition of its delegation to particular meetings of the Joint Liaison Group or sub-group in accordance with the subjects to be discussed and the venue chosen.

13. The working procedures of the Joint Liaison Group shall be discussed and decided upon by the two sides within the guidelines laid down in this Annex.

ANNEX III

Land Leases

The Government of the United Kingdom and the Government of the People's Republic of China have agreed that, with effect from the entry into force of the Joint Declaration, land leases in Hong Kong and other related matters shall be dealt with in accordance with the following provisions:

1. All leases of land granted or decided upon before the entry into force of the Joint Declaration and those granted thereafter in accordance with paragraph 2 or 3 of this Annex, and which extend beyond 30 June 1997, and all rights in relation to such leases shall continue to be recognised and protected under the law of the Hong Kong Special Administrative Region.
2. All leases of land granted by the British Hong Kong Government not containing a right of renewal that expire before 30 June 1997, except short term tenancies and leases for special purposes, may be extended if the lessee so wishes for a period expiring not later than 30 June 2047 without payment of an additional premium. An annual rent shall be charged from the date of extension equivalent to 3 per cent of the rateable value of the property at that date, adjusted in step with any changes in the rateable value thereafter. In the case of old schedule lots, village lots, small houses and similar rural holdings, where the property was on 30 June 1984 held by, or, in the case of small houses granted after that date, the property is granted to, a person descended through the male line from a person who was in 1898 a resident of an established village in Hong Kong, the rent shall remain unchanged so long as the property is held by that person or by one of his lawful successors in the male line. Where leases of land not having a right of renewal expire after 30 June 1997, they shall be dealt with in accordance with the relevant land laws and policies of the Hong Kong Special Administrative Region.
3. From the entry into force of the Joint Declaration until 30 June 1997, new leases of land may be granted by the British Hong Kong Government for terms expiring not later than 30 June 2047. Such leases shall be granted at a premium and nominal rental until 30 June 1997, after which date they shall not require payment of an additional premium but an annual rent

equivalent to 3 per cent of the rateable value of the property at that date, adjusted in step with changes in the rateable value thereafter, shall be charged.

4. The total amount of new land to be granted under paragraph 3 of this Annex shall be limited to 50 hectares a year (excluding land to be granted to the Hong Kong Housing Authority for public rental housing) from the entry into force of the Joint Declaration until 30 June 1997.

5. Modifications of the conditions specified in leases granted by the British Hong Kong Government may continue to be granted before 1 July 1997 at a premium equivalent to the difference between the value of the land under the previous conditions and its value under the modified conditions.

6. From the entry into force of the Joint Declaration until 30 June 1997, premium income obtained by the British Hong Kong Government from land transactions shall, after deduction of the average cost of land production, be shared equally between the British Hong Kong Government and the future Hong Kong Special Administrative Region Government. All the income obtained by the British Hong Kong Government, including the amount of the above mentioned deduction, shall be put into the Capital Works Reserve Fund for the financing of land development and public works in Hong Kong. The Hong Kong Special Administrative Region Government's share of the premium income shall be deposited in banks incorporated in Hong Kong and shall not be drawn on except for the financing of land development and public works in Hong Kong in accordance with the provisions of paragraph 7(d) of this Annex.

7. A Land Commission shall be established in Hong Kong immediately upon the entry into force of the Joint Declaration. The Land Commission shall be composed of an equal number of officials designated respectively by the Government of the United Kingdom and the Government of the People's Republic of China together with necessary supporting staff. The officials of the two sides shall be responsible to their respective governments. The Land Commission shall be dissolved on 30 June 1997.

The terms of reference of the Land Commission shall be:
(*a*) to conduct consultations on the implementation of this Annex;
(*b*) to monitor observance of the limit specified in paragraph 4 of this Annex, the amount of land granted to the Hong Kong Housing Authority for public rental housing, and the division and use of premium income referred to in paragraph 6 of this Annex;

(c) to consider and decide on proposals from the British Hong Kong Government for increasing the limit referred to in paragraph 4 of this Annex;

(d) to examine proposals for drawing on the Hong Kong Special Administrative Region Government's share of premium income referred to in paragraph 6 of this Annex and to make recommendations to the Chinese side for decision.

Matters on which there is disagreement in the Land Commission shall be referred to the Government of the United Kingdom and the Government of the People's Republic of China for decision.

8. Specific details regarding the establishment of the Land Commission shall be finalised separately by the two sides through consultations.

[Exchange of Memoranda]

UNITED KINGDOM MEMORANDUM

In connection with the Joint Declaration of the Government of the United Kingdom of Great Britain and Northern Ireland and the Government of the People's Republic of China on the question of Hong Kong to be signed this day, the Government of the United Kingdom declares that, subject to the completion of the necessary amendments to the relevant United Kingdom legislation:

(a) All persons who on 30 June 1997 are, by virtue of a connection with Hong Kong, British Dependent Territories citizens (BDTCs) under the law in force in the United Kingdom will cease to be BDTCs with effect from 1 July 1997, but will be eligible to retain an appropriate status which, without conferring the right of abode in the United Kingdom, will entitle them to continue to use passports issued by the Government of the United Kingdom. This status will be acquired by such persons only if they hold or are included in such a British passport issued before 1 July 1997, except that eligible persons born on or after 1 January 1997 but before 1 July 1997 may obtain or be included in such a passport up to 31 December 1997.

(b) No person will acquire BDTC status on or after 1 July 1997 by virtue of a connection with Hong Kong. No person born on or after 1 July 1997 will acquire the status referred to as being appropriate in sub-paragraph (a).

(c) United Kingdom consular officials in the Hong Kong Special Administrative Region and elsewhere may renew and replace passports of persons mentioned in sub-paragraph (a) and may also issue them to persons, born before 1 July 1997 of such persons, who had previously been included in the passport of their parent.

(d) Those who have obtained or been included in passports issued by the Government of the United Kingdom under sub-paragraphs (a) and (c) will be entitled to receive, upon request, British consular services and protection when in third countries.

Beijing, 19 December 1984.

CHINESE MEMORANDUM

The Government of the People's Republic of China has received the memorandum from the Government of the United Kingdom of Great Britain and Northern Ireland dated 19 December 1984.

Under the Nationality Law of the People's Republic of China, all Hong Kong Chinese compatriots, whether they are holders of the 'British Dependent Territories citizens' Passport' or not, are Chinese nationals.

Taking account of the historical background of Hong Kong and its realities, the competent authorities of the Government of the People's Republic of China will, with effect from 1 July 1997, permit Chinese nationals in Hong Kong who were previously called 'British Dependent Territories citizens' to use travel documents issued by the Government of the United Kingdom for the purpose of travelling to other states and regions.

The above Chinese nationals will not be entitled to British consular protection in the Hong Kong Special Administrative Region and other parts of the People's Republic of China on account of their holding the above-mentioned British travel documents.

Beijing, 19 December 1984.

Index

Acts of state
 Basic Law, no jurisdiction under, 133
 common law legal system, under, 132–4
 Congo case, 138–9, 140–2
 Court of Final Appeal (CFA) and, 83, 85–7, 132
 Department of Justice position, 135–6
 diplomatic immunity and, 136–7
 National Security Law and, 143–4
 non-justiciability versus lack of jurisdiction, 132–3
 PRC law and, 135
 public order and, 144–6
 Sino-British Joint Liaison Group and, 132, 143–4
 state immunity and, 138–9
Air services agreements, 125–6
Allegiance
 Exchange of Memoranda and, 185–6
 Hong Kong allegiance to PRC, 185–6, 198–9
 'Missing booksellers' affair and, 189, 190–1
Annex I to Joint Declaration
 Basic Law and, 9
 binding nature of, 39–40
 defence exception, 129, 132, 231
 elaborations in, 6–7, 10, 14, 36, 42–3, 207–8
 elections under, 65–6, 154, 161
 foreign affairs exception, 129, 132, 231
 ICCPR and, 148–9, 207, 227–8
 ICESCR and, 227–8
 internal affairs under, 129
 judiciary and, 82, 92
 post-handover arrangements and, 36
 public order, defence and foreign affairs distinguished, 145, 231–2
 relations and agreements with states under, 117–18
 right of abode under, 52
 text of, 268–80
Annex II to Joint Declaration
 alleged breaches by UK, 74
 Sino-British Joint Liaison Group, 8, 36, 38, 42, 281–2
 text of, 281–2
Annex III to Joint Declaration
 land leases and, 42, 52, 283–5
 text of, 283–5
Appleyard, Len, 38
Arrest under Joint Declaration, 192
Atkin, James, 215
Aust, Anthony, 116, 206
Australia
 extradition agreement with Hong Kong, 128
 on National Security Law, 151–2, 216
 Privy Council and, 81
 suspension of extradition treaty, 240
Autonomy
 Basic Law and, 68, 195–6
 immigration, autonomy of Hong Kong regarding, 196
 PRC view of, 13

Badinter, Robert, 221
Badinter Commission, 221
Bagehot, Walter, 66
Balancing approach, 100–1
Barbados, Privy Council and, 81
Bar Council (UK), 229
Basic Law of the Hong Kong Special Administrative Region (1990)

288

Index

accountability of Chief Executive to central government, 70–1, 245
acts of state, no jurisdiction over, 133
air services agreements and, 125–6
amendment of, 222
Annex I and, 9
authority of NPCSC to enact laws, 234–5
autonomy and, 68, 195–6
Basic Law Consultative Committee (BLCC), 68–9
Basic Law Drafting Committee (BLDC), 68–9
Bill of Rights compared, 72–3, 90
boundaries of Hong Kong and, 197
breaches by PRC, UK position on, 68
Constitutional court, proposal for, 219–21
constitutional status of, 106
Court of Final Appeal (CFA) and, 82, 84, 86, 94–6
customs territory, Hong Kong as, 245
defence exception, 132, 143, 230–1
democratic reforms and, 58
as domestic legislation, 167
Drafting Committee, 220
elections under, 66–7, 75, 158, 162–4, 165
emergency declaration under, 236
enactment of, 72
Extradition Bill and, 210, 212, 215
first draft, 70
foreign affairs exception, 132, 142, 230–1
fully implementing Joint Declaration, viewed as, 8, 37
Hong Kong to enact 'own law', 234
ICCPR, incorporation of, 72–3, 90, 150, 152–3, 197, 202, 214, 227–8
ICESCR, incorporation of, 72–3, 90, 150, 227–8
implementation of Joint Declaration by, 214, 221
interpretation by NPCSC, 9, 69–70, 81, 91–2, 94–6, 131, 215, 219, 222–3
investment agreements and, 125
Joint Declaration compared, 201
judiciary and, 81
lack of fundamental rights in, 5
legislative disqualifications and, 257
list of laws extended to Hong Kong, 135, 187, 195–6
National Security Law, UK alleging to be breach, 219, 224–5
non-interference by central government, 177–8

PRC Constitution, relationship to, 106–7, 186–7
public order, defence and foreign affairs distinguished, 144, 146
review of laws by NPCSC, 131–2
second draft, 70
selection of Chief Executive under, 165, 179
success of, 263
tax agreements and, 125
Tiananmen Square incident, effect of, 69, 72
treaty law and, 237–8
Vienna Convention on the Law of Treaties and, 153, 214
Biden, Joe, 246
Bilateral investment treaties (BITs)
air services agreements, 125–6
Hong Kong lacking authority to enter, 120, 125
investment agreements, 125
PRC-Lao PDR Bilateral Investment Treaty, 110–11, 113
tax agreements, 125
Bill of Rights Ordinance (1991) (Hong Kong)
generally, 72
Basic Law compared, 72–3, 90
citations of, 75
elections under, 149
Extradition Bill and, 212
ICCPR, incorporation of, 72–3, 148, 150, 152–3, 161, 197, 202, 227
purpose of, 72
BN(O) passports. *See* British Nationals (Overseas) passports
Bodin, Jean, 261
Bokhary, Kemal
on Basic Law, 96–9
Congo case and, 138–9
on Court of Final Appeal (CFA), 93
flag desecration case and, 96–9
freedom of assembly and, 96–9, 101
freedom of speech and, 96–9
on individual rights, 257
on interpretation, 100
Boundaries of Hong Kong, 197
Brandeis, Louis, 99
British Nationals (Overseas) passports
change in UK policy, 260–1
countermeasure, derecognition as, 251
derecognition by PRC, 250–2, 258
Exchange of Memoranda and, 250

British Nationals (Overseas) passports (cont.)
  pathway to citizenship for passport holders, 52, 185–6, 192, 193, 240, 249
  PRC allegation of breach of Joint Declaration regarding, 249–50, 254
  right of abode and, 252
  as travel documents, 250, 251
Buttes Gas, 133

Cab-rank rule, 229–30
Cameron, David, 216
Canada
  on National Security Law, 151–2, 216
  Privy Council and, 81
  suspension of extradition treaty, 240
Carroll, Lewis, 215
CFA. *See* Court of Final Appeal (CFA) (Hong Kong)
Chan, Patrick, 138–9
Chen, Albert, 166
Cheng, Teresa, 169, 249
Chen Zuo'er, 85
Chief Executive (Hong Kong)
  accountability issue, 70–1
  Basic Law, under, 165, 179
  central government, accountability to, 70–1, 245
  Election Committee, 165, 178–9, 222, 246, 252–3
  elections and, 75, 144, 161, 164–5, 166
  Extradition Bill and, 212
  Joint Declaration, under, 165, 167
  Legislative Council, accountability to, 169
  National People's Congress and, 222
  Nominating Committee, 165, 178–9
  NPCSC and, 165, 166–7, 178–9, 246, 252–3
  'one country, two systems' and, 178–9
  selection of, 165, 167, 178–9, 257–8
China. *See specific topic*
China Railway Group, 138
Chinese Extradition Ordinance 1889 (Hong Kong), 210–11
Chung, S.Y., 27, 30, 45, 57–8
Churchill, Winston, 56, 159
Clark, Alan, 204
Clarke, Kenneth, 84
Closer Economic Partnership Arrangement, 123
Coke, Edward, 219
Coles, John, 9
Collins, Lawrence, 103

Colonialism, 20
Common law legal system
  acts of state under, 132–4
  conflict with PRC legal system, 95–6
  extradition in, 208
  Joint Declaration, under, 51–2, 87
  prerogative powers in, 142–3
Communist Party of China (CPC), 10, 105
Congo case, 138–9, 140–2
Conservative Party (UK), 18, 20–1
Constitutional court, proposal for, 219–21
Constitution (PRC)
  amendments to, 105
  Basic Law, relationship to, 106–7, 186–7
  Hong Kong, applicability to, 186–7
  Joint Declaration, relationship to, 106
Contract law, 123–4
Convention on the International Sale of Goods (CISG) (1979)
  governing law, 121–2
  Hong Kong not participating country in, 121–2
  PRC law inapplicable to, 121–2
Convention on the Jurisdictional Immunities of States, 142
Convention on the Law of the Sea, 241
Convention Respecting an Extension of the Hong Kong Territory (1898) (New Territories Lease), 16–20, 24
Cottrell, Robert
  aphorism on rights, 75
  on democratic reforms, 56–7
  on Hong Kong delegations to London, 45
  on negotiation of Joint Declaration, 21, 23, 34, 41
Countermeasures
  derecognition of BN(O) passports as, 251
  as response, 239
  sanctions as, 246–7
  treaty suspension or withdrawal as, 254–6
Court of Appeal (Hong Kong), 138
Court of Final Appeal (CFA) (Hong Kong)
  acts of state and, 83, 85–7, 132
  Basic Law and, 82, 84, 86
  Congo case, 138–9, 140–2
  flag desecration case, 96–9, 101, 103, 197, 225–6
  foreign judges on, 83
  foreign sovereign immunity and, 196
  freedom of assembly and, 96–9, 101
  freedom of speech and, 96–9

Joint Declaration and, 84, 87
judges, 82–3
judicial review, 83, 85, 93
  Legislative Council (LegCo) and, 83, 84
  NPCSC and, 87
  on NPCSC interpretation of Basic Law, 94–6
  power of final adjudication, 83, 85, 90, 223
  Privy Council, replacing, 81, 82
  Provisional Legislative Council and, 87
  right of abode and, 93
  Sino-British Joint Liaison Group and, 83, 85
  state immunity and, 138–9, 140–2
  tolerance of diversity versus guaranteed rights, 99, 100
  UK judges on, 103–5, 107–8
Court of First Instance (Hong Kong), 142
Cowen, Zelman, 169
Cradock, Percy
  generally, 54, 150, 162
  on Annex I, 43
  on continued UK administration, 28–9
  on democratic reforms, 57, 73–4, 162–3
  on elections, 154–5
  Hong Kong delegations to London and, 46
  negotiation of Joint Declaration and, 8, 26, 29–32, 33–4, 35, 39, 217
Crawford, James, 119–20, 205–6, 247
Criminal law
  extradition (*See* Extradition)
  National Security Law, offences under, 232–4
  in PRC, 210
  problems with, 124
  secession, 232–3
  subversion (*See* Subversion)
  terrorism, 232–3
  treason, 187–8, 232–3
Cross, Grenville, 210
Crown Proceedings Act 1947 (UK), 142–3
Crown Proceedings Ordinance (Hong Kong), 142–3
Cultural Revolution, 20–1
Currency under Joint Declaration, 51
Customs territories
  free trade agreements (FTAs) and, 120, 123
  Hong Kong as, 245

Decolonisation
  democratic reforms and, 159
  sovereignty and, 183
  Special Committee on Decolonisation (C-24), 58–64, 262

United Nations and, 262–3
Defence
  Annex I exception, 129, 132, 231
  Basic Law exception, 130–1, 132, 143, 230–1
  Joint Declaration exception, 230
  National Security Law offences and, 233
  prerogative powers and, 143
  public order distinguished, 144–6, 231–2
Defence White Paper (2019) (PRC), 248
Delegated authority, 182
deLisle, Jacques, 15
Democratic reforms
  Basic Law and, 58
  decolonisation and, 159
  disagreement between PRC and UK regarding, 65–6
  elections (*See* Elections)
  interim period, attempts during, 56–8, 66–8, 147–8
  Joint Declaration and, 58, 147, 172
  UK 'carve-out' to ICCPR, 147, 149, 150, 152, 153–4
  UK position on, 167
Democratic Republic of the Congo case (*Congo* case), 138–9, 140–2
Deng Xiaoping
  on binding nature of Joint Declaration, 41
  Heath meeting, 18–19, 23, 28
  on Joint Declaration, 14, 15, 180
  MacLehose meeting, 16–17, 18
  negotiation of Joint Declaration and, 12, 22–3, 32–3, 35, 259
  'Nine Points', 18
  'one country, two systems' and, 183
  signing of Joint Declaration, 53
  on Sino-British Joint Liaison Group, 58
  Thatcher and, 12, 20, 22–3, 65
  on timetable of Joint Declaration, 40–1
  on West, 13
Department of Justice (Hong Kong), 135–6, 140
Department of Trade and Industry (UK), 133
Dicks, Anthony, 17
Dimbleby, Jonathan, 84, 86
Diplomatic immunity, 136–7
Duffy, Peter
  on democratic reforms, 148
  on elections, 160
  on ICCPR, 119, 205, 228
  on Joint Declaration, 88–9, 90–1
  Patten's plan under Joint Declaration and, 74

Economic and cultural relations
  contract law, 123–4
  economic relations with Mainland PRC, 123–4
  Joint Declaration, under, 51, 116–17, 120
  trade, importance of to Hong Kong, 126
Economic system under Joint Declaration, 50
Education Bureau (Hong Kong), 160–1
Elections
  Annex I, under, 65–6, 154, 161
  Basic Law, under, 66–7, 75, 158, 162–4, 165
  Bill of Rights, under, 149
  Chief Executive and, 75, 144, 161, 164–5, 166
  disagreement between PRC and UK regarding, 72–6
  ICCPR and, 167
  Joint Declaration, under, 154, 155–6, 160, 161–2, 165, 167, 257–8
  Legislative Council and, 75, 156, 162–4, 167, 257–8
  NPCSC on, 163, 165, 166–7
  postponement of 2020 elections, 75
  White Paper (1984) and, 156–9
Elizabeth I (England), 261
Emergency declaration, 235–7
European Convention on Human Rights, 101–2, 149
European Law of Nations, 261–2
European Union
  extradition agreement with Hong Kong, 128
  on National Security Law, 216
Evans, Richard, 41–2, 47–8
Exchange of Memoranda. *See* Sino-British Exchange of Memoranda on British Nationals Overseas
Executive Council (ExCo), 8–9, 31, 44, 57–8
Executive-led system, 66, 161
Extradition
  authority for agreements, 125
  in common law legal system, 208
  Extradition Bill (*See* Extradition Bill (2019) (Hong Kong))
  habeas corpus and, 212
  historical background, 210–11
  Joint Declaration and, 192, 211
  problems involving, 124
  protests against, 200–1
  Soering rule, 213, 214–15
  suspension of extradition treaties, 240
  third country agreements, 128
Extradition Act 1989 (UK), 209, 212

Extradition Act 2003 (UK), 209, 213
Extradition Bill (2019) (Hong Kong)
  ad hoc nature of extradition under, 209, 212
  Basic Law and, 210, 212, 215
  basic principles, 211–12
  Bill of Rights and, 212
  breach of Joint Declaration, UK viewing as, 208–9
  central government, authority of, 215
  Chief Executive and, 212
  conflicting views of PRC and UK, 209
  fundamental rights and, 201
  Joint Declaration and, 212, 215
  UK law compared, 209, 212–13
  UK position on, 204
  unrest in response to, 177, 179–80, 194, 209–10, 215
  withdrawal of, 215
Extraterritorial jurisdiction of National Security Law, 233–4

Falconer, Charlie, 108
Falklands War (1982), 19, 20
Featherstonehaugh, Guy, 107–8
FG Hemisphere, 138
Fifoot, Paul, 169, 223
Finland, suspension of extradition treaty, 240
First International, 262
First Opium War (1839–1842), 10, 44
First Peking Convention (1860), 10–11, 115
Fitzmaurice, Gerald, 203–4
'Five Eyes', 151–2, 216
Flag desecration case, 96–9, 101, 103, 197, 198, 225–6
Foreign affairs
  Annex I exception, 129, 132, 231
  Basic Law exception, 130–1, 132, 142, 230–1
  Congo case and, 138–9, 140–2
  Joint Declaration exception, 230
  National Security Law offences and, 233
  prerogative powers and, 134–5, 143
  public order distinguished, 144–6, 231–2
  state immunity and, 140–2
Foreign and Commonwealth Office (UK)
  continued UK administration and, 24
  on Exchange of Memoranda, 250
  India and, 150–1
  Joint Declaration and, 20–1, 54–5
  on National Security Law, 239
  negotiation of Joint Declaration and, 21, 27
Foreign Jurisdiction Act 1890 (UK), 17

Index 293

Foreign Jurisdiction Act 1913 (UK), 17
Foreign Ministry (PRC), 142
Foreign sovereign immunity, 196
France, suspension of extradition treaty, 240
Freedom of assembly, 96–9, 101
Freedom of speech, 96–9
Free port and financial centre, Hong Kong as under Joint Declaration, 50–1
Free trade agreements (FTAs)
  customs territories and, 120, 123
  Hong Kong having authority to enter, 120–1, 123
Frontier regions, administration of, 13, 183
Fugitive Offenders Ordinance (Hong Kong), 212

Gadamer, Hans Georg, 65
Galsworthy, Anthony, 31
General Agreement on Tariffs and Trade (GATT) (1947)
  generally, 242
  free trade agreements (FTAs) and, 123
  Hong Kong and, 118, 120, 241
  withdrawal of recognition and, 239–40
General Agreement on Trade in Services (GATS) (1994), 120, 123
Gentili, Alberico, 261
Germany, suspension of extradition treaty, 240
Ghai, Yash, 12, 95–6
Goodall, David, 48
Green Paper on Constitutional Development (2007), 166
Guomindang, 10
Guyana, Privy Council and, 81

Habeas corpus, 212
Haddon-Cave, Philip, 30, 62, 63
Hague Rules (1924), 120, 197
Hale, Brenda, 103, 108, 228–9
Hammer, Armand, 133, 134
Hammond, Philip, xii, 188–9, 224
Hang Seng Index, 27
Hassett, Kevin, 244
Heath, Edward, 18–19, 23, 28
Heseltine, Michael, 84
High Court (Hong Kong), 138
Historical background, 11–12
Hoare, Richard, 85
Hodge, Patrick, 79–80, 108, 230
Hoffman, Lennie, 103
Holmes, Oliver Wendell Jr, 67, 99, 103

Hong Kong. *See specific topic*
Howe, Geoffrey
  generally, 154–5, 220
  announcement of Joint Declaration, 43, 44
  on Basic Law, 91
  on binding nature of Joint Declaration, 40
  on decolonisation, 63–4
  on Deng-Heath meeting, 18–19
  Hong Kong delegations to London and, 45–6
  on immigration, 250–1
  on Joint Declaration, 54–5
  on judiciary, 81
  negotiation of Joint Declaration and, 15, 28–9, 30, 31–2, 33, 39, 49
  on PLA in Hong Kong, 46–7
  on PRC intentions, 36–8
  on Sino-British Joint Liaison Group, 44
  on timetable of Joint Declaration, 40–1
  visit to Hong Kong, 47–8
Huang Hua
  generally, 64, 115
  on decolonisation, 60, 61, 62, 63
  on sovereignty, 19–20, 23
Human Rights Act 1998 (UK), 149
Human Rights Committee
  on applicability of ICCPR to Hong Kong, 205–6
  reporting obligations, 87–8, 90, 118–20, 205, 228, 237
Hunt, Jeremy, 209, 210
Hurd, Douglas, 73, 84

ICCPR. *See* International Covenant on Civil and Political Rights (ICCPR) (1966)
ICESCR. *See* International Covenant on Economic, Social, and Cultural Rights (ICESCR) (1966)
Immigration
  Exchange of Memoranda and, 250–1
  Hong Kong, autonomy regarding, 196
  from Hong Kong to UK, 18
Impartiality, duty of, 104–5
India
  political liberalism in, 259
  Privy Council and, 81
Individual rights
  elections (*See* Elections)
  freedom of assembly, 96–9, 101
  freedom of speech, 96–9
  Fugitive Offenders Ordinance, under, 212
  Joint Declaration, under, 177

Individual rights (cont.)
  National Security Law, under, 177
    in PRC context, 177
    PRC law versus Hong Kong law, 179
  Internal affairs
    Annex I, under, 129
    Joint Declaration, under, 51, 129
  International Bill of Rights, 208
  International Court of Justice, 124
  International Covenant on Civil and Political Rights (ICCPR) (1966)
    Annex I and, 148–9, 207, 227–8
    Basic Law incorporating, 72–3, 150, 152–3, 197, 202, 214, 227–8
    Bill of Rights incorporating, 72–3, 148, 150, 152–3, 161, 197, 202, 227
    elections and, 167
    emergency declaration and, 236–7
    First Optional Protocol, 88–9
    Hong Kong, applicability to, 110, 118–20, 121, 126, 198, 205–6, 227–8
    Hong Kong not party to, 204, 206
    Human Rights Committee and, 160, 167
    Joint Declaration and, 5, 87, 90, 149, 172, 205
    National Security Law and, 227–9
    PRC as signatory only, 89, 118, 205
    PRC not party to, 89, 118, 177, 204
    reporting obligations, 87–8, 90, 118–20, 205, 228, 237
    UK 'carve-out', 147, 149, 150, 152, 153–4
    United Nations, notification of regarding, 205
  International Covenant on Economic, Social, and Cultural Rights (ICESCR) (1966)
    Annex I and, 227–8
    Basic Law incorporating, 72–3, 90, 150, 227–8
    National Security Law and, 227–8
    PRC party to, 89
  International law, 261–2
  International Law Commission, 247
  Investment agreements, 125
  Iran, oil concessions and, 134
  Iraq, invasion of Kuwait, 133–4

Japan
  defeat of, 159
  Manchuria crisis and, 159
  Shandong, possession of, 159
  treaties and, 260
Jessel, George, 113

Jiang Shigong, 71–2, 180, 181, 183, 186–7
Ji Pengfei, 155, 157–8, 160
Johnson, Boris
  generally, 21, 230
  Basic Law, allegation of National Security Law as breach of, 224–5
  Joint Declaration, allegation of National Security Law as breach of, 68, 151, 218, 224–5
  path to citizenship for BN(O) passport holders and, 216–17
Joint Declaration. See Sino-British Joint Declaration (1984)
Joint Liaison Group. See Sino-British Joint Liaison Group
Jowitt, William, 187–8, 190
Joyce, William, 187–8, 189, 190–1, 192
Judicial review, 83, 85, 93
Judiciary of Hong Kong
  adjudication versus interpretation, 92–3
  administrators, judges viewed as, 180
  Annex I and, 82, 92
  balancing approach, 100–1
  Basic Law and, 81
  Congo case, 138–9, 140–2
  Constitutional court, proposal for, 219–21
  Court of Appeal, 138
  Court of Final Appeal (CFA) (*See* Court of Final Appeal (CFA) (Hong Kong))
  Court of First Instance, 142
  criticism of, 181–2
  diplomatic immunity and, 136–7
  foreign judges in, 82, 83
  High Court, 138
  impartiality, duty of, 104–5
  Joint Declaration and, 81
  judicial independence and, 180–1, 184
  jurisdiction of central government over, 180–1, 183–4
  margin of appreciation, 101–2
  National Security Law and, 84
  NPCSC authority regarding, 92–3
  'one country, two systems' and, 106, 180–1
  overview, 81
  patriotism, duty of in White Paper, 180–2, 198–9
  prerogative powers and, 181
  proportionality test, 101
  protection of fundamental rights, 90–1
  state immunity and, 138–9, 140–2

Index

tolerance of diversity versus guaranteed
rights, 99, 100
Jurisdiction
acts of state, no jurisdiction over in Basic
Law, 133
judiciary, jurisdiction of central government
over, 180–1, 183–4
National Security Law, extraterritorial
jurisdiction of, 233–4
non-justiciability versus lack of jurisdiction,
132–3
sovereignty versus, 11
Jus gentium, 261

Keller, Perry, 74
Kellogg-Briand Pact (1928), 63
Kennedy, Helena, 229
Kenya, Mau Mau insurgents, 253
Ke Zaishuo, 31, 49
Kissinger, Henry, 257
Kuwait, Iraqi invasion of, 133–4

Labour Party (UK), 18
Land leases, 42, 52, 283–5
Lao PDR-PRC Bilateral Investment Treaty,
110–11, 113
Law of the People's Republic of China on
Safeguarding National Security in the
Hong Kong Special Administrative
Region (2020) (PRC)
generally, 26–7, 135
acts of state and, 143–4
Basic Law, UK allegation of breach of, 219,
224–5
citizenship offered by UK in response to, 185–6
defence and, 233
emergency declaration under, 236
enactment of, 218
extraterritorial jurisdiction, 233–4
foreign affairs and, 233
ICCPR and, 227–9
ICESCR and, 227–8
individual rights under, 257
Joint Declaration, UK allegation of breach
of, 68, 138–9, 151, 172, 218, 224–5, 226, 251,
252–3
judiciary and, 84
lack of fundamental rights in, 5
Legislative Council, erosion of autonomy,
177–8
offences under, 232–4

public order, defence and foreign affairs
distinguished, 145–6
reaction to, 216–17, 239–42
as response to unrest, 151, 177, 179–80,
194, 201
secession under, 232–3
as subject to Hong Kong law, 226
subversion under, 168–9, 232–3
terrorism under, 232–3
treason under, 232–3
UK judges, pressure on as result of, 103–4
Law of the People's Republic of China on the
Garrisoning of the Hong Kong Special
Administrative Region (PRC), 198
League of Nations
Covenant, 20, 59
failure of, 159
Mandates System, 59
Lee, Martin, 84, 86
Lee Po, 188–93
Legislative Council (LegCo) (Hong Kong)
generally, 57
Chief Executive, accountability of, 169
Court of Final Appeal (CFA) and, 83, 84
disqualifications, 168, 198, 252–3, 257
elections and, 75, 156, 162–4, 167, 257–8
erosion of autonomy, 177–8
National People's Congress and, 222
NPCSC and, 246, 252–3
Provisional Legislative Council
becoming, 67
Security Panel, 211
subversion and, 168–9
Leung, C.Y., 164, 166
Li, Andrew
generally, 182
on Court of Final Appeal (CFA), 93
flag desecration case and, 96–9, 101
freedom of assembly and, 101
freedom of speech and, 96–9
on interpretation, 100
on judicial independence, 180–1
on UK judges, 104–5
Liaison Office (PRC), 177, 250
Li Fei, 139
Lisbon Protocol, 115
Liu Xiaoming, 42
Local governance under Joint Declaration, 51
Luard, Evan, 63
Luce, Richard, 30, 46
Lu Ping, 31

Ma, Geoffrey, 182
Macao
  administration of, 13
  Portuguese rule in, 10, 115
  Sino-Portuguese Joint Declaration and, 110–14
  sovereignty and, 19–20, 23
  treaty law and, 110–14, 116
  UN Special Committee on Decolonisation (C-24) and, 60
MacLehose, Murray, 16–17, 18, 42, 56
'Made in China' dispute, 118, 177, 241, 242–5
Major, John, 54, 150, 162
Major, Pamela, 106–7, 186
Malaysia, Privy Council and, 81
Manchuria crisis, 159
Mao Zedong, 17, 183
Margin of appreciation, 101–2
Marrakesh Agreement, 243
Mason, Anthony, 138–9
Maude, Francis, 220–1
Ma Xinmin, 115, 116
Menon, Sundaresh, 127
Millett, Peter, 103
'Missing booksellers' affair
  generally, 177, 179
  allegiance and, 189, 190–1
  diplomatic solution, 192–3
  dual nationality and, 189–90, 191
  Joint Declaration, UK allegation of breach of, 188, 223–4
  passports and, 190–1, 193
  UK position on, 192
  West Kowloon Terminus in context of, 195
Mitchell-Heggs, Christopher, 220–1
Moon Treaty (1969), 201
Mortimer, John B., 138–9
Mountbatten, Louis, 150–1
'Moving treaty frontiers' rule, 63, 111, 112, 114, 116
Mugabe, Bona, 136–7, 140
Mugabe, Grace, 136–7
Mugabe, Robert, 136–7

National anthem, 198
National People's Congress (PRC)
  Basic Law and, 68–9
  Chief Executive and, 222
  Constitutional Revision Committee, 18
  Court of Final Appeal (CFA) and, 83
  on Hong Kong delegations to London, 45

  Legislative Council and, 222
  Standing Committee (*See* Standing Committee of the National People's Congress (NPCSC) (PRC))
National Security Law. *See* Law of the People's Republic of China on Safeguarding National Security in the Hong Kong Special Administrative Region (2020) (PRC)
Negotiation of Joint Declaration
  continued administration, UK position on, 20–1, 29–32, 33–4
  fallback position of UK, 29–31, 32
  overview, 5, 12
  post-handover arrangements, 34–40
  PRC position, 26–7
  sovereignty and, 12, 19, 27–34
  sovereignty plus administration, PRC position on, 26–7
  UK position, 27–34
Neuberger, David, 103, 107–8, 228–9
'New States' problem, 22
New Zealand
  extradition agreement with Hong Kong, 128
  on National Security Law, 151–2, 216
  Privy Council and, 81
  suspension of extradition treaty, 240
Nie Er, 198
'Nine Points', 18, 20
Non-self-governing territories, 58–64
NPC. *See* National People's Congress (PRC)
NPCSC. *See* Standing Committee of the National People's Congress (NPCSC) (PRC)

Occidental Petroleum, 133, 134
'Occupy Movement', 165–6, 177, 178
Office for Safeguarding National Security in the Hong Kong SAR (PRC), 177–8
Office of the Commissioner of the Ministry of Foreign Affairs (OCMFA) (Hong Kong), 137, 152
'One country, two systems'
  Chief Executive and, 178–9
  judiciary and, 106, 180–1
  sovereignty and, 183
  Taiwan and, 18
  UK position on, 13, 42
Oppenheim, L.F.L., 204, 255
Owen, David, 18

Index

Pakistan, Privy Council and, 81
Panel on Security and Panel on Administration of Justice and Legal Services, 135
Passports
  BN(O) passports (*See* British Nationals (Overseas) passports)
  'missing booksellers' affair and, 190–1, 193
Patten, Chris
  generally, 253
  on acts of state, 132
  on Court of Final Appeal (CFA), 84–6
  criticism of, 76
  on democratic reforms, 57, 66, 67, 147–8, 150–1, 162–3, 223–4, 259
  on elections, 71, 73, 74, 75, 155–6, 158, 160
  as Governor, 58, 66
  on Joint Declaration, 217
  support from 'three different teams' of international lawyers, 147–8 (*See also* Duffy, Peter; Keller, Perry; Slinn, Peter)
People's Liberation Army (PLA) in Hong Kong, 46–7, 231–2
People's Republic of China (PRC). *See specific topic*
Perez de Cuellar, Javier, 53
Perry, David, 229
Phillips, Nick, 103
Piggott, George Bettesworth, 210–11
Political activities under Joint Declaration, 52
Political liberalism, 259
Pomerance, Michla, 61, 65
Ponsonby, Arthur, 40
Ponsonby Rule, 40
Porter, Samuel, 187–8
Powell, Charles, 38
Power of final adjudication, 83, 85, 90, 223
PRC-Lao PDR Bilateral Investment Treaty, 110–11, 113
Preliminary Working Committee (PWC) (Hong Kong), 83
Preparatory Committee (Hong Kong), 75, 83
Prerogative powers
  in common law legal system, 142–3
  defence and, 143
  foreign affairs and, 134–5, 143
  judiciary and, 181
Privy Council (UK), 81, 82
Proportionality test, 101
Protective principle, 234
Provisional Legislative Council (Hong Kong), 67, 75, 87

Public order
  acts of state and, 144–6
  defence distinguished, 144–6
  foreign affairs distinguished, 144–6
  Joint Declaration, under, 52
Purchas, Francis, 143

Qian Qichen, 73, 83
Qing Dynasty, 13
Qin Huasun, 112–13, 120, 206

Raab, Dominic
  generally, 229
  Basic Law, allegation of National Security Law as breach of, 219
  on defence and foreign affairs exceptions, 230, 231, 232
  on elections, 154
  on individual rights, 235, 236–7
  Joint Declaration, allegation of National Security Law as breach of, 138–9, 172, 218, 226
  on mass arrests, 170–1
Randelzhofer, Abrecht, 247
Recognition, withdrawal of, 239–40
Reed, Robert, 79–80, 108–9, 230
Regulations of the People's Republic of China Concerning Diplomatic Privileges and Immunities (PRC), 137
Rendition. *See* Extradition
Renton, Tim, 158
Reprisals, 239
'Resumption' of sovereignty, 11–12, 19, 21, 126–7, 195, 202, 205, 213–14
Retorsion, 239
Reyes, Anselmo, 138
Ribeiro, Roberto, 138–9
Ricketts, Peter, 9, 48–9
Right of abode
  Annex I, under, 52
  BN(O) passports and, 252
  Court of Final Appeal (CFA) and, 93
  Exchange of Memoranda and, 250, 252, 260–1
Roosevelt, Franklin Delano, 44, 56, 159
Rules of Origin Agreement, 244
Russian Revolution, 262

Sanctions
  as countermeasures, 246–7
  economic coercion as use of force, 247–8

Sanctions (cont.)
  smart sanctions, 246
  by UK, 241–2
  unilateral sanctions, 239
  United Nations and, 239
  by United States, 241, 246–8
Sanum Investments Limited, 110–11
Seawright, Stephen, 27–8
Secession, 232–3
Second Opium War (1856–1860), 10
Second Peking Convention (1898), 10–11, 115
Self-determination, 170
'Semi-civilised' peoples, 53–4
Separation of powers, 160–1, 169
Shandong, Japanese possession of, 159
Shao Tianren, 169
Shenzhen Bay, 195
Silke, William, 100–1
Sinclair, Ian, 62, 63–4, 203–4, 263
Singapore
  Court of Appeal, 111–14, 116, 127
  High Court, 111
  International Arbitration Act, 110–11
  Privy Council and, 81
  Singapore-PRC treaty on judicial assistance, applicability to Hong Kong, 127
Single nationality requirement, 186
Sino-British Commission. *See* Sino-British Joint Liaison Group
Sino-British Exchange of Memoranda on British Nationals Overseas
  allegiance and, 185–6
  BN(O) passports and, 250
  citizenship and, 260–1
  as compromise, 254
  disagreement between PRC and UK regarding, 42, 177, 185–6, 193
  immigration and, 250–1
  interpretation of, 241
  Joint Declaration and, 252
  pathway to citizenship for BN(O) passport holders, 52, 185–6, 192, 193, 240
  right of abode and, 250, 252, 260–1
  status of, 241
  text of, 286–7
Sino-British Joint Declaration (1984)
  Annex I (*See* Annex I to Joint Declaration)
  Annex II (*See* Annex II to Joint Declaration)
  Annex III (*See* Annex III to Joint Declaration)
  Appendix I, 23

  arrest under, 192
  Basic Law compared, 201
  Basic Law viewed as fully implementing, 8, 37
  bespoke solution to treaty law issues, 124
  binding nature of, 40, 41
  BN(O) passports, PRC allegation of breach of Joint Declaration regarding, 249–50
  Chief Executive under, 165, 167
  common law legal system under, 51–2, 81–2, 87
  conflicting views of PRC and UK, 6–7, 20–2, 42–3, 195, 202–4, 213–14
  contents of, 42, 49–52
  Court of Final Appeal (CFA) and, 84, 87
  currency under, 51
  defence and, 230
  democratic reforms and, 58, 147, 172
  economic and cultural relations under, 51, 116–17, 120
  economic system under, 50
  elections under, 154, 155–6, 160, 161–2, 165, 167, 257–8
  Exchange of Memoranda and, 252
  existing systems to be maintained under, 7, 13, 50
  extradition and, 192, 211
  Extradition Bill, UK viewing as breach, 208–9
  Extradition Bill and, 212, 215
  foreign affairs and, 230
  free port and financial centre under, 50–1
  fully executed, PRC viewing as, 6–7, 8, 22, 195, 207–8, 213–14, 218, 232
  governing law under, 226–7
  historical background, 16–20
  Hong Kong delegations to London, 45–6
  Hong Kong representatives, views of, 43–7
  ICCPR and, 5, 87–90, 149, 172, 205
  implementation by Basic Law, 214, 221
  intention not to jeopardise, 253–4
  internal affairs under, 51, 129
  interpretation of, 24–5
  judiciary and, 81–2
  lack of exchange in, 15
  lack of fundamental rights in, 5
  legal nature of, 15–16
  local governance under, 51
  'missing booksellers' affair, UK alleging as breach, 188, 223–4
  National Security Law, UK alleging to be breach, 68, 145, 151, 172, 218, 224–5, 226, 251, 252–3

Index

negotiation of (*See* Negotiation of Joint Declaration)
political activities under, 52
PRC Constitution, relationship to, 106
property rights and, 24
public order, defence and foreign affairs distinguished, 146
public order under, 52
rationale for UK acceptance of, 54–5
reactions to, 53–4
'restoration' and, 48–9, 58
resumption, PRC position on, 21
signing of, 53
social reforms under, 52
sovereignty and, 22–5, 48–9, 182
success of, 263
text of, 264–7
third country acceptance of, 126–7
timetable of, 40–1
travel documents under, 51, 116–17
as treaty, 14, 15–16, 43
treaty law and, 237
unequal treaties doctrine and, 20–2
United Nations, notification of regarding, 112–13, 204
weaknesses of, 258–61
Sino-British Joint Liaison Group
acts of state and, 132, 143–4
Annex II and, 8, 36, 38, 42, 281–2
as bargaining chip, 36, 38–9
Court of Final Appeal (CFA) and, 83, 85
functions of, 47
Hong Kong representatives, views of, 44
negotiation regarding, 8–9, 43
public order, defence and foreign affairs distinguished, 145
renaming, 47, 58
on treaty law, 113, 120
UK administration under, 52
Sino-Japanese War (1894–1895), 10
Sino-Portuguese Joint Declaration (1987), 110–14
Sino-Portuguese Treaty of Friendship and Commerce (1888), 115
Sino-Portuguese Treaty of Peking (1887), 115
Slinn, Peter, 71–2, 74
Smart sanctions, 246
Smith, Ewan, 207, 214
Socialism, 262
Social reforms under Joint Declaration, 52
Soering rule, 213, 214–15

South China Sea Arbitration, 22
Sovereignty
delegated authority versus, 182
importance to PRC, 217
Joint Declaration and, 22–5, 182
jurisdiction versus, 11
negotiation of Joint Declaration and, 12, 19, 27–34
'one country, two systems' and, 183
'resumption' of, 11–12, 19, 21, 126–7, 195, 202, 205, 213–14
sovereignty plus administration, PRC position on, 26–7
Sri Lanka, Privy Council and, 81
Standing Committee of the National People's Congress (NPCSC) (PRC)
authority to enact laws, 234–5
Basic Law Committee, 166
Chief Executive and, 165, 166–7, 178–9, 246, 252–3
Congo case and, 139, 140–2
Court of Final Appeal (CFA) and, 87, 94–6
on elections, 163, 165, 166–7
interpretation of Basic Law by, 9, 69–70, 81, 91–2, 94–6, 131, 215, 219, 222–3
judiciary, authority regarding, 92–3
Legislative Council and, 246, 252–3
list of laws extended to Hong Kong, 135
review of laws, 131–2
on state immunity, 139, 140–2
West Kowloon Terminus and, 198
State Council (PRC)
Hong Kong and Macao Office, 20, 177
White Paper (2014), 177, 178–9, 183–4, 207
State immunity, 138–9, 140–2
State Immunity Act 1978 (UK), 138
State of emergency, 235–7
Stock, Frank, 140
Stone, William, 184
Subversion
Legislative Council and, 168–9
National Security Law, under, 168–9, 232–3
PRC position on, 171
Sumption, Jonathan, 103, 108, 228–9
Swire, Hugo, xii

Taiwan
administration of, 13
Hong Kong compared, 13
'one country, two systems' and, 18
PRC approach to, 183

Taiwan (cont.)
  United States policy regarding, 248
Tam Yiu-chung, 249
Tax agreements, 125
Technical Barriers to Trade (TBT) Agreement, 243–4
Templeman, Sydney, 184
Terrorism, 232–3
Thatcher, Margaret
  generally, 8–9, 16, 238
  Deng and, 12, 20, 22–3, 65
  on Exchange of Memoranda, 254
  negotiation of Joint Declaration and, 17, 20, 22–3, 26, 32, 39
  signing of Joint Declaration, 53
  scepticism of, 13
  on treaties, 217–18
Thorn, Gaston, 32–3
Tiananmen Square incident (1989), 69, 72
Tian Han, 198
Tibet
  administration of, 13, 183
  United States policy regarding, 248
Travel documents
  BN(O) passports as, 250, 251
  Joint Declaration, under, 51, 116–17
Treason, 187–8, 232–3
Treaties. *See also specific Treaty*
  Basic Law, treaty law and, 237–8
  bespoke solution to treaty law issues, 124–6
  extradition treaties, suspension of, 240
  Hong Kong, 'own' treaty regime of, 110
  interpretation of, 24–5, 203–4, 263
  Joint Declaration, treaty law and, 237
  limitations of treaty law in Hong Kong, 127–8
  'moving treaty frontiers' rule, 63, 111, 112, 114, 116
  suspension or withdrawal from, 239, 254–6
  travaux preparatoires, 24–5, 203–4
  unequal treaties doctrine (*See* Unequal treaties doctrine)
  unjust treaties doctrine, 24, 90
  Vienna Convention on the Law of Treaties (*See* Vienna Convention on the Law of Treaties (1969))
Treaty of Nanjing (1842), 10, 115
Treaty of Nanjing (1868), 210–11
Treaty of Shimonoseki (1895), 10
Trump, Donald, 118, 216, 242, 244, 248
Trust territories, 59
Tsang, Donald, 164

Tugendhat, Tom, 103–4, 228
Tung Chee-hwa, 95, 163–4
'Twelve Point Plan', 20, 23, 26, 49, 183

'Umbrella Movement', 165–6, 177, 178
Umm al Quwain, 134
'Uncivilised' peoples, 53–4, 261–2
Unequal treaties doctrine
  PRC position on, 18–22, 64, 115, 126–7, 217
  UK position on, 22
Unilateral sanctions, 239
United Kingdom. *See specific topic*
United Nations
  Charter (*See* United Nations Charter)
  Conference on the Law of Treaties of China, 24
  Convention on the Jurisdictional Immunities of States, 142
  Convention on the Law of the Sea, 241
  Declaration on Non-Self-Governing Territories, 59
  decolonisation and, 262–3
  dispute settlement and, 256
  General Assembly Resolutions, 58–60, 61, 62, 64–5, 262–3
  Human Rights Committee, 88–9, 119, 121, 160, 167
  ICCPR, notification regarding, 205
  Joint Declaration, notification regarding, 112–13, 204
  sanctions and, 239
  Special Committee on Decolonisation (C-24), 58–64, 262
  use of force and, 247–8
United Nations Charter
  generally, 20
  breaches of, 134
  dispute settlement and, 256
  non-self-governing territories and, 63, 64–5
  PRC and, 257
  sanctions and, 239
  self-determination and, 60
  Trust Territories, 59
  use of force and, 247–8
United States
  Alaska, purchase of, 195
  Constitution, 124
  Customs and Border Protection, 242–3, 244
  Executive Order 13936, 242–3, 244, 246
  extradition agreement with Hong Kong, 128

Global Magnitsky Human Rights
  Accountability Act of 2016, 246
Hong Kong Autonomy Act of 2020, 118,
  242, 246
Hong Kong Human Rights and Democracy
  Act of 2019, 239
Hong Kong Policy Act of 1992, 239
'Made in China' dispute, 118, 177, 241, 242–5
Magnitsky Act, 246
on National Security Law, 151–2, 216
PRC sanctions against, 248
product labelling requirements, 118, 177, 241,
  242–5
relations with PRC, 256–7, 261
Republican Party, 248
Russia and Moldova Jackson-Vanik Repeal
  and Sergei Magnitsky Rule of Law
  Accountability Act of 2012, 246
sanctions by, 241, 246–8
suspension of extradition treaty, 240
WTO dispute with Hong Kong, 118, 177, 241,
  242–5
Unjust treaties doctrine, 24, 90
Unofficial Members of the Executive and
  Legislative Councils (OMELCO)
  (Hong Kong), 222
Uruguay Round, 243, 245

Vienna Convention on Consular Relations
  (1963), 124
Vienna Convention on Diplomatic Relations
  (1961), 124
Vienna Convention on Succession of States in
  respect of Treaties (1978), 111–12, 116
Vienna Convention on the Law of Treaties (1969)
  Basic Law and, 153, 214
  colonialism and, 62
  interpretation under, 203–4
  'moving treaty frontiers'/'moving frontiers'
    rule and, 63, 114
  rebus sic stantibus and, 255–6
  treaty suspension or withdrawal and, 254–6
  United Nations Charter and, 256
  unjust treaties and, 24
Vogel, Ezra, 21
Voting. *See* Elections

Wade, William, 169
Walden, John, 56–7
Waldock, Humphrey, 101–2, 203–4
Walker, Michael, 103

Wang Tieya, 11, 24
Wang Yi, 188–9
Wang Zhenmin, 186
Wesley-Smith, Peter, 17
West Kowloon Terminus
  generally, 194
  extension of PRC law to, 177, 179, 196
  Hong Kong law, applicability of, 200
  lease of land to Mainland PRC, 194–5,
    196–7, 201
  'missing booksellers' affair, in context of, 195
  NPCSC and, 198
  Shenzhen Bay analogy, 195
Wilberforce, Richard, 133, 134, 143
Wilson, David, 46, 49, 66, 162
Wilson, Woodrow, 159, 262
Wong Yan Lung, 137
World Health Organisation, 206
World Trade Organisation (WTO)
  Beau Rivage Group, 245
  Buick Group, 245
  Cairns Group, 245
  dispute between Hong Kong and United
    States in, 118, 177, 241, 242–5
  Friends of Fish, 245
  Friends of Geographical Indications, 245
  Friends of the Development Box, 245
  Hong Kong and, 111, 118, 120, 125, 241
  informal groups in, 245
  Invisibles Group, 245
  Like-Minded Group, 245
  'Made in China' dispute, 118, 177, 241, 242–5
  Marrakesh Agreement, 243
  non-discrimination principle, 243–4
  Paradisus Group, 245
  PRC and, 67, 244
  Technical Barriers to Trade (TBT)
    Agreement, 243–4
  Uruguay Round, 243, 245
  West African Cotton Four, 245
  withdrawal of recognition and, 239–40
WTO. *See* World Trade Organisation (WTO)
Wu Xueqian, 28–9, 40–1, 115

Xiao Weiyun, 223
Xinjiang, United States policy regarding,
  241–2, 248
Xu Hong, 207–8

Yang Ti-liang, 82, 93
Yao Guang, 31, 34–5

Youde, Edward
 generally, 156
 on elections, 157–8, 161
 Hong Kong delegations to London and, 46
 negotiation of Joint Declaration and, 8–9, 29, 30, 33
Young Plan, 56
Yuen, Maria, 141

Yuen, Rimsky, 127, 200
Yugoslavia, breakup of, 170

Zhao Ziyang, 8–9, 23, 41–2
Zhou Nan
 generally, 31
 negotiation of Joint Declaration and, 28–9, 39, 41–2, 47, 48, 49

Lightning Source UK Ltd.
Milton Keynes UK
UKHW052127100123
414916UK00040B/699